P9-DWS-624

尾田栄一郎

The wrappers for the old-fashioned candies have certain characters printed on them. They usually announce how the candies taste. I think it'd be funny if all products had these. For example, on a bag of kimchi, it'd say, "Spicy!" For pervy DVDs, it'd say "Sexy!" For cigarettes, it'd say "Smoky!" For drugs, it'd say "Dangerous!" Anyway, volume 64 is starting! Tasty!

-Eiichiro Oda, 2011

Eiichiro Oda began his manga career at the age of 17, when his one-shot cowboy manga **Wanted!** won second place in the coveted Tezuka manga awards. Oda went on to work as an assistant to some of the biggest manga artists in the industry, including Nobuhiro Watsuki, before winning the Hop Step Award for new artists. His pirate adventure **One Piece**, which debuted in **Weekly Shonen Jump** in 1997, quickly became one of the most popular manga in Japan.

ONE PIECE VOL. 64
NEW WORLD PART 4

SHONEN JUMP Manga Edition

STORY AND ART BY EIICHIRO ODA

English Adaptation/Lance Caselman
Translation/Laabaman, HC Language Solutions, Inc., Stephen Paul
Touch-up Art & Lettering/Elena Diaz
Design/Fawn Lau
Editor/Alexis Kirsch

ONE PIECE © 1997 by Eiichiro Oda. All rights reserved.
First published in Japan in 1997 by SHUEISHA Inc., Tokyo.
English translation rights arranged by SHUEISHA Inc.

The rights of the author(s) of the work(s) in this publication to be so
identified have been asserted in accordance with the Copyright, Designs
and Patents Act 1988. A CIP catalogue record for this book is available
from the British Library.

The stories, characters and incidents mentioned in this publication are
entirely fictional.

No portion of this book may be reproduced or transmitted in any form
or by any means without written permission from the copyright holders.

Printed in the U.S.A.

Published by VIZ Media, LLC
P.O. Box 77010
San Francisco, CA 94107

10 9 8 7 6 5 4 3 2 1
First printing, September 2012

www.viz.com

PARENTAL ADVISORY
ONE PIECE is rated T for Teen and is recommended
for ages 13 and up. This volume contains fantasy
violence and tobacco usage.
ratings.viz.com

THE WORLD'S
MOST POPULAR MANGA
SHONEN JUMP
www.shonenjump.com

SHONEN JUMP MANGA

ONE PIECE

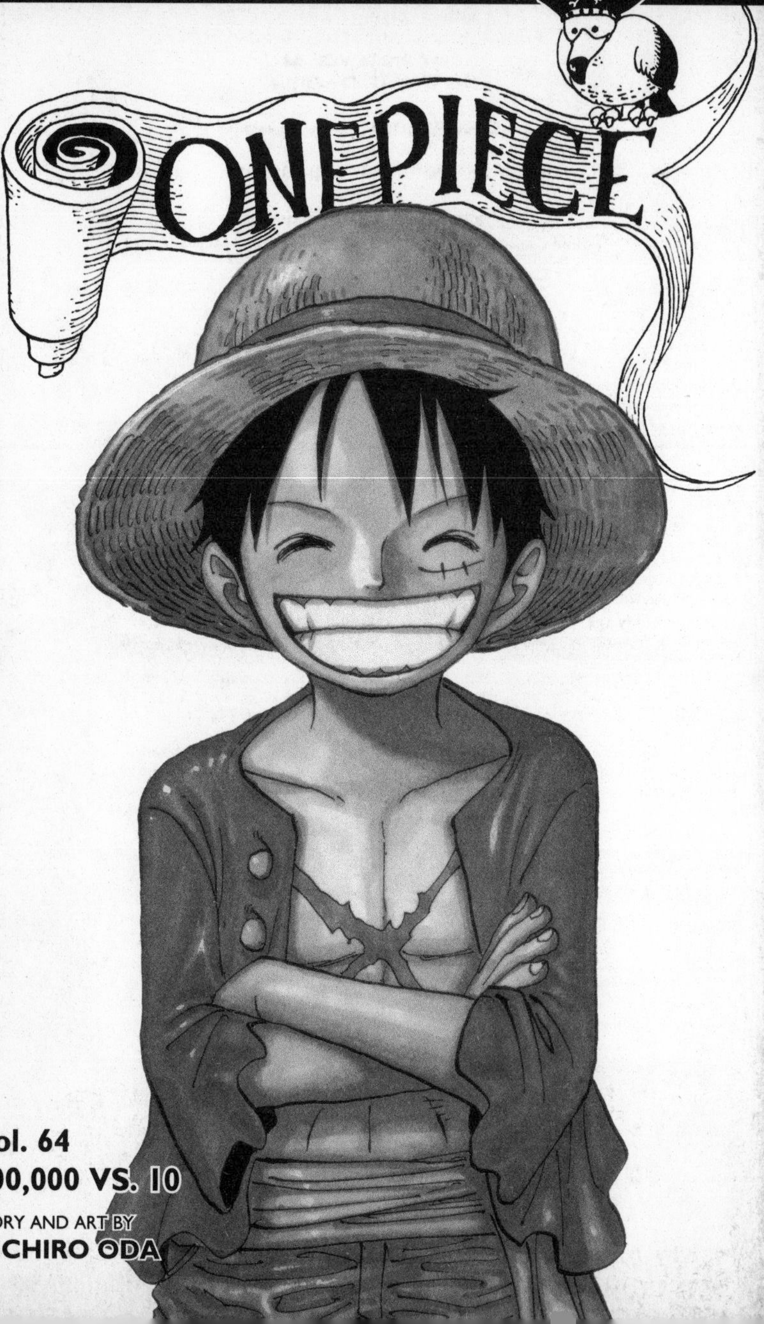

Vol. 64

100,000 VS. 10

STORY AND ART BY
EIICHIRO ODA

The Straw Hat Crew

Monkey D. Luffy

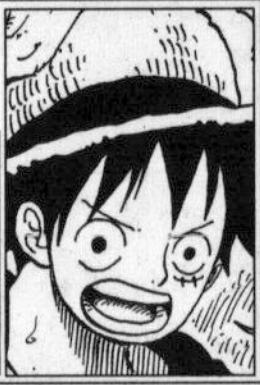

A young man who dreams of becoming the Pirate King. After training with Rayleigh, he and his crew head for the New World!

Captain, Bounty: 400 million berries

Roronoa Zolo

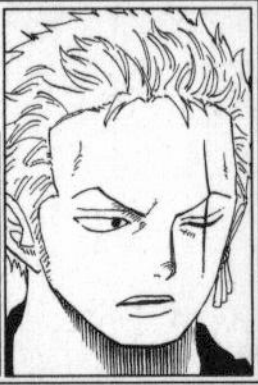

He swallowed his pride and asked to be trained by Mihawk on Gloom Island before reuniting with the rest of the crew.

Fighter, Bounty: 120 million berries

Tony Tony Chopper

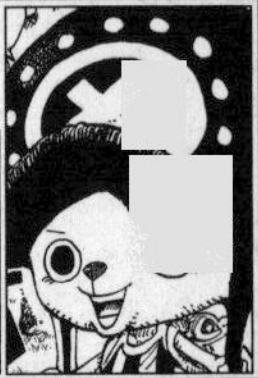

After researching powerful medicine in Birdie Kingdom, he reunites with the rest of the crew.

Ship's Doctor, Bounty: 50 berries

Nami

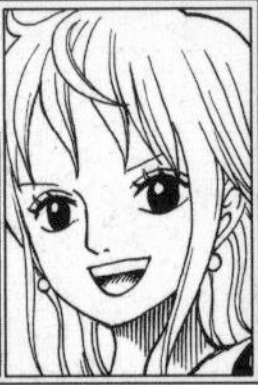

She studied the weather of the New World on the small Sky Island Weatheria, a place where weather is studied as a science.

Navigator, Bounty: 16 million berries

Nico Robin

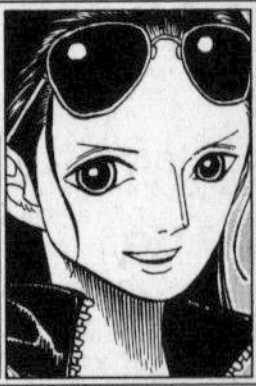

She spent her time in Baltigo with the leader of the Revolutionary Army: Luffy's father, Dragon.

Archeologist, Bounty: 80 million berries

Usopp

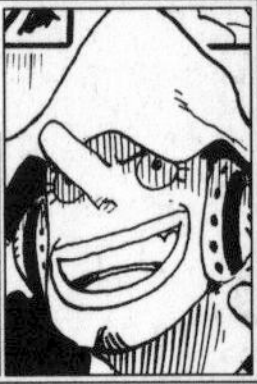

He trained under Heracles at the Bowin Islands to become the King of Snipers.

Sniper, Bounty: 30 million berries

Franky

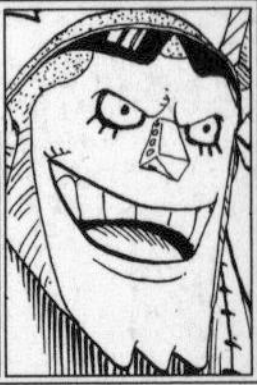

He modified himself in Future Land Baldimore and turned himself into Armored Franky before reuniting with the rest of the crew.

Shipwright, Bounty: 44 million berries

Sanji

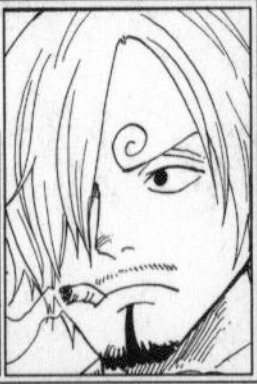

After fighting the New Kama Karate masters in the Kamabakka Kingdom, he returned to the crew.

Cook, Bounty: 77 million berries

Brook

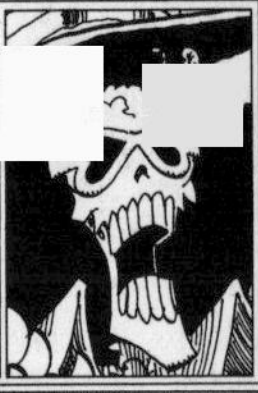

After being captured and used as a freak show by the Longarm Tribe, he became a famous rock star called "Soul King" Brook.

Musician, Bounty: 33 million berries

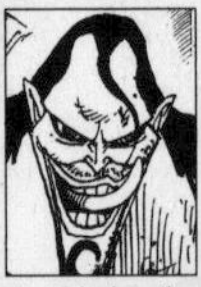

Wet-Haired Caribou

Captain of the Caribou Pir

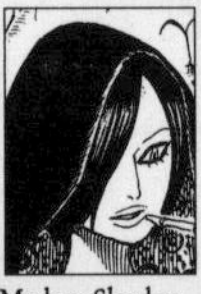

Madam Sharley

Owner of the Mermaid Café

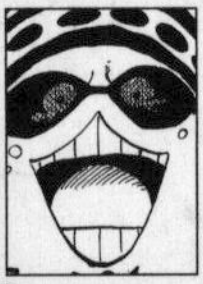

Pappagu

The Designer/President of the Criminal brand

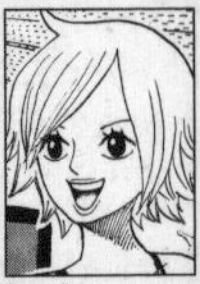

Camie

Works at the Mermaid Café

The story of ONE PIECE 1»64

Shanks

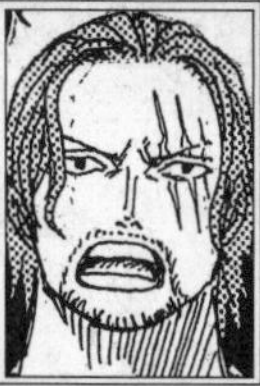

One of the Four Emperors. He continues to wait for Luffy in the second half of the Grand Line, called the New World.

Captain of the Red-Haired Pirates

Jimbei

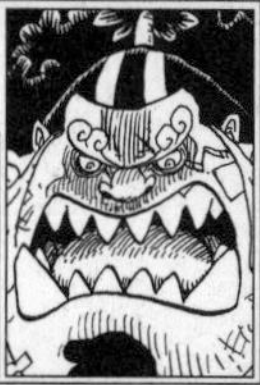

He left Luffy before he started his training and returned to Fish-Man Island.

Former Warlord of the Sea

The Ryugu Kingdom

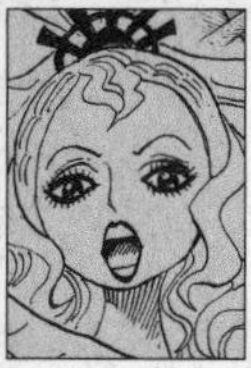

Queen Otohime

Neptune's Wife

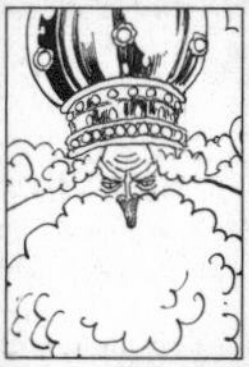

Neptune the Sea God

King of the Ryugu Kingdom

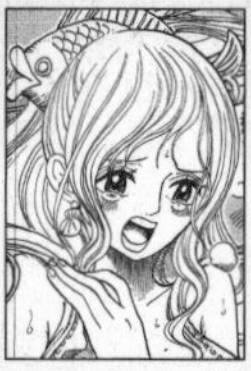

Princess Shirahoshi

Princess of the Ryugu Kingdom

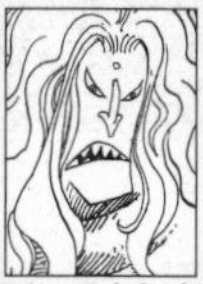

Prince Fukaboshi

Eldest of Neptune's Three Sons

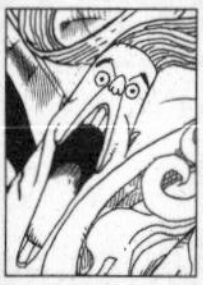

Prince Ryuboshi

Second of Neptune's Three Sons

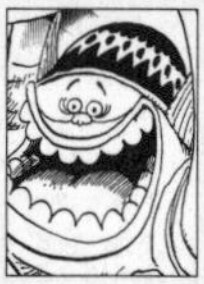

Prince Mamboshi

Youngest of Neptune's Three Sons

Proposed to ↑

Allied

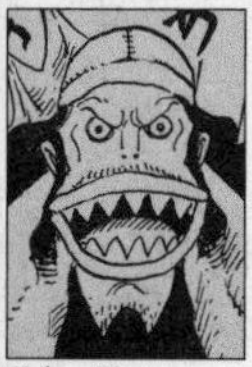

Fisher Tiger

Sun Pirates Captain

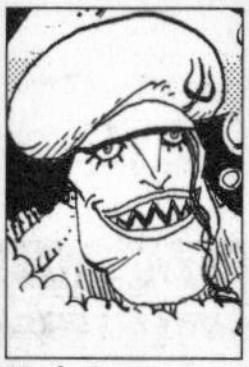

Hody Jones

Captain of the New Fish-Man Pirates

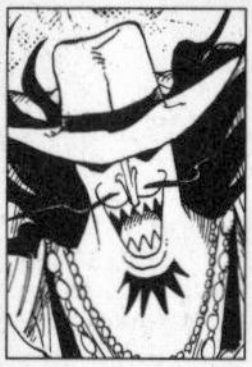

Vander Decken IX

Captain of the Flying Pirates

Flying Pirates

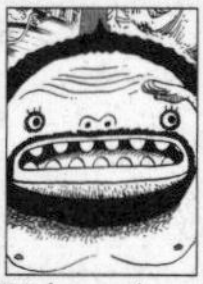

Wadatsumi

Member of the Flying Pirates

The New Fish-Man Pirates

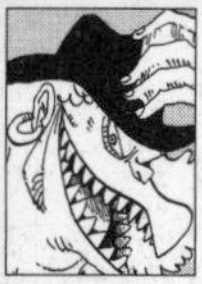

Hammond

New Fish-Man Pirate

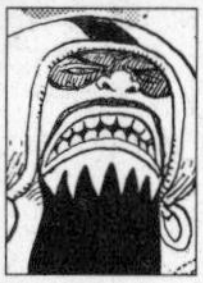

Ikaros Much

New Fish-Man Pirate

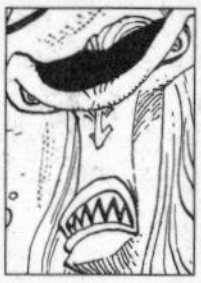

Dosun

New Fish-Man Pirate

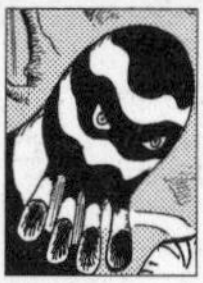

Zeo

New Fish-Man Pirate

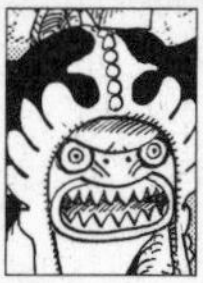

Daruma

New Fish-Man Pirate

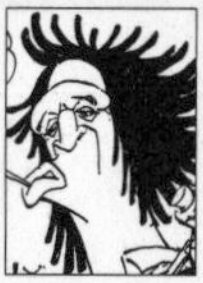

Hyouzou

New Fish-Man Pirate

Story

Having finished their two years of training, the Straw Hat crew reunites on the Sabaody Archipelago. They set sail more determined than ever to reach the New World!

The Straw Hats finally reach Fish-Man Island but are quickly ambushed by the New Fish-Man Pirates. Luffy and his crew then hear from Jimbei why the Fish-Men hate humans. One reason is that the death of their hero, Fisher Tiger, was caused by humans. Another part of the story concerned Queen Otohime, who worked to bring humans and Fish-Men together until she was assassinated. Shirahoshi and her siblings inherited their mother's will, but…

NEW WORLD
ONE PIECE

Vol. 64
100,000 vs. 10

CONTENTS

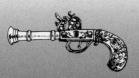

Chapter 627:
THANK YOU

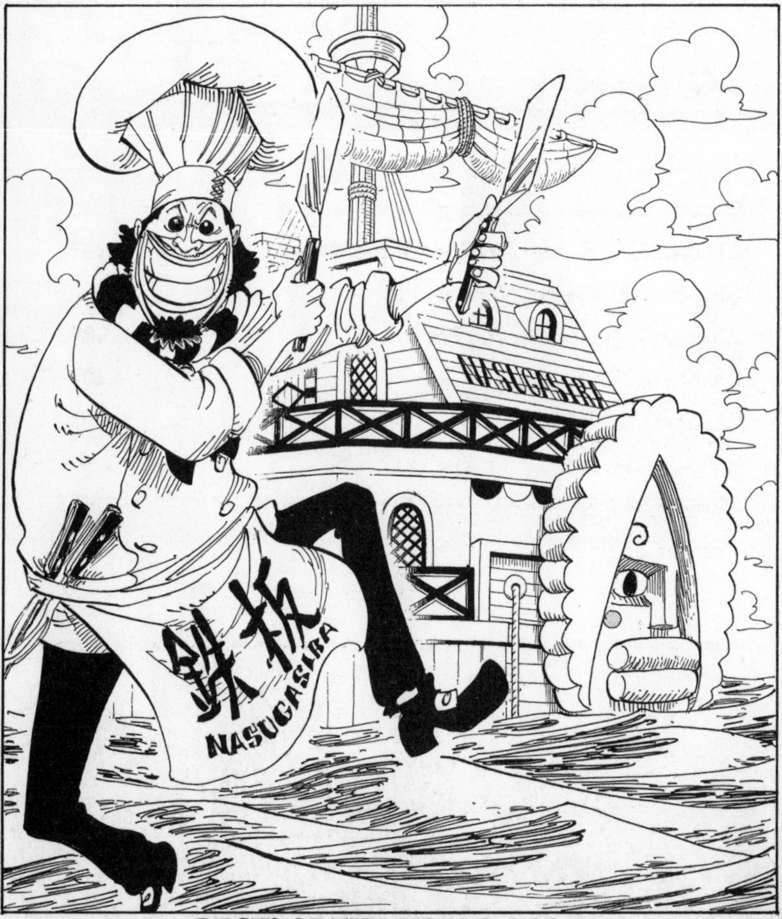
NASUGASHIRA
鉄板
NASUGASHIRA

DECKS OF THE WORLD, VOL. 13:
"BARATIE—JOINT TEPPANYAKI SHIP NASUGASHIRA"

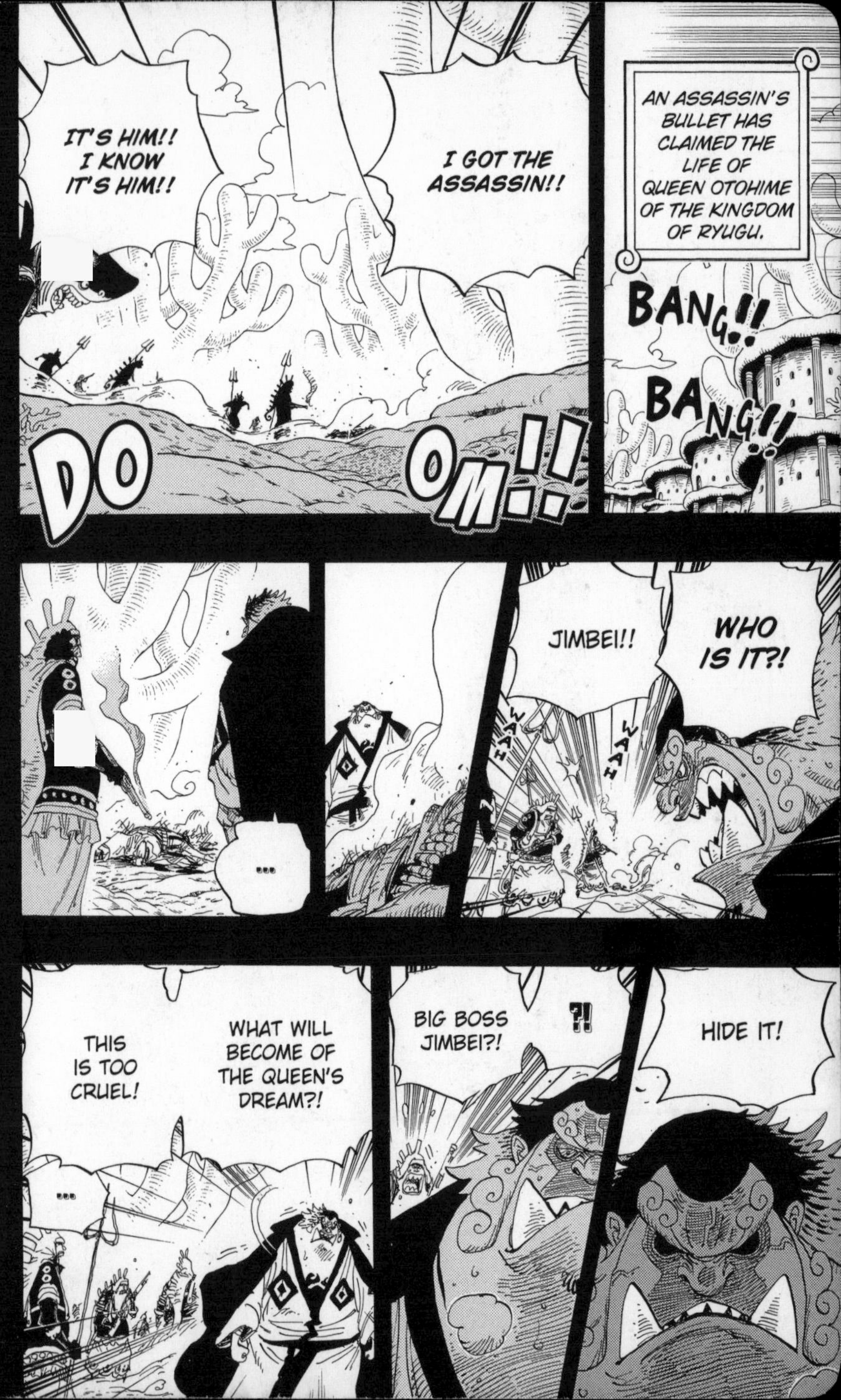
AN ASSASSIN'S BULLET HAS CLAIMED THE LIFE OF QUEEN OTOHIME OF THE KINGDOM OF RYUGU.
BANG!!
BANG!!
I GOT THE ASSASSIN!!
IT'S HIM!! I KNOW IT'S HIM!!
DOOM!!
WHO IS IT?!
JIMBEI!!
WAAH
WAAH
...
HIDE IT!
?!
BIG BOSS JIMBEI?!
WHAT WILL BECOME OF THE QUEEN'S DREAM?!
THIS IS TOO CRUEL!
...

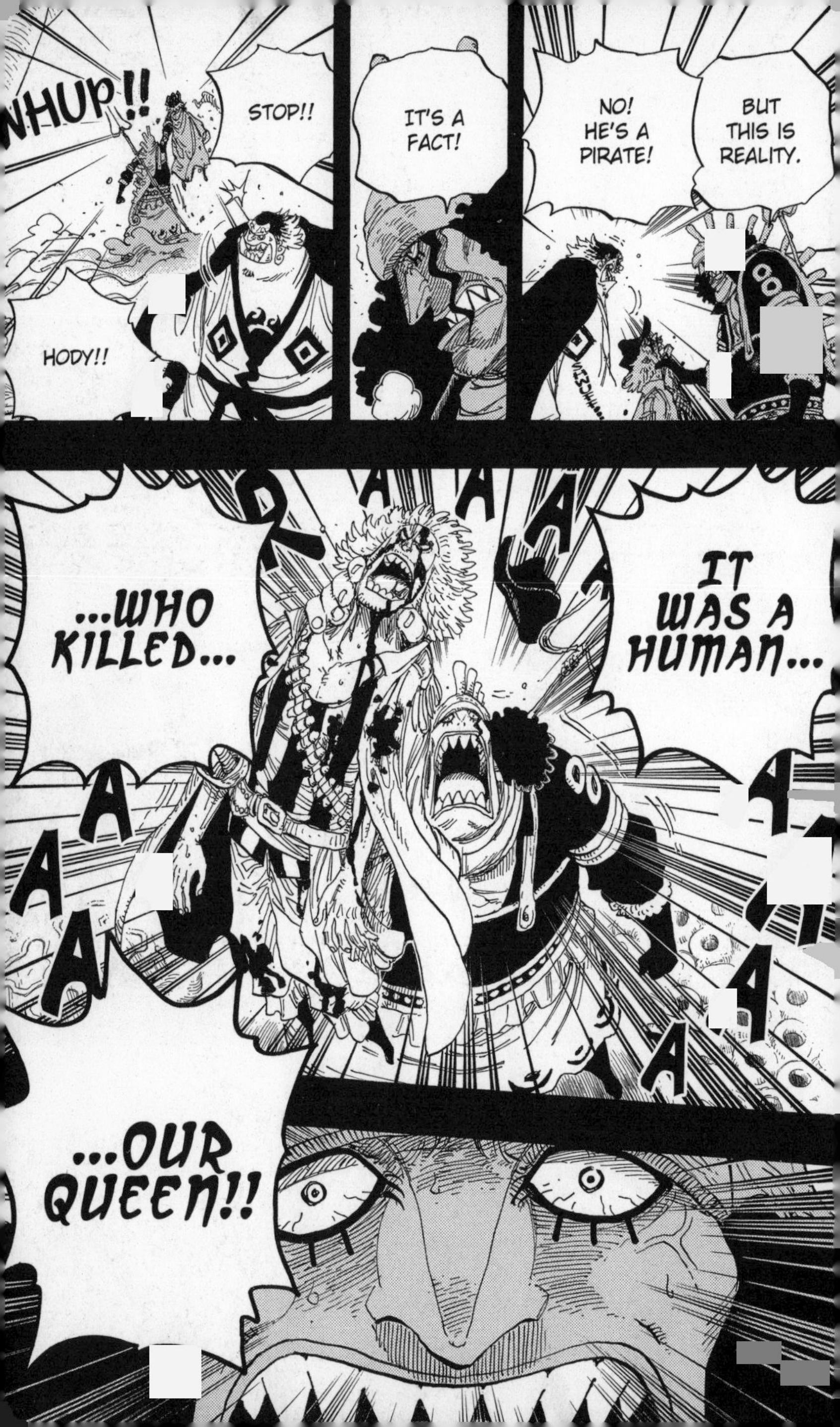
BUT THIS IS REALITY.
NO! HE'S A PIRATE!
IT'S A FACT!
STOP!!
WHUP!!
HODY!!
IT WAS A HUMAN...
...WHO KILLED...
...OUR QUEEN!!

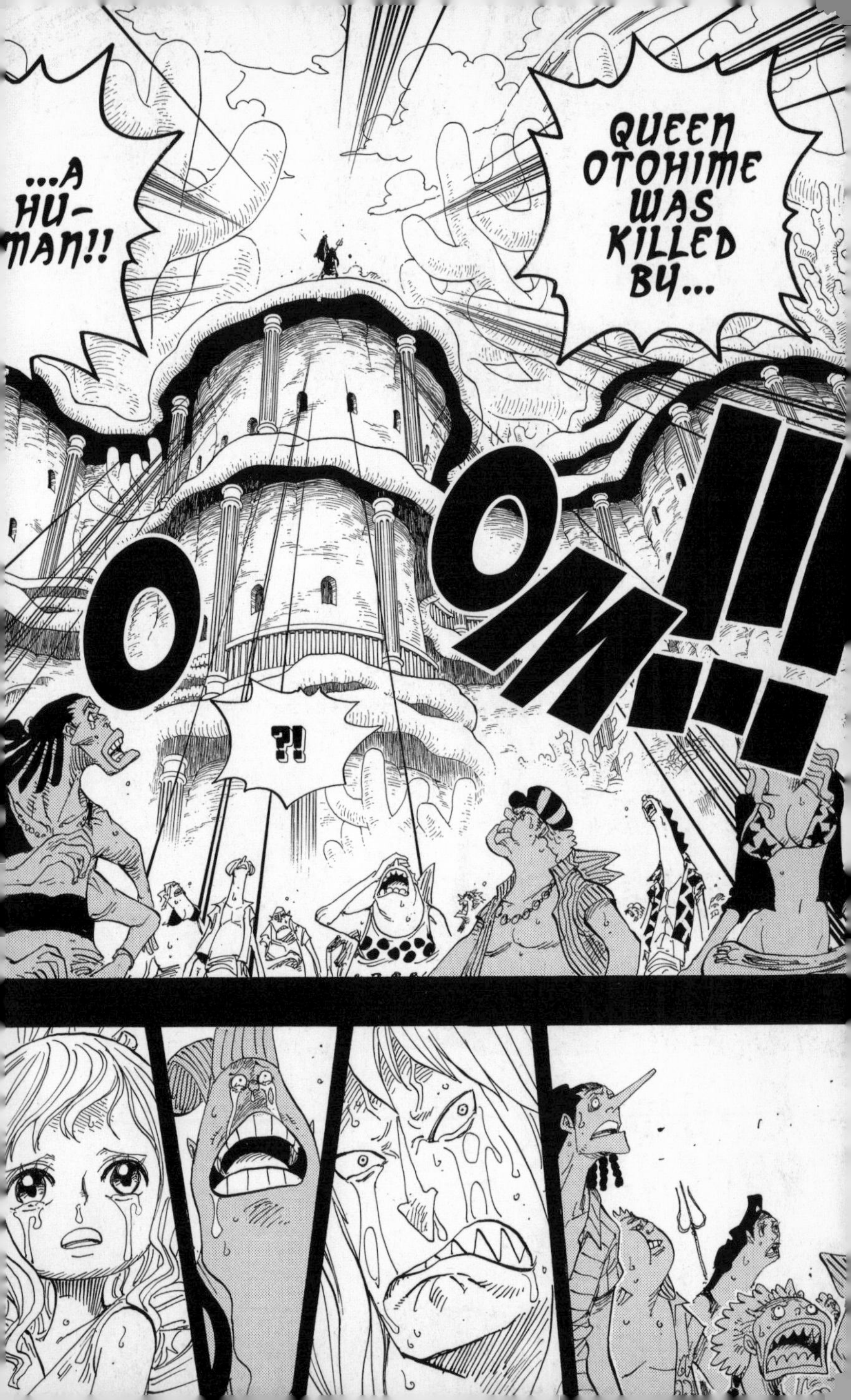
QUEEN OTOHIME WAS KILLED BY...
...A HU-MAN!!
?!
OOH!!

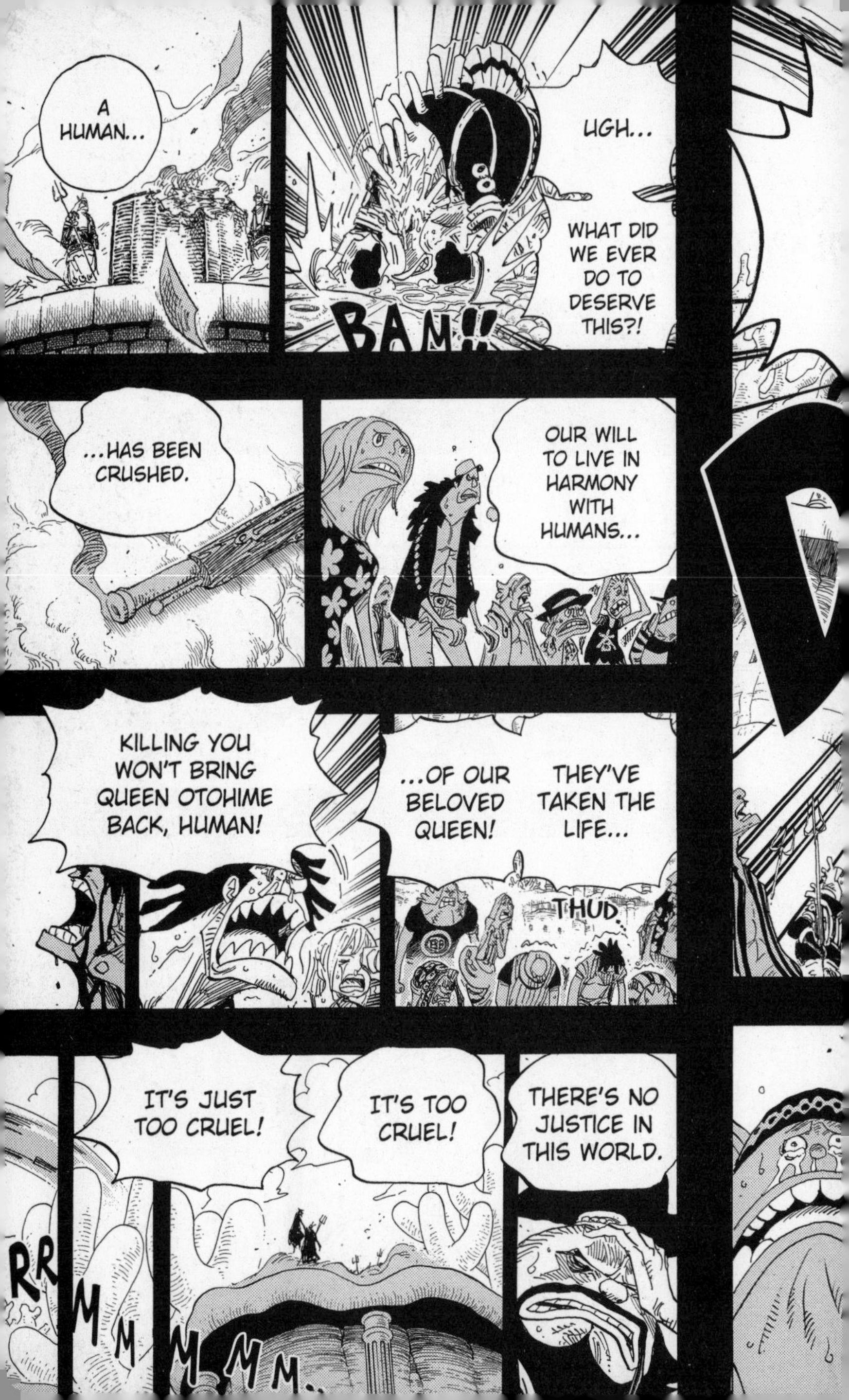
UGH...
WHAT DID WE EVER DO TO DESERVE THIS?!
BAM!!
A HUMAN...
OUR WILL TO LIVE IN HARMONY WITH HUMANS...
...HAS BEEN CRUSHED.
THEY'VE TAKEN THE LIFE...
...OF OUR BELOVED QUEEN!
THUD
KILLING YOU WON'T BRING QUEEN OTOHIME BACK, HUMAN!
THERE'S NO JUSTICE IN THIS WORLD.
IT'S TOO CRUEL!
IT'S JUST TOO CRUEL!
RRMMMMMM..

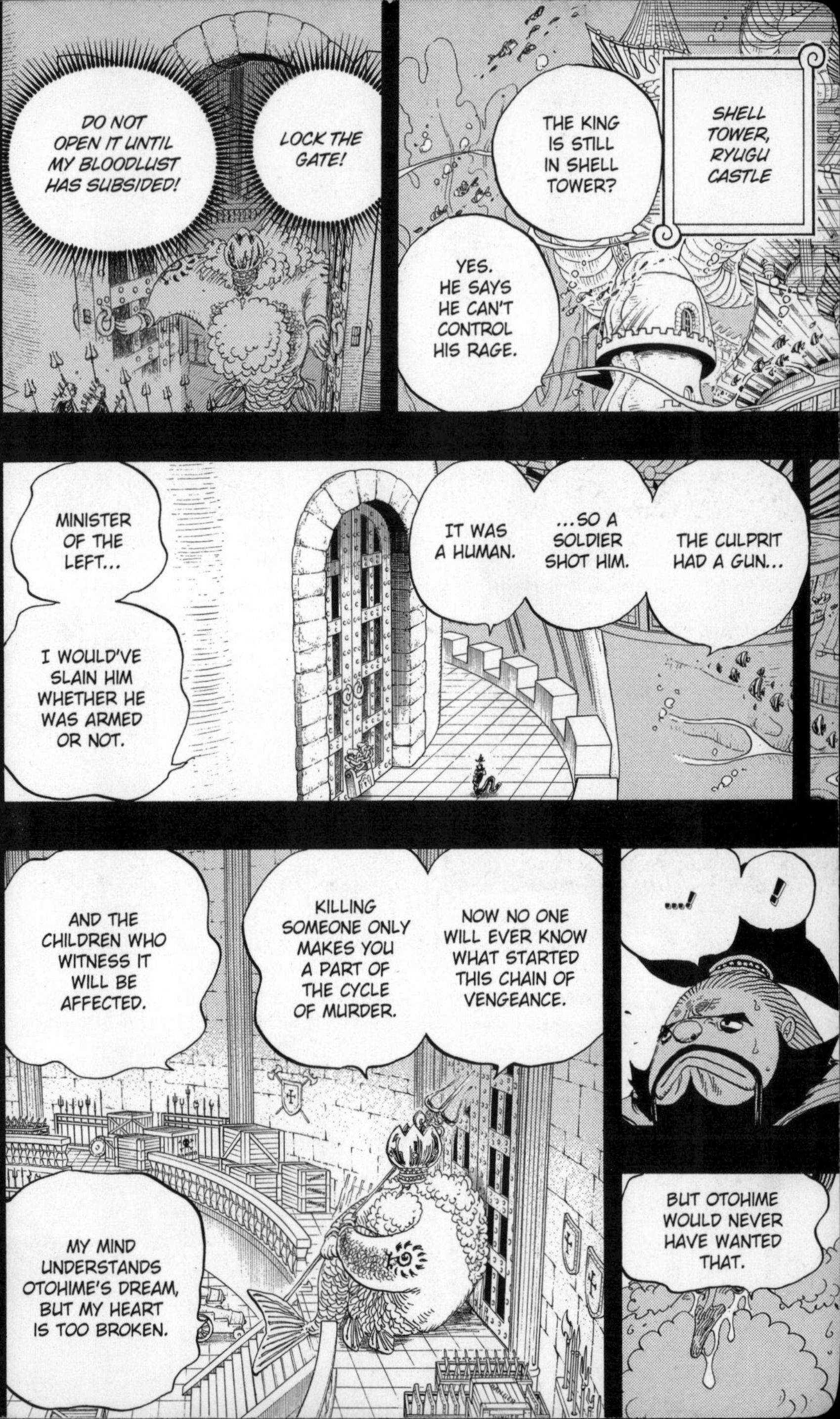
SHELL TOWER, RYUGU CASTLE
THE KING IS STILL IN SHELL TOWER?
YES. HE SAYS HE CAN'T CONTROL HIS RAGE.
LOCK THE GATE!
DO NOT OPEN IT UNTIL MY BLOODLUST HAS SUBSIDED!
THE CULPRIT HAD A GUN...
...SO A SOLDIER SHOT HIM.
IT WAS A HUMAN.
MINISTER OF THE LEFT...
I WOULD'VE SLAIN HIM WHETHER HE WAS ARMED OR NOT.
!
...!
BUT OTOHIME WOULD NEVER HAVE WANTED THAT.
NOW NO ONE WILL EVER KNOW WHAT STARTED THIS CHAIN OF VENGEANCE.
KILLING SOMEONE ONLY MAKES YOU A PART OF THE CYCLE OF MURDER.
AND THE CHILDREN WHO WITNESS IT WILL BE AFFECTED.
MY MIND UNDERSTANDS OTOHIME'S DREAM, BUT MY HEART IS TOO BROKEN.

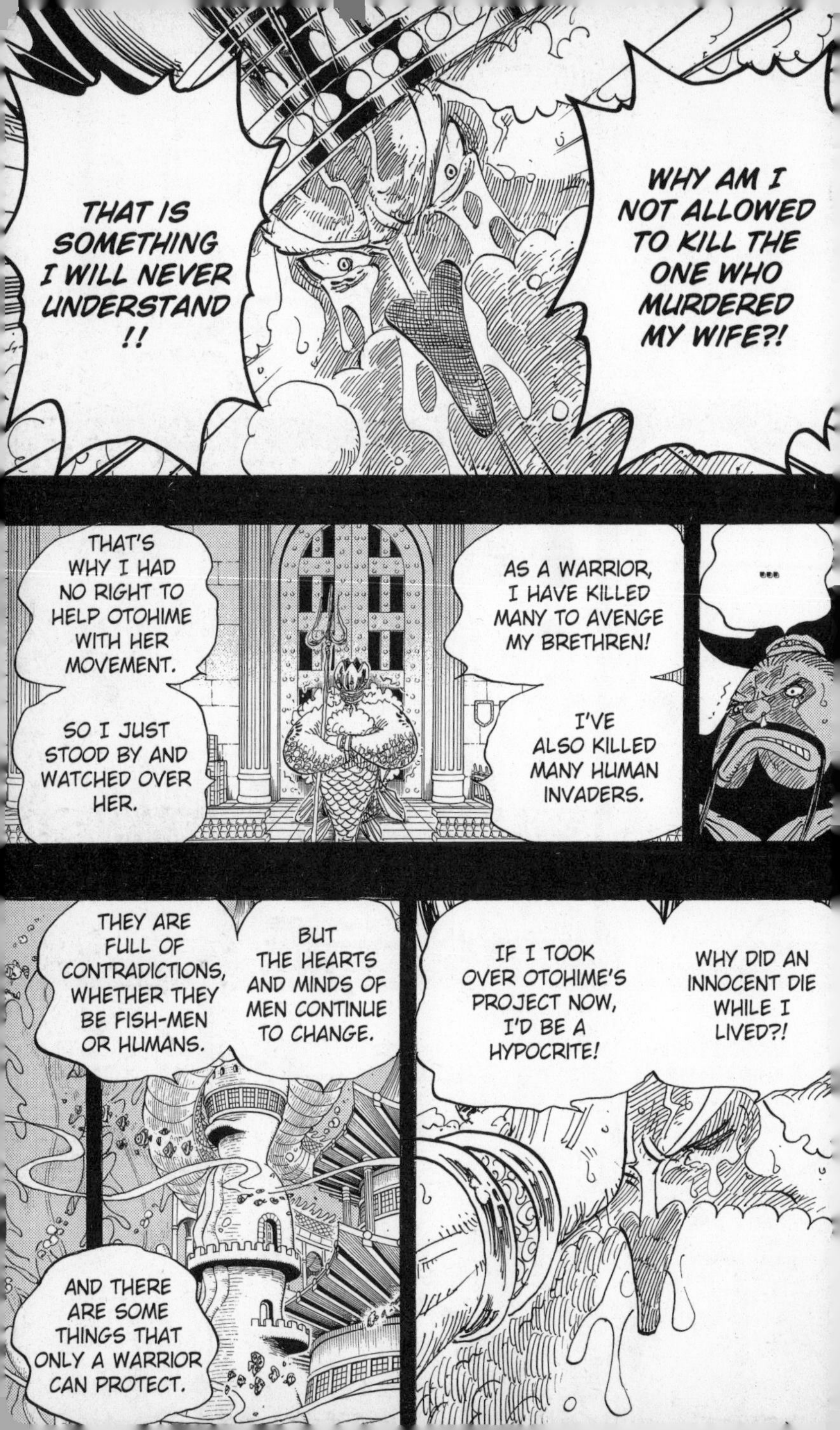
WHY AM I NOT ALLOWED TO KILL THE ONE WHO MURDERED MY WIFE?!
THAT IS SOMETHING I WILL NEVER UNDERSTAND !!
...
AS A WARRIOR, I HAVE KILLED MANY TO AVENGE MY BRETHREN!
I'VE ALSO KILLED MANY HUMAN INVADERS.
THAT'S WHY I HAD NO RIGHT TO HELP OTOHIME WITH HER MOVEMENT.
SO I JUST STOOD BY AND WATCHED OVER HER.
WHY DID AN INNOCENT DIE WHILE I LIVED?!
IF I TOOK OVER OTOHIME'S PROJECT NOW, I'D BE A HYPOCRITE!
BUT THE HEARTS AND MINDS OF MEN CONTINUE TO CHANGE.
THEY ARE FULL OF CONTRADICTIONS, WHETHER THEY BE FISH-MEN OR HUMANS.
AND THERE ARE SOME THINGS THAT ONLY A WARRIOR CAN PROTECT.

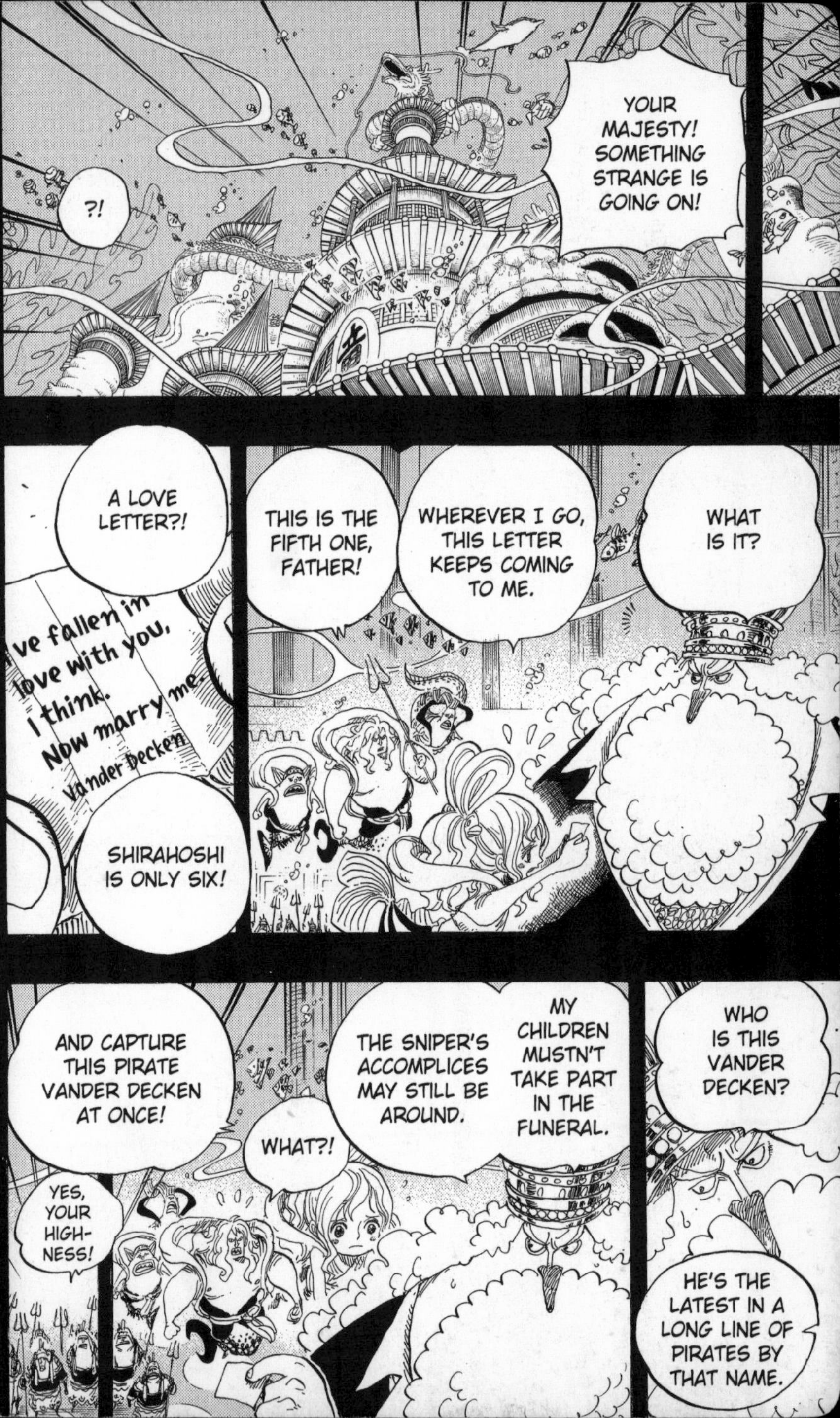
YOUR MAJESTY! SOMETHING STRANGE IS GOING ON!
?!
WHAT IS IT?
WHEREVER I GO, THIS LETTER KEEPS COMING TO ME.
THIS IS THE FIFTH ONE, FATHER!
A LOVE LETTER?!
ve fallen in love with you, I think. Now marry me.
Vander Decken
SHIRAHOSHI IS ONLY SIX!
WHO IS THIS VANDER DECKEN?
HE'S THE LATEST IN A LONG LINE OF PIRATES BY THAT NAME.
MY CHILDREN MUSTN'T TAKE PART IN THE FUNERAL.
THE SNIPER'S ACCOMPLICES MAY STILL BE AROUND.
WHAT?!
AND CAPTURE THIS PIRATE VANDER DECKEN AT ONCE!
YES, YOUR HIGHNESS!

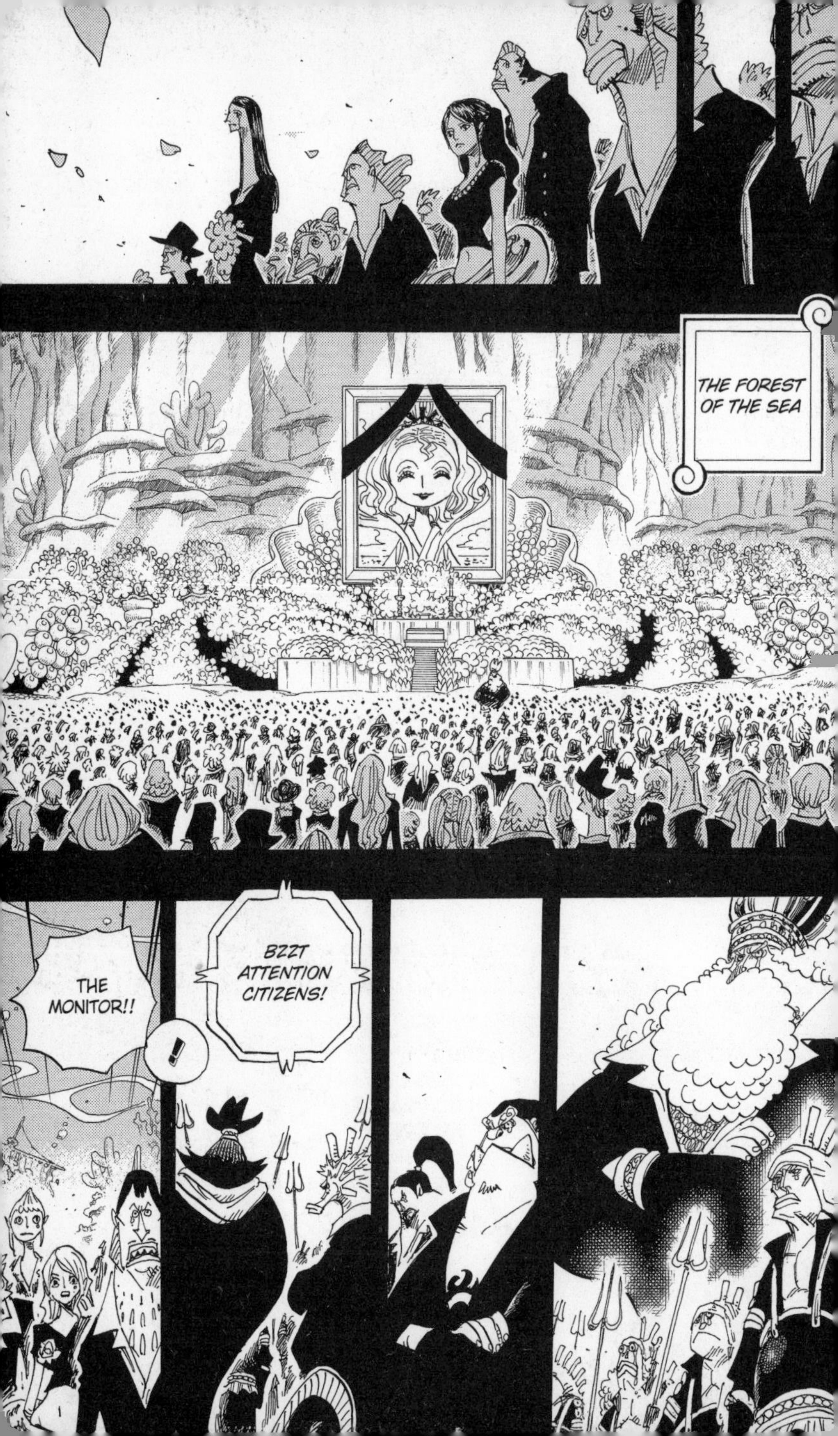
THE FOREST OF THE SEA
BZZT ATTENTION CITIZENS!
!
THE MONITOR!!

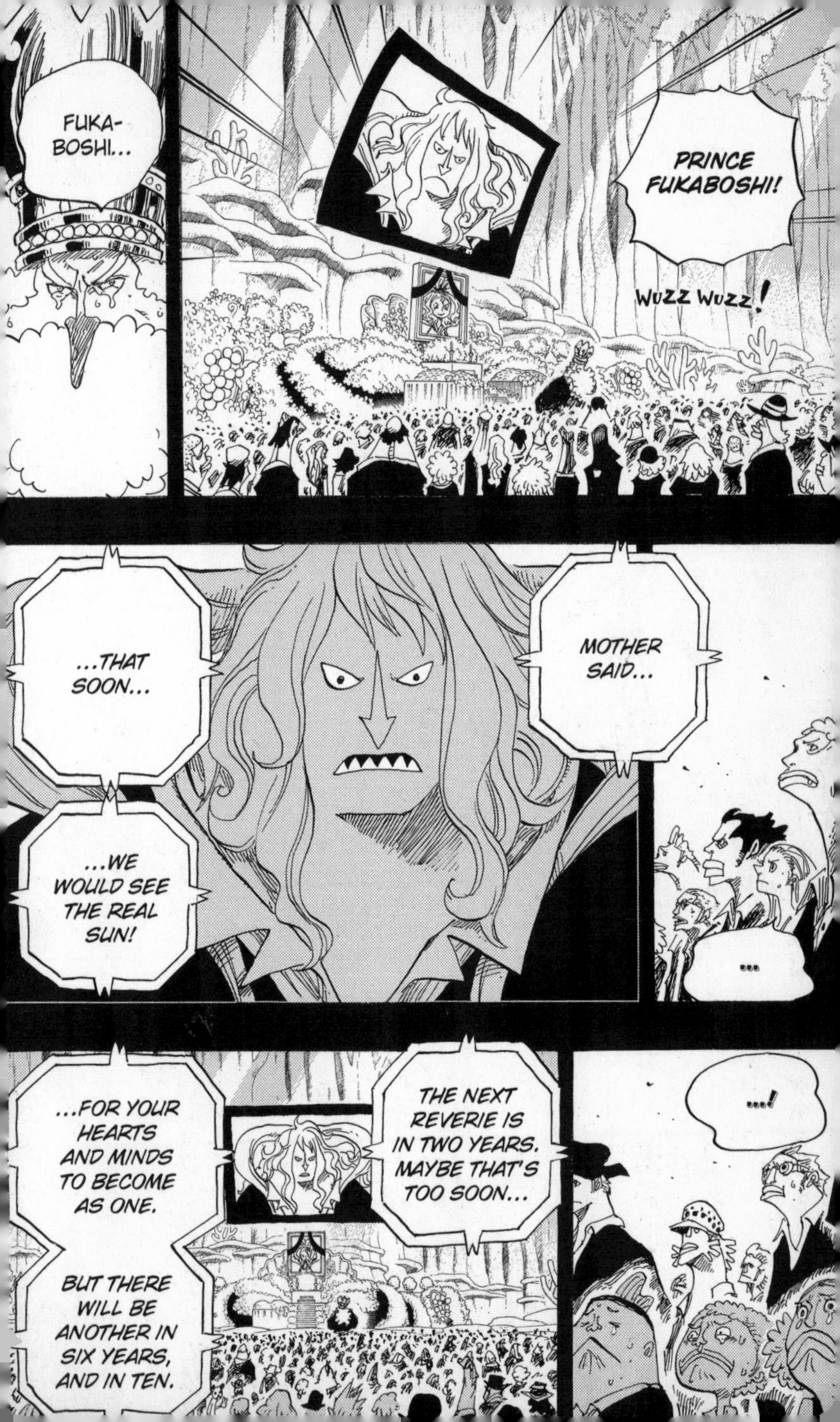
PRINCE FUKABOSHI!
WUZZ WUZZ!
FUKA-BOSHI...
...
MOTHER SAID...
...THAT SOON...
...WE WOULD SEE THE REAL SUN!
...!
THE NEXT REVERIE IS IN TWO YEARS. MAYBE THAT'S TOO SOON...
...FOR YOUR HEARTS AND MINDS TO BECOME AS ONE.
BUT THERE WILL BE ANOTHER IN SIX YEARS, AND IN TEN.

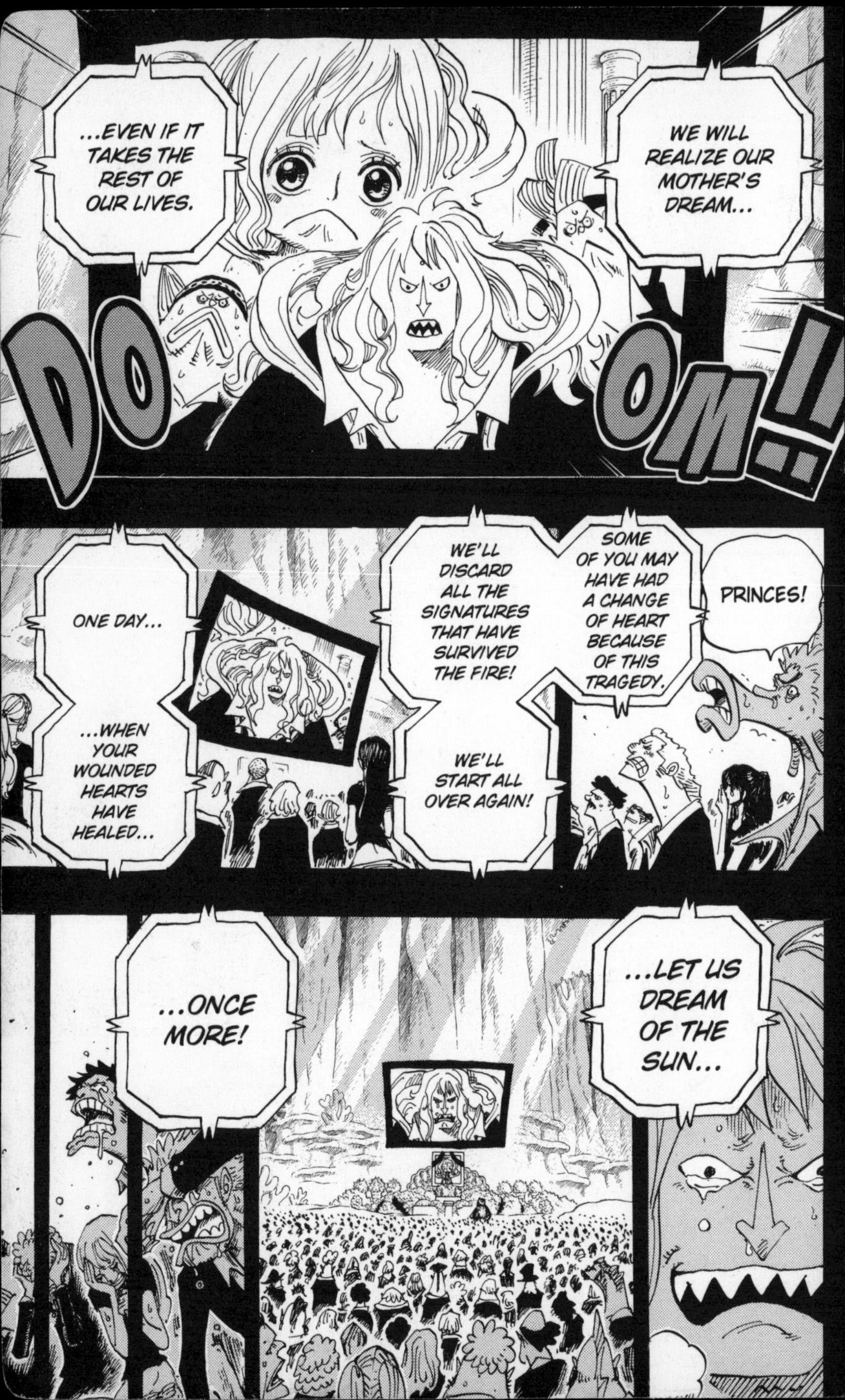
WE WILL REALIZE OUR MOTHER'S DREAM...
...EVEN IF IT TAKES THE REST OF OUR LIVES.
DOOM!!
PRINCES!
SOME OF YOU MAY HAVE HAD A CHANGE OF HEART BECAUSE OF THIS TRAGEDY.
WE'LL DISCARD ALL THE SIGNATURES THAT HAVE SURVIVED THE FIRE!
WE'LL START ALL OVER AGAIN!
ONE DAY...
...WHEN YOUR WOUNDED HEARTS HAVE HEALED...
...LET US DREAM OF THE SUN...
...ONCE MORE!

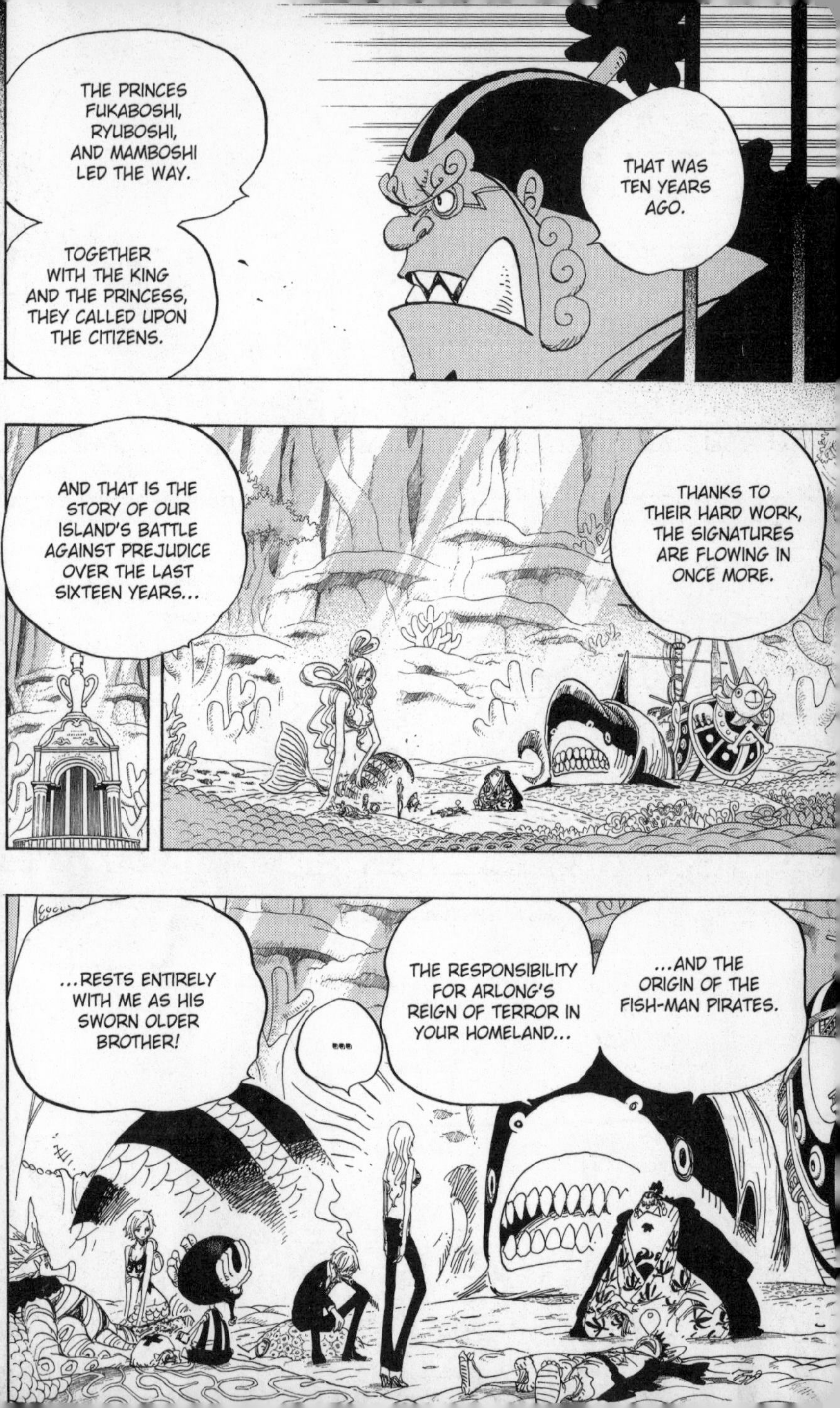
THAT WAS TEN YEARS AGO.
THE PRINCES FUKABOSHI, RYUBOSHI, AND MAMBOSHI LED THE WAY.
TOGETHER WITH THE KING AND THE PRINCESS, THEY CALLED UPON THE CITIZENS.
THANKS TO THEIR HARD WORK, THE SIGNATURES ARE FLOWING IN ONCE MORE.
AND THAT IS THE STORY OF OUR ISLAND'S BATTLE AGAINST PREJUDICE OVER THE LAST SIXTEEN YEARS...
...AND THE ORIGIN OF THE FISH-MAN PIRATES.
THE RESPONSIBILITY FOR ARLONG'S REIGN OF TERROR IN YOUR HOMELAND...
...
...RESTS ENTIRELY WITH ME AS HIS SWORN OLDER BROTHER!

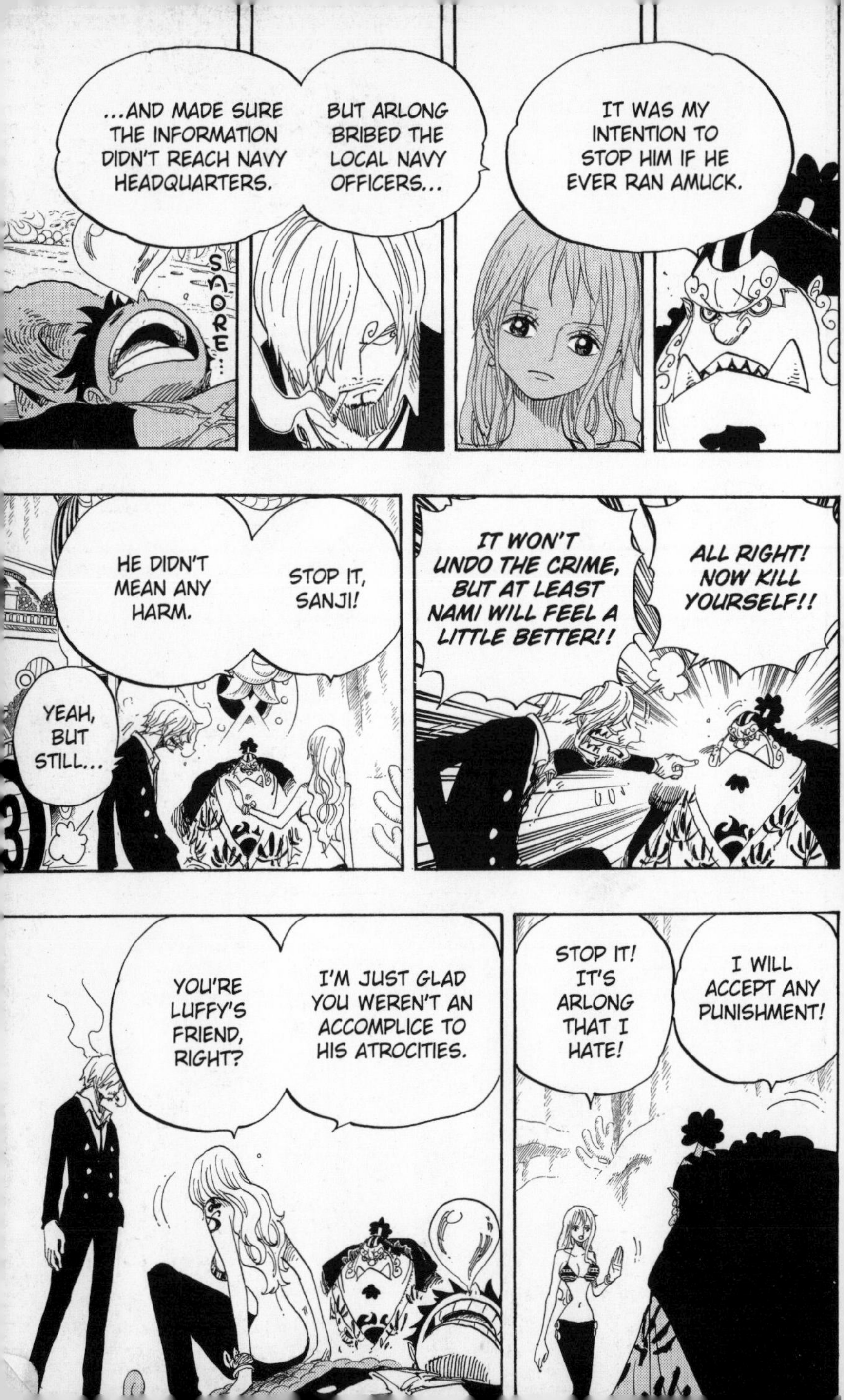
IT WAS MY INTENTION TO STOP HIM IF HE EVER RAN AMUCK.
BUT ARLONG BRIBED THE LOCAL NAVY OFFICERS...
...AND MADE SURE THE INFORMATION DIDN'T REACH NAVY HEADQUARTERS.
SNORE...
ALL RIGHT! NOW KILL YOURSELF!!
IT WON'T UNDO THE CRIME, BUT AT LEAST NAMI WILL FEEL A LITTLE BETTER!!
STOP IT, SANJI!
HE DIDN'T MEAN ANY HARM.
YEAH, BUT STILL...
I WILL ACCEPT ANY PUNISHMENT!
STOP IT! IT'S ARLONG THAT I HATE!
I'M JUST GLAD YOU WEREN'T AN ACCOMPLICE TO HIS ATROCITIES.
YOU'RE LUFFY'S FRIEND, RIGHT?

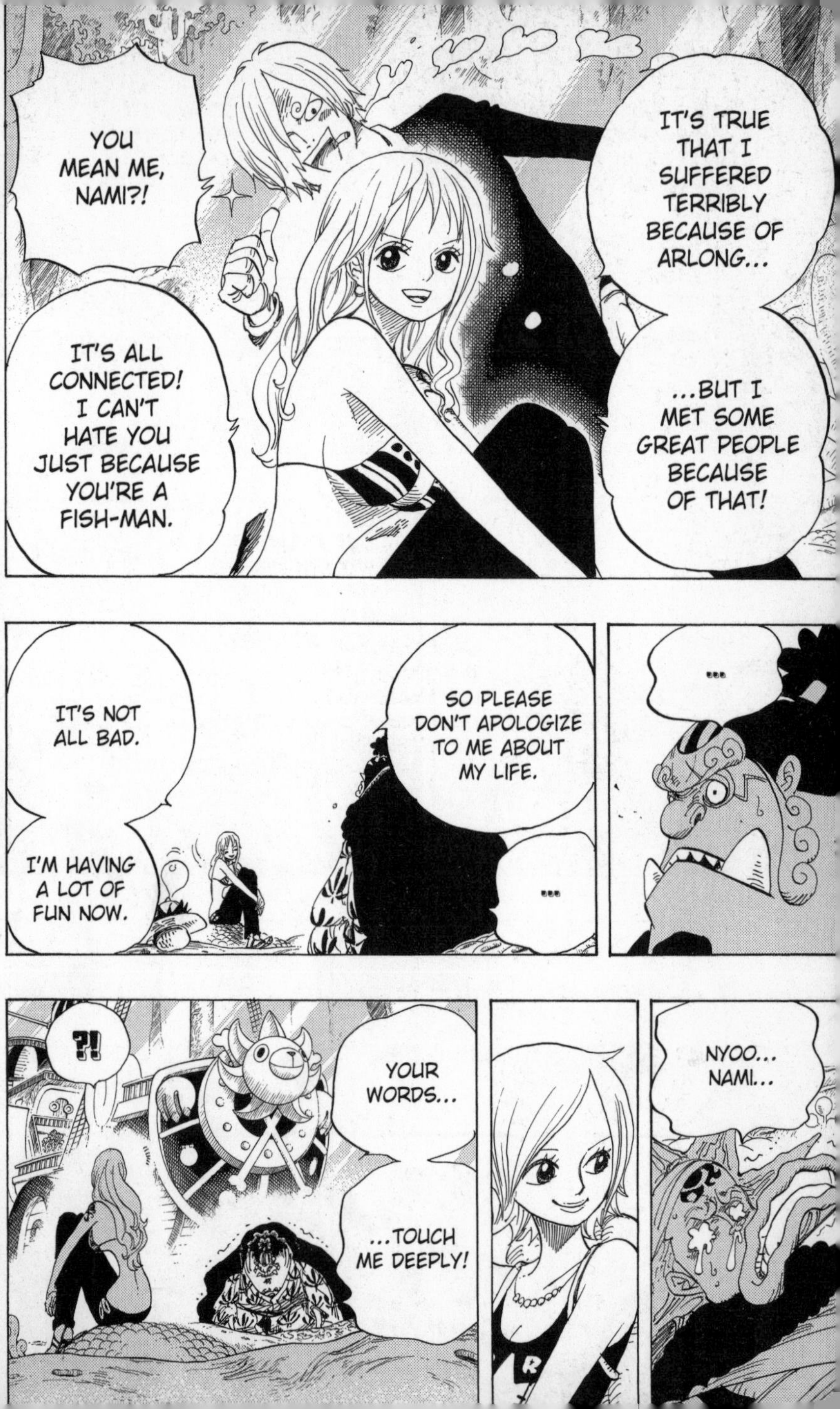
IT'S TRUE THAT I SUFFERED TERRIBLY BECAUSE OF ARLONG...
...BUT I MET SOME GREAT PEOPLE BECAUSE OF THAT!
YOU MEAN ME, NAMI?!
IT'S ALL CONNECTED! I CAN'T HATE YOU JUST BECAUSE YOU'RE A FISH-MAN.
...
SO PLEASE DON'T APOLOGIZE TO ME ABOUT MY LIFE.
IT'S NOT ALL BAD.
...
I'M HAVING A LOT OF FUN NOW.
NYOO... NAMI...
YOUR WORDS...
?!
...TOUCH ME DEEPLY!

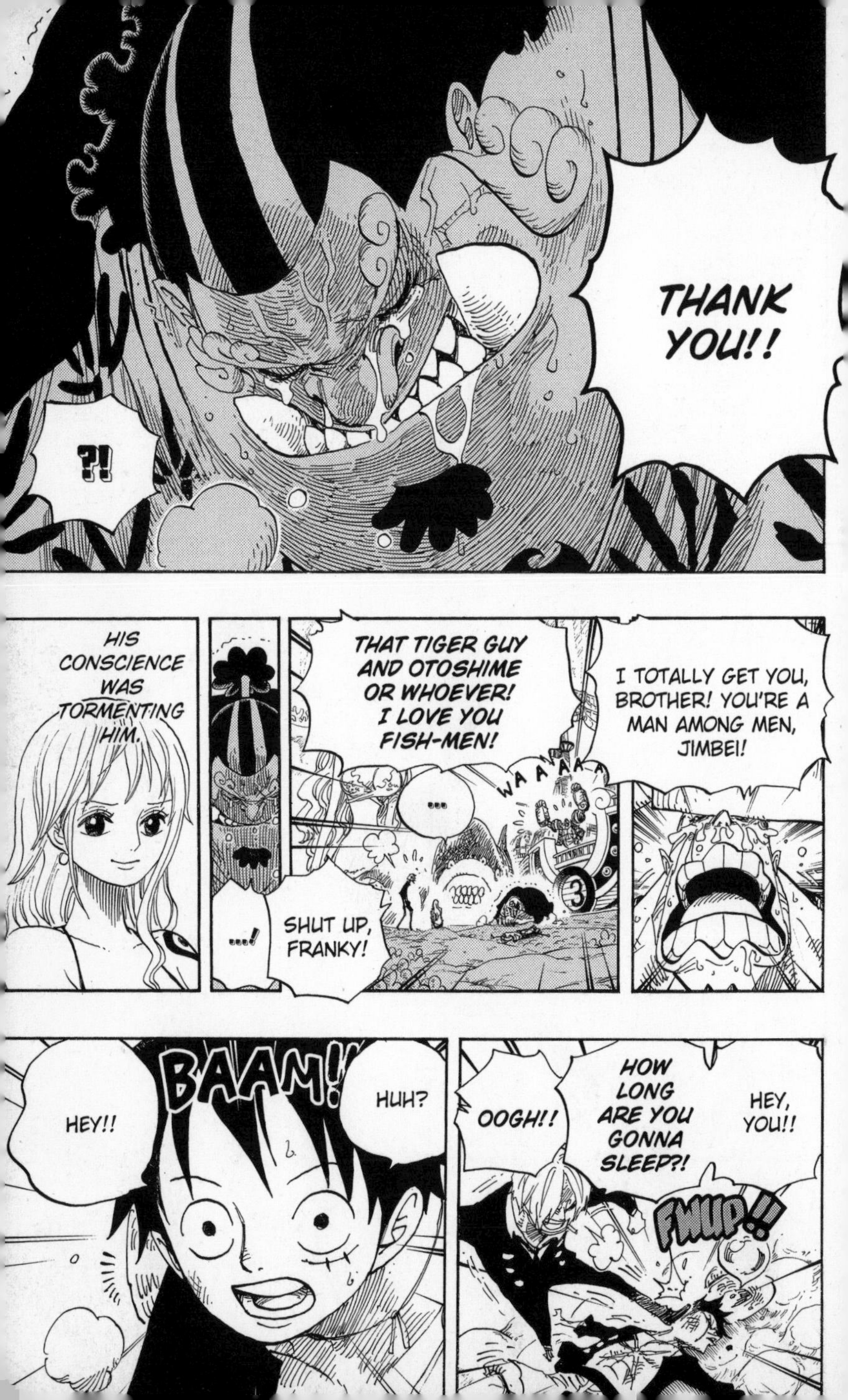
THANK YOU!!
?!
I TOTALLY GET YOU, BROTHER! YOU'RE A MAN AMONG MEN, JIMBEI!
THAT TIGER GUY AND OTOSHIME OR WHOEVER! I LOVE YOU FISH-MEN!
WA A A A A
...
SHUT UP, FRANKY!
...!
HIS CONSCIENCE WAS TORMENTING HIM.
HEY, YOU!!
HOW LONG ARE YOU GONNA SLEEP?!
OOGH!!
FWUP!!
HUH?
BAAM!!
HEY!!

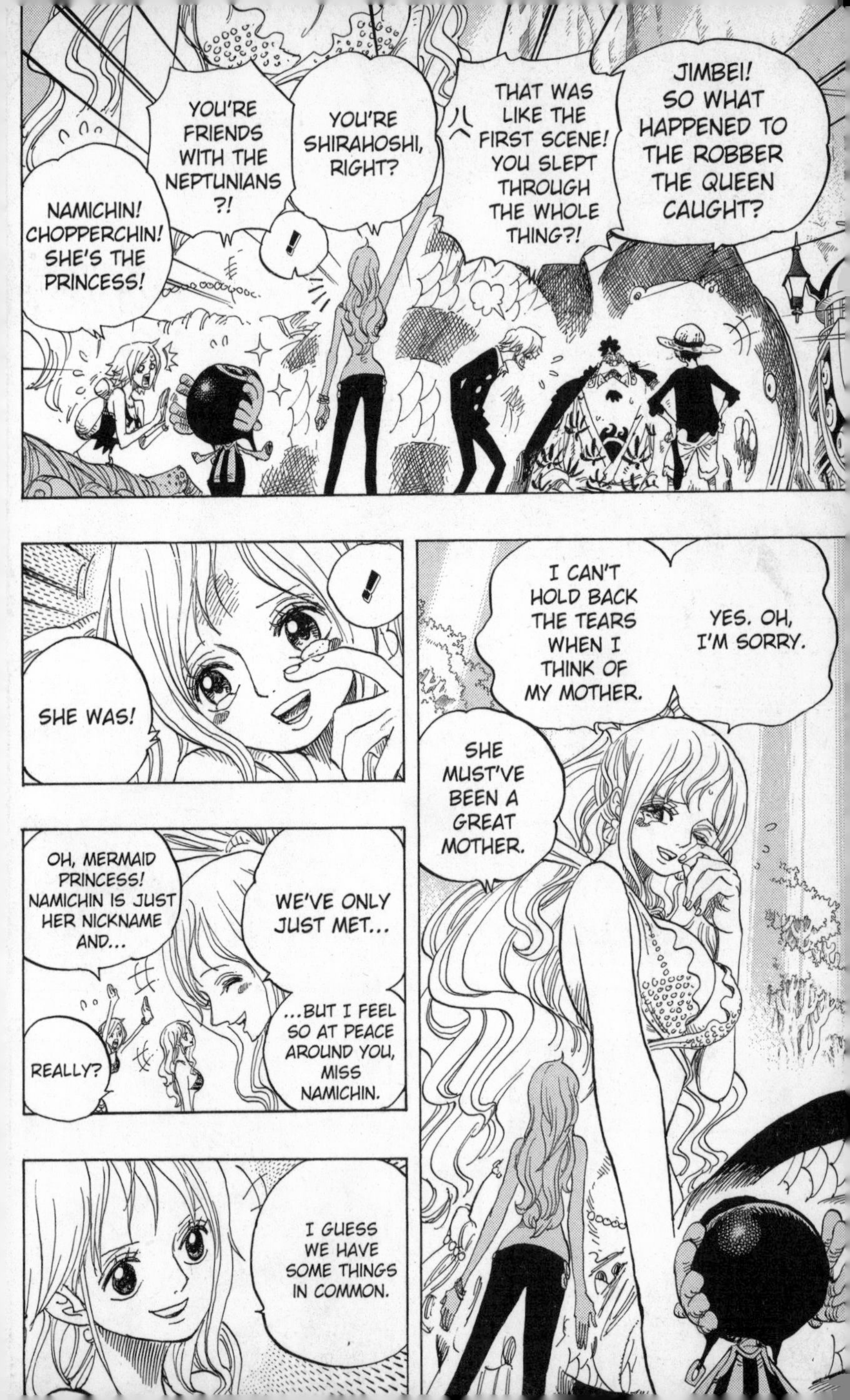
JIMBEI! SO WHAT HAPPENED TO THE ROBBER THE QUEEN CAUGHT?
THAT WAS LIKE THE FIRST SCENE! YOU SLEPT THROUGH THE WHOLE THING?!
YOU'RE SHIRAHOSHI, RIGHT?
YOU'RE FRIENDS WITH THE NEPTUNIANS?!
NAMICHIN! CHOPPERCHIN! SHE'S THE PRINCESS!
YES. OH, I'M SORRY.
I CAN'T HOLD BACK THE TEARS WHEN I THINK OF MY MOTHER.
SHE MUST'VE BEEN A GREAT MOTHER.
SHE WAS!
WE'VE ONLY JUST MET...
...BUT I FEEL SO AT PEACE AROUND YOU, MISS NAMICHIN.
OH, MERMAID PRINCESS! NAMICHIN IS JUST HER NICKNAME AND...
REALLY?
I GUESS WE HAVE SOME THINGS IN COMMON.

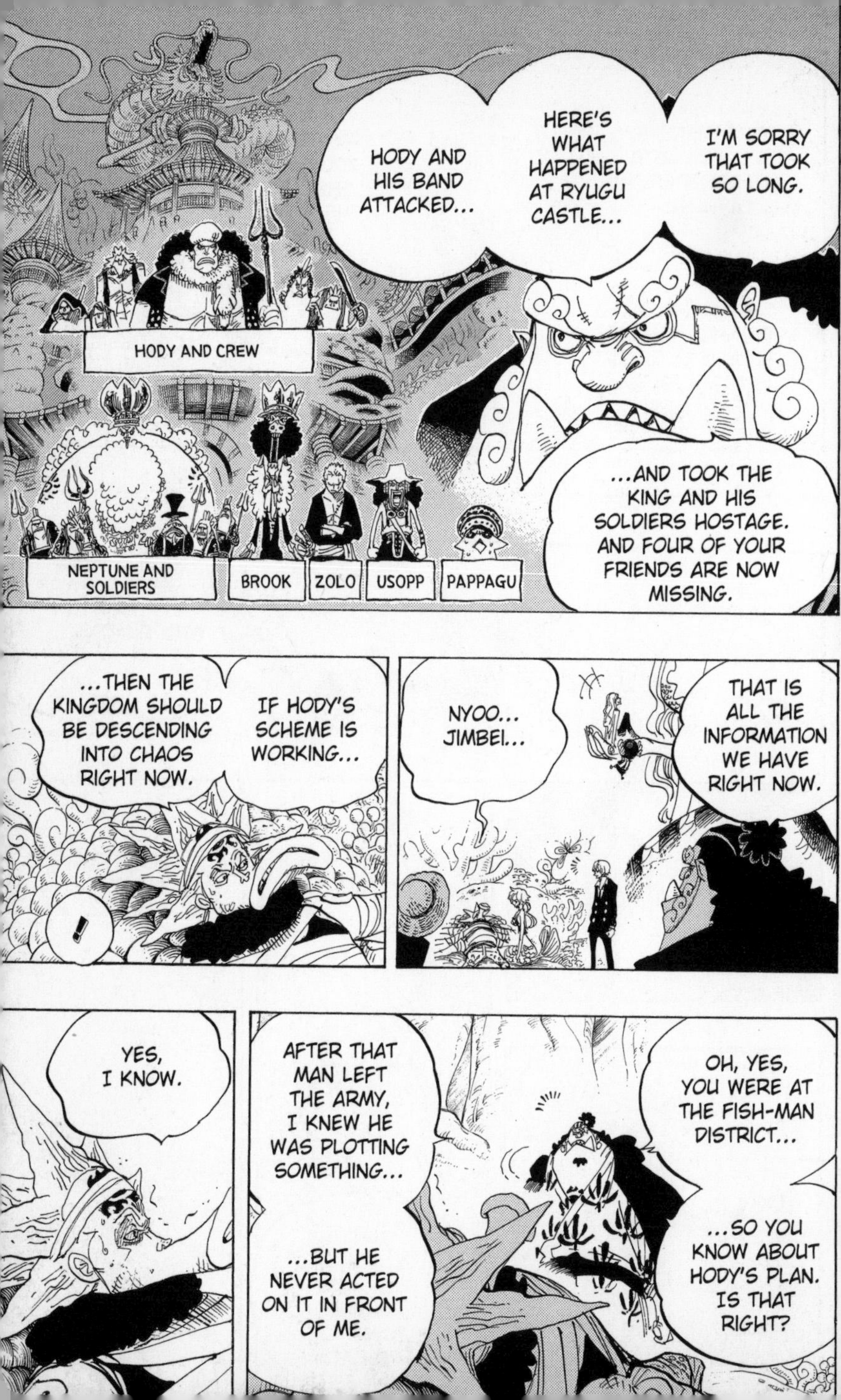
I'M SORRY THAT TOOK SO LONG.
HERE'S WHAT HAPPENED AT RYUGU CASTLE...
HODY AND HIS BAND ATTACKED...
...AND TOOK THE KING AND HIS SOLDIERS HOSTAGE. AND FOUR OF YOUR FRIENDS ARE NOW MISSING.
HODY AND CREW
PAPPAGU
USOPP
ZOLO
BROOK
NEPTUNE AND SOLDIERS
THAT IS ALL THE INFORMATION WE HAVE RIGHT NOW.
NYOO... JIMBEI...
IF HODY'S SCHEME IS WORKING...
...THEN THE KINGDOM SHOULD BE DESCENDING INTO CHAOS RIGHT NOW.
!
OH, YES, YOU WERE AT THE FISH-MAN DISTRICT...
...SO YOU KNOW ABOUT HODY'S PLAN. IS THAT RIGHT?
AFTER THAT MAN LEFT THE ARMY, I KNEW HE WAS PLOTTING SOMETHING...
...BUT HE NEVER ACTED ON IT IN FRONT OF ME.
YES, I KNOW.

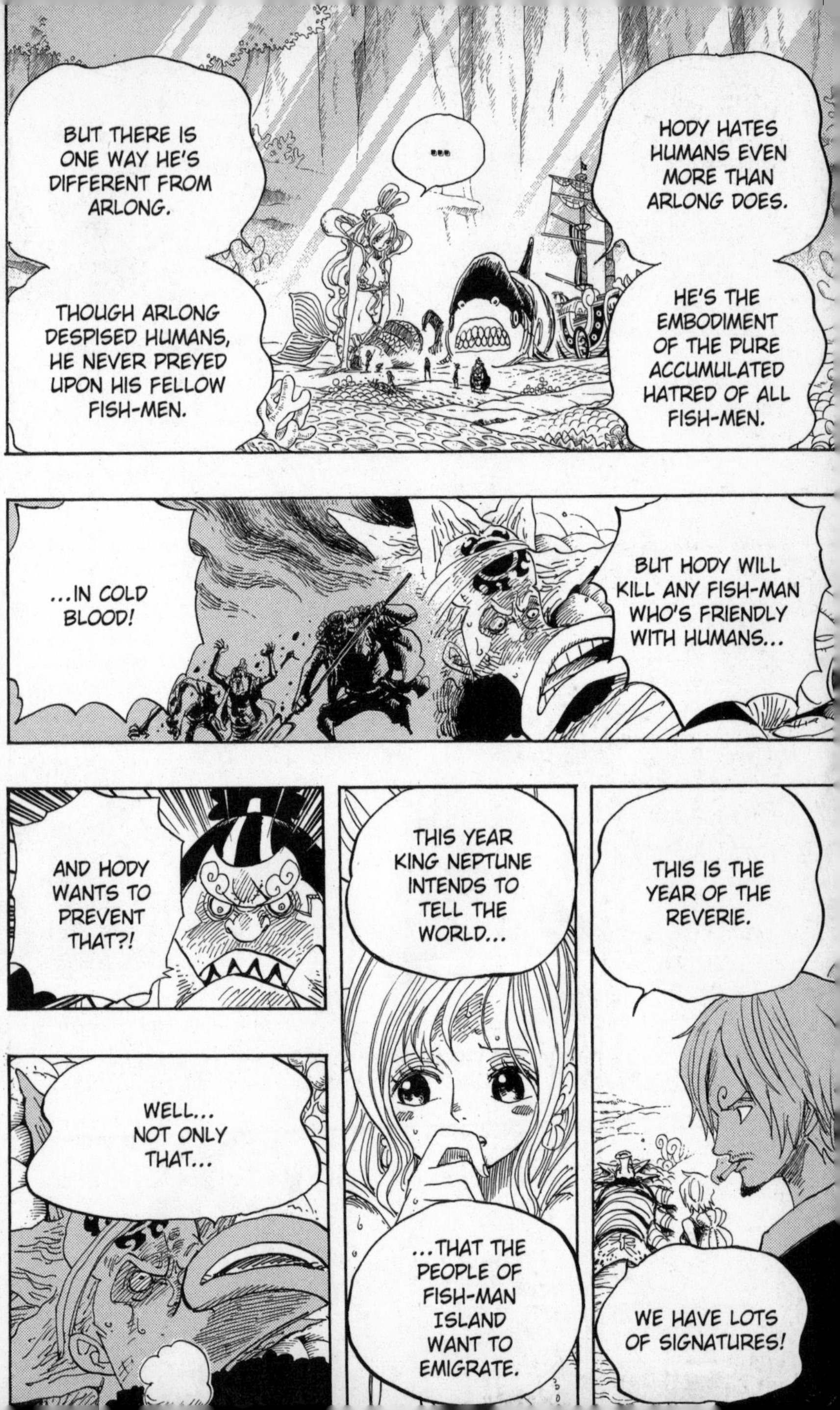
HODY HATES HUMANS EVEN MORE THAN ARLONG DOES.
HE'S THE EMBODIMENT OF THE PURE ACCUMULATED HATRED OF ALL FISH-MEN.
...
BUT THERE IS ONE WAY HE'S DIFFERENT FROM ARLONG.
THOUGH ARLONG DESPISED HUMANS, HE NEVER PREYED UPON HIS FELLOW FISH-MEN.
BUT HODY WILL KILL ANY FISH-MAN WHO'S FRIENDLY WITH HUMANS...
...IN COLD BLOOD!
THIS IS THE YEAR OF THE REVERIE.
WE HAVE LOTS OF SIGNATURES!
THIS YEAR KING NEPTUNE INTENDS TO TELL THE WORLD...
...THAT THE PEOPLE OF FISH-MAN ISLAND WANT TO EMIGRATE.
AND HODY WANTS TO PREVENT THAT?!
WELL... NOT ONLY THAT...

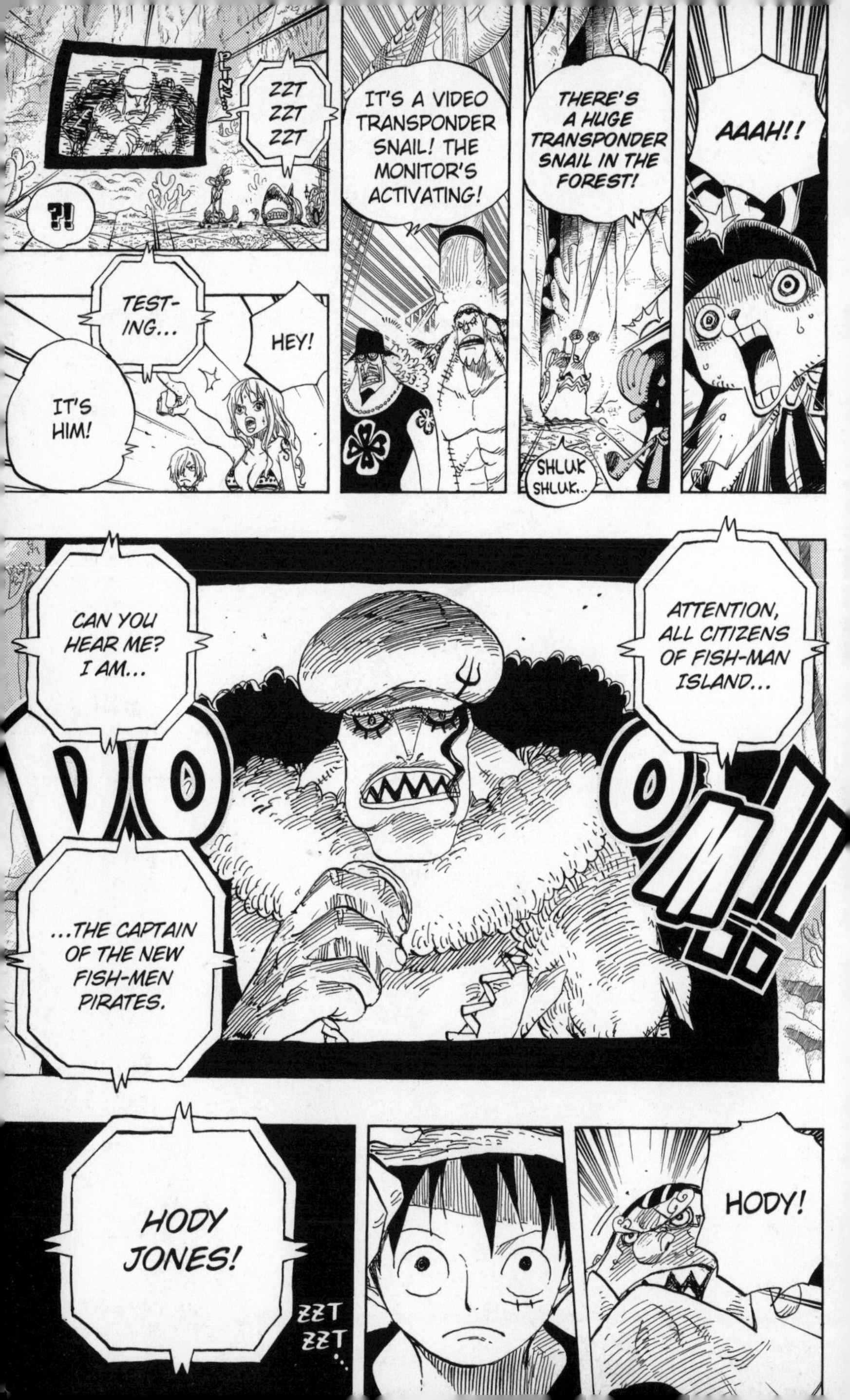
AAAH!!
THERE'S A HUGE TRANSPONDER SNAIL IN THE FOREST!
SHLUK SHLUK...
IT'S A VIDEO TRANSPONDER SNAIL! THE MONITOR'S ACTIVATING!
ZZT ZZT ZZT
PLINK
?!
TEST-ING...
HEY!
IT'S HIM!
ATTENTION, ALL CITIZENS OF FISH-MAN ISLAND...
CAN YOU HEAR ME? I AM...
DOOM!!
...THE CAPTAIN OF THE NEW FISH-MEN PIRATES.
HODY!
HODY JONES!
ZZT ZZT

SPRING CLEANING

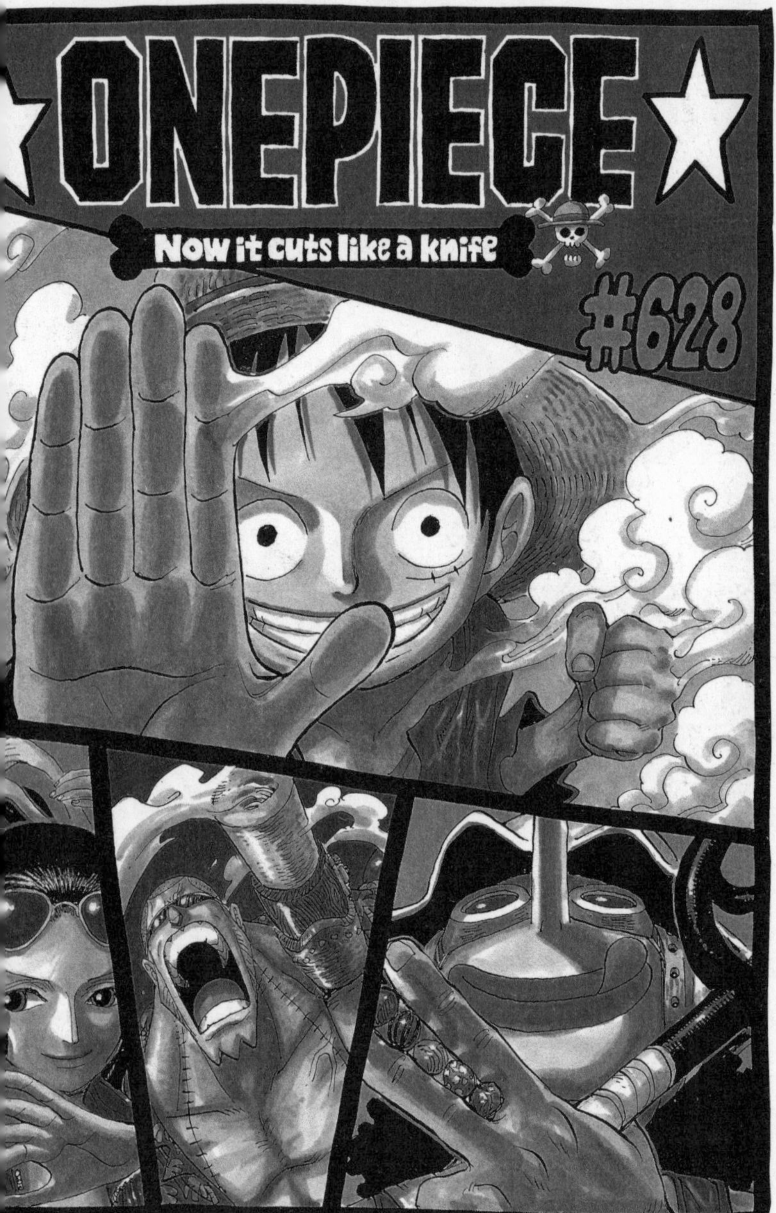
ONEPIECE
Now it cuts like a knife
#628

Chapter 628:

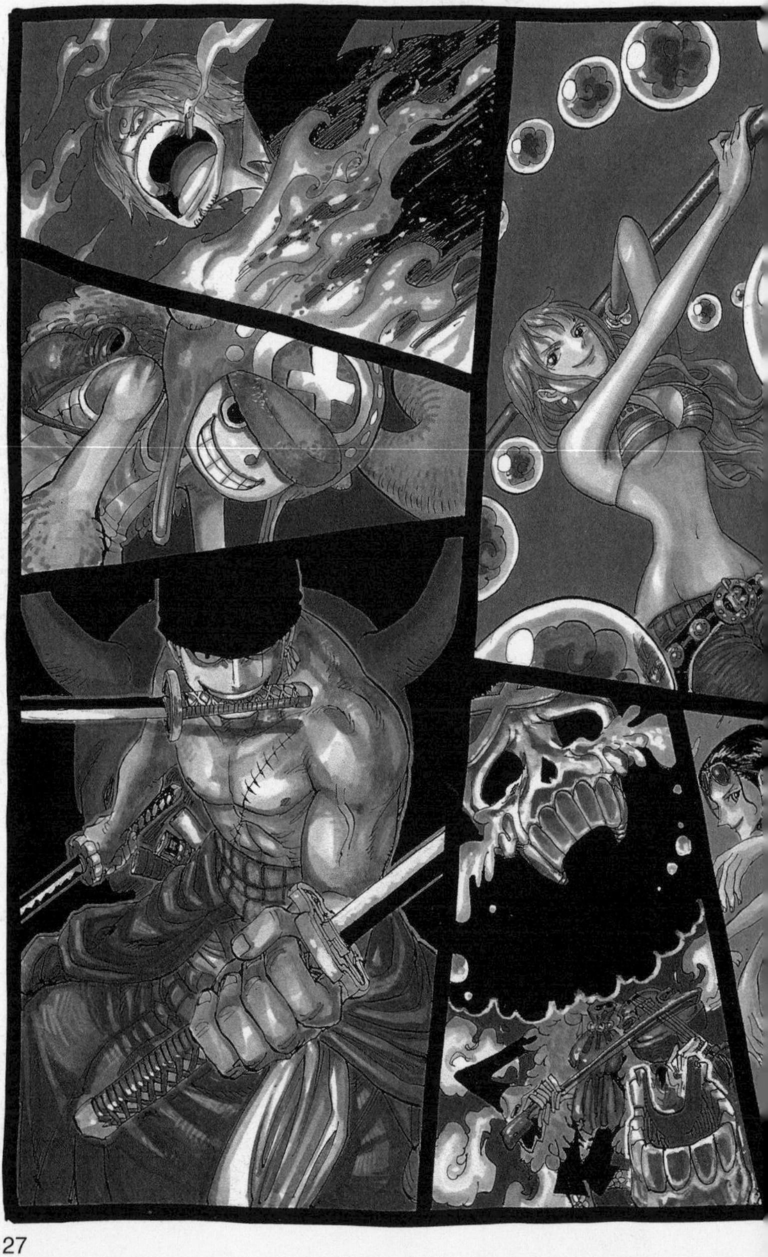

ONE PIECE vol.64

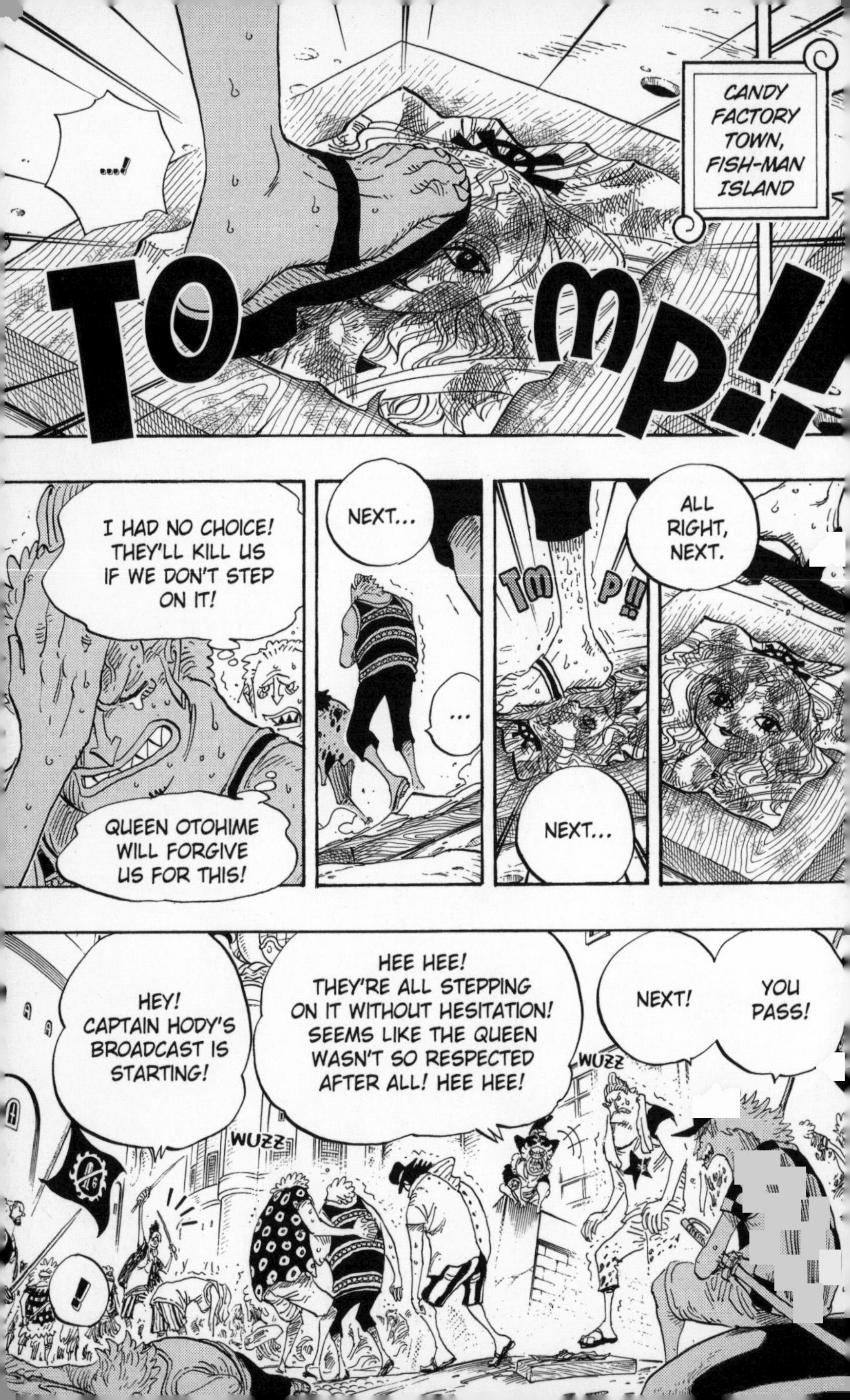
CANDY FACTORY TOWN, FISH-MAN ISLAND
...!
TOMP!!
ALL RIGHT, NEXT.
TMP!!
NEXT...
NEXT...
...
I HAD NO CHOICE! THEY'LL KILL US IF WE DON'T STEP ON IT!
QUEEN OTOHIME WILL FORGIVE US FOR THIS!
YOU PASS!
NEXT!
WUZZ
HEE HEE! THEY'RE ALL STEPPING ON IT WITHOUT HESITATION! SEEMS LIKE THE QUEEN WASN'T SO RESPECTED AFTER ALL! HEE HEE!
HEY! CAPTAIN HODY'S BROADCAST IS STARTING!
WUZZ
!

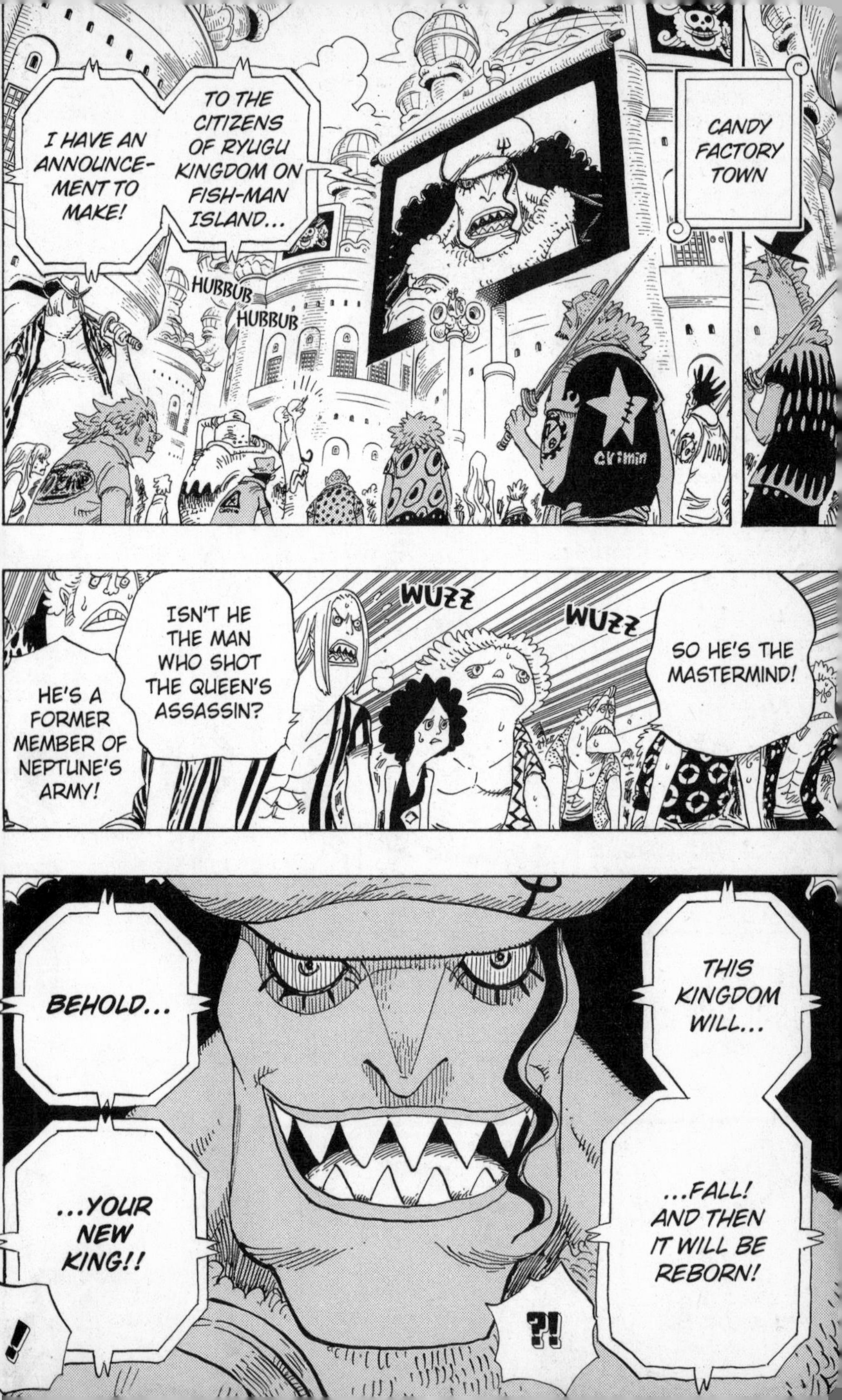
CANDY FACTORY TOWN
TO THE CITIZENS OF RYUGU KINGDOM ON FISH-MAN ISLAND...
I HAVE AN ANNOUNCEMENT TO MAKE!
HUBBUB
HUBBUB
SO HE'S THE MASTERMIND!
WUZZ
WUZZ
ISN'T HE THE MAN WHO SHOT THE QUEEN'S ASSASSIN?
HE'S A FORMER MEMBER OF NEPTUNE'S ARMY!
THIS KINGDOM WILL...
...FALL! AND THEN IT WILL BE REBORN!
BEHOLD...
...YOUR NEW KING!!
?!
!

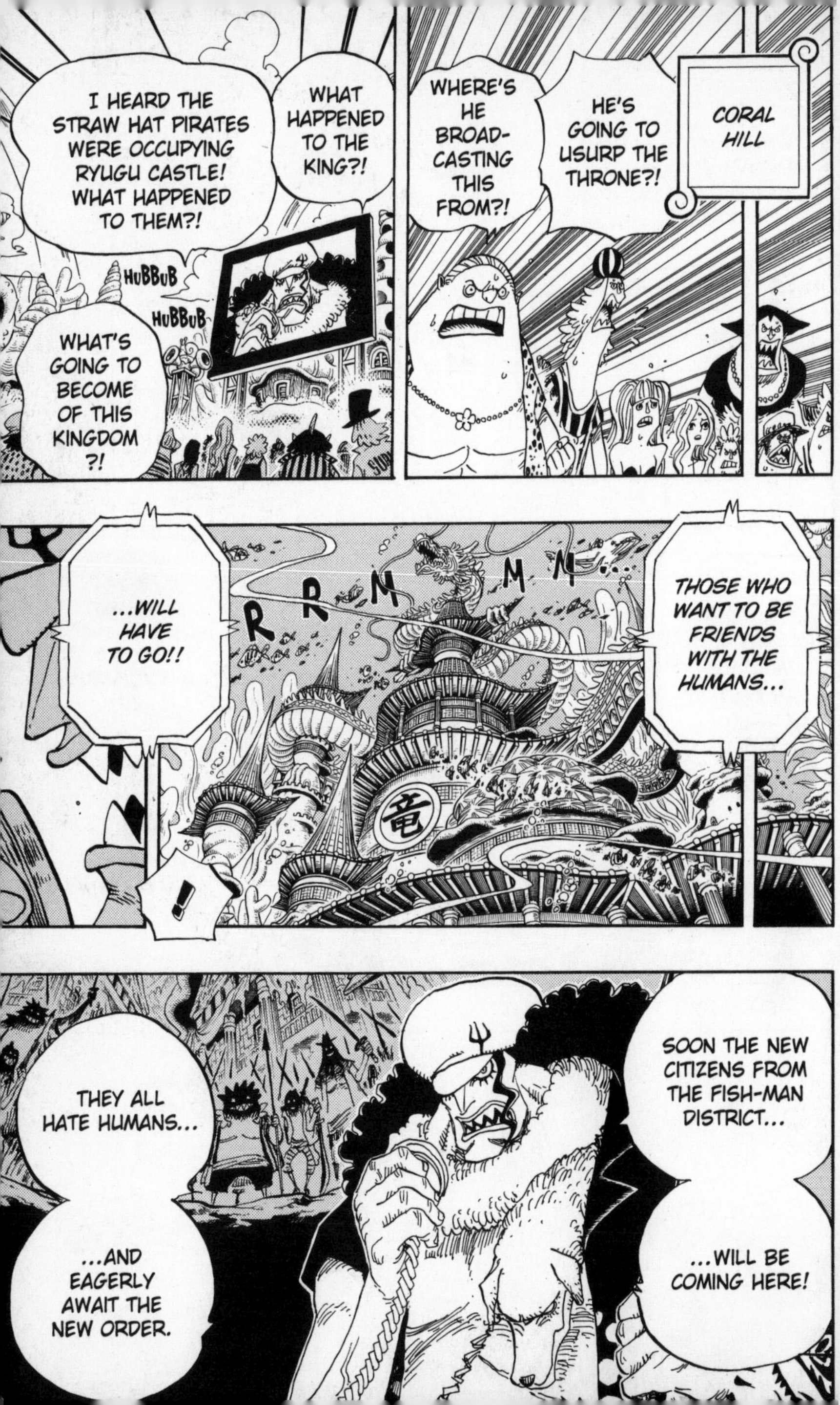
CORAL HILL
HE'S GOING TO USURP THE THRONE?!
WHERE'S HE BROADCASTING THIS FROM?!
WHAT HAPPENED TO THE KING?!
I HEARD THE STRAW HAT PIRATES WERE OCCUPYING RYUGU CASTLE! WHAT HAPPENED TO THEM?!
HUBBUB
HUBBUB
WHAT'S GOING TO BECOME OF THIS KINGDOM?!
THOSE WHO WANT TO BE FRIENDS WITH THE HUMANS...
RRMMM
...WILL HAVE TO GO!!
!
SOON THE NEW CITIZENS FROM THE FISH-MAN DISTRICT...
...WILL BE COMING HERE!
THEY ALL HATE HUMANS...
...AND EAGERLY AWAIT THE NEW ORDER.

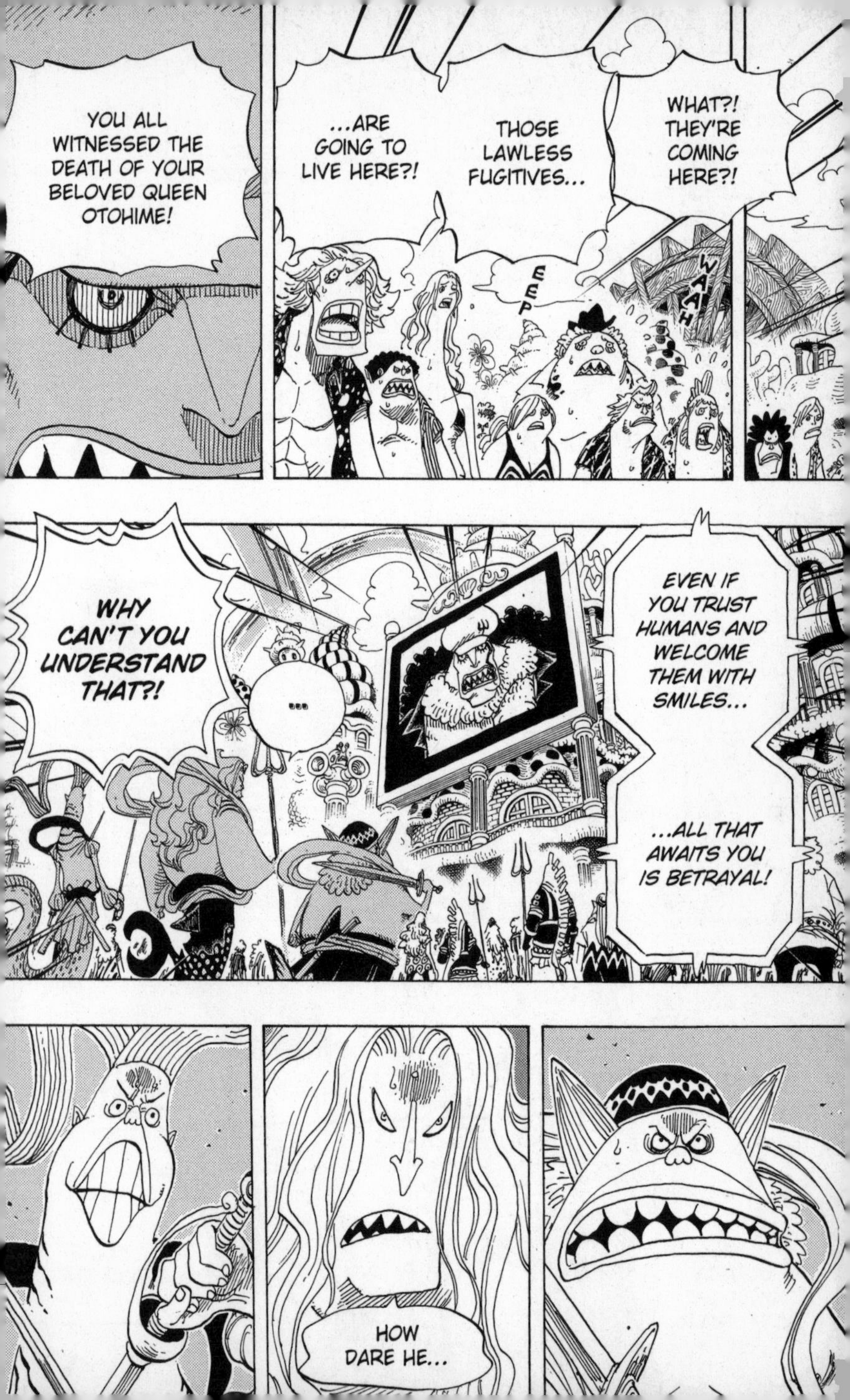
WHAT?! THEY'RE COMING HERE?!
WAAH
THOSE LAWLESS FUGITIVES...
...ARE GOING TO LIVE HERE?!
EEP
YOU ALL WITNESSED THE DEATH OF YOUR BELOVED QUEEN OTOHIME!
EVEN IF YOU TRUST HUMANS AND WELCOME THEM WITH SMILES...
...ALL THAT AWAITS YOU IS BETRAYAL!
...
WHY CAN'T YOU UNDERSTAND THAT?!
HOW DARE HE...

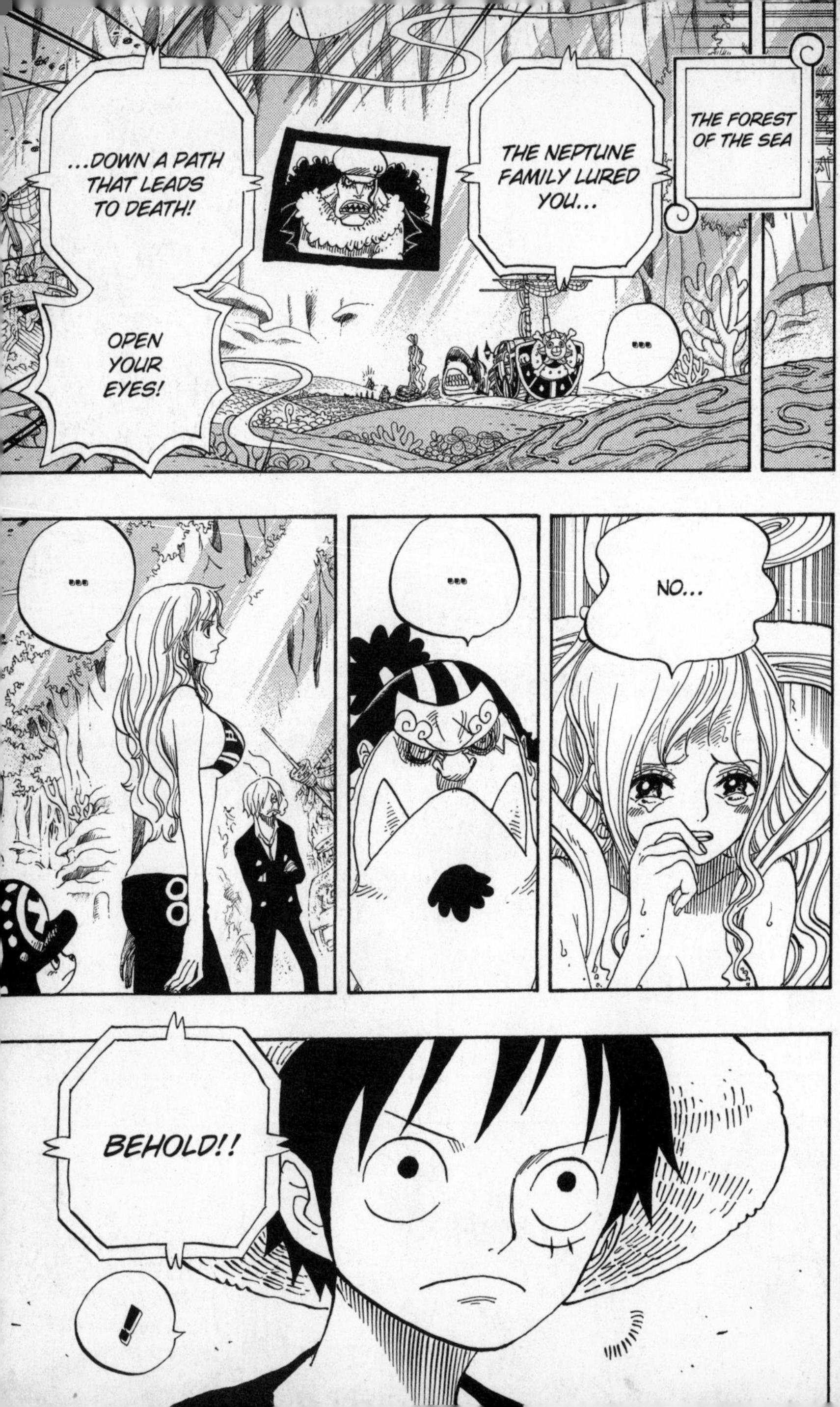
THE FOREST OF THE SEA
THE NEPTUNE FAMILY LURED YOU...
...
...DOWN A PATH THAT LEADS TO DEATH!
OPEN YOUR EYES!
NO...
...
...
BEHOLD!!
!

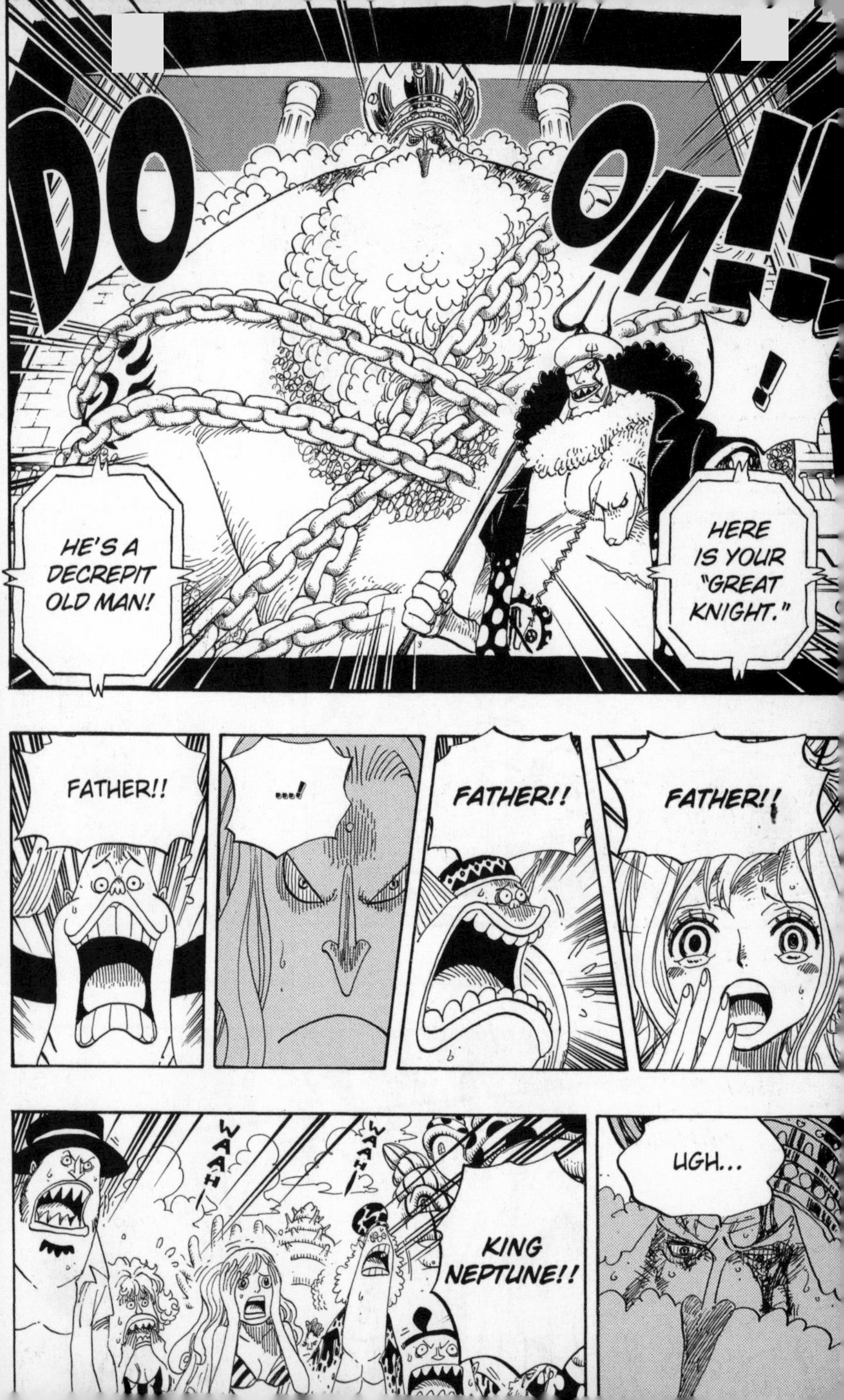

DO
OM!!
!
HERE IS YOUR "GREAT KNIGHT."
HE'S A DECREPIT OLD MAN!
FATHER!!
FATHER!!
...!
FATHER!!
UGH...
KING NEPTUNE!!
WAAH!
WAAH!

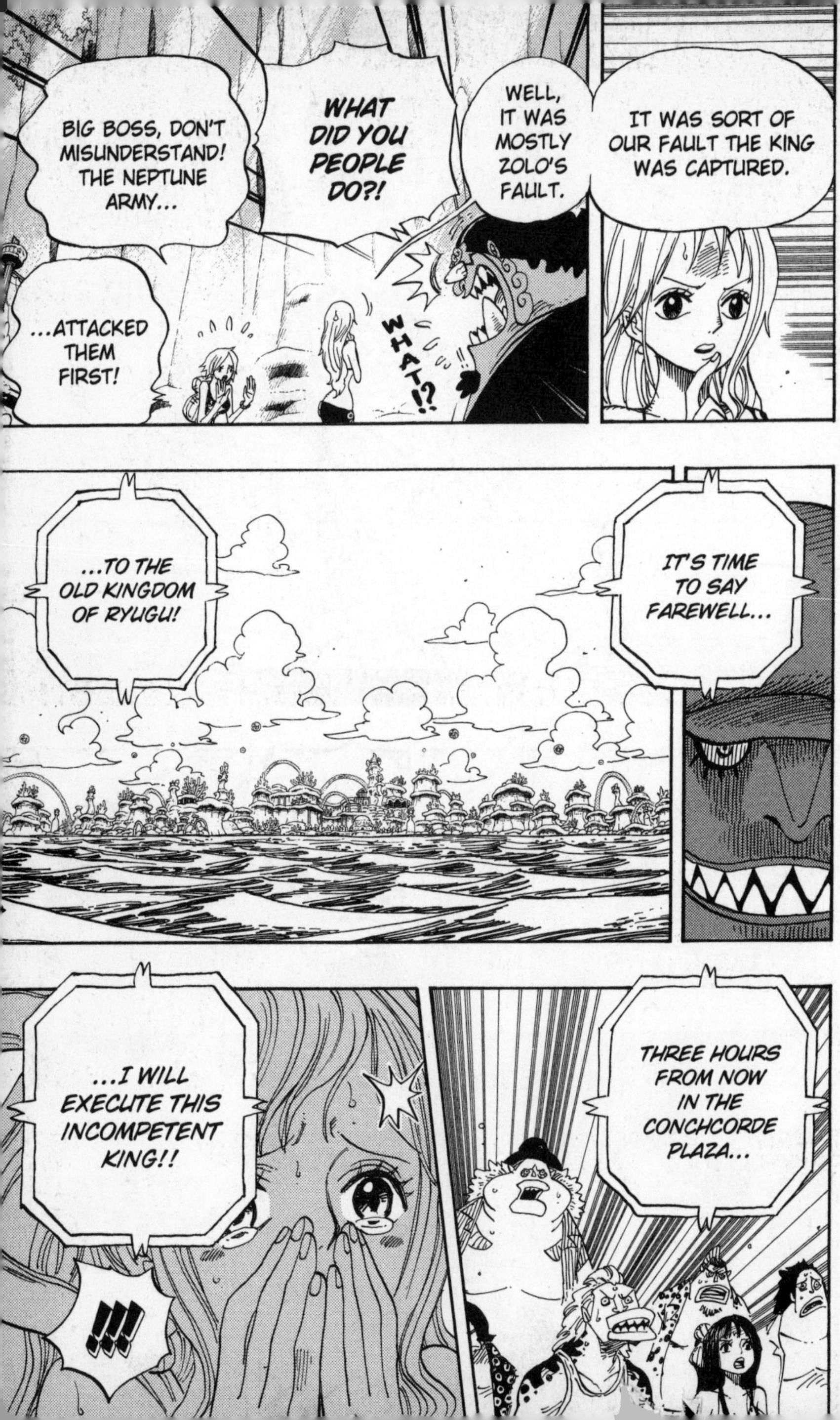
IT WAS SORT OF OUR FAULT THE KING WAS CAPTURED.
WELL, IT WAS MOSTLY ZOLO'S FAULT.
WHAT!?
WHAT DID YOU PEOPLE DO?!
BIG BOSS, DON'T MISUNDERSTAND! THE NEPTUNE ARMY...
...ATTACKED THEM FIRST!
IT'S TIME TO SAY FAREWELL...
...TO THE OLD KINGDOM OF RYUGU!
THREE HOURS FROM NOW IN THE CONCHCORDE PLAZA...
...I WILL EXECUTE THIS INCOMPETENT KING!!
!!!

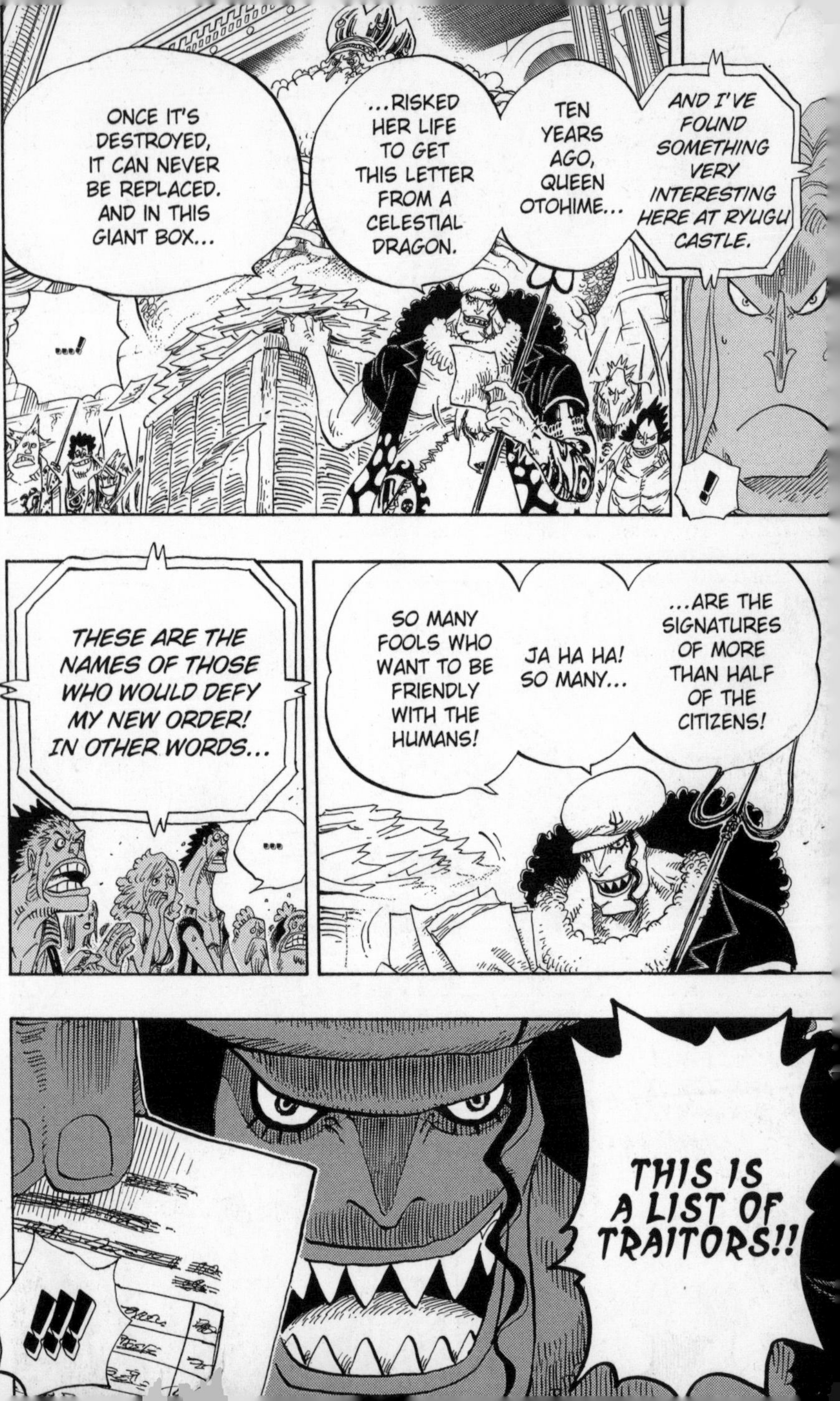
AND I'VE FOUND SOMETHING VERY INTERESTING HERE AT RYUGU CASTLE.
!
TEN YEARS AGO, QUEEN OTOHIME...
...RISKED HER LIFE TO GET THIS LETTER FROM A CELESTIAL DRAGON.
ONCE IT'S DESTROYED, IT CAN NEVER BE REPLACED. AND IN THIS GIANT BOX...
...!
...ARE THE SIGNATURES OF MORE THAN HALF OF THE CITIZENS!
JA HA HA! SO MANY...
SO MANY FOOLS WHO WANT TO BE FRIENDLY WITH THE HUMANS!
THESE ARE THE NAMES OF THOSE WHO WOULD DEFY MY NEW ORDER! IN OTHER WORDS...
...
THIS IS A LIST OF TRAITORS!!
!!!

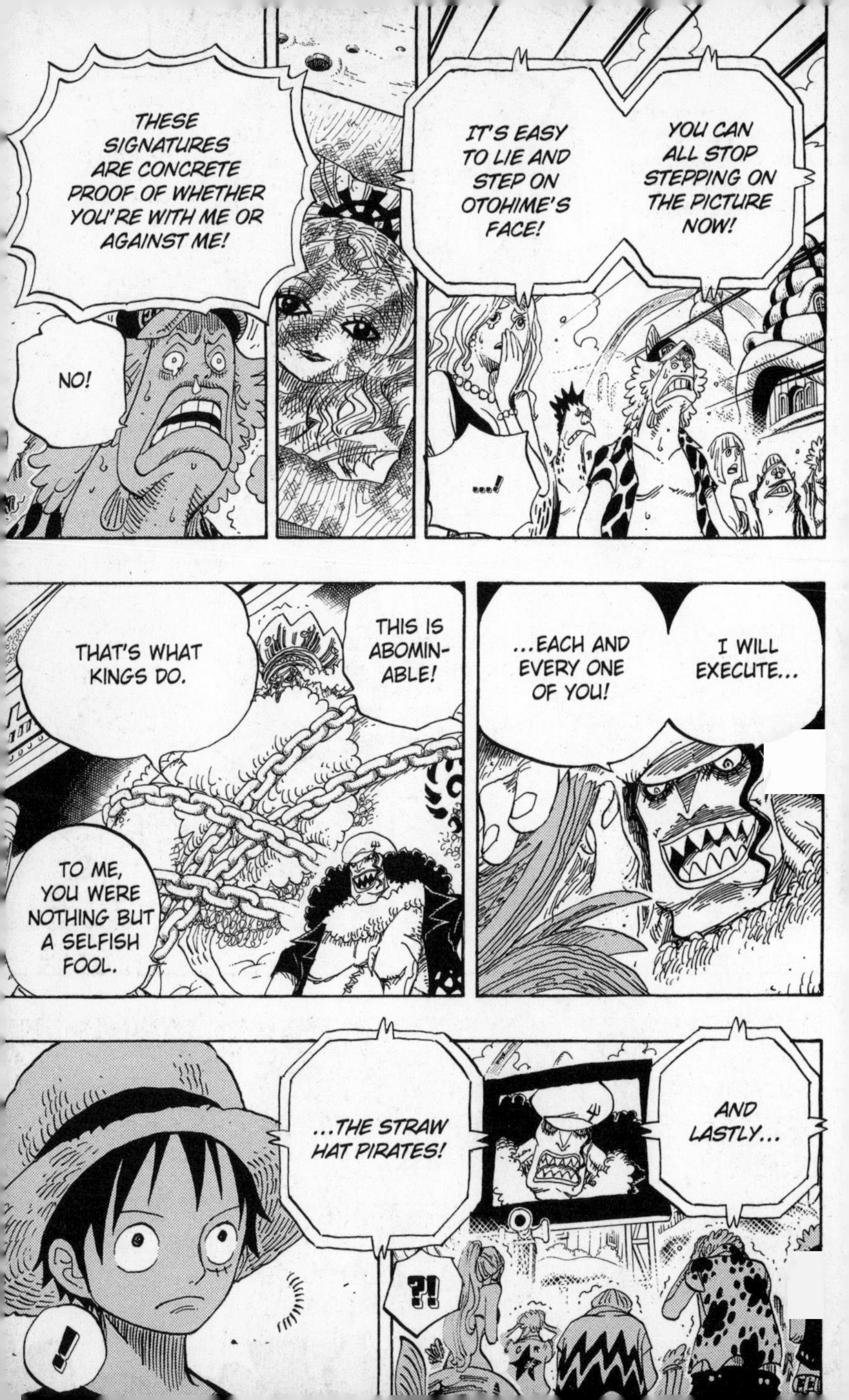
YOU CAN ALL STOP STEPPING ON THE PICTURE NOW!
IT'S EASY TO LIE AND STEP ON OTOHIME'S FACE!
...!
THESE SIGNATURES ARE CONCRETE PROOF OF WHETHER YOU'RE WITH ME OR AGAINST ME!
NO!
I WILL EXECUTE...
...EACH AND EVERY ONE OF YOU!
THIS IS ABOMIN-ABLE!
THAT'S WHAT KINGS DO.
TO ME, YOU WERE NOTHING BUT A SELFISH FOOL.
AND LASTLY...
...THE STRAW HAT PIRATES!
?!
!

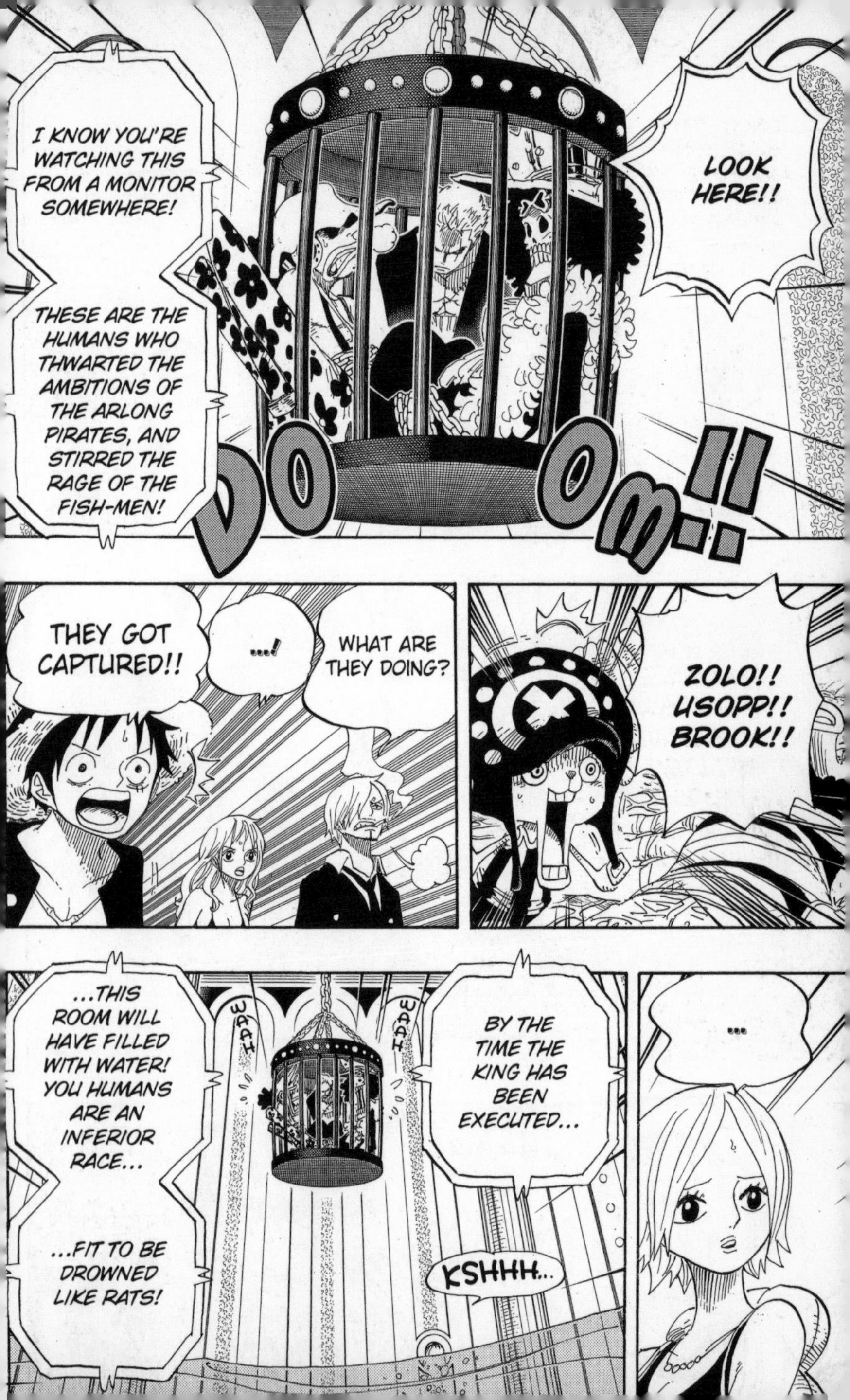
LOOK HERE!!
I KNOW YOU'RE WATCHING THIS FROM A MONITOR SOMEWHERE!
THESE ARE THE HUMANS WHO THWARTED THE AMBITIONS OF THE ARLONG PIRATES, AND STIRRED THE RAGE OF THE FISH-MEN!
DOOM!!
ZOLO!! USOPP!! BROOK!!
WHAT ARE THEY DOING?
...!
THEY GOT CAPTURED!!
...
BY THE TIME THE KING HAS BEEN EXECUTED...
...THIS ROOM WILL HAVE FILLED WITH WATER! YOU HUMANS ARE AN INFERIOR RACE...
WAAH
WAAH
KSHHH...
...FIT TO BE DROWNED LIKE RATS!

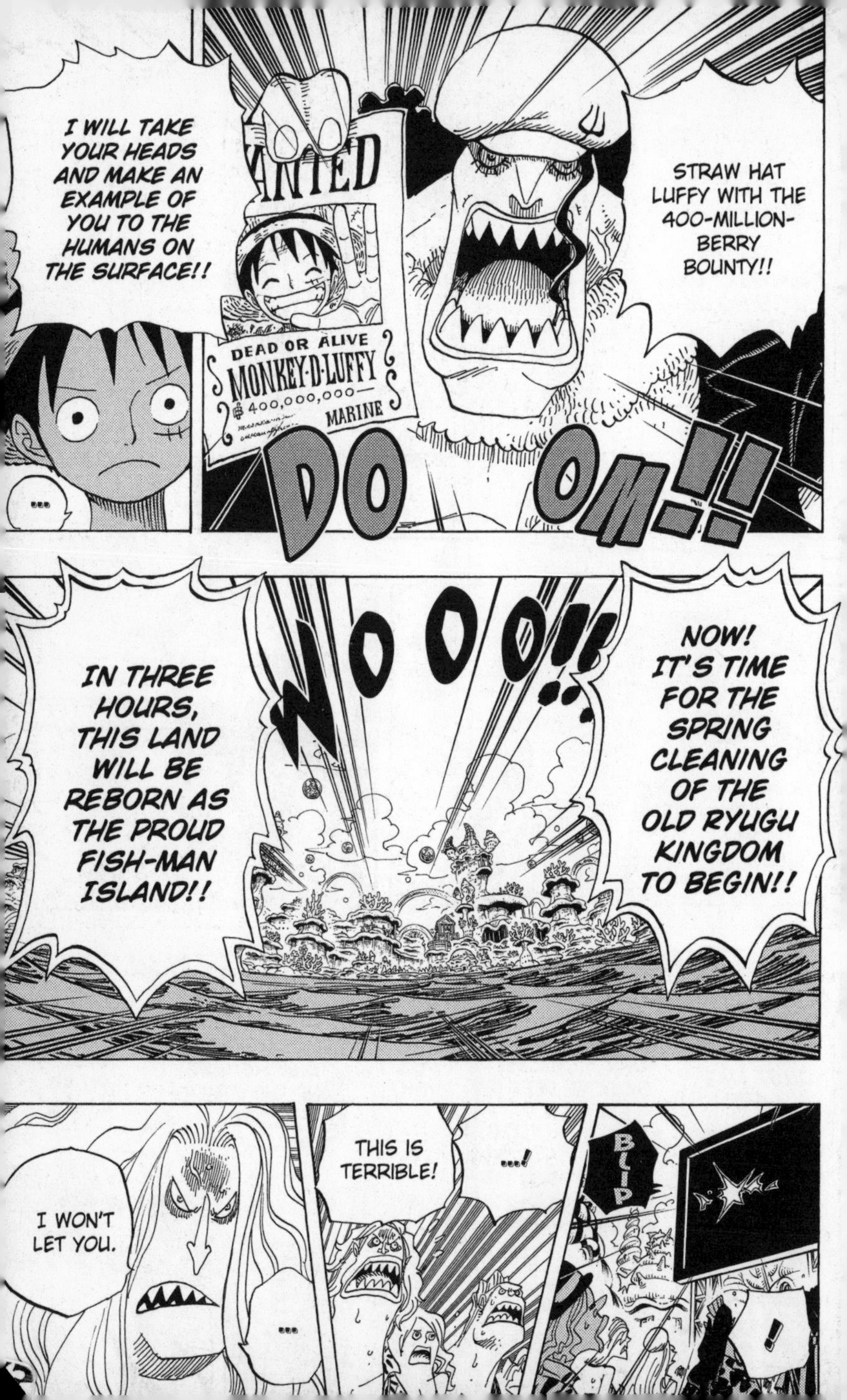
STRAW HAT LUFFY WITH THE 400-MILLION-BERRY BOUNTY!!
I WILL TAKE YOUR HEADS AND MAKE AN EXAMPLE OF YOU TO THE HUMANS ON THE SURFACE!!
WANTED
DEAD OR ALIVE
MONKEY·D·LUFFY
฿400,000,000—
MARINE
DOOM!!
...
NOW! IT'S TIME FOR THE SPRING CLEANING OF THE OLD RYUGU KINGDOM TO BEGIN!!
IN THREE HOURS, THIS LAND WILL BE REBORN AS THE PROUD FISH-MAN ISLAND!!
WOOO!!
BLIP
!
...!
THIS IS TERRIBLE!
I WON'T LET YOU.
...

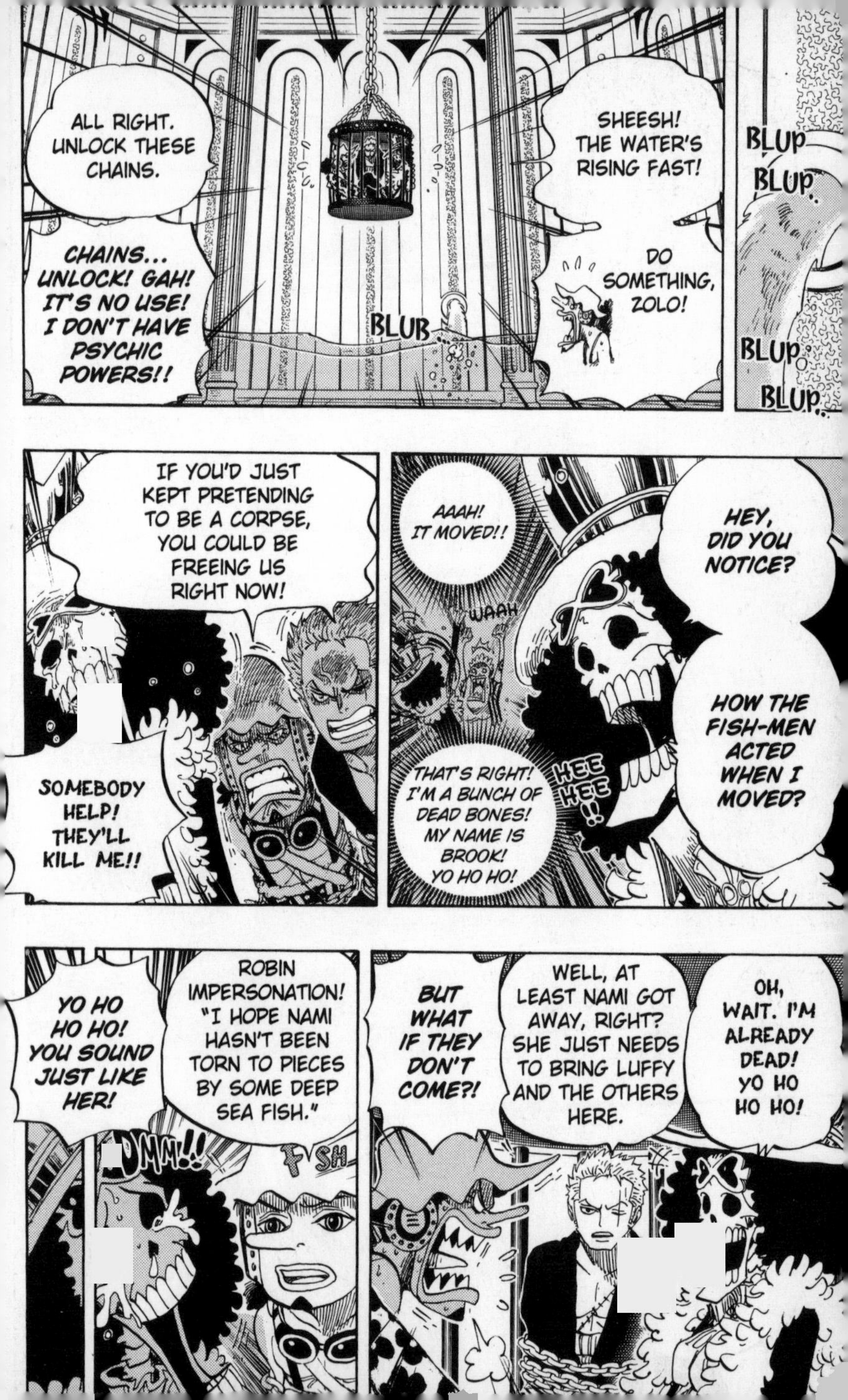
BLUP
BLUP..
BLUP
BLUP..
SHEESH! THE WATER'S RISING FAST!
DO SOMETHING, ZOLO!
ALL RIGHT. UNLOCK THESE CHAINS.
CHAINS... UNLOCK! GAH! IT'S NO USE! I DON'T HAVE PSYCHIC POWERS!!
BLUB
HEY, DID YOU NOTICE?
HOW THE FISH-MEN ACTED WHEN I MOVED?
AAAH! IT MOVED!!
WAAH
HEE HEE!!
THAT'S RIGHT! I'M A BUNCH OF DEAD BONES! MY NAME IS BROOK! YO HO HO!
IF YOU'D JUST KEPT PRETENDING TO BE A CORPSE, YOU COULD BE FREEING US RIGHT NOW!
SOMEBODY HELP! THEY'LL KILL ME!!
OH, WAIT. I'M ALREADY DEAD! YO HO HO HO!
WELL, AT LEAST NAMI GOT AWAY, RIGHT? SHE JUST NEEDS TO BRING LUFFY AND THE OTHERS HERE.
BUT WHAT IF THEY DON'T COME?!
ROBIN IMPERSONATION! "I HOPE NAMI HASN'T BEEN TORN TO PIECES BY SOME DEEP SEA FISH."
FSH
YO HO HO HO! YOU SOUND JUST LIKE HER!

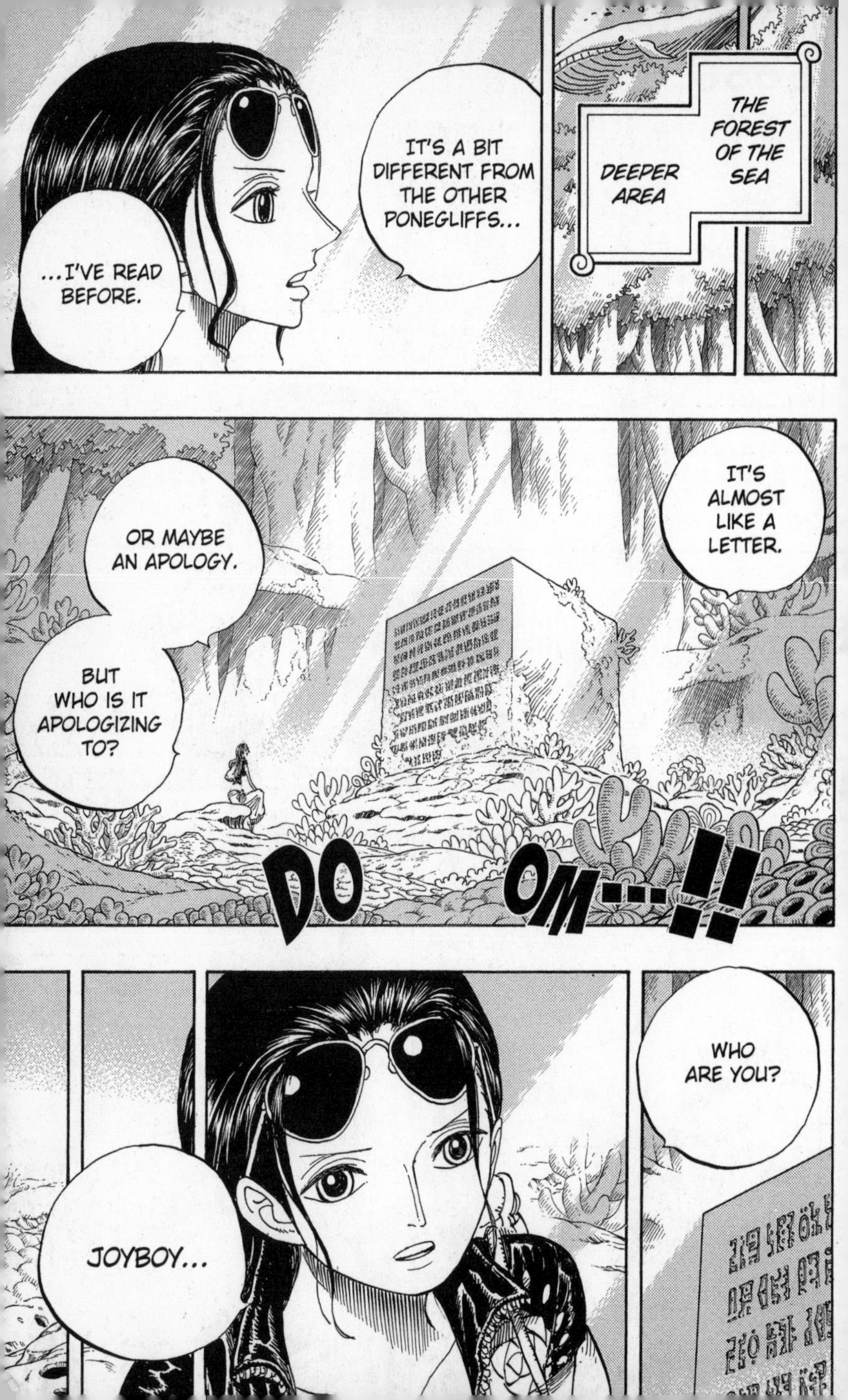
THE FOREST OF THE SEA
DEEPER AREA
IT'S A BIT DIFFERENT FROM THE OTHER PONEGLIFFS...
...I'VE READ BEFORE.
IT'S ALMOST LIKE A LETTER.
OR MAYBE AN APOLOGY.
BUT WHO IS IT APOLOGIZING TO?
DOOM...!!
WHO ARE YOU?
JOYBOY...

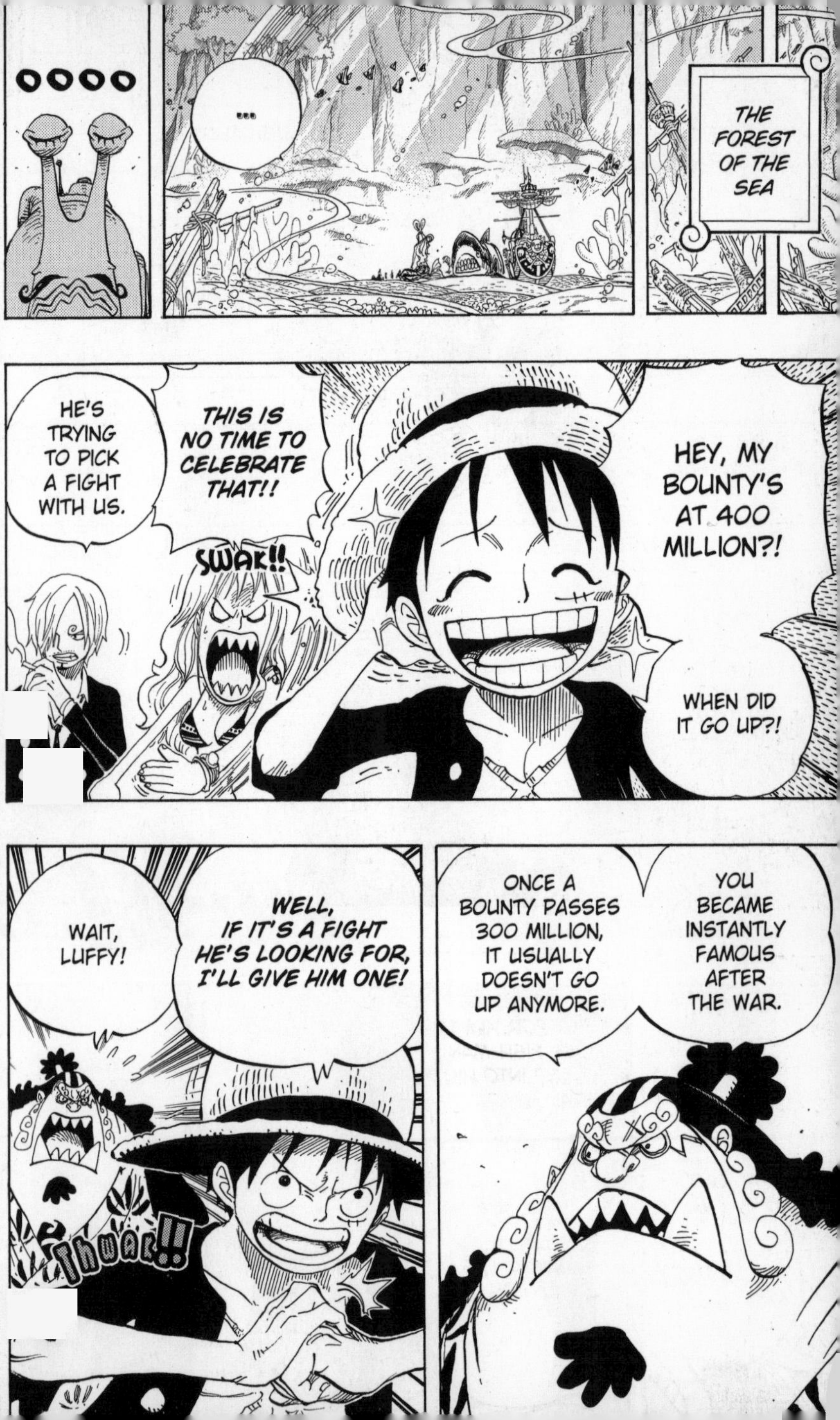
THE FOREST OF THE SEA
...
OOOO
HEY, MY BOUNTY'S AT 400 MILLION?!
WHEN DID IT GO UP?!
THIS IS NO TIME TO CELEBRATE THAT!!
SWAK!!
HE'S TRYING TO PICK A FIGHT WITH US.
YOU BECAME INSTANTLY FAMOUS AFTER THE WAR.
ONCE A BOUNTY PASSES 300 MILLION, IT USUALLY DOESN'T GO UP ANYMORE.
WELL, IF IT'S A FIGHT HE'S LOOKING FOR, I'LL GIVE HIM ONE!
WAIT, LUFFY!
THWAK!!

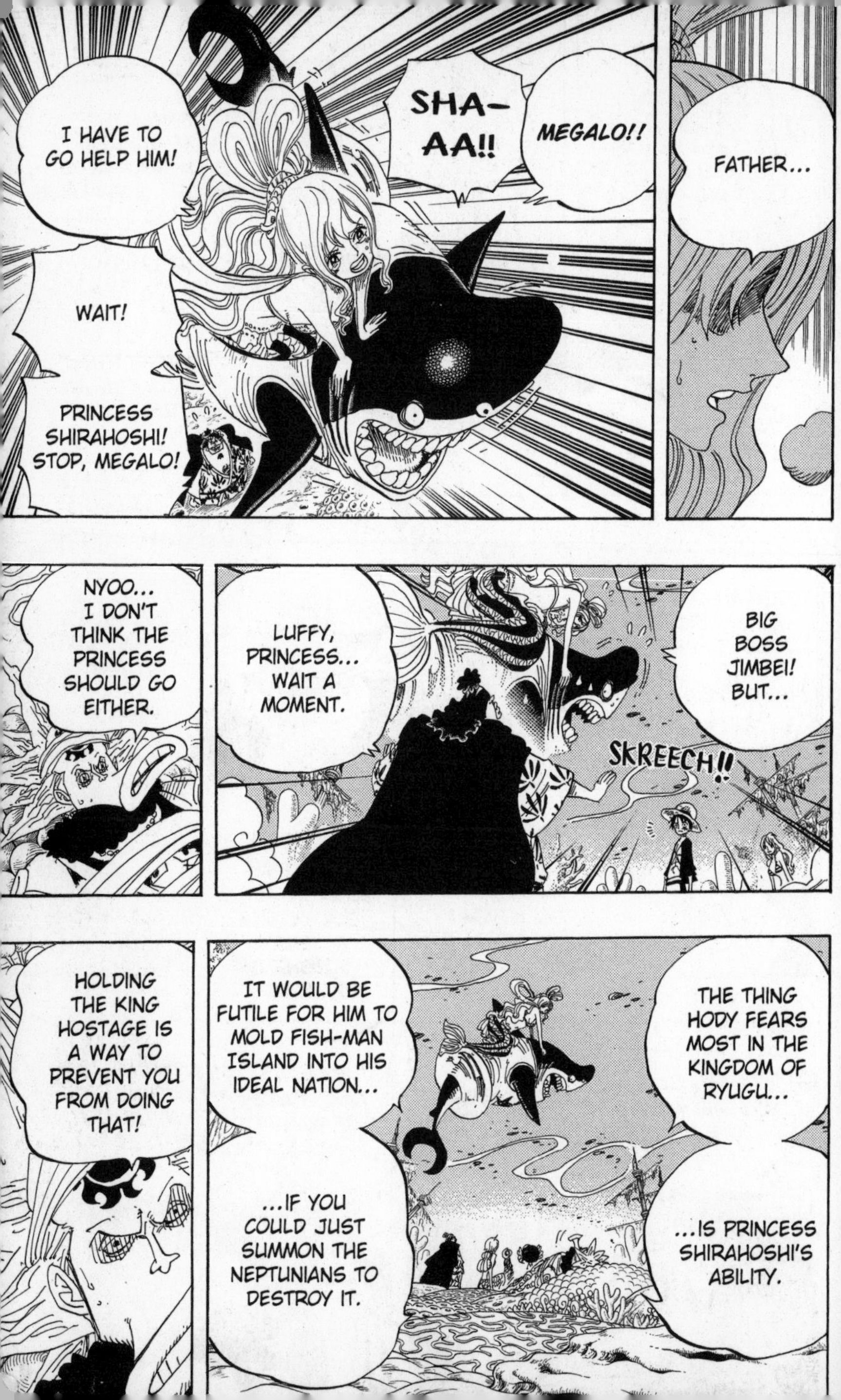
FATHER...
MEGALO!!
SHA-AA!!
I HAVE TO GO HELP HIM!
WAIT!
PRINCESS SHIRAHOSHI! STOP, MEGALO!
BIG BOSS JIMBEI! BUT...
SKREECH!!
LUFFY, PRINCESS... WAIT A MOMENT.
NYOO... I DON'T THINK THE PRINCESS SHOULD GO EITHER.
THE THING HODY FEARS MOST IN THE KINGDOM OF RYUGU...
...IS PRINCESS SHIRAHOSHI'S ABILITY.
IT WOULD BE FUTILE FOR HIM TO MOLD FISH-MAN ISLAND INTO HIS IDEAL NATION...
...IF YOU COULD JUST SUMMON THE NEPTUNIANS TO DESTROY IT.
HOLDING THE KING HOSTAGE IS A WAY TO PREVENT YOU FROM DOING THAT!

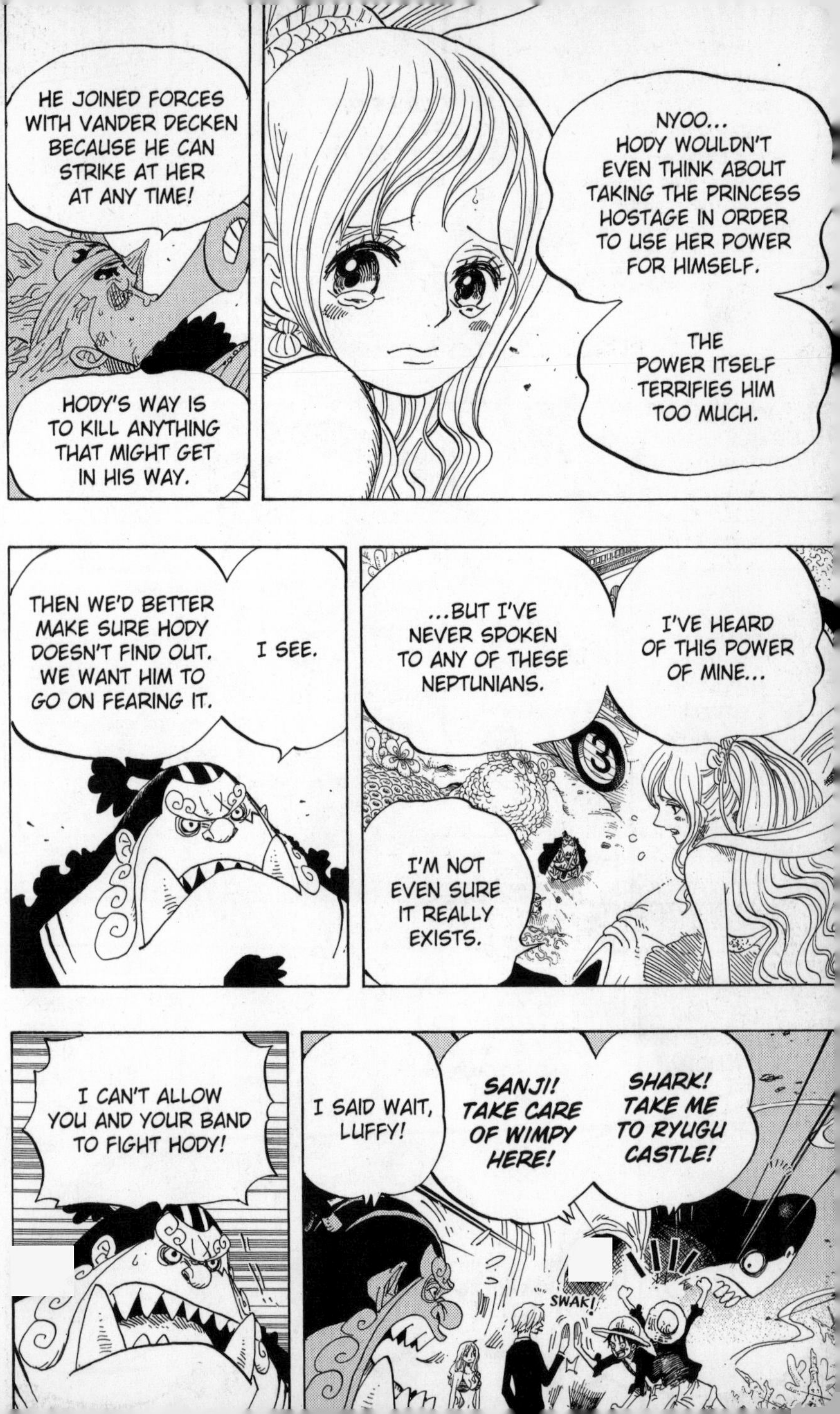
NYOO... HODY WOULDN'T EVEN THINK ABOUT TAKING THE PRINCESS HOSTAGE IN ORDER TO USE HER POWER FOR HIMSELF.
THE POWER ITSELF TERRIFIES HIM TOO MUCH.
HE JOINED FORCES WITH VANDER DECKEN BECAUSE HE CAN STRIKE AT HER AT ANY TIME!
HODY'S WAY IS TO KILL ANYTHING THAT MIGHT GET IN HIS WAY.
I'VE HEARD OF THIS POWER OF MINE...
...BUT I'VE NEVER SPOKEN TO ANY OF THESE NEPTUNIANS.
I'M NOT EVEN SURE IT REALLY EXISTS.
I SEE.
THEN WE'D BETTER MAKE SURE HODY DOESN'T FIND OUT. WE WANT HIM TO GO ON FEARING IT.
SHARK! TAKE ME TO RYUGU CASTLE!
SANJI! TAKE CARE OF WIMPY HERE!
I SAID WAIT, LUFFY!
SWAK!
I CAN'T ALLOW YOU AND YOUR BAND TO FIGHT HODY!

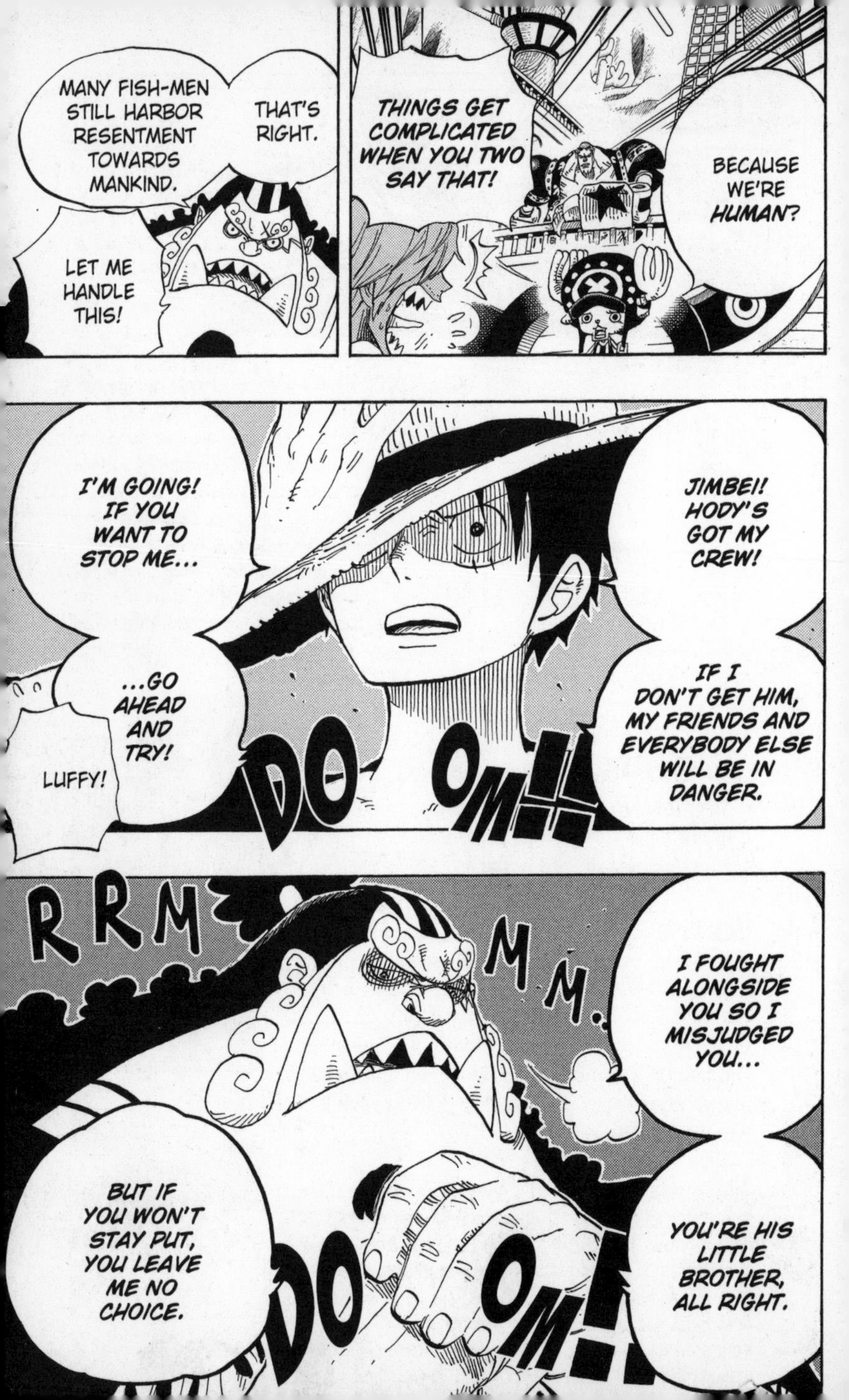
BECAUSE WE'RE HUMAN?
THINGS GET COMPLICATED WHEN YOU TWO SAY THAT!
THAT'S RIGHT.
MANY FISH-MEN STILL HARBOR RESENTMENT TOWARDS MANKIND.
LET ME HANDLE THIS!
JIMBEI! HODY'S GOT MY CREW!
IF I DON'T GET HIM, MY FRIENDS AND EVERYBODY ELSE WILL BE IN DANGER.
I'M GOING! IF YOU WANT TO STOP ME...
...GO AHEAD AND TRY!
DOOM!!
LUFFY!
I FOUGHT ALONGSIDE YOU SO I MISJUDGED YOU...
YOU'RE HIS LITTLE BROTHER, ALL RIGHT.
RRRMMMM...
BUT IF YOU WON'T STAY PUT, YOU LEAVE ME NO CHOICE.
DOOM!!

SBS Question Corner

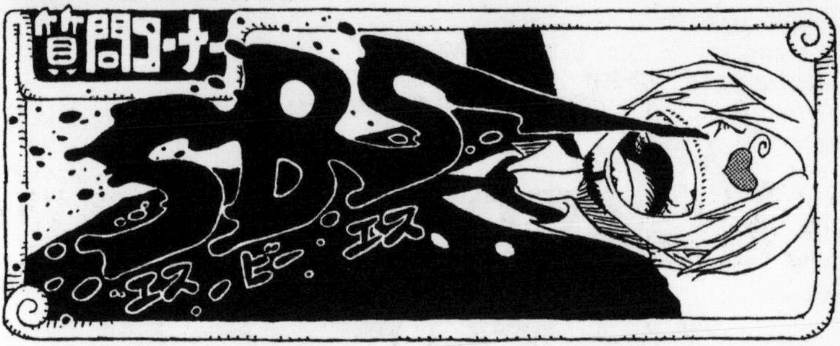
質問コーナー
SBS
エス・ビー・エス

(Hiroshi Suyama, Tokyo)

Reader (Q):

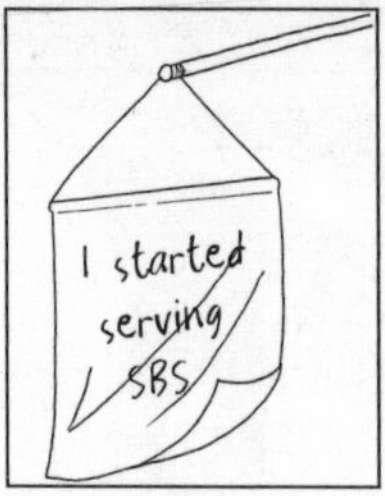
I started serving SBS

--N-ji

Oda (A): Hi, everyone. How do you do? The weather sure is hot recently. Oh, I guess summer is coming. (It's actually winter right now.) But you know how we always feel like eating some Chinese food during summer? Oh, look, a common street sign in summer. It started this year also. Let's have ice cold SBS! Wait, what?!

Q: Odacchi! Sneeze for me!

--Kirikirimai

A: O-O-Okaychooo! Sniff... Ahh...

Q: If you woke up in the morning and found out that your left hand turned into Crab-hand Gyro's hand, what would you do? I'd boil it.

--Maeda

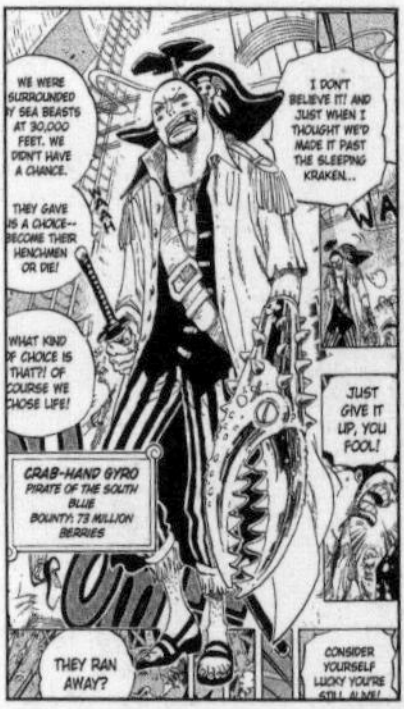
I DON'T BELIEVE IT! AND JUST WHEN I THOUGHT WE'D MADE IT PAST THE SLEEPING KRAKEN...
WE WERE SURROUNDED Y SEA BEASTS AT 30,000 FEET. WE DIDN'T HAVE A CHANCE.
THEY GAVE S A CHOICE-- BECOME THEIR HENCHMEN OR DIE!
WHAT KIND F CHOICE IS THAT?! OF OURSE WE HOSE LIFE!
JUST GIVE IT UP, YOU FOOL!
CRAB-HAND GYRO PIRATE OF THE SOUTH BLUE BOUNTY: 73 MILLION BERRIES
THEY RAN AWAY?
CONSIDER YOURSELF LUCKY YOU'RE

A: You're gonna eat it?! It's your own hand! Well, if you're going to eat it anyway, I'll have some too. I won't be eating my hand. But I'll have some of yours.

Q: I have a question! It's about Megalo. Let me guess... Did you base that on the ancient giant shark called Megalodon? Don't they say that there are still a few surviving ones?

--Miha

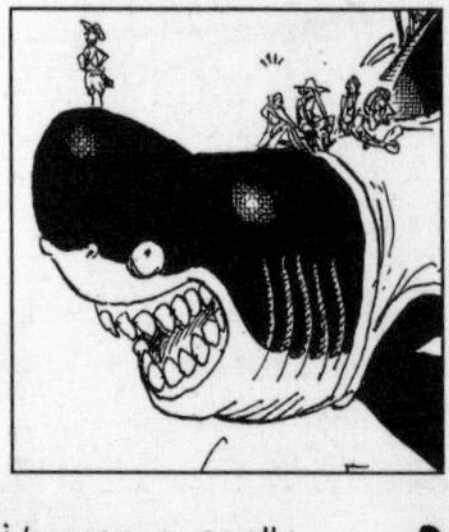

A: That's exactly right. It's megalodon. They are the ancestors of the great white sharks and fossils of their teeth have been found. By studying those fossils, they think that the length of those sharks were anywhere from 13 meters to 20 meters. Even the scary great white is 5 meters long. I'm sure it was a really powerful monster. And yes, I based Megalo on Megalodon.

Chapter 629:
FORMER WARLORD IN THE WAY

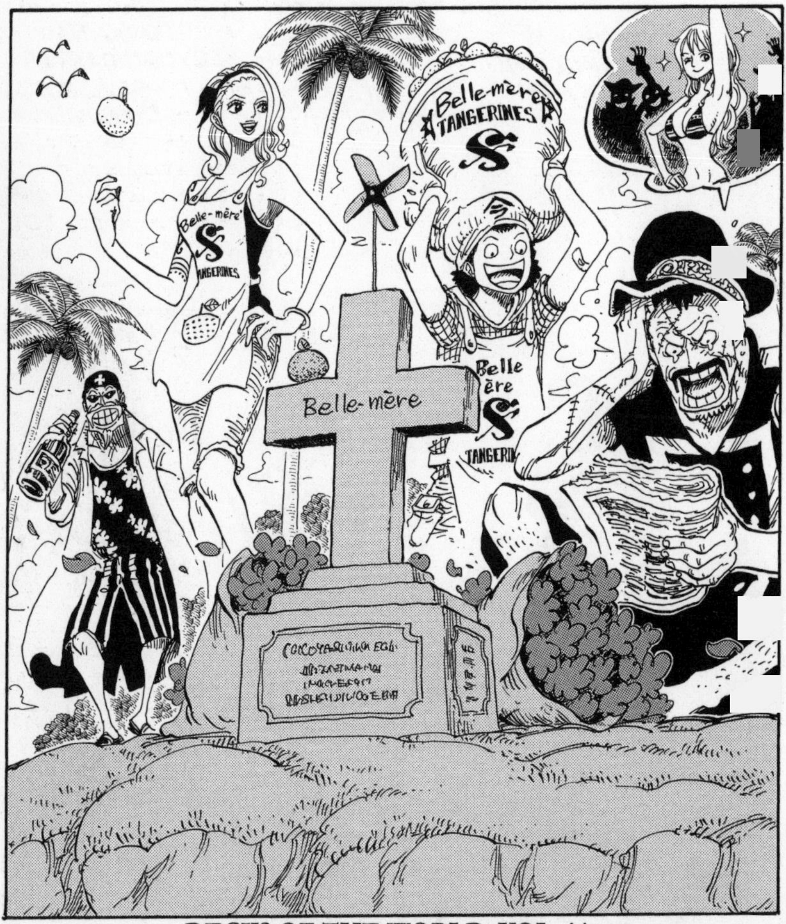
Belle-mère
TANGERINES
Belle-mère'
TANGERINES
Belle-mère
Belle
ère
TANGERI

DECKS OF THE WORLD, VOL. 14:
"COCO VILLAGE"

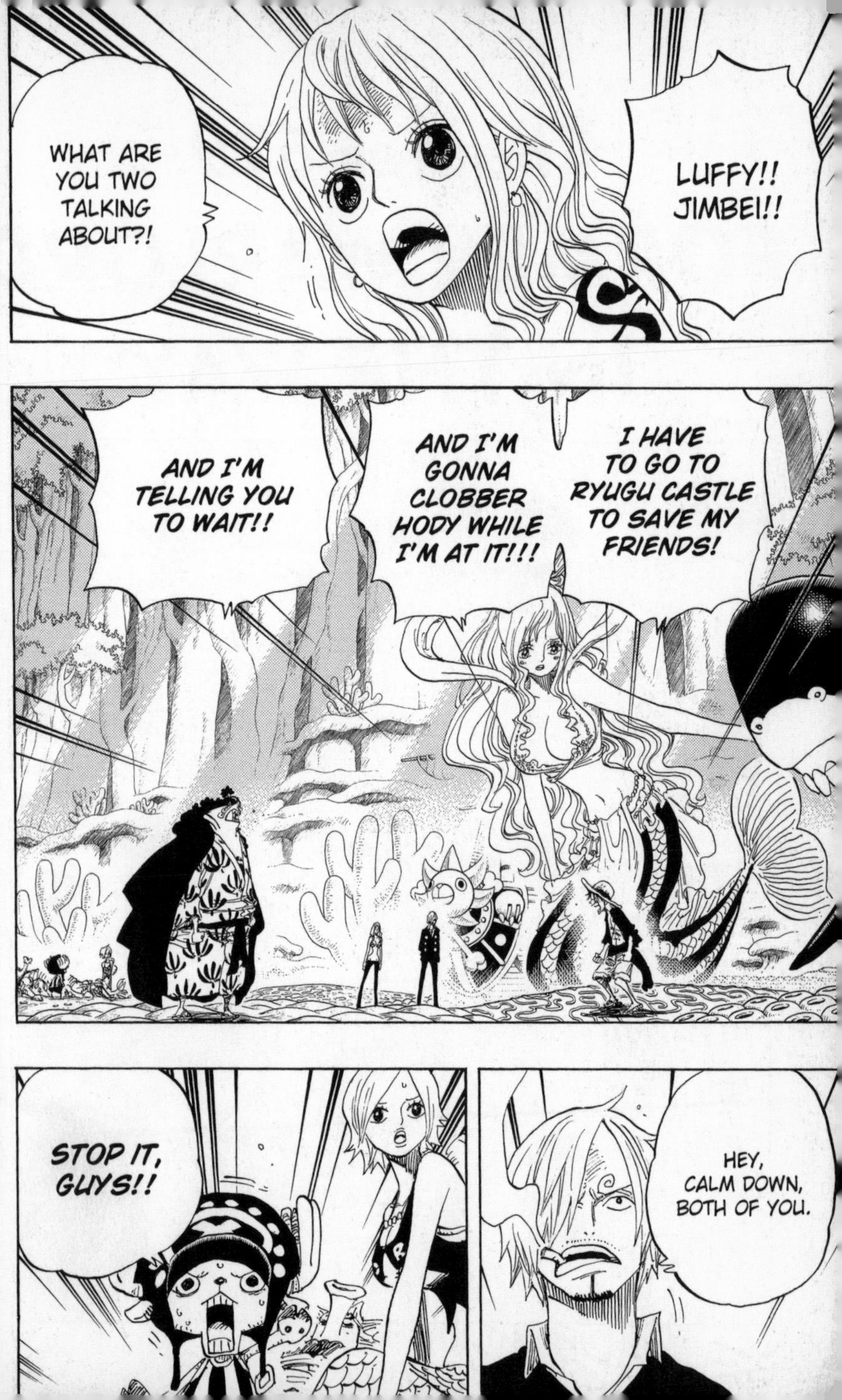
LUFFY!! JIMBEI!!
WHAT ARE YOU TWO TALKING ABOUT?!
I HAVE TO GO TO RYUGU CASTLE TO SAVE MY FRIENDS!
AND I'M GONNA CLOBBER HODY WHILE I'M AT IT!!!
AND I'M TELLING YOU TO WAIT!!
HEY, CALM DOWN, BOTH OF YOU.
STOP IT, GUYS!!

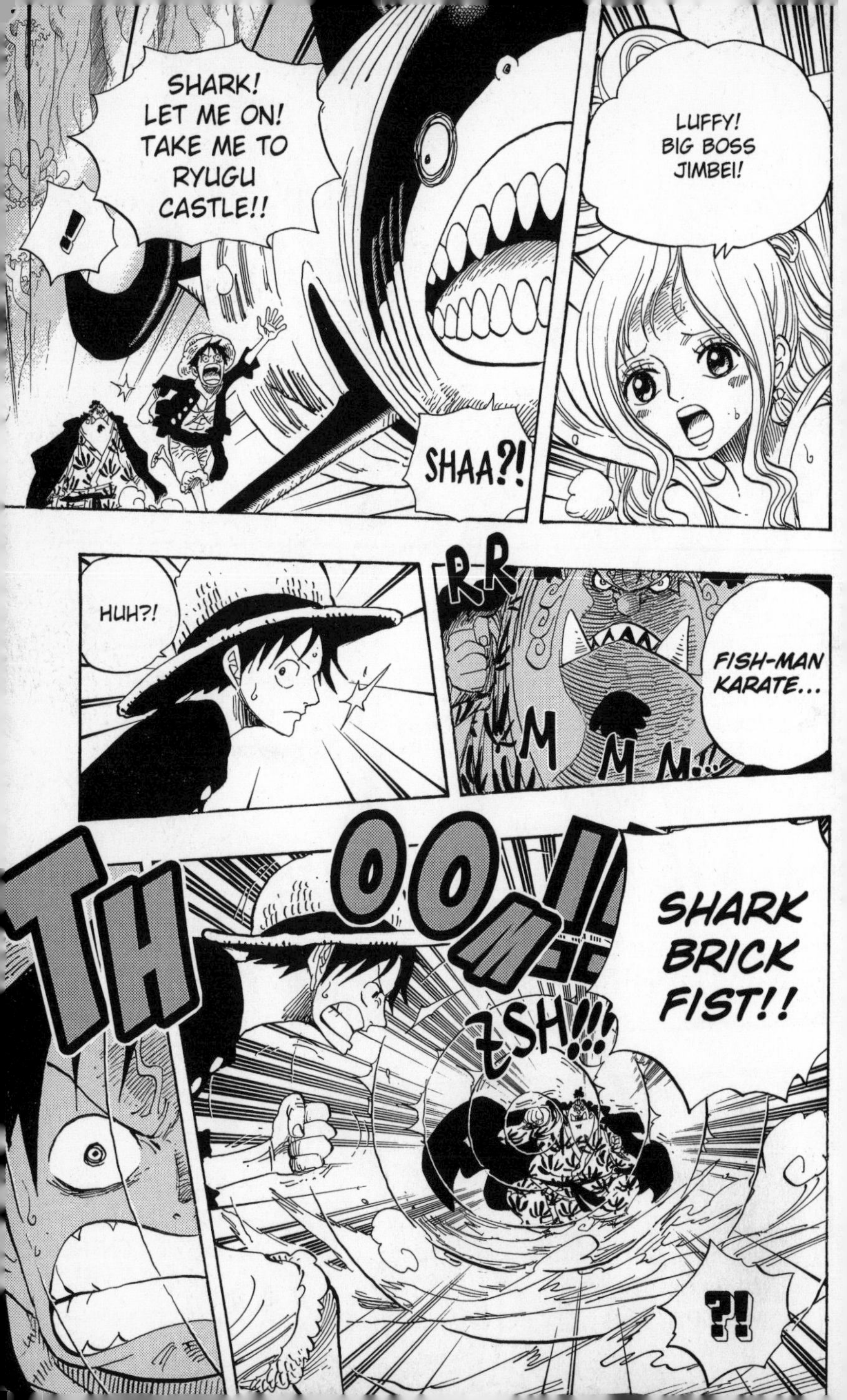
LUFFY! BIG BOSS JIMBEI!
SHARK! LET ME ON! TAKE ME TO RYUGU CASTLE!!
!
SHAA?!
RR
FISH-MAN KARATE...
MMM..!!
HUH?!
SHARK BRICK FIST!!
THOOM!
ZSH!!!
?!

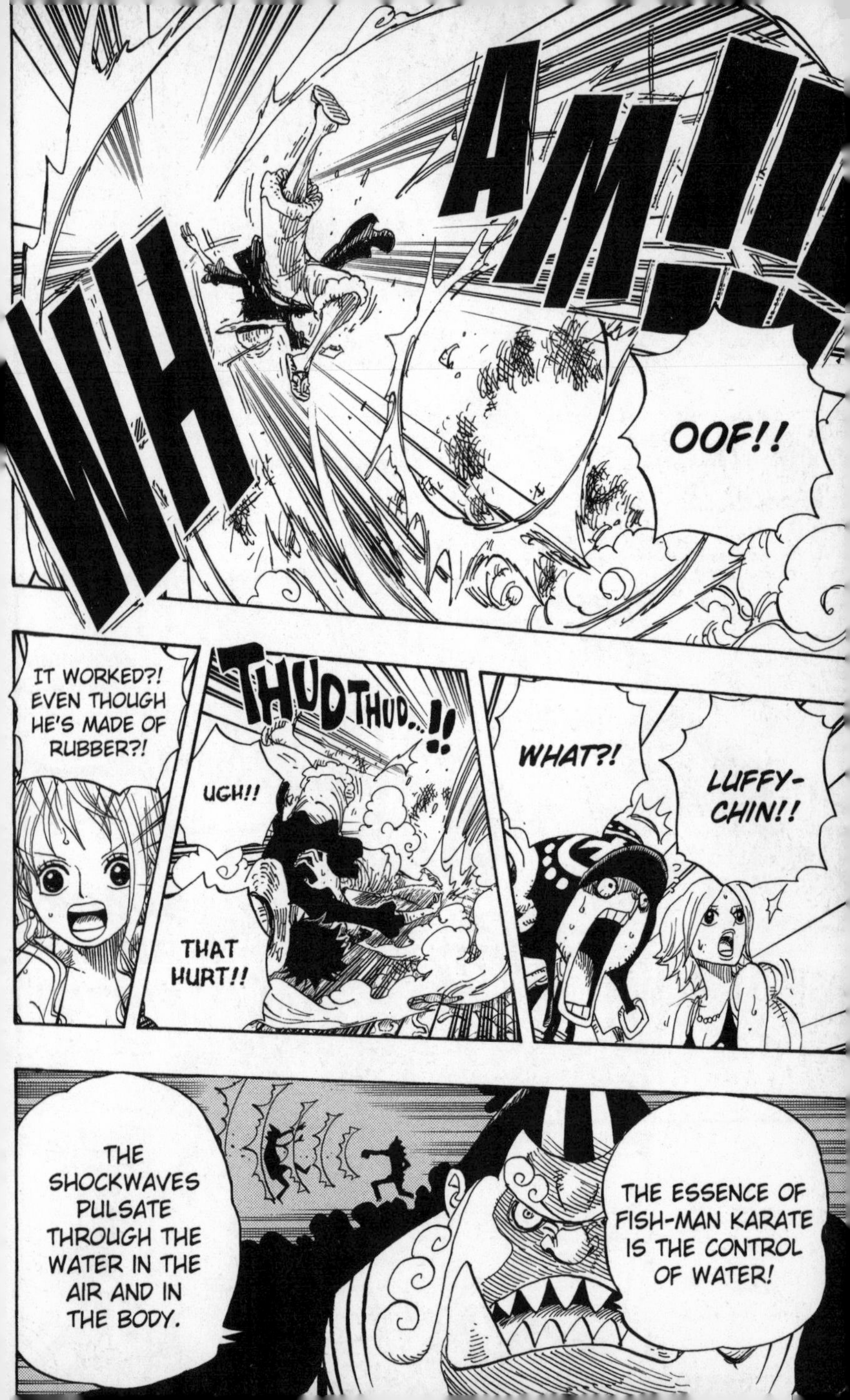

WHAM!!
OOF!!
LUFFY-CHIN!!
WHAT?!
THUD THUD...!!
UGH!!
THAT HURT!!
IT WORKED?! EVEN THOUGH HE'S MADE OF RUBBER?!
THE ESSENCE OF FISH-MAN KARATE IS THE CONTROL OF WATER!
THE SHOCKWAVES PULSATE THROUGH THE WATER IN THE AIR AND IN THE BODY.

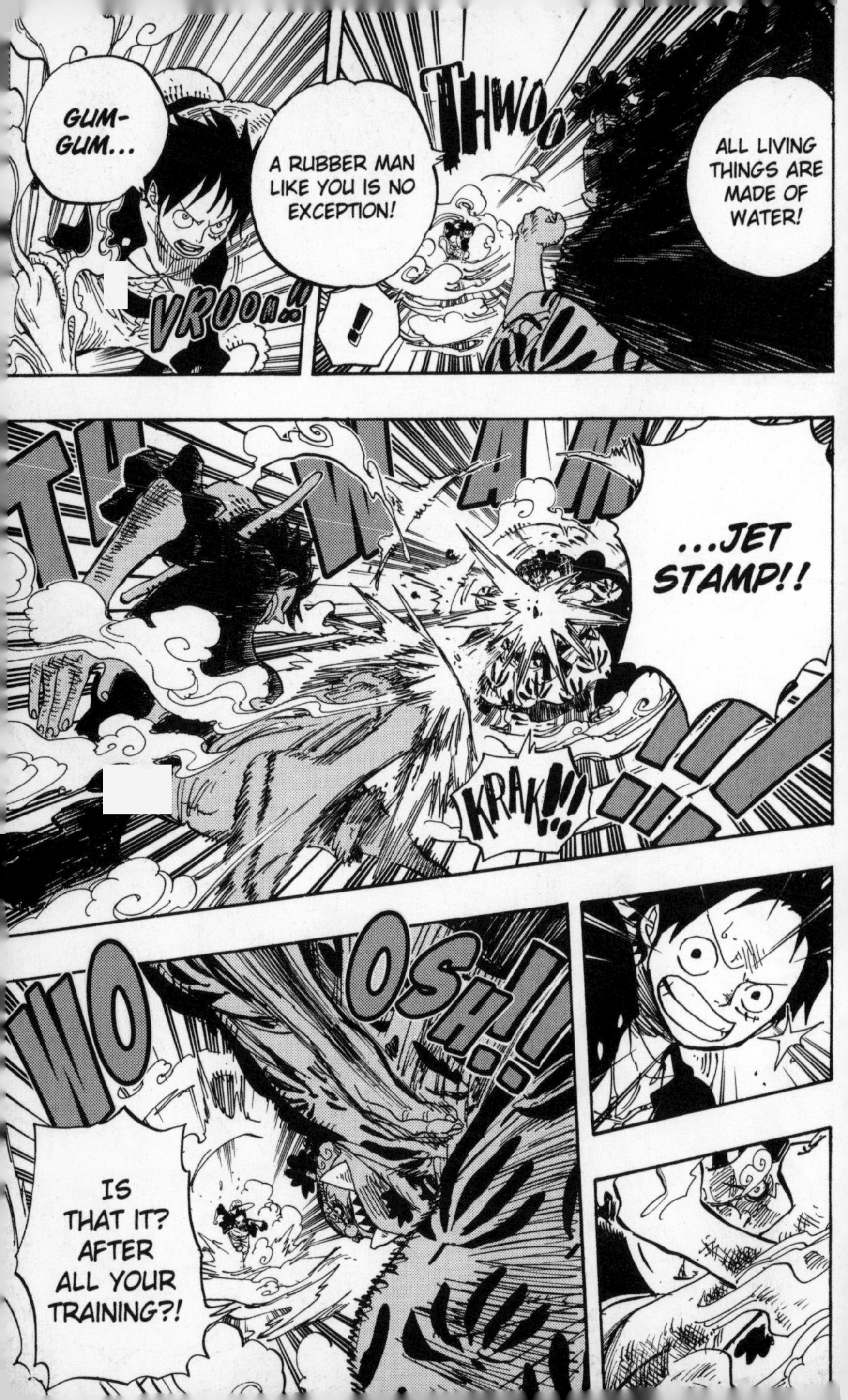
ALL LIVING THINGS ARE MADE OF WATER!
THWOO
A RUBBER MAN LIKE YOU IS NO EXCEPTION!
!
GUM-GUM...
...JET STAMP!!
KRAK!!!
WHOOSH!!
IS THAT IT? AFTER ALL YOUR TRAINING?!

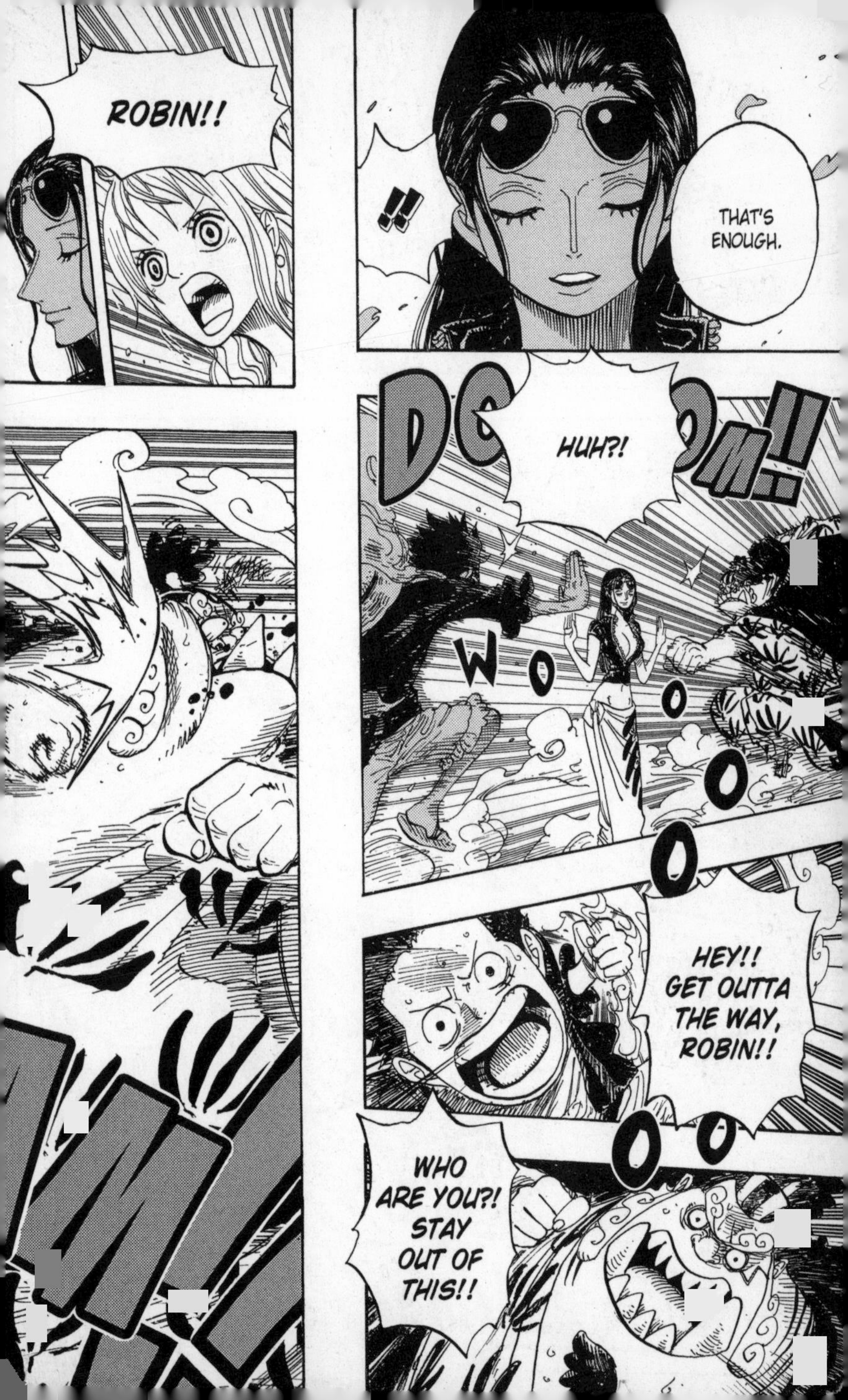
THAT'S ENOUGH.
ROBIN!!
HUH?!
HEY!! GET OUTTA THE WAY, ROBIN!!
WHO ARE YOU?! STAY OUT OF THIS!!

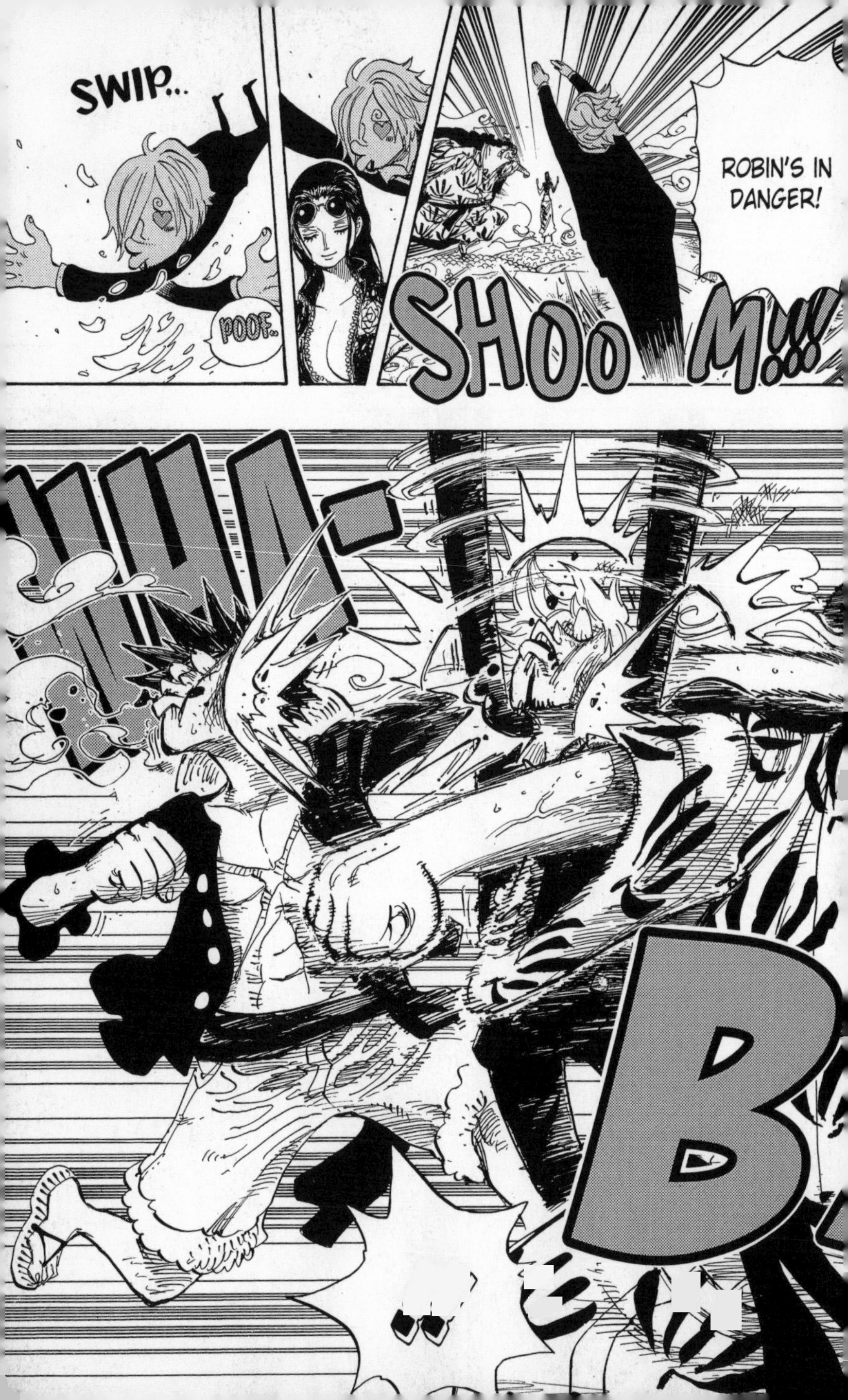
ROBIN'S IN DANGER!
SHOOM!!
SWIP...
POOF..

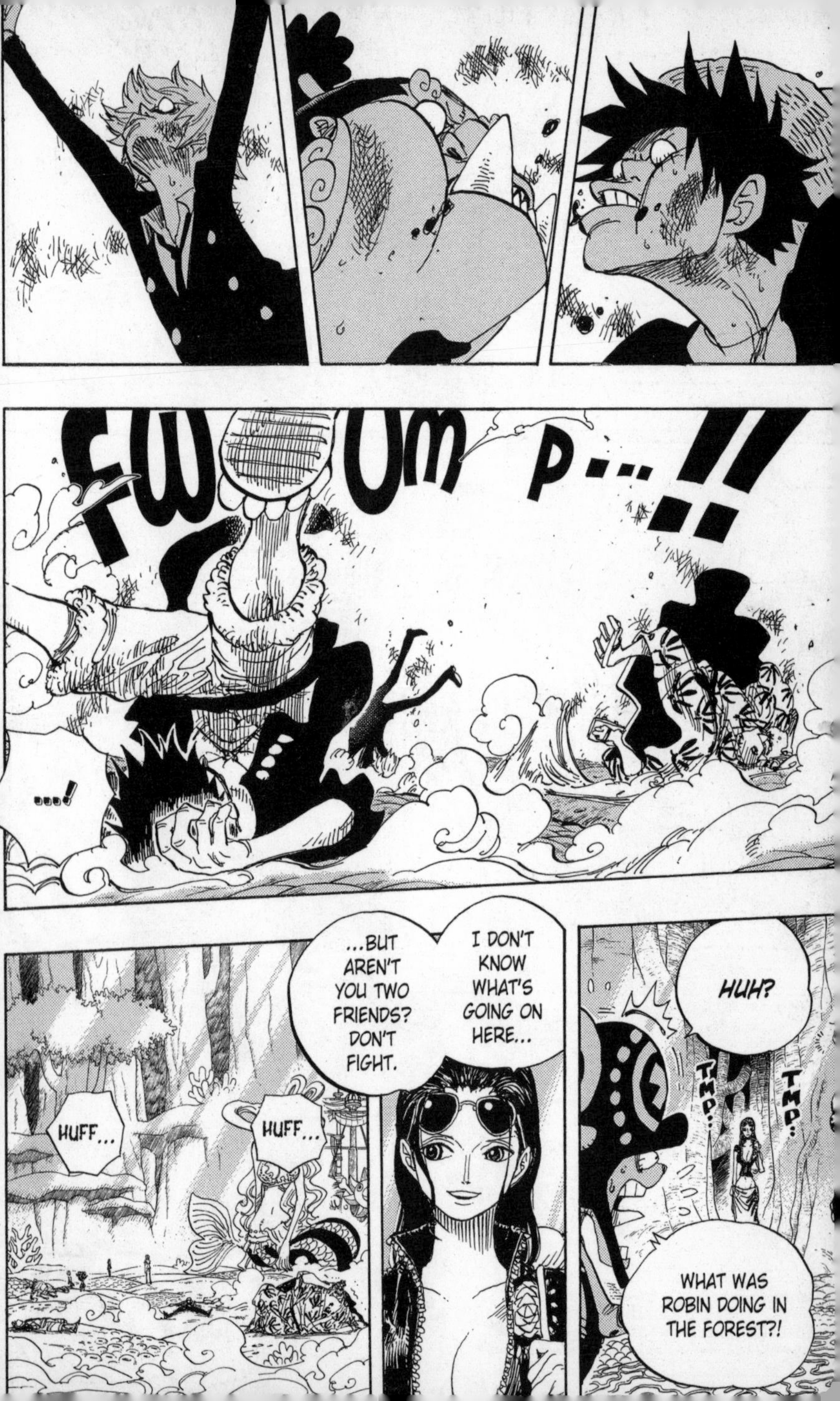
FWUMP...!!
...!
HUH?
TMP...
TMP...
WHAT WAS ROBIN DOING IN THE FOREST?!
I DON'T KNOW WHAT'S GOING ON HERE...
...BUT AREN'T YOU TWO FRIENDS? DON'T FIGHT.
HUFF...
HUFF...

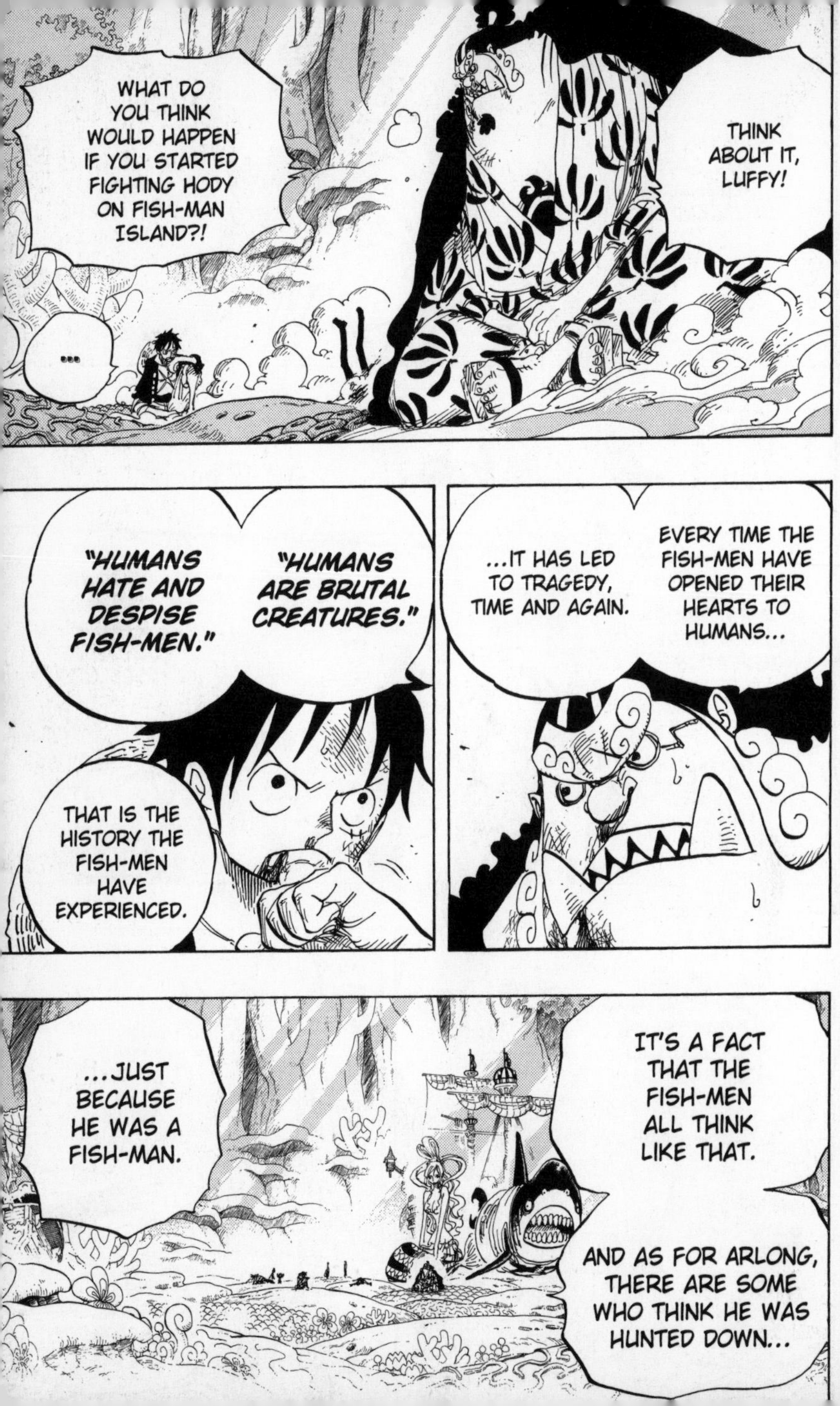
THINK ABOUT IT, LUFFY!
WHAT DO YOU THINK WOULD HAPPEN IF YOU STARTED FIGHTING HODY ON FISH-MAN ISLAND?!
...
EVERY TIME THE FISH-MEN HAVE OPENED THEIR HEARTS TO HUMANS...
...IT HAS LED TO TRAGEDY, TIME AND AGAIN.
"HUMANS ARE BRUTAL CREATURES."
"HUMANS HATE AND DESPISE FISH-MEN."
THAT IS THE HISTORY THE FISH-MEN HAVE EXPERIENCED.
IT'S A FACT THAT THE FISH-MEN ALL THINK LIKE THAT.
AND AS FOR ARLONG, THERE ARE SOME WHO THINK HE WAS HUNTED DOWN...
...JUST BECAUSE HE WAS A FISH-MAN.

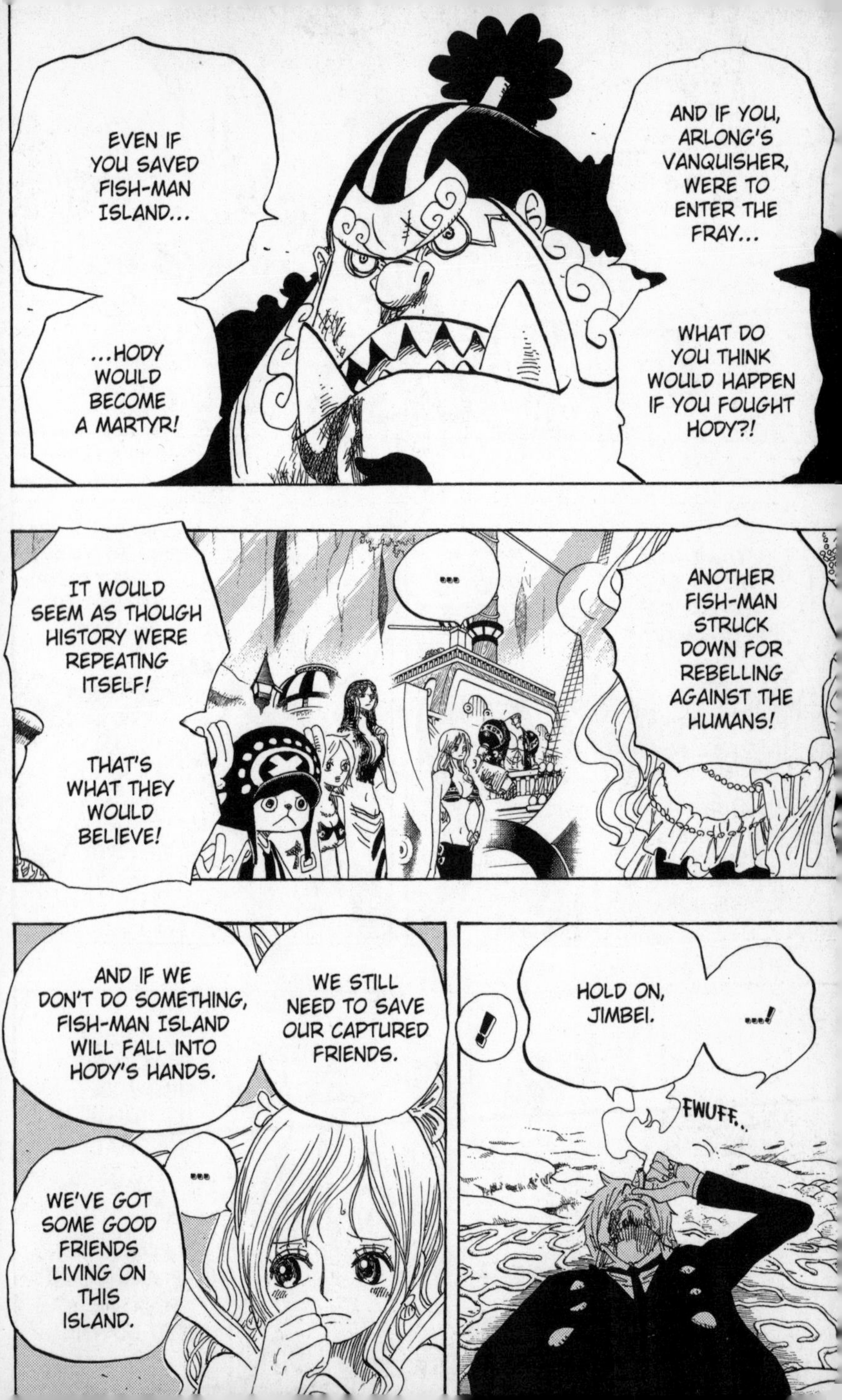
AND IF YOU, ARLONG'S VANQUISHER, WERE TO ENTER THE FRAY...
WHAT DO YOU THINK WOULD HAPPEN IF YOU FOUGHT HODY?!
EVEN IF YOU SAVED FISH-MAN ISLAND...
...HODY WOULD BECOME A MARTYR!
ANOTHER FISH-MAN STRUCK DOWN FOR REBELLING AGAINST THE HUMANS!
...
IT WOULD SEEM AS THOUGH HISTORY WERE REPEATING ITSELF!
THAT'S WHAT THEY WOULD BELIEVE!
HOLD ON, JIMBEI.
...!
!
FWUFF..
WE STILL NEED TO SAVE OUR CAPTURED FRIENDS.
AND IF WE DON'T DO SOMETHING, FISH-MAN ISLAND WILL FALL INTO HODY'S HANDS.
...
WE'VE GOT SOME GOOD FRIENDS LIVING ON THIS ISLAND.

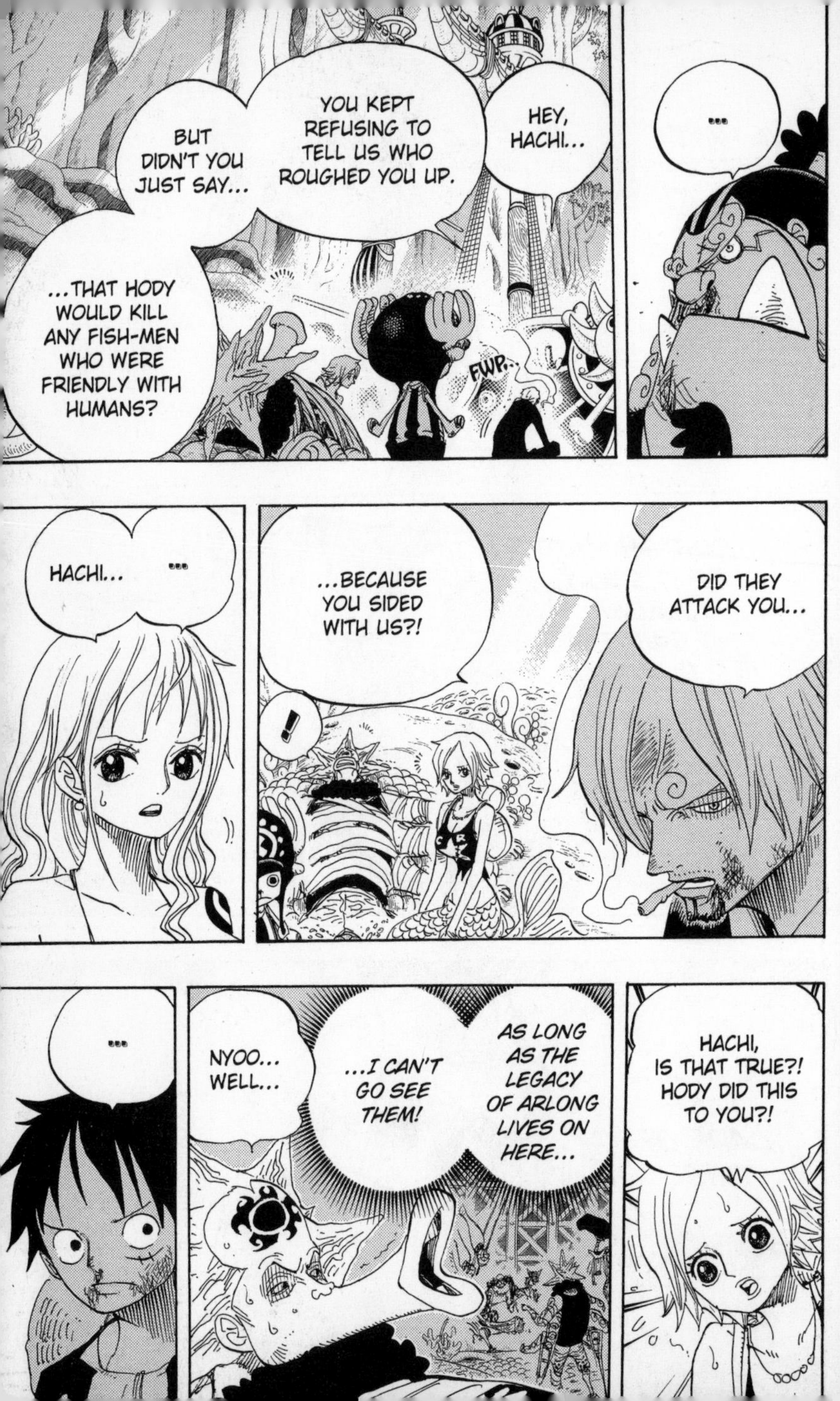
...
HEY, HACHI...
YOU KEPT REFUSING TO TELL US WHO ROUGHED YOU UP.
BUT DIDN'T YOU JUST SAY...
...THAT HODY WOULD KILL ANY FISH-MEN WHO WERE FRIENDLY WITH HUMANS?
FWP...
DID THEY ATTACK YOU...
...BECAUSE YOU SIDED WITH US?!
!
...
HACHI...
HACHI, IS THAT TRUE?! HODY DID THIS TO YOU?!
AS LONG AS THE LEGACY OF ARLONG LIVES ON HERE...
...I CAN'T GO SEE THEM!
NYOO... WELL...
...

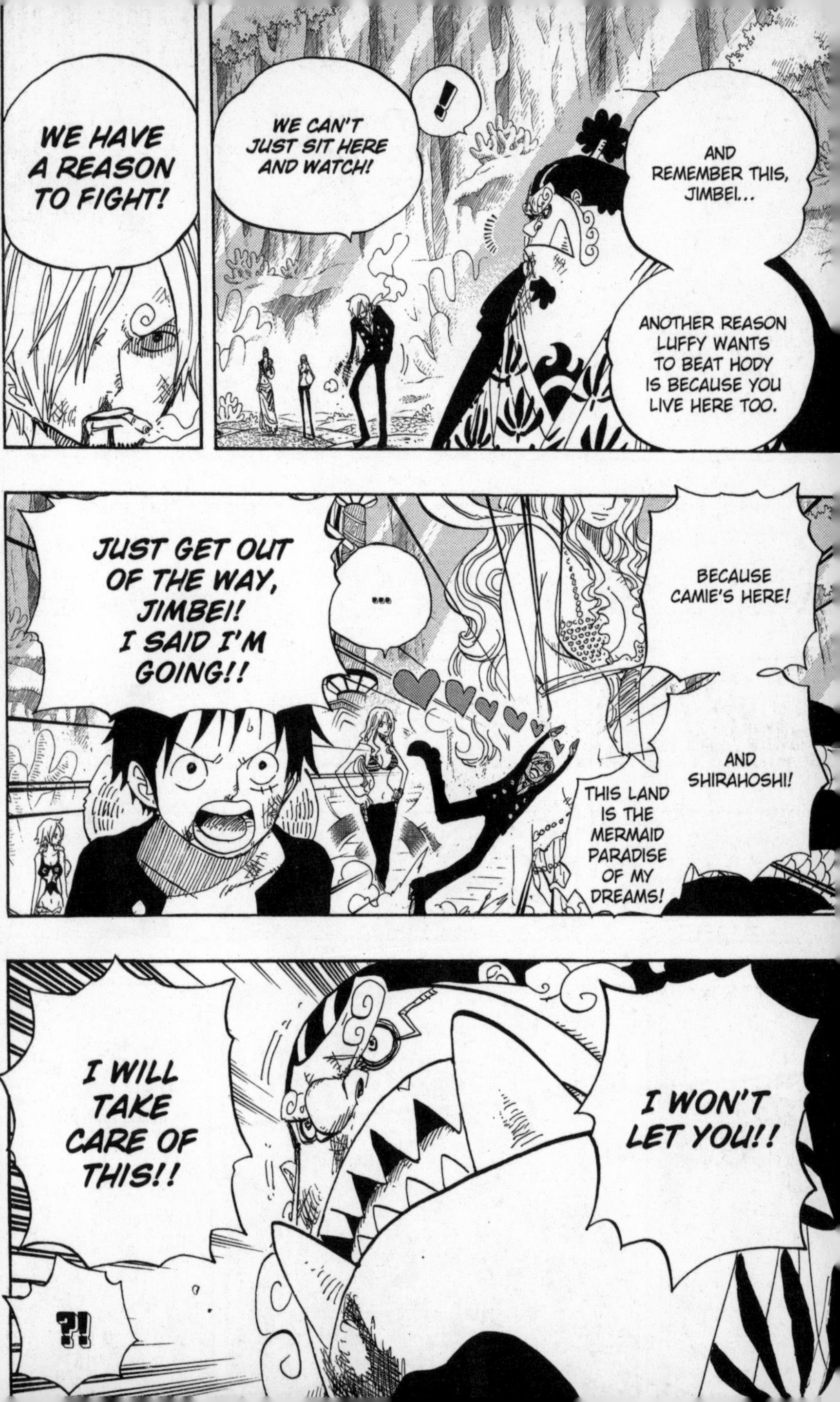
AND REMEMBER THIS, JIMBEI...
ANOTHER REASON LUFFY WANTS TO BEAT HODY IS BECAUSE YOU LIVE HERE TOO.
!
WE CAN'T JUST SIT HERE AND WATCH!
WE HAVE A REASON TO FIGHT!
BECAUSE CAMIE'S HERE!
AND SHIRAHOSHI!
THIS LAND IS THE MERMAID PARADISE OF MY DREAMS!
...
JUST GET OUT OF THE WAY, JIMBEI! I SAID I'M GOING!!
I WON'T LET YOU!!
I WILL TAKE CARE OF THIS!!
?!

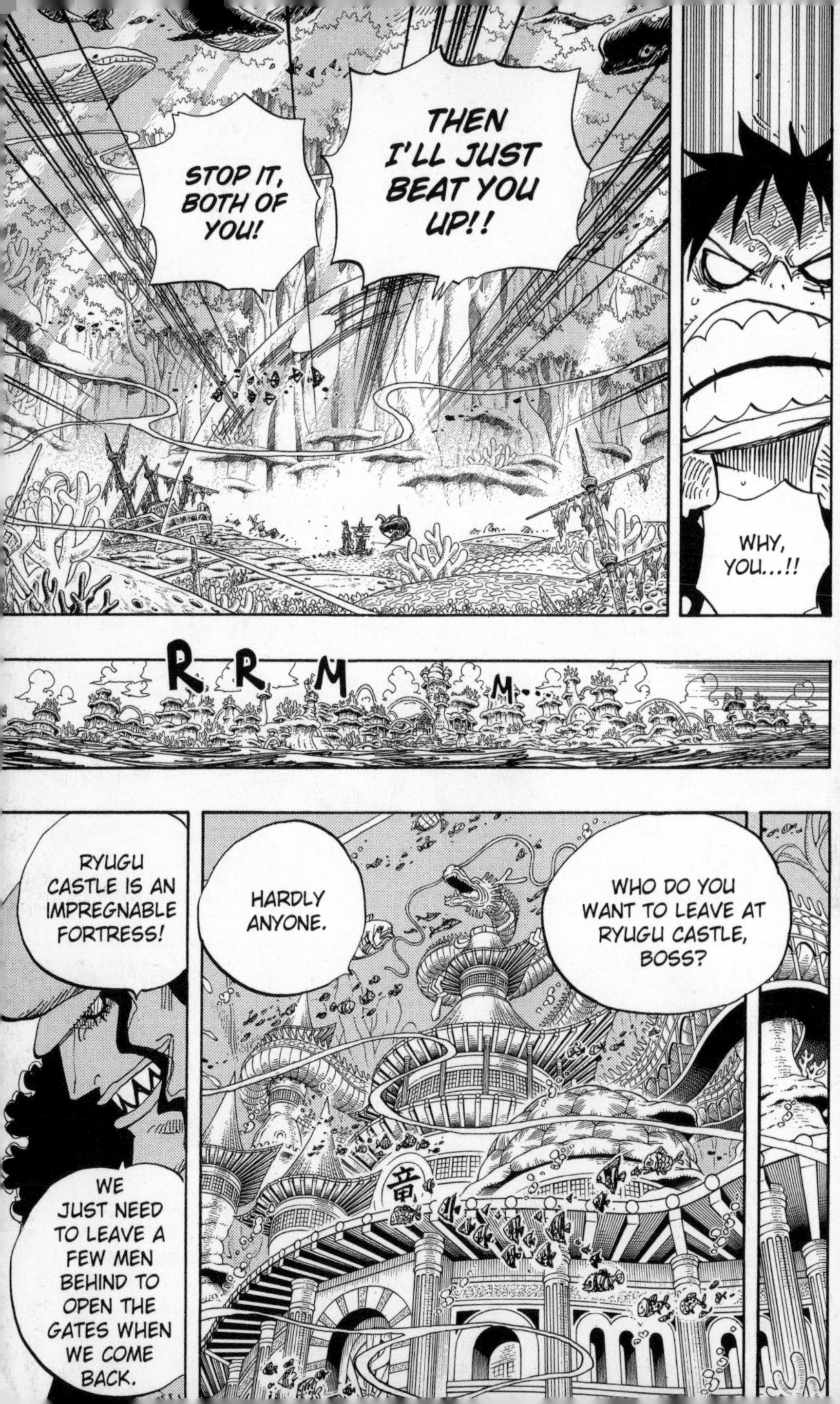
WHY, YOU...!!
THEN I'LL JUST BEAT YOU UP!!
STOP IT, BOTH OF YOU!
RRMM..
WHO DO YOU WANT TO LEAVE AT RYUGU CASTLE, BOSS?
HARDLY ANYONE.
RYUGU CASTLE IS AN IMPREGNABLE FORTRESS!
WE JUST NEED TO LEAVE A FEW MEN BEHIND TO OPEN THE GATES WHEN WE COME BACK.

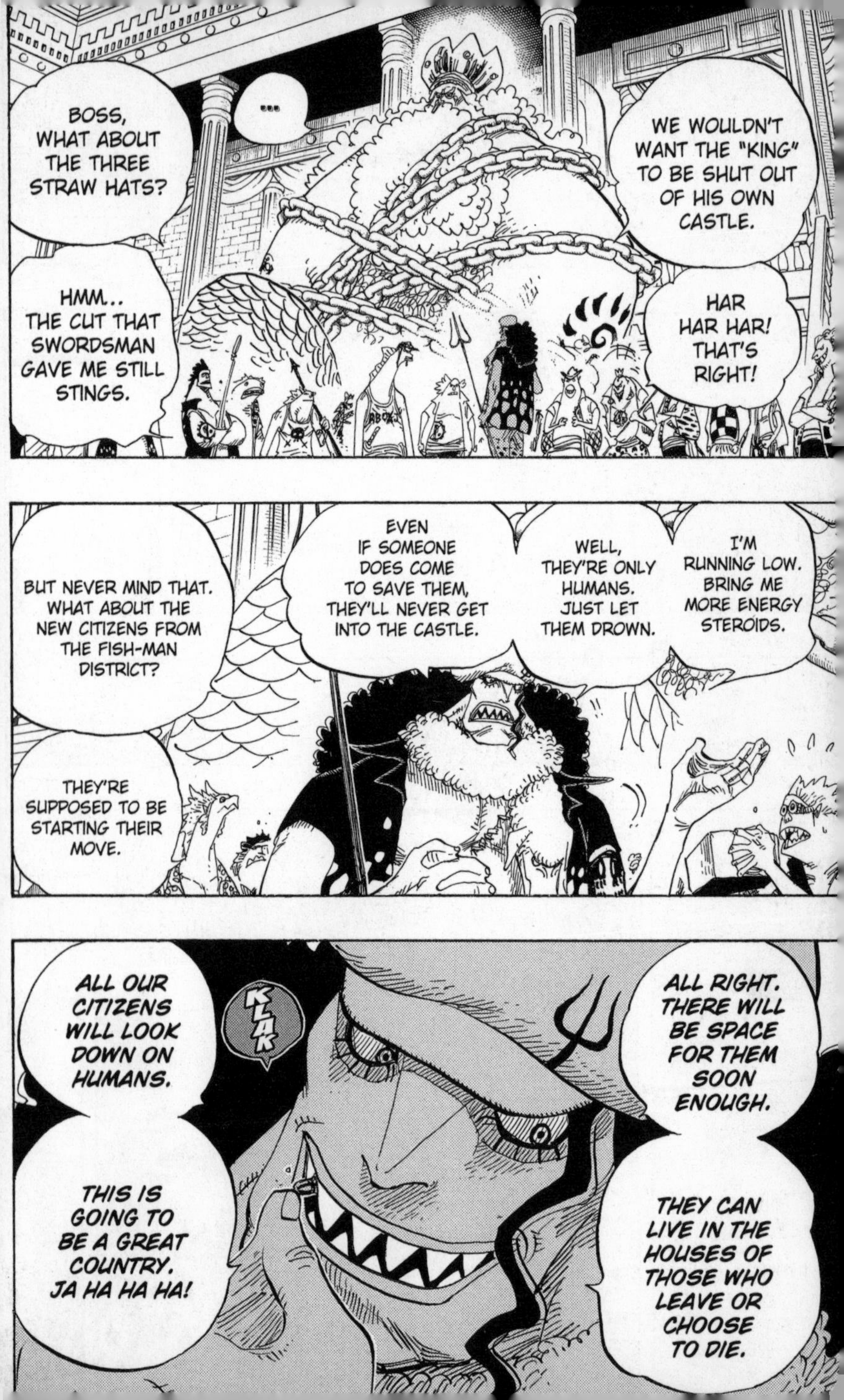
WE WOULDN'T WANT THE "KING" TO BE SHUT OUT OF HIS OWN CASTLE.
HAR HAR HAR! THAT'S RIGHT!
...
BOSS, WHAT ABOUT THE THREE STRAW HATS?
HMM... THE CUT THAT SWORDSMAN GAVE ME STILL STINGS.
I'M RUNNING LOW. BRING ME MORE ENERGY STEROIDS.
WELL, THEY'RE ONLY HUMANS. JUST LET THEM DROWN.
EVEN IF SOMEONE DOES COME TO SAVE THEM, THEY'LL NEVER GET INTO THE CASTLE.
BUT NEVER MIND THAT. WHAT ABOUT THE NEW CITIZENS FROM THE FISH-MAN DISTRICT?
THEY'RE SUPPOSED TO BE STARTING THEIR MOVE.
ALL RIGHT. THERE WILL BE SPACE FOR THEM SOON ENOUGH.
THEY CAN LIVE IN THE HOUSES OF THOSE WHO LEAVE OR CHOOSE TO DIE.
KLAK
ALL OUR CITIZENS WILL LOOK DOWN ON HUMANS.
THIS IS GOING TO BE A GREAT COUNTRY. JA HA HA HA!

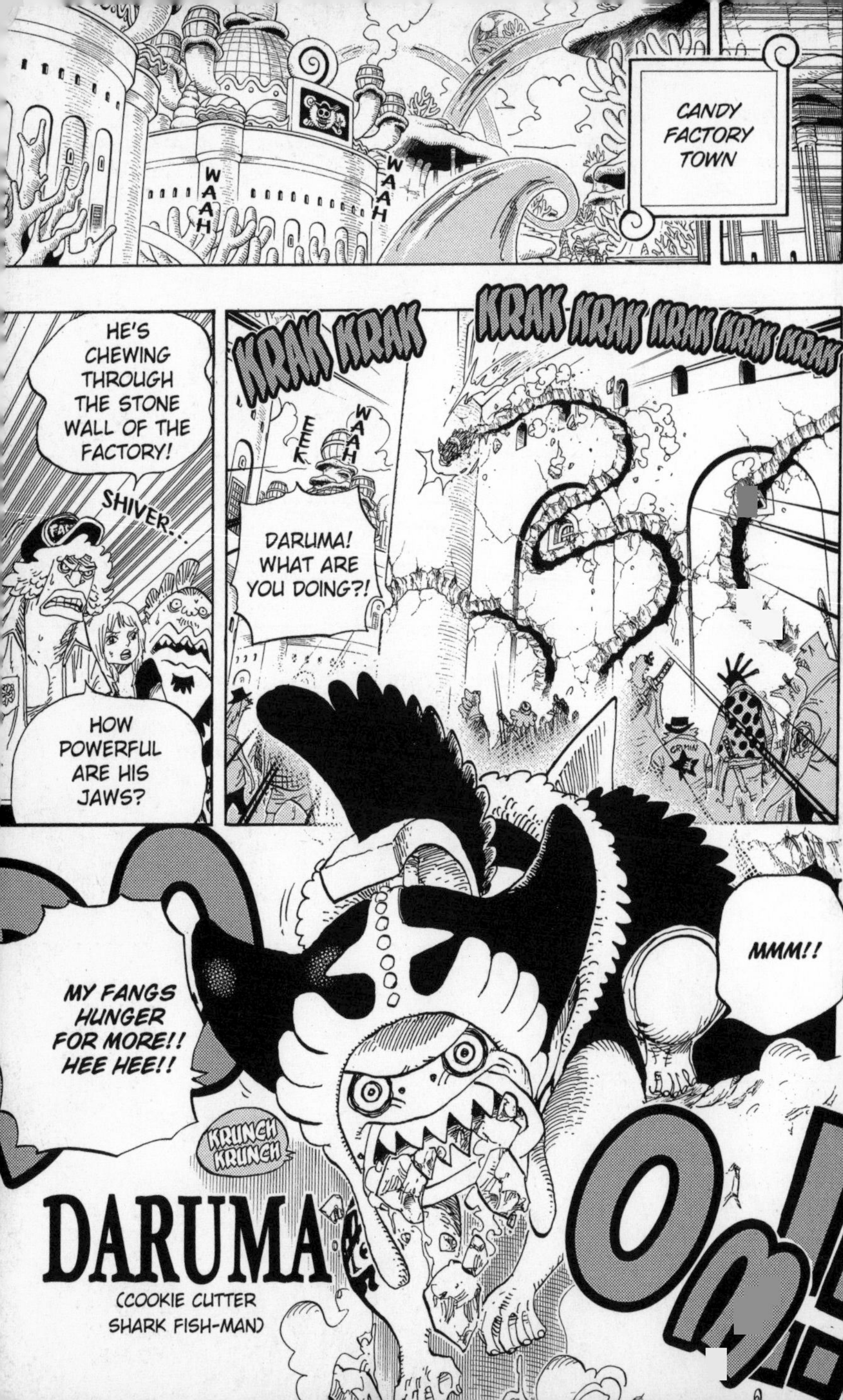
CANDY FACTORY TOWN
WAAH
WAAH
KRAK KRAK
KRAK KRAK KRAK KRAK KRAK
WAAH
EEK
DARUMA! WHAT ARE YOU DOING?!
HE'S CHEWING THROUGH THE STONE WALL OF THE FACTORY!
SHIVER...
HOW POWERFUL ARE HIS JAWS?
MMM!!
MY FANGS HUNGER FOR MORE!! HEE HEE!!
KRUNCH KRUNCH
DARUMA
(COOKIE CUTTER SHARK FISH-MAN)

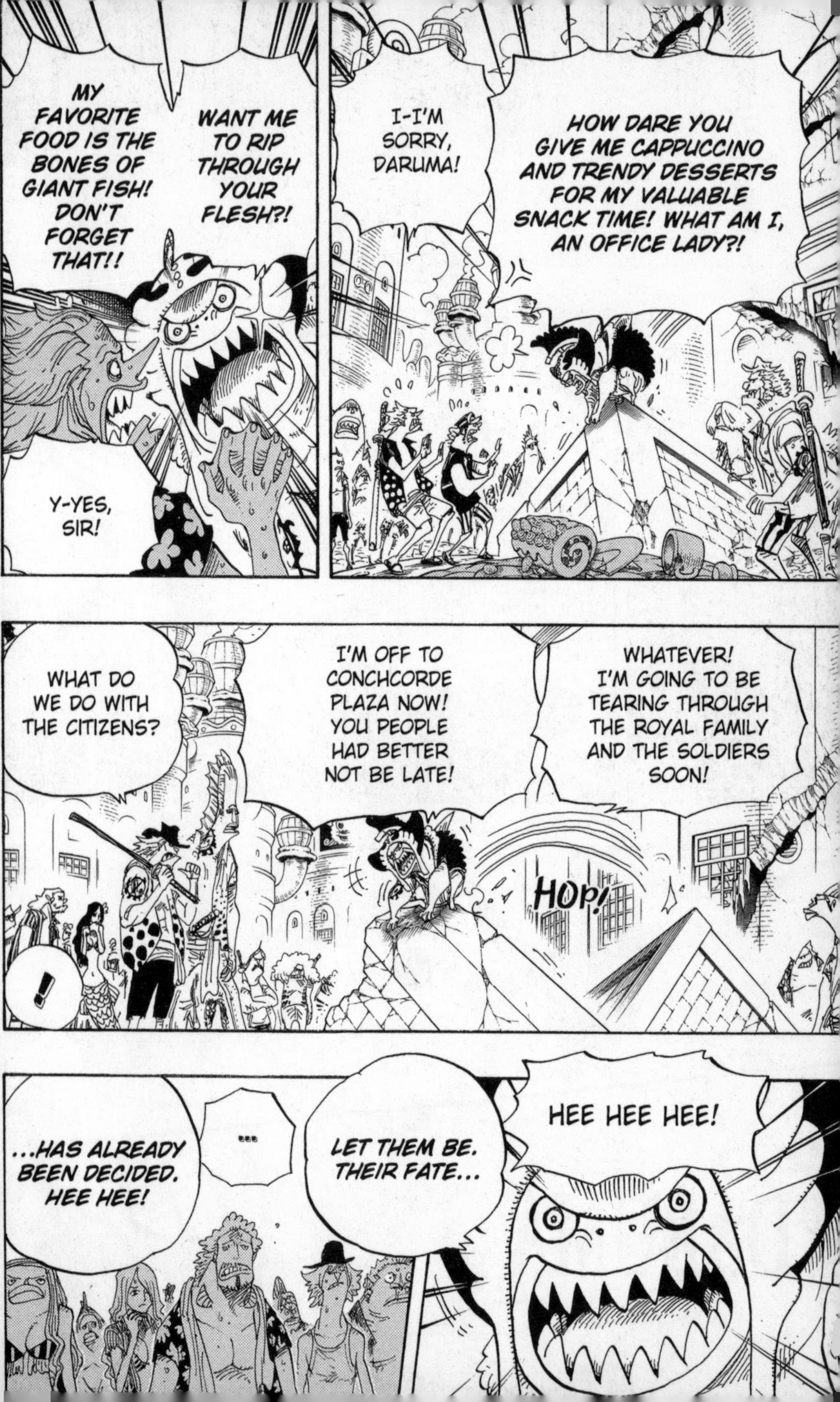
HOW DARE YOU GIVE ME CAPPUCCINO AND TRENDY DESSERTS FOR MY VALUABLE SNACK TIME! WHAT AM I, AN OFFICE LADY?!
I-I'M SORRY, DARUMA!
WANT ME TO RIP THROUGH YOUR FLESH?!
MY FAVORITE FOOD IS THE BONES OF GIANT FISH! DON'T FORGET THAT!!
Y-YES, SIR!
WHATEVER! I'M GOING TO BE TEARING THROUGH THE ROYAL FAMILY AND THE SOLDIERS SOON!
I'M OFF TO CONCHCORDE PLAZA NOW! YOU PEOPLE HAD BETTER NOT BE LATE!
HOP!
WHAT DO WE DO WITH THE CITIZENS?
!
HEE HEE HEE!
LET THEM BE. THEIR FATE...
...
...HAS ALREADY BEEN DECIDED. HEE HEE!

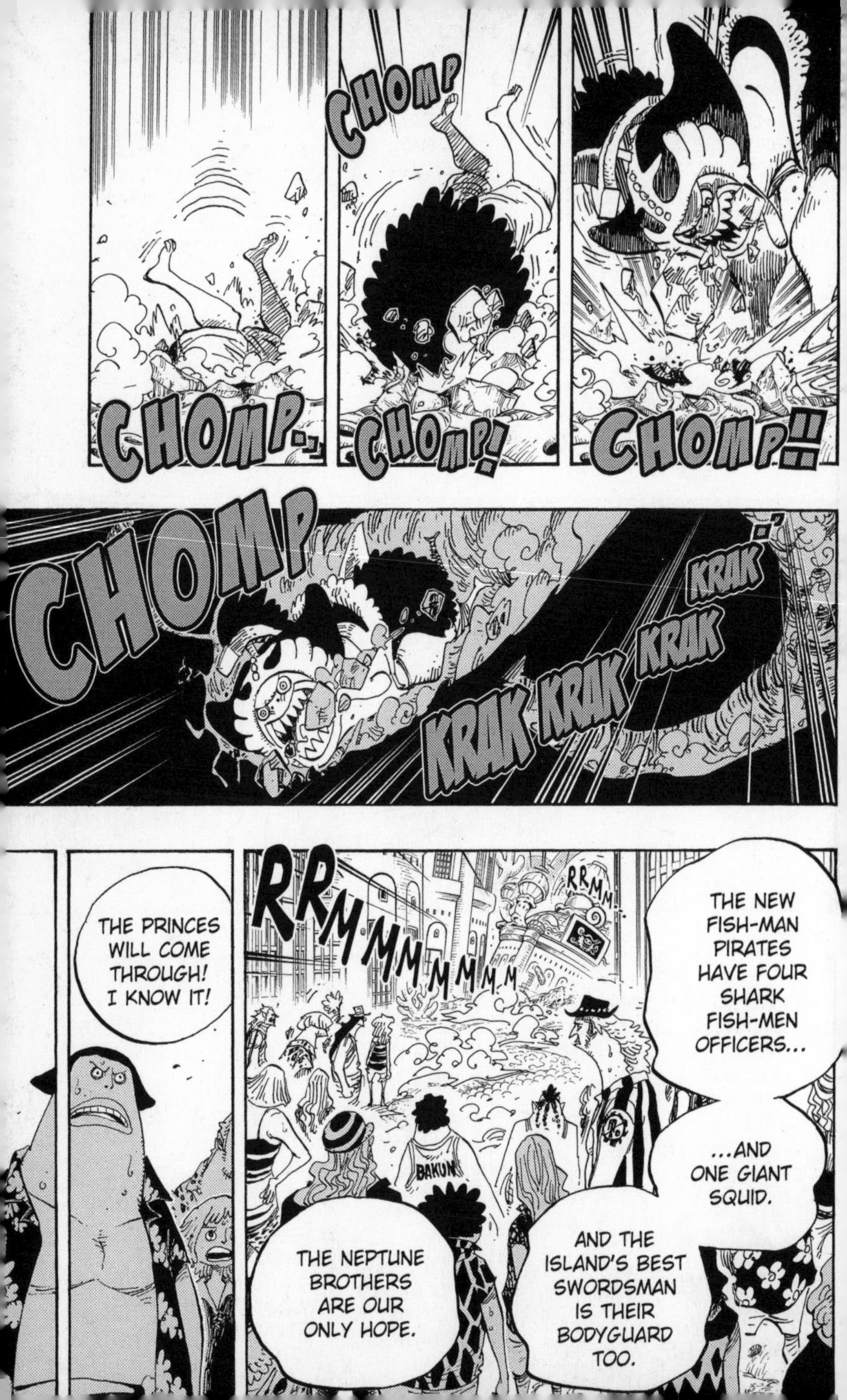
CHOMP!!
CHOMP
CHOMP!
CHOMP..
CHOMP
KRAK
KRAK KRAK KRAK
RRMM..
RRMMMMMMM
THE NEW FISH-MAN PIRATES HAVE FOUR SHARK FISH-MEN OFFICERS...
...AND ONE GIANT SQUID.
AND THE ISLAND'S BEST SWORDSMAN IS THEIR BODYGUARD TOO.
THE NEPTUNE BROTHERS ARE OUR ONLY HOPE.
BAKUN
THE PRINCES WILL COME THROUGH! I KNOW IT!

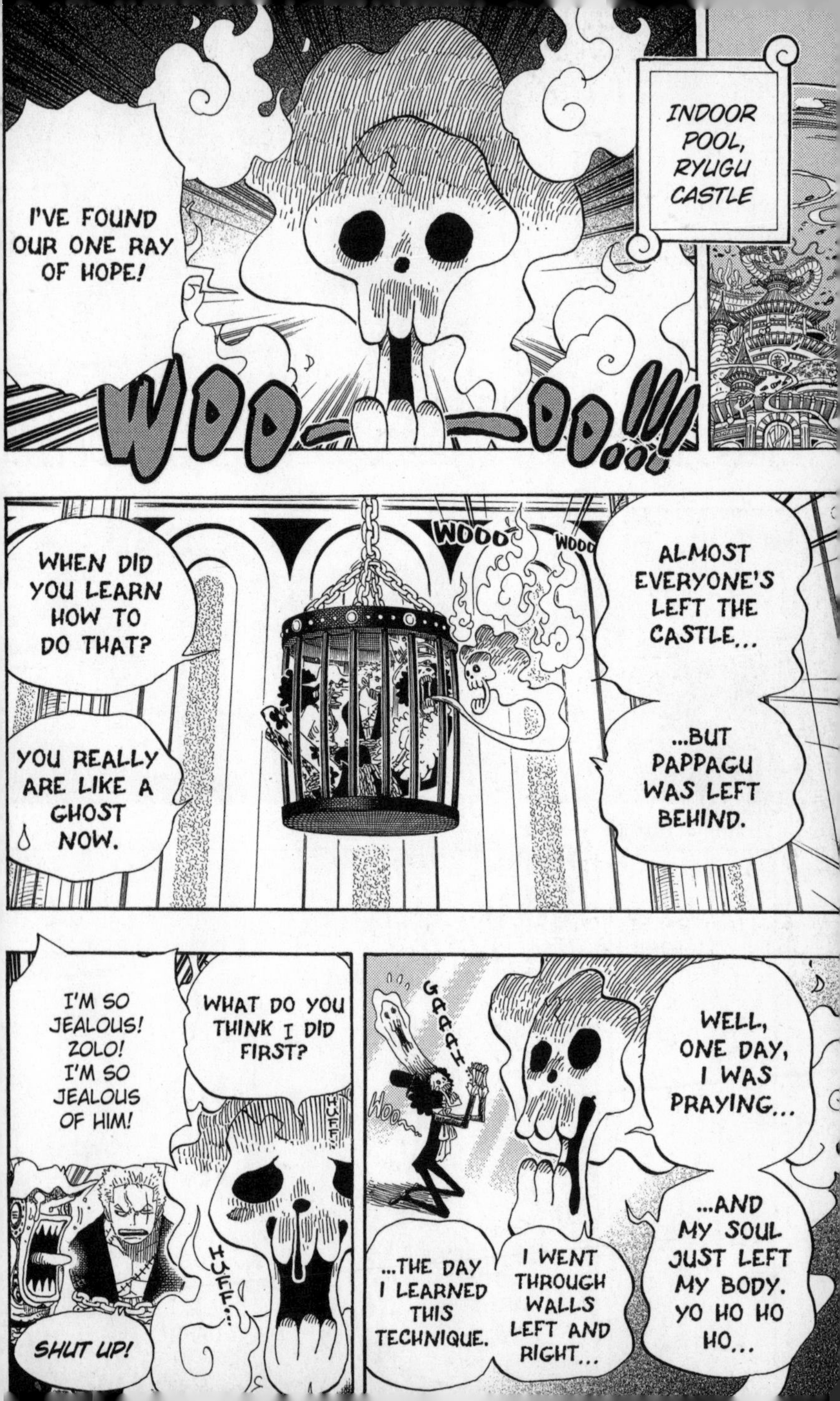
INDOOR POOL, RYUGU CASTLE
I'VE FOUND OUR ONE RAY OF HOPE!
WOO—OO!!!
ALMOST EVERYONE'S LEFT THE CASTLE...
...BUT PAPPAGU WAS LEFT BEHIND.
WOOO
WOOO
WHEN DID YOU LEARN HOW TO DO THAT?
YOU REALLY ARE LIKE A GHOST NOW.
WELL, ONE DAY, I WAS PRAYING...
...AND MY SOUL JUST LEFT MY BODY. YO HO HO HO...
GAAAH
HOO
I WENT THROUGH WALLS LEFT AND RIGHT...
...THE DAY I LEARNED THIS TECHNIQUE.
WHAT DO YOU THINK I DID FIRST?
HUFF
HUFF
I'M SO JEALOUS! ZOLO! I'M SO JEALOUS OF HIM!
SHUT UP!

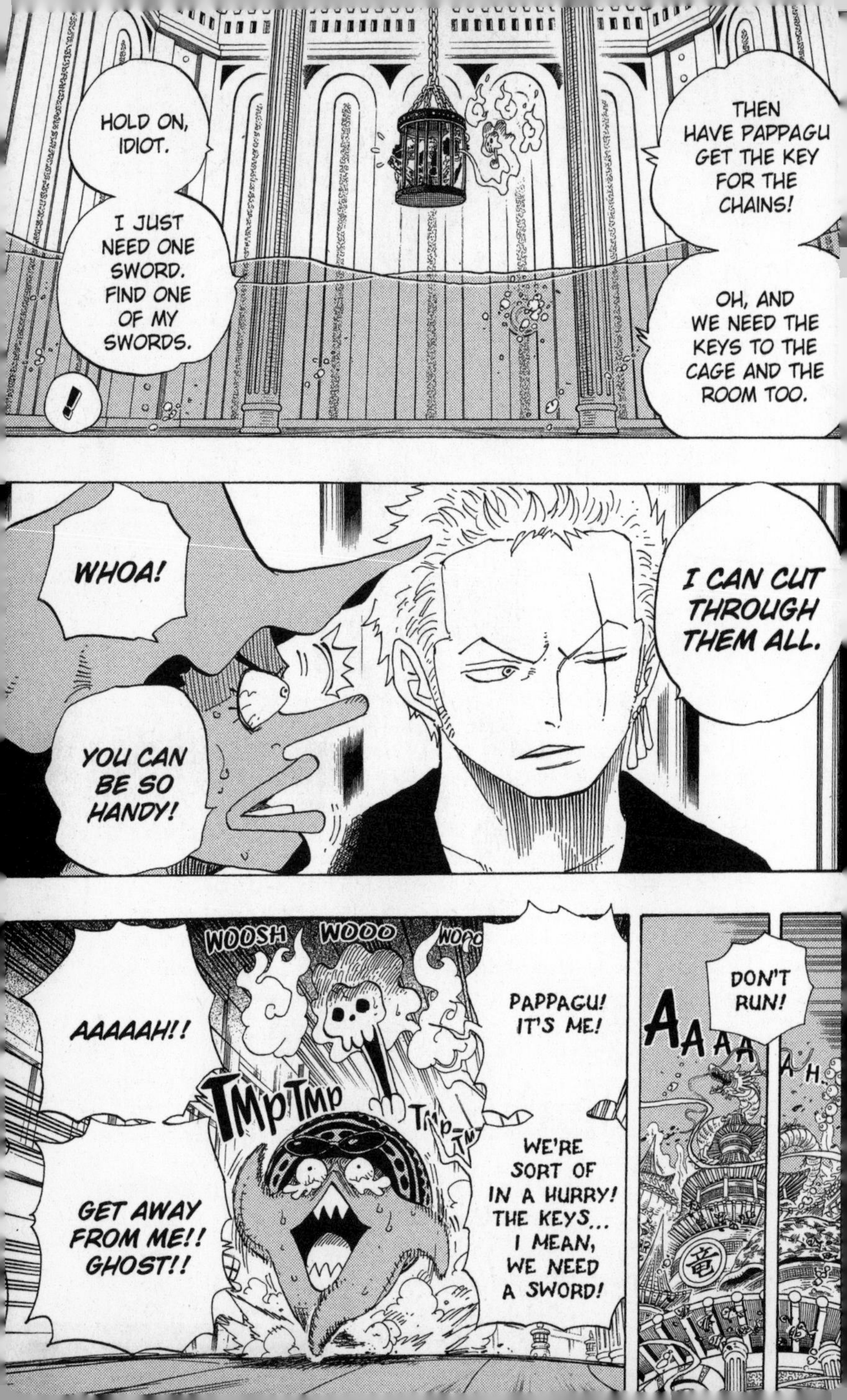
THEN HAVE PAPPAGU GET THE KEY FOR THE CHAINS!
OH, AND WE NEED THE KEYS TO THE CAGE AND THE ROOM TOO.
HOLD ON, IDIOT.
I JUST NEED ONE SWORD. FIND ONE OF MY SWORDS.
!
I CAN CUT THROUGH THEM ALL.
WHOA!
YOU CAN BE SO HANDY!
DON'T RUN!
AAAAAH...
竜
PAPPAGU! IT'S ME!
WE'RE SORT OF IN A HURRY! THE KEYS... I MEAN, WE NEED A SWORD!
WOOO
WOOSH
TMPTMP
AAAAAH!!
GET AWAY FROM ME!! GHOST!!

質問コーナー

(Kurumekko, Saitama)

Q: Mr. Odacchi, I have a question. It's a serious one! In volume 63, page 144, there's a partial message behind Kizaru. Aokiji's motto is "lazy justice." So what are Kizaru's and Akainu's and Odacchi's mottos? Please tell me. --K. Z. K. Jones

A: What? Mine too? Well, here's what they are.

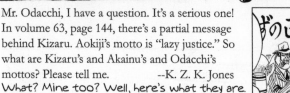

Akainu Absolute Justice

Kizaru Uncertain Justice

Aokiji Lazy Justice

Oda I love Anpanman

Well, anyway, if you have a lot of free time, you can think about what I meant by that. I love Takashi Yanase. Akainu's justice involves his eradicating all forms of evil, as shown by the destruction of Robin's hometown of Ohara. At the time, Aokiji based his thinking on "Burning Justice," but through lots of thinking, he resorted to his current "Lazy Justice." Kizaru probably saw everything from a distance and chose whatever he thought fit best. Over the past two years, a lot of things happened in the Navy. I can't wait to draw out exactly what happened, so please look forward to them in the main chapters.

Q: Dear Mr. Odacchi. Hello. I thought about Drake's and Bege's birthdays.

X Drake October 24
X is the roman number for 10 and it's also the 24th letter in the alphabet.

Capone "Gang" Bege January 17
Same birthday as Al Capone

What do you think? --Eraser-Eraser Stamp!

A: Oh, right. I forgot that I had suspended thinking about the birthdays of these two supernovas. Hmmmm... (pretending to think hard) Sure.

Q: It might be kind of late but I don't quite understand the system behind the bounties. If you kill the bounty, you'll get money from the Navy, right? But if a pirate comes to deliver the bounty, won't the Navy capture the guy too? --Sakimaru

DEAD OR ALIVE
MONKEY·D·LUFFY
400,000,000
MARINE

A: Yes, they will. That's why even if pirates defeat other pirates, they can't obtain bounties. All they will get is "infamy."

Chapter 630:
GETTING VIOLENT

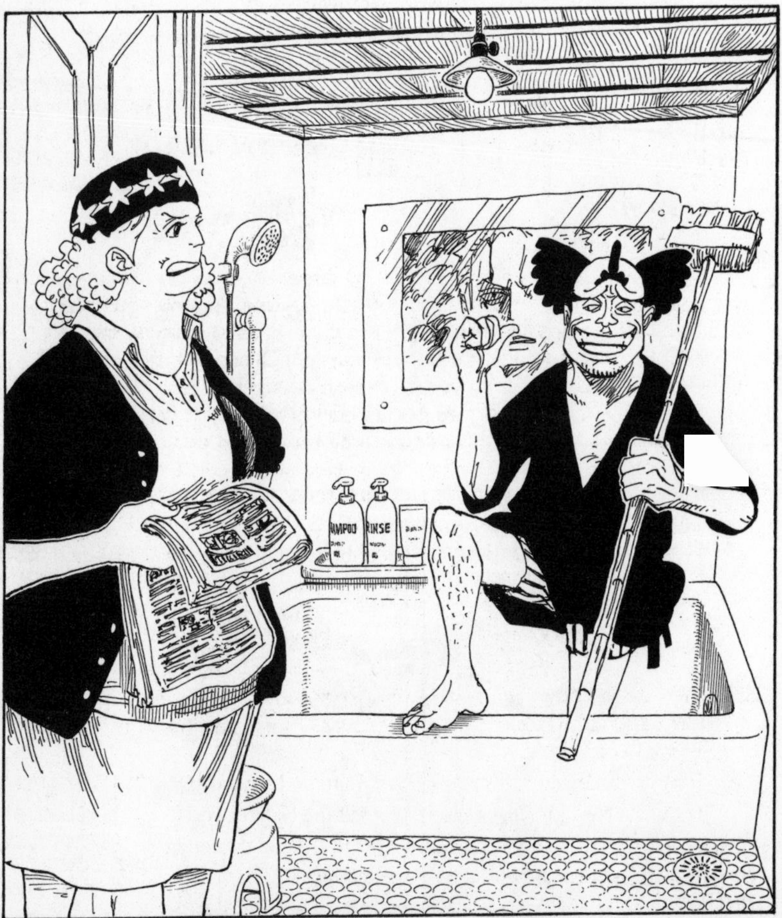
RINSE

DECKS OF THE WORLD, VOL. 15:
"ROGUETOWN"

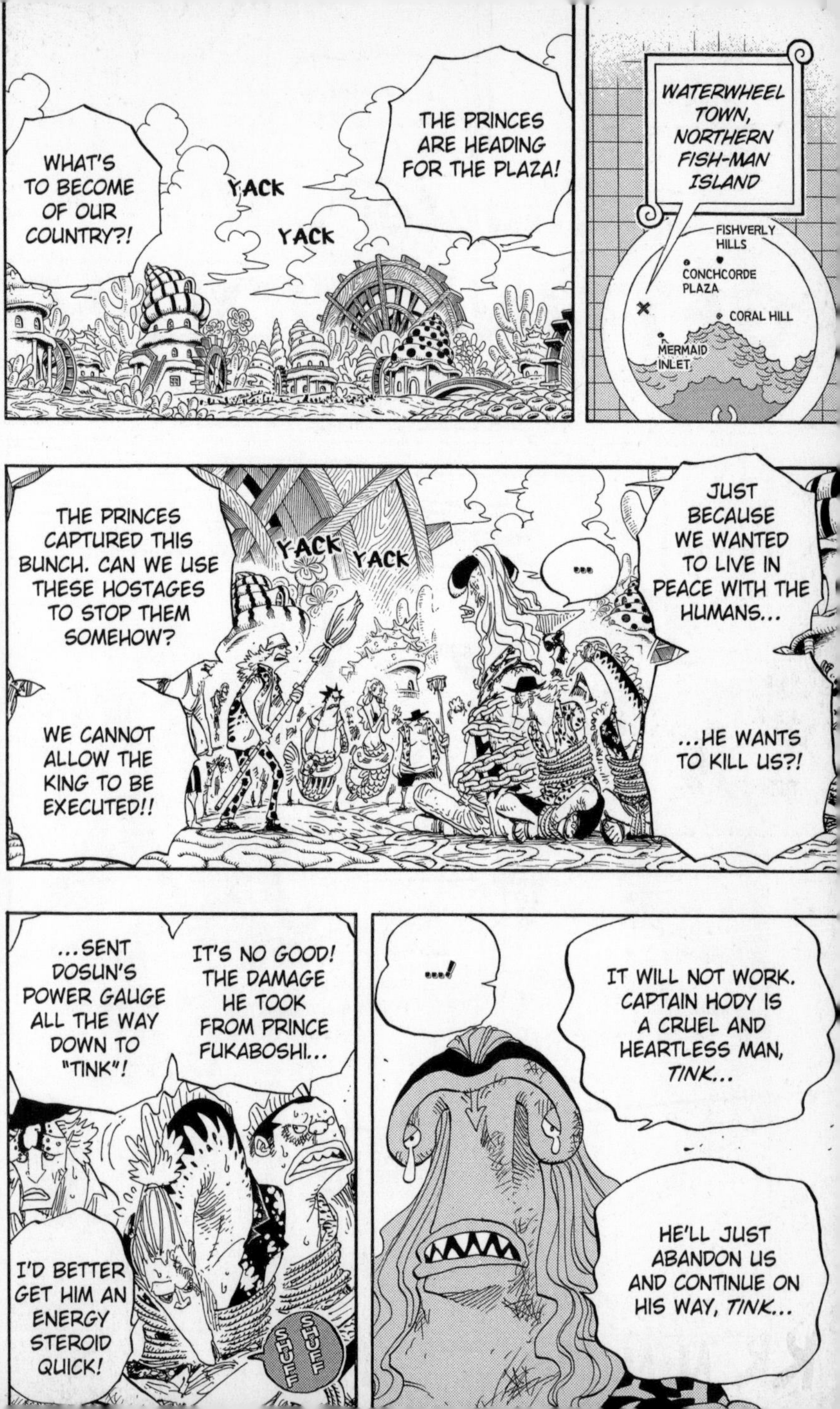
WATERWHEEL TOWN, NORTHERN FISH-MAN ISLAND
FISHVERLY HILLS
CONCHCORDE PLAZA
CORAL HILL
MERMAID INLET
THE PRINCES ARE HEADING FOR THE PLAZA!
YACK
YACK
WHAT'S TO BECOME OF OUR COUNTRY?!
JUST BECAUSE WE WANTED TO LIVE IN PEACE WITH THE HUMANS...
...HE WANTS TO KILL US?!
...
YACK
YACK
THE PRINCES CAPTURED THIS BUNCH. CAN WE USE THESE HOSTAGES TO STOP THEM SOMEHOW?
WE CANNOT ALLOW THE KING TO BE EXECUTED!!
...!
IT WILL NOT WORK. CAPTAIN HODY IS A CRUEL AND HEARTLESS MAN, *TINK*...
HE'LL JUST ABANDON US AND CONTINUE ON HIS WAY, *TINK*...
IT'S NO GOOD! THE DAMAGE HE TOOK FROM PRINCE FUKABOSHI...
...SENT DOSUN'S POWER GAUGE ALL THE WAY DOWN TO "TINK"!
I'D BETTER GET HIM AN ENERGY STEROID QUICK!
STUFF
STUFF

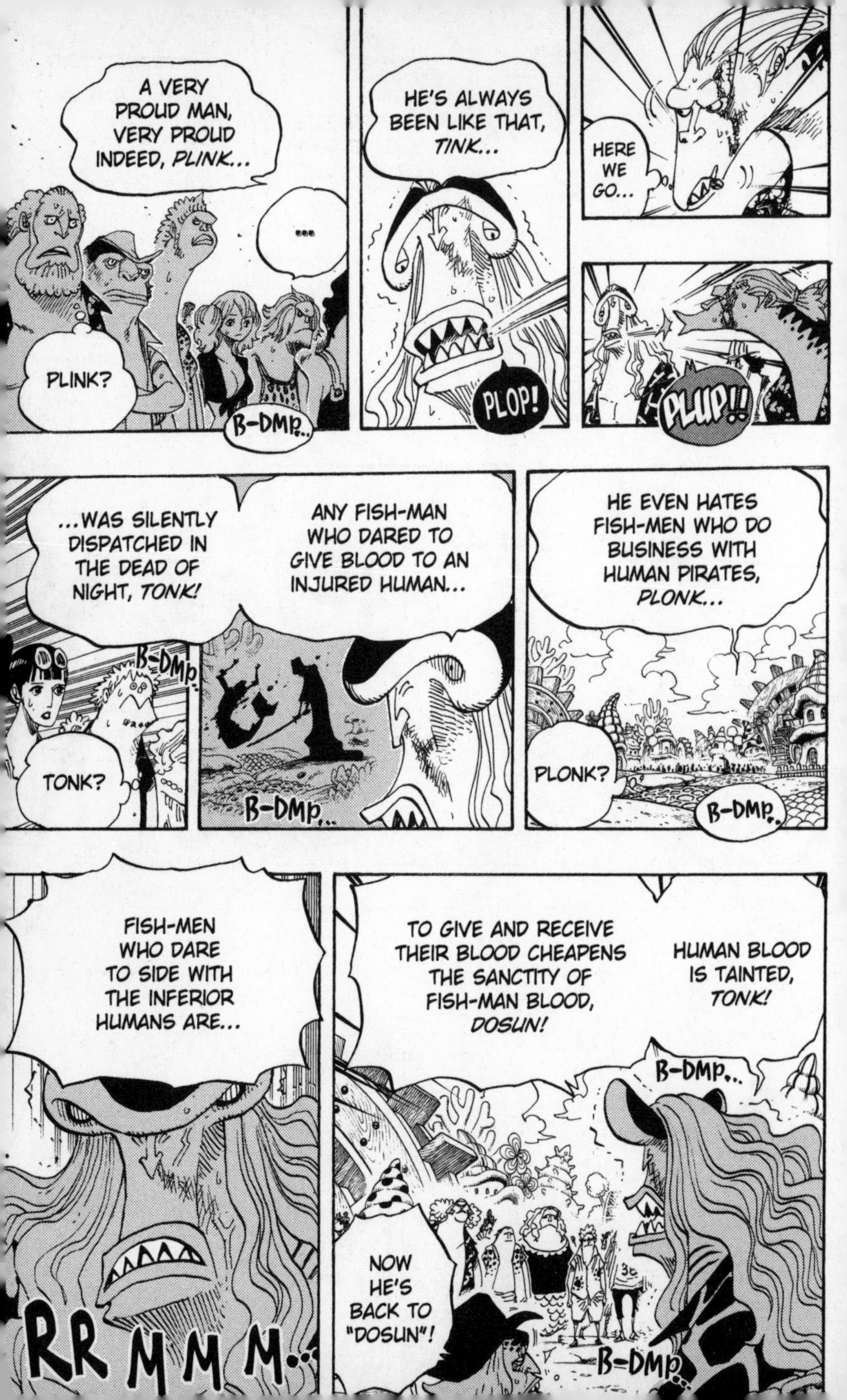
HERE WE GO...
PLUP!!
HE'S ALWAYS BEEN LIKE THAT, *TINK*...
PLOP!
A VERY PROUD MAN, VERY PROUD INDEED, *PLINK*...
...
PLINK?
B-DMP..
HE EVEN HATES FISH-MEN WHO DO BUSINESS WITH HUMAN PIRATES, *PLONK*...
PLONK?
B-DMP..
ANY FISH-MAN WHO DARED TO GIVE BLOOD TO AN INJURED HUMAN...
B-DMP..
...WAS SILENTLY DISPATCHED IN THE DEAD OF NIGHT, *TONK!*
B-DMP
TONK?
HUMAN BLOOD IS TAINTED, *TONK!*
TO GIVE AND RECEIVE THEIR BLOOD CHEAPENS THE SANCTITY OF FISH-MAN BLOOD, *DOSUN!*
B-DMP..
NOW HE'S BACK TO "DOSUN"!
B-DMP..
FISH-MEN WHO DARE TO SIDE WITH THE INFERIOR HUMANS ARE...
RRMMM..

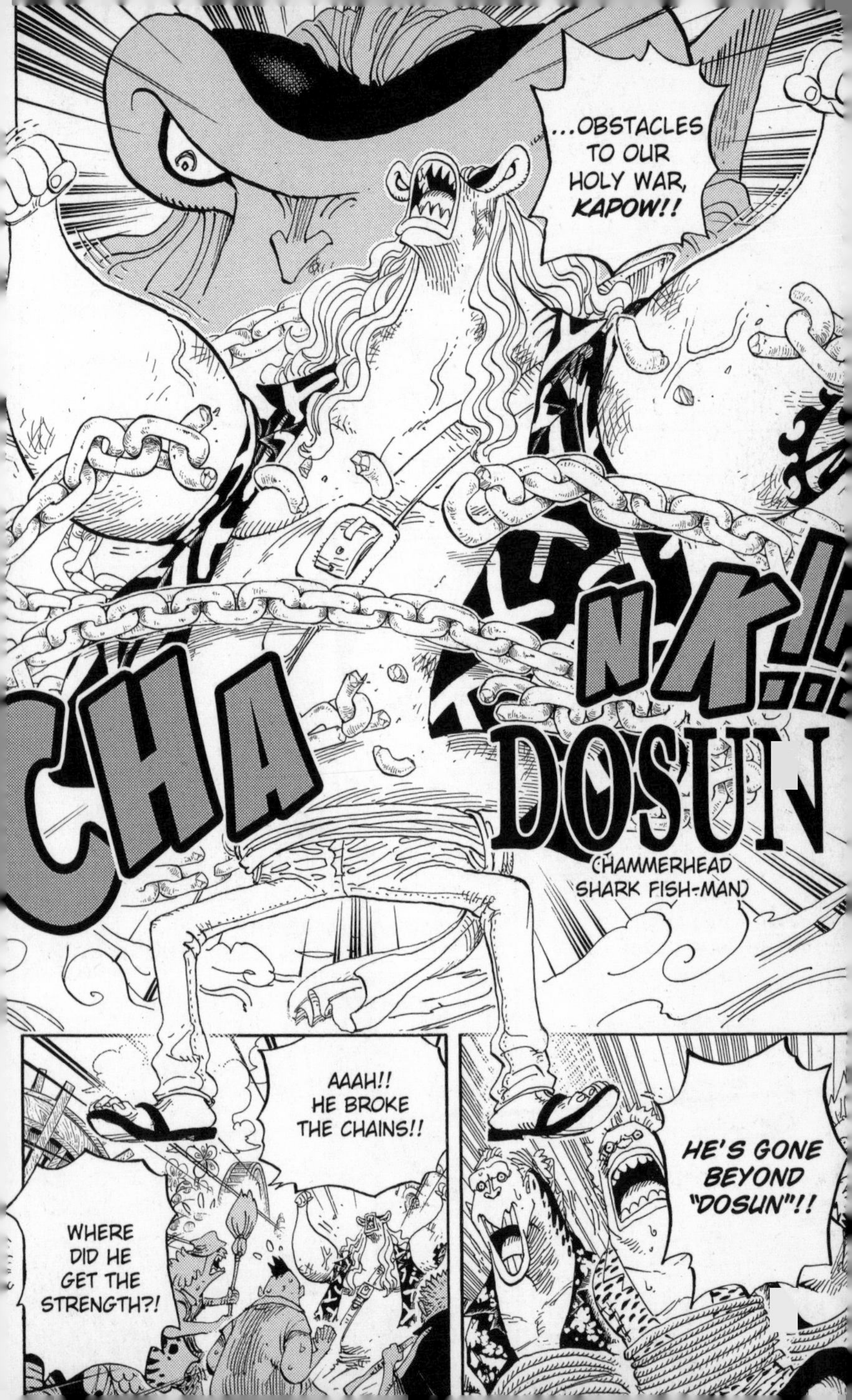
...OBSTACLES TO OUR HOLY WAR, *KAPOW!!*
CHANK!!
DOSUN
(HAMMERHEAD SHARK FISH-MAN)
HE'S GONE BEYOND "DOSUN"!!
AAAH!! HE BROKE THE CHAINS!!
WHERE DID HE GET THE STRENGTH?!

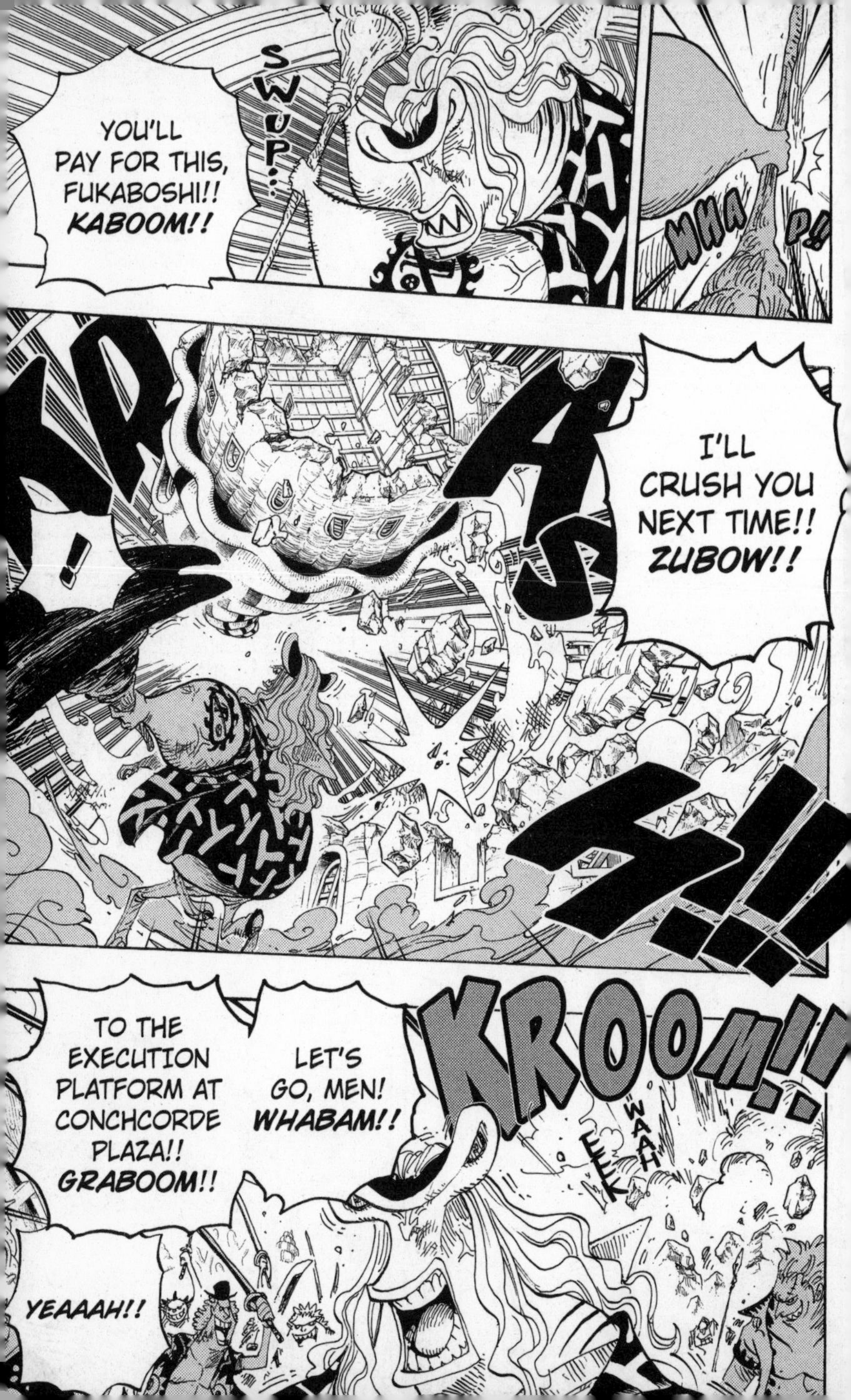
WHAP!
SWUP...
YOU'LL PAY FOR THIS, FUKABOSHI!! KABOOM!!
I'LL CRUSH YOU NEXT TIME!! ZUBOW!!
KROOM!!
LET'S GO, MEN! WHABAM!!
TO THE EXECUTION PLATFORM AT CONCHCORDE PLAZA!! GRABOOM!!
WAAH
YEAAAH!!

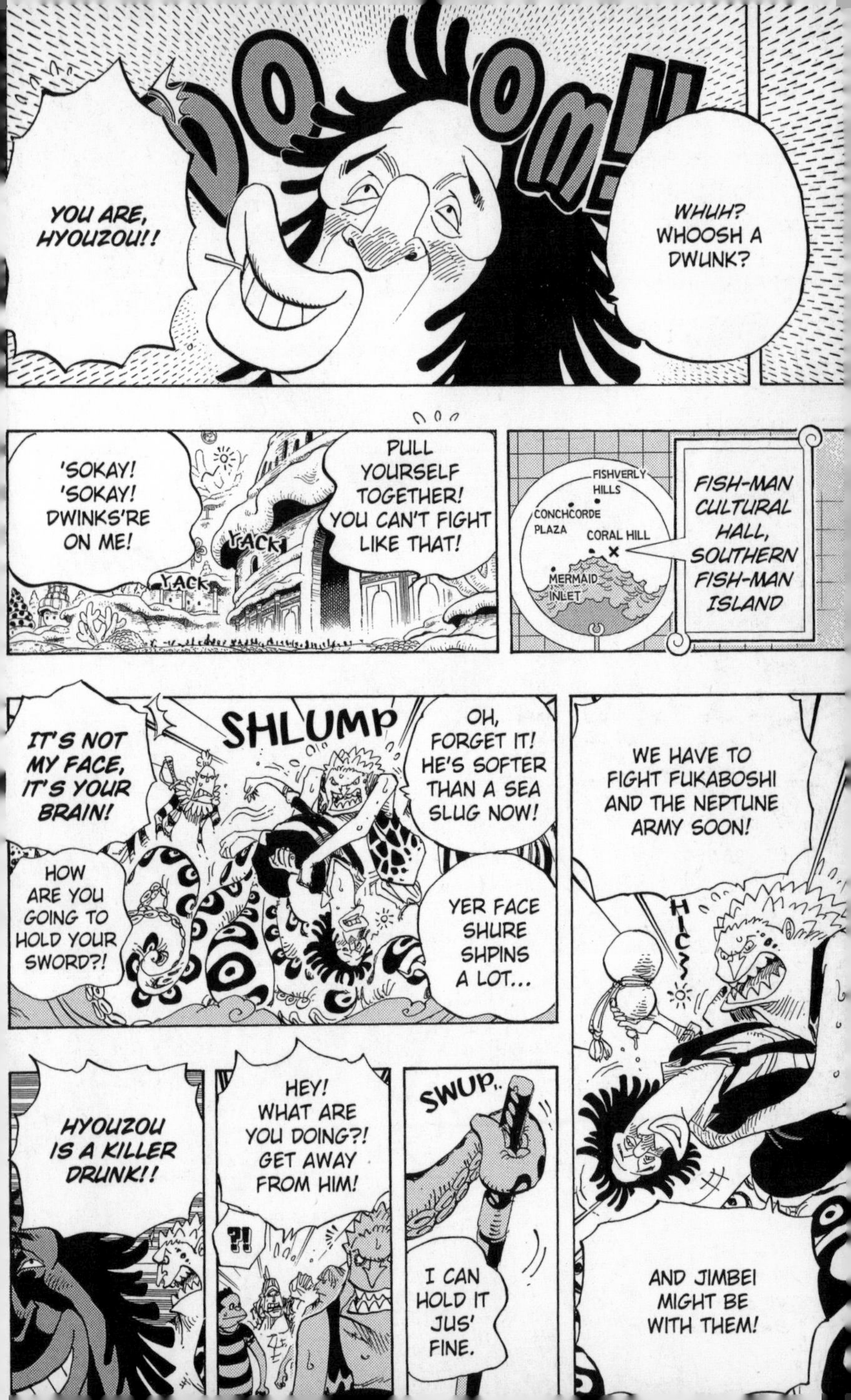
WHUH? WHOOSH A DWUNK?
YOU ARE, HYOUZOU!!
FISH-MAN CULTURAL HALL, SOUTHERN FISH-MAN ISLAND
FISHVERLY HILLS
CONCHCORDE PLAZA
CORAL HILL
MERMAID INLET
PULL YOURSELF TOGETHER! YOU CAN'T FIGHT LIKE THAT!
YACK
YACK
'SOKAY! 'SOKAY! DWINKS'RE ON ME!
WE HAVE TO FIGHT FUKABOSHI AND THE NEPTUNE ARMY SOON!
HIC
AND JIMBEI MIGHT BE WITH THEM!
OH, FORGET IT! HE'S SOFTER THAN A SEA SLUG NOW!
SHLUMP
IT'S NOT MY FACE, IT'S YOUR BRAIN!
YER FACE SHURE SHPINS A LOT...
HOW ARE YOU GOING TO HOLD YOUR SWORD?!
SWUP..
I CAN HOLD IT JUS' FINE.
HEY! WHAT ARE YOU DOING?! GET AWAY FROM HIM!
?!
HYOUZOU IS A KILLER DRUNK!!

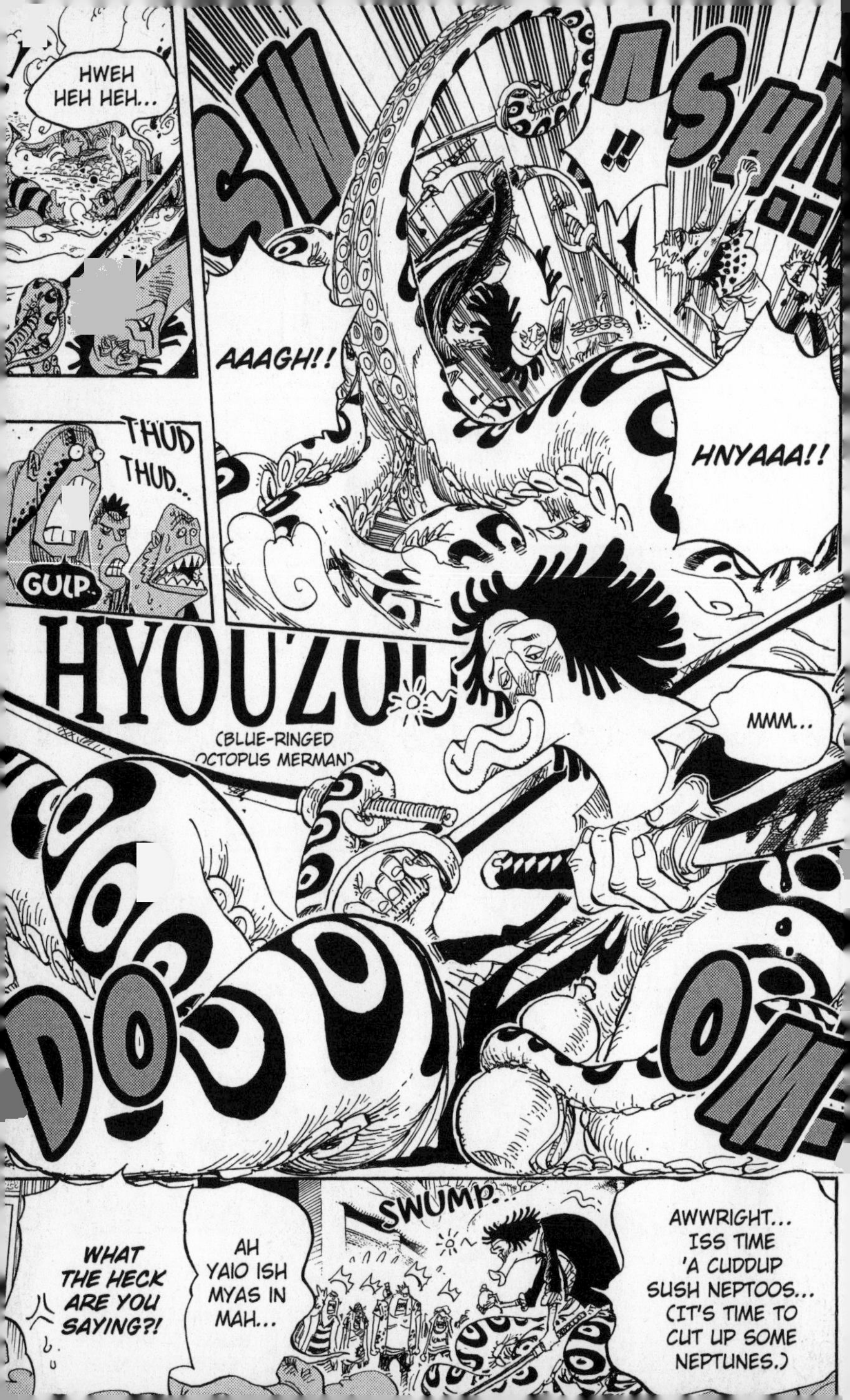

SWASH!!
!!
HNYAAA!!
AAAGH!!
HWEH HEH HEH...
THUD THUD...
GULP
MMM...
HYOUZOU
(BLUE-RINGED OCTOPUS MERMAN)
DOGOOM!!
SWUMP...
AWWRIGHT... ISS TIME 'A CUDDUP SUSH NEPTOOS... (IT'S TIME TO CUT UP SOME NEPTUNES.)
AH YAIO ISH MYAS IN MAH...
WHAT THE HECK ARE YOU SAYING?!

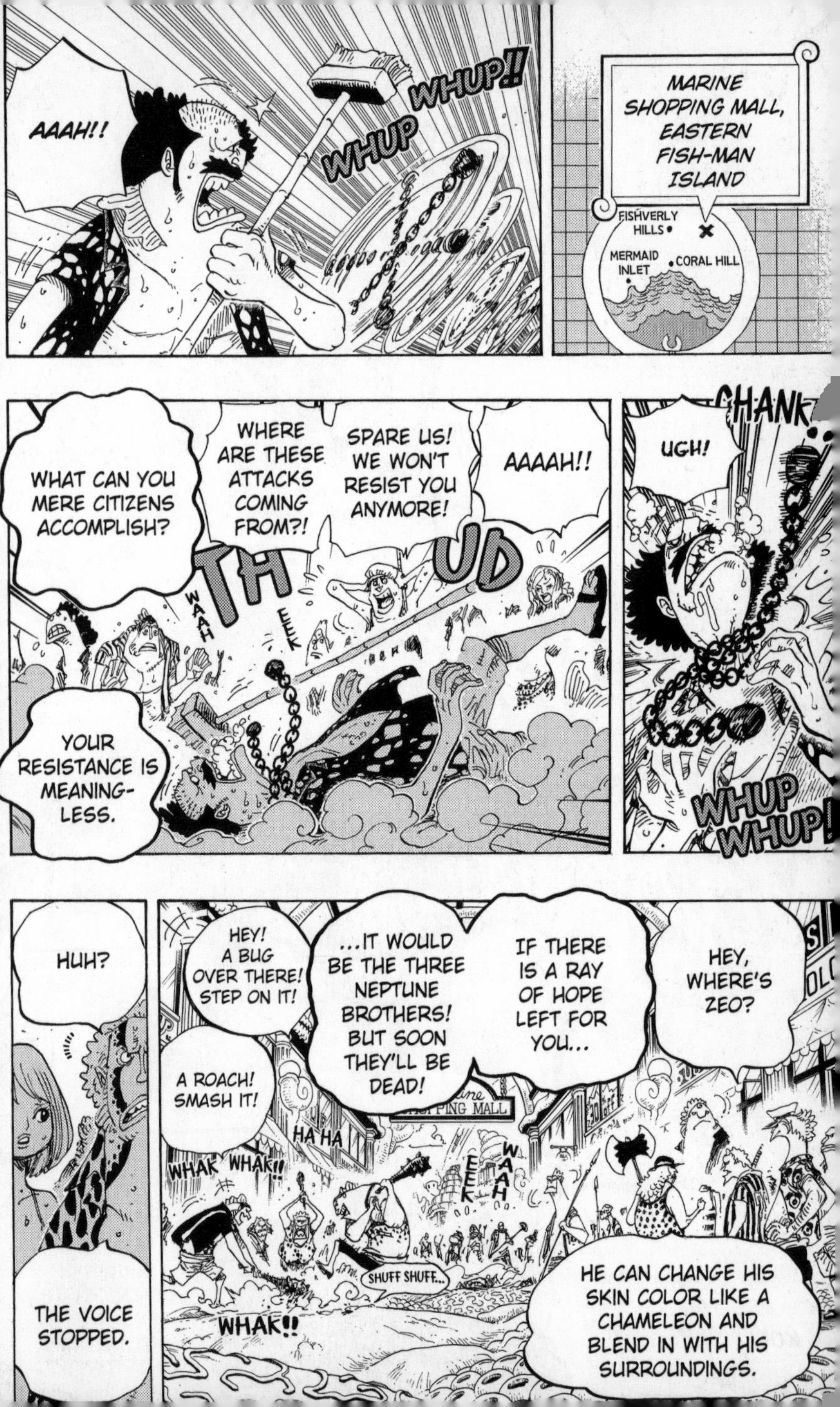
MARINE SHOPPING MALL, EASTERN FISH-MAN ISLAND
FISHVERLY HILLS
MERMAID INLET
CORAL HILL
WHUP WHUP!!
AAAH!!
CHANK
UGH!
WHUP WHUP!
AAAAH!!
SPARE US! WE WON'T RESIST YOU ANYMORE!
WHERE ARE THESE ATTACKS COMING FROM?!
WHAT CAN YOU MERE CITIZENS ACCOMPLISH?
THUD
EEK
WAAH
YOUR RESISTANCE IS MEANING-LESS.
HEY, WHERE'S ZEO?
IF THERE IS A RAY OF HOPE LEFT FOR YOU...
...IT WOULD BE THE THREE NEPTUNE BROTHERS! BUT SOON THEY'LL BE DEAD!
HEY! A BUG OVER THERE! STEP ON IT!
A ROACH! SMASH IT!
SHOPPING MALL
HA HA
WAAH
EEK
WHAK WHAK!!
SHUFF SHUFF...
WHAK!!
HE CAN CHANGE HIS SKIN COLOR LIKE A CHAMELEON AND BLEND IN WITH HIS SURROUNDINGS.
HUH?
THE VOICE STOPPED.

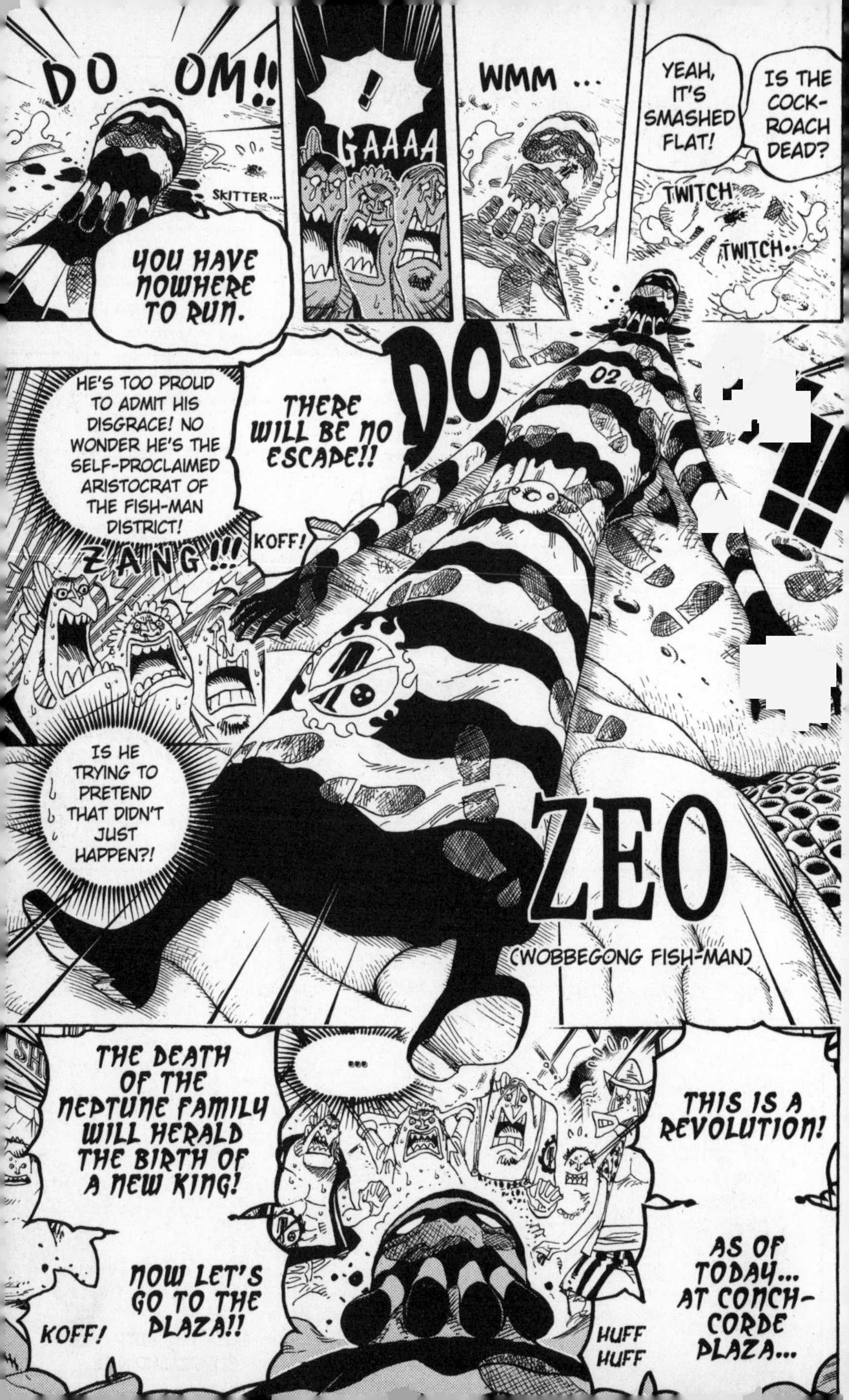
IS THE COCK-ROACH DEAD?
YEAH, IT'S SMASHED FLAT!
TWITCH
TWITCH...
WMM...
!
GAAAA
DO OM!!
SKITTER...
YOU HAVE NOWHERE TO RUN.
DO
!!
THERE WILL BE NO ESCAPE!!
HE'S TOO PROUD TO ADMIT HIS DISGRACE! NO WONDER HE'S THE SELF-PROCLAIMED ARISTOCRAT OF THE FISH-MAN DISTRICT!
KOFF!
ZANG!!!
IS HE TRYING TO PRETEND THAT DIDN'T JUST HAPPEN?!
ZEO
(WOBBEGONG FISH-MAN)
THIS IS A REVOLUTION!
AS OF TODAY... AT CONCH-CORDE PLAZA...
HUFF HUFF
...
THE DEATH OF THE NEPTUNE FAMILY WILL HERALD THE BIRTH OF A NEW KING!
NOW LET'S GO TO THE PLAZA!!
KOFF!

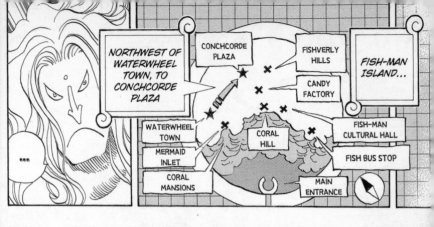

FISH-MAN ISLAND...
FISHVERLY HILLS
CANDY FACTORY
CONCHCORDE PLAZA
NORTHWEST OF WATERWHEEL TOWN, TO CONCHCORDE PLAZA
FISH-MAN CULTURAL HALL
CORAL HILL
FISH BUS STOP
WATERWHEEL TOWN
MERMAID INLET
CORAL MANSIONS
MAIN ENTRANCE
...
HOW LONG UNTIL WE REACH CONCHCORDE PLAZA?
竜宮
LESS THAN ONE HOUR, SIR.
WHY WOULD THEY GO TO ALL THE TROUBLE OF EXECUTING THE KING IN THE PLAZA?
IT'S SURE MADNESS. IT MUST BE A TRAP CAST FOR YOUR GRACE!
...
SO BE IT! I ACCEPT THEIR CHALLENGE!!
I WILL NOT ALLOW THAT FIEND TO HARM MY FATHER!!
THE CITIZENS HAVE FINALLY BEGUN TO OPEN THEIR HEARTS AGAIN! I WON'T ALLOW HIM TO SHUT THEM DOWN!!

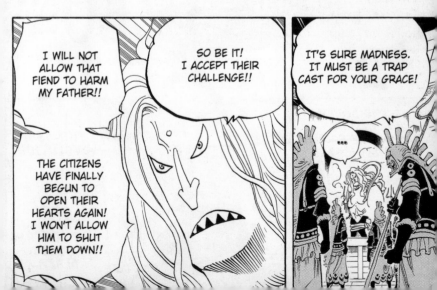

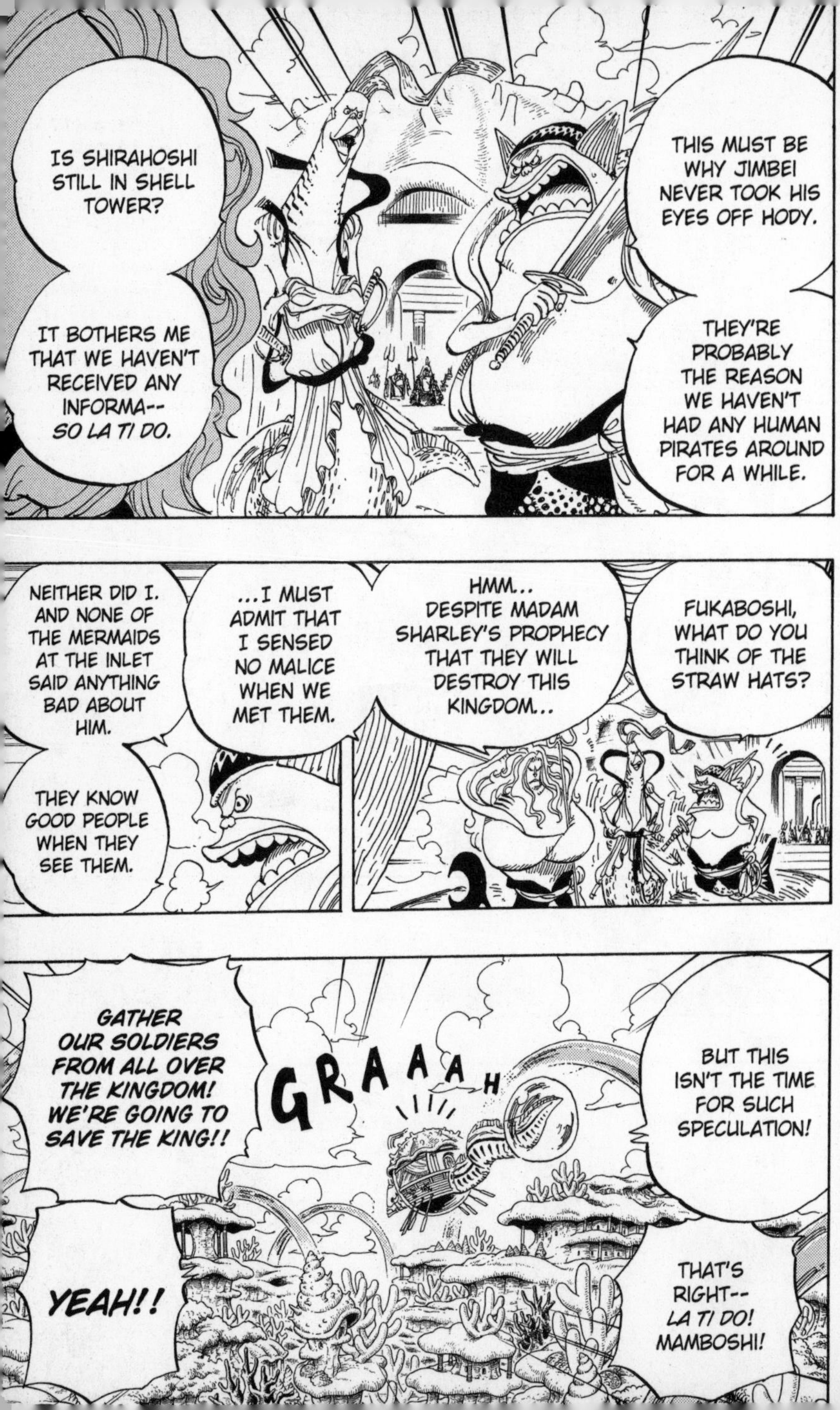
THIS MUST BE WHY JIMBEI NEVER TOOK HIS EYES OFF HODY.
THEY'RE PROBABLY THE REASON WE HAVEN'T HAD ANY HUMAN PIRATES AROUND FOR A WHILE.
IS SHIRAHOSHI STILL IN SHELL TOWER?
IT BOTHERS ME THAT WE HAVEN'T RECEIVED ANY INFORMA-- *SO LA TI DO.*
FUKABOSHI, WHAT DO YOU THINK OF THE STRAW HATS?
HMM... DESPITE MADAM SHARLEY'S PROPHECY THAT THEY WILL DESTROY THIS KINGDOM...
...I MUST ADMIT THAT I SENSED NO MALICE WHEN WE MET THEM.
NEITHER DID I. AND NONE OF THE MERMAIDS AT THE INLET SAID ANYTHING BAD ABOUT HIM.
THEY KNOW GOOD PEOPLE WHEN THEY SEE THEM.
BUT THIS ISN'T THE TIME FOR SUCH SPECULATION!
THAT'S RIGHT-- *LA TI DO!* MAMBOSHI!
GATHER OUR SOLDIERS FROM ALL OVER THE KINGDOM! WE'RE GOING TO SAVE THE KING!!
GRAAAAH
YEAH!!

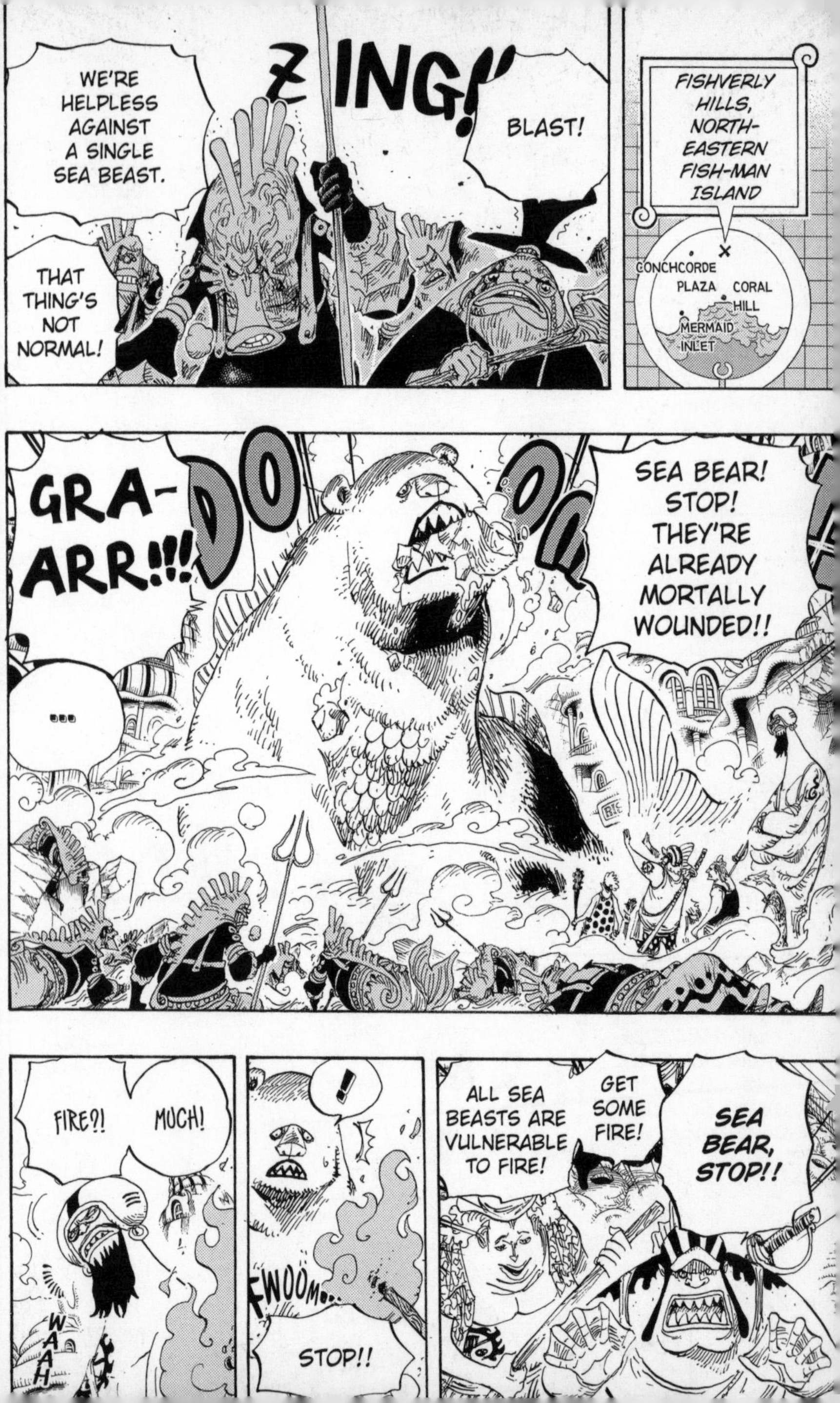
FISHVERLY HILLS, NORTH-EASTERN FISH-MAN ISLAND
CONCHCORDE PLAZA
CORAL HILL
MERMAID INLET
ZING!
BLAST!
WE'RE HELPLESS AGAINST A SINGLE SEA BEAST.
THAT THING'S NOT NORMAL!
SEA BEAR! STOP! THEY'RE ALREADY MORTALLY WOUNDED!!
DOOO
GRA-ARR!!!
...
SEA BEAR, STOP!!
GET SOME FIRE!
ALL SEA BEASTS ARE VULNERABLE TO FIRE!
!
FWOOM...
STOP!!
MUCH!
FIRE?!
WAAH

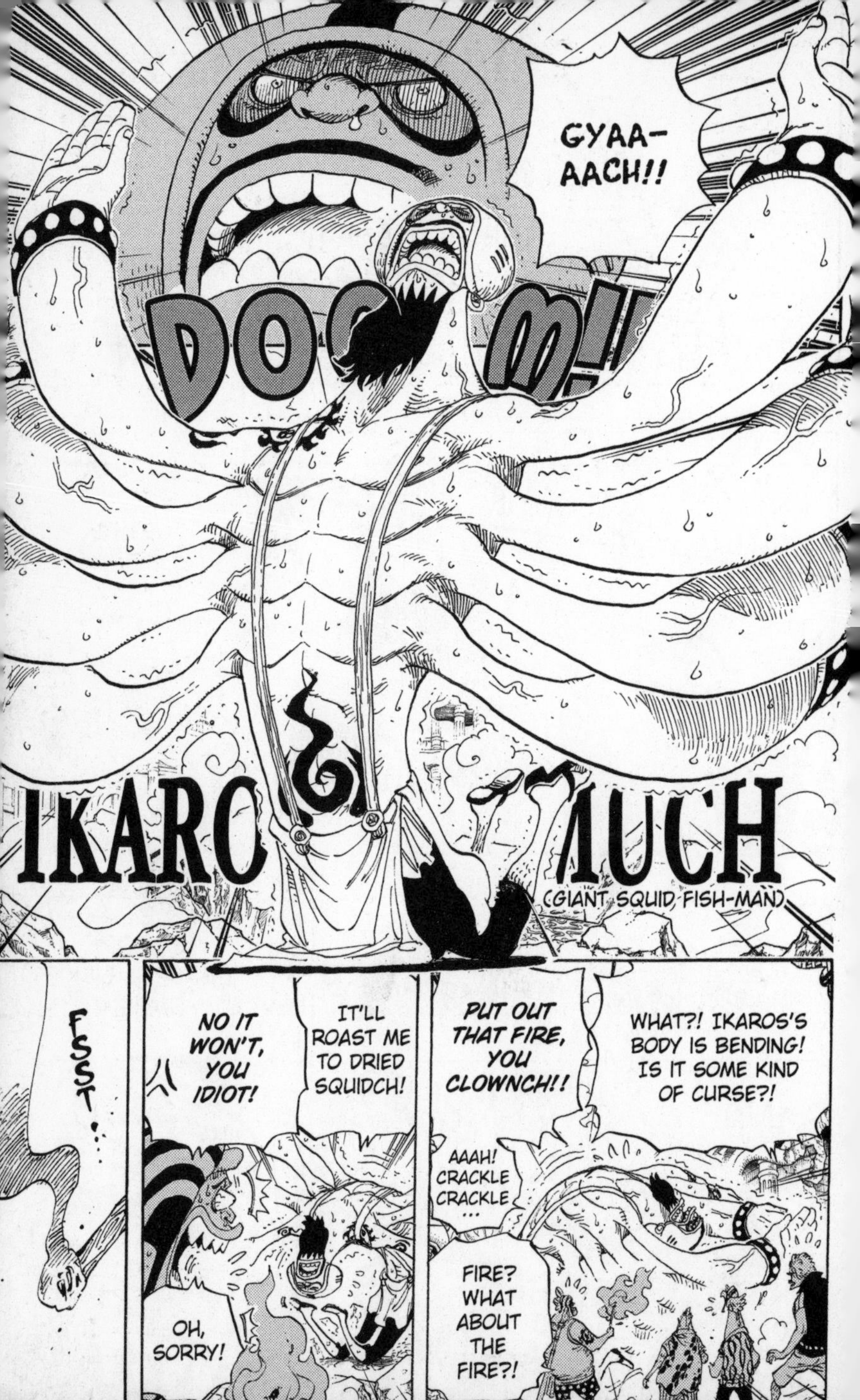
GYAA-AACH!!
DOOM!!
IKARO MUCH
(GIANT SQUID FISH-MAN)
WHAT?! IKAROS'S BODY IS BENDING! IS IT SOME KIND OF CURSE?!
PUT OUT THAT FIRE, YOU CLOWNCH!!
AAAH! CRACKLE CRACKLE ...
FIRE? WHAT ABOUT THE FIRE?!
IT'LL ROAST ME TO DRIED SQUIDCH!
NO IT WON'T, YOU IDIOT!
OH, SORRY!
FSST...

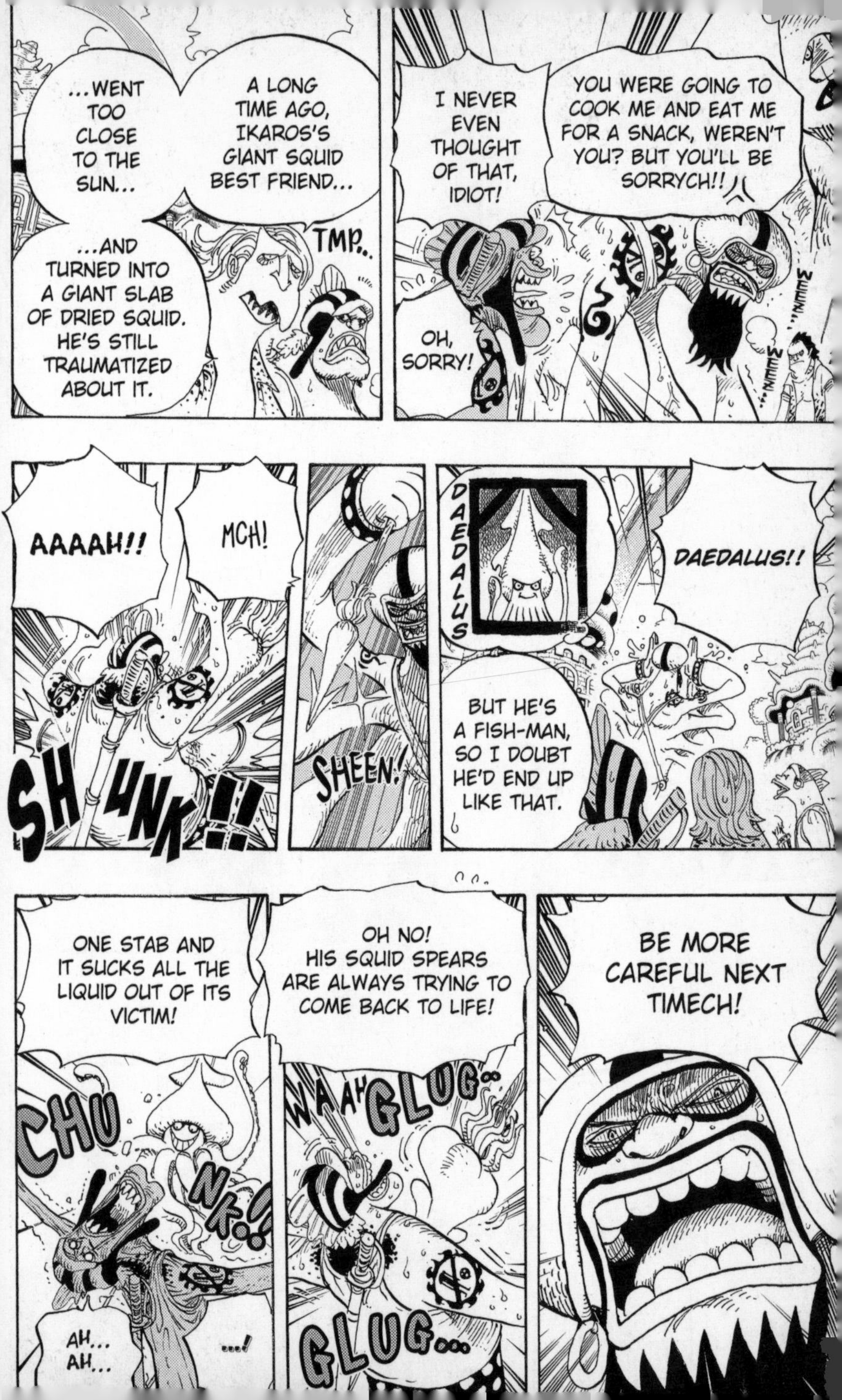
YOU WERE GOING TO COOK ME AND EAT ME FOR A SNACK, WEREN'T YOU? BUT YOU'LL BE SORRYCH!!
I NEVER EVEN THOUGHT OF THAT, IDIOT!
OH, SORRY!
WEEN...
WEEN...
A LONG TIME AGO, IKAROS'S GIANT SQUID BEST FRIEND...
...WENT TOO CLOSE TO THE SUN...
TMP...
...AND TURNED INTO A GIANT SLAB OF DRIED SQUID. HE'S STILL TRAUMATIZED ABOUT IT.
DAEDALUS!!
DAEDALUS
BUT HE'S A FISH-MAN, SO I DOUBT HE'D END UP LIKE THAT.
SHEEN!
MCH!
AAAAH!!
SHUNK!!
BE MORE CAREFUL NEXT TIMECH!
OH NO! HIS SQUID SPEARS ARE ALWAYS TRYING TO COME BACK TO LIFE!
WAAH
GLUG
GLUG...
ONE STAB AND IT SUCKS ALL THE LIQUID OUT OF ITS VICTIM!
CHUNK!!
AH... AH...
...!

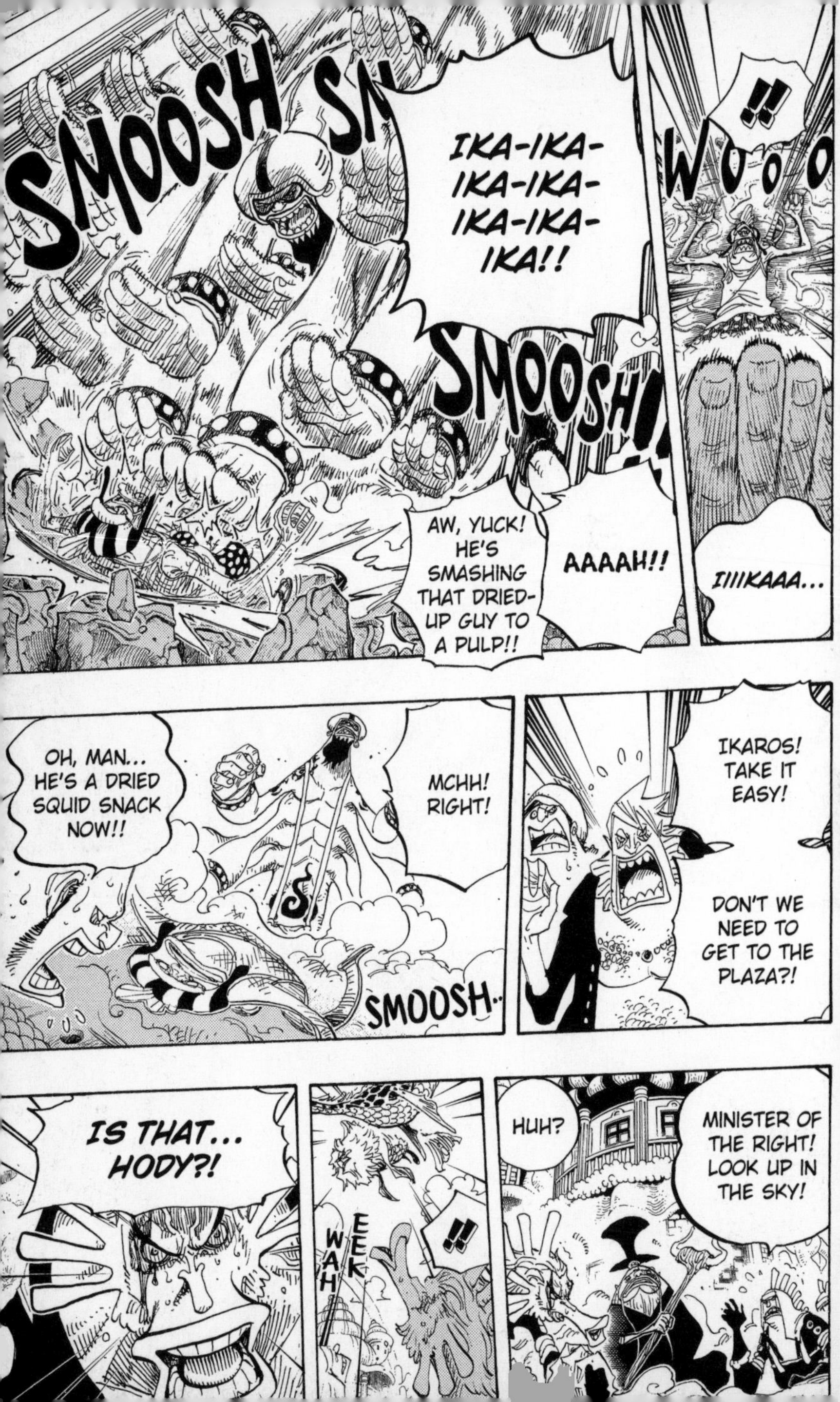
!!
WOOO
IIIIKAAA...
IKA-IKA-IKA-IKA-IKA-IKA-IKA!!
SMOOSH SM
SMOOSH
AAAAH!!
AW, YUCK! HE'S SMASHING THAT DRIED-UP GUY TO A PULP!!
IKAROS! TAKE IT EASY!
DON'T WE NEED TO GET TO THE PLAZA?!
MCHH! RIGHT!
OH, MAN... HE'S A DRIED SQUID SNACK NOW!!
SMOOSH..
MINISTER OF THE RIGHT! LOOK UP IN THE SKY!
HUH?
!!
EEK
WAH
IS THAT... HODY?!

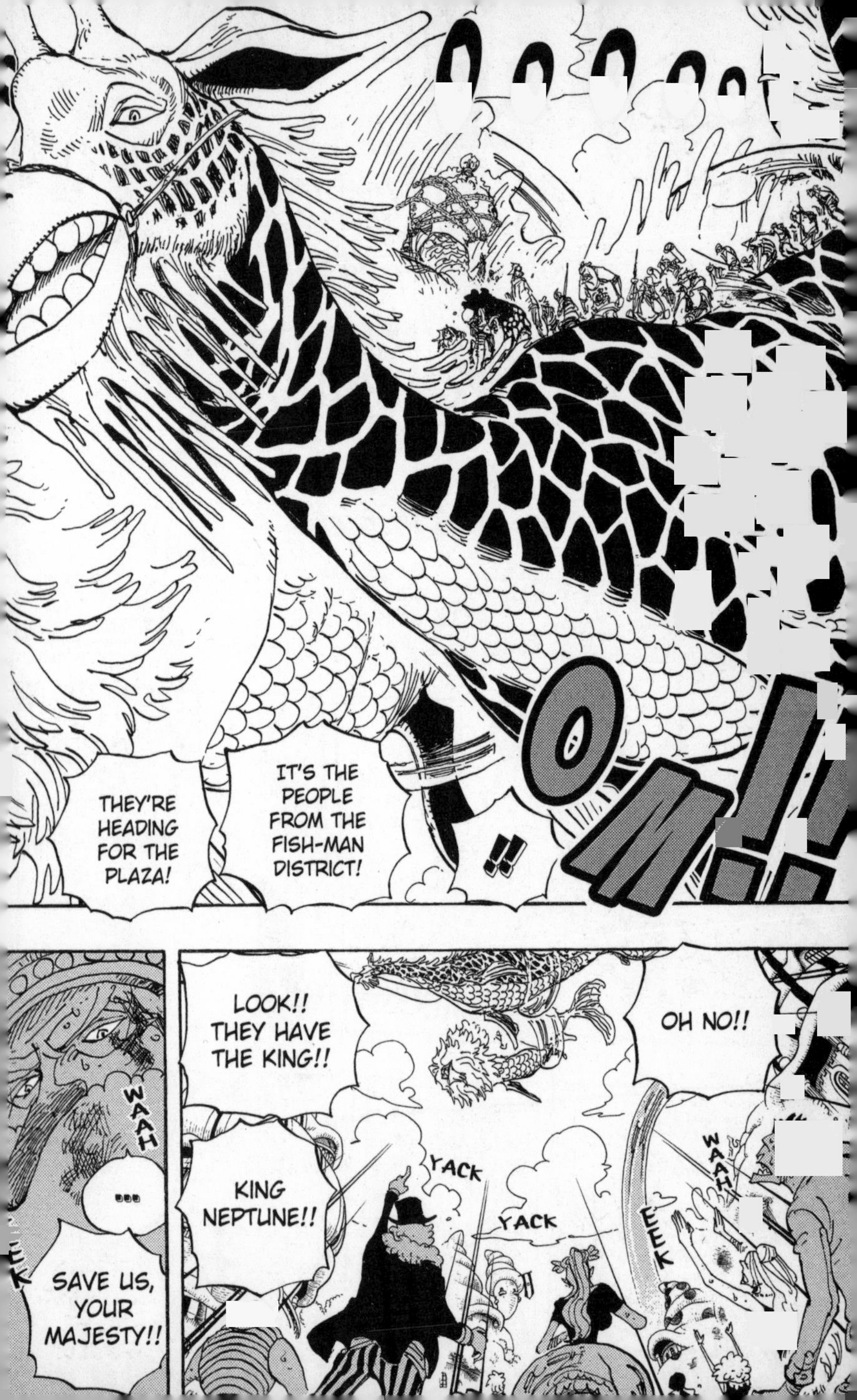
IT'S THE PEOPLE FROM THE FISH-MAN DISTRICT!
THEY'RE HEADING FOR THE PLAZA!
OH NO!!
WAAH
EEK
LOOK!! THEY HAVE THE KING!!
YACK
YACK
KING NEPTUNE!!
WAAH
...
SAVE US, YOUR MAJESTY!!

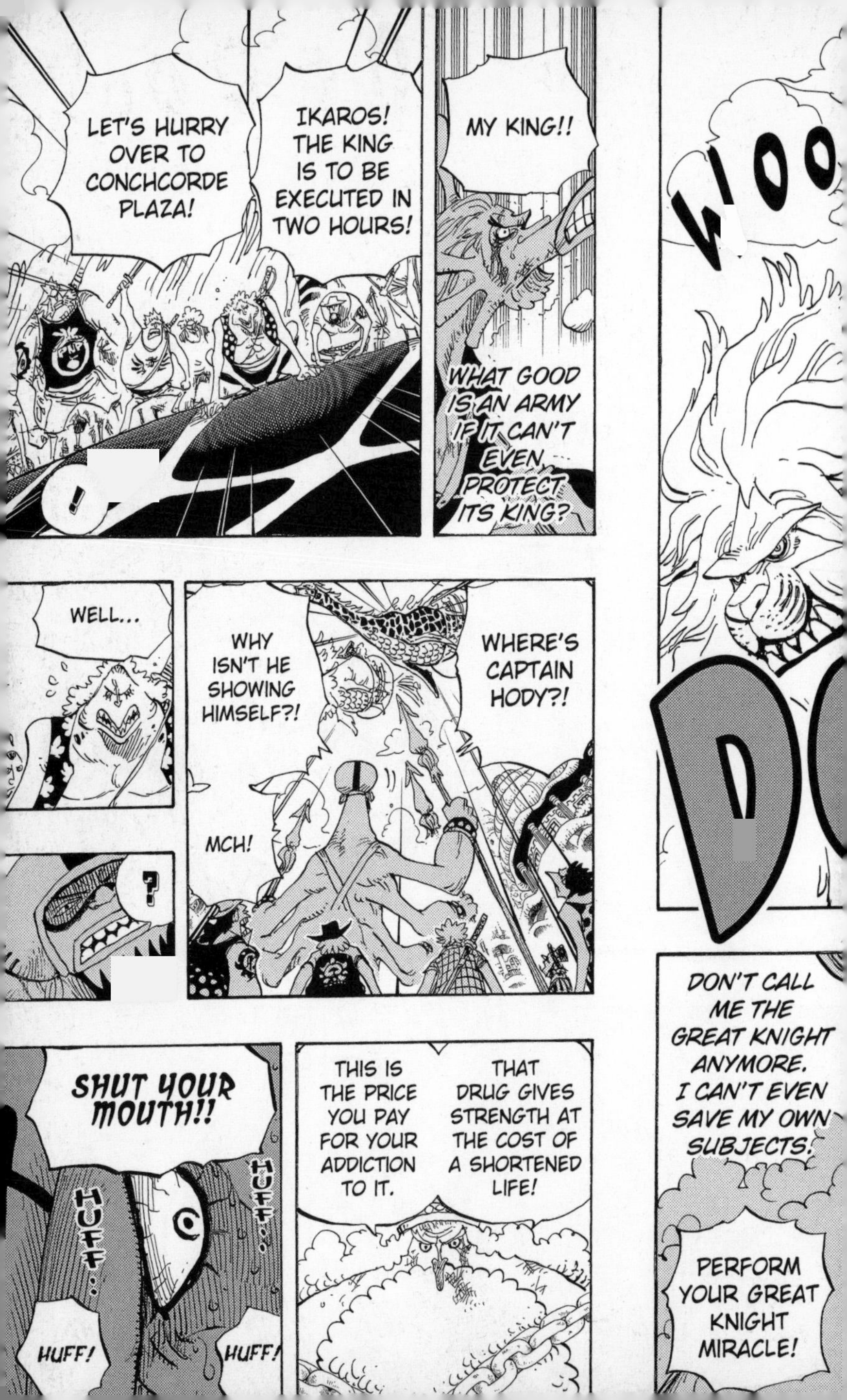
WHOO
DO
MY KING!!
WHAT GOOD IS AN ARMY IF IT CAN'T EVEN PROTECT ITS KING?
IKAROS! THE KING IS TO BE EXECUTED IN TWO HOURS!
LET'S HURRY OVER TO CONCHCORDE PLAZA!
!
WHERE'S CAPTAIN HODY?!
WHY ISN'T HE SHOWING HIMSELF?!
MCH!
WELL...
?
DON'T CALL ME THE GREAT KNIGHT ANYMORE. I CAN'T EVEN SAVE MY OWN SUBJECTS.
PERFORM YOUR GREAT KNIGHT MIRACLE!
THAT DRUG GIVES STRENGTH AT THE COST OF A SHORTENED LIFE!
THIS IS THE PRICE YOU PAY FOR YOUR ADDICTION TO IT.
SHUT YOUR MOUTH!!
HUFF...
HUFF...
HUFF!
HUFF!

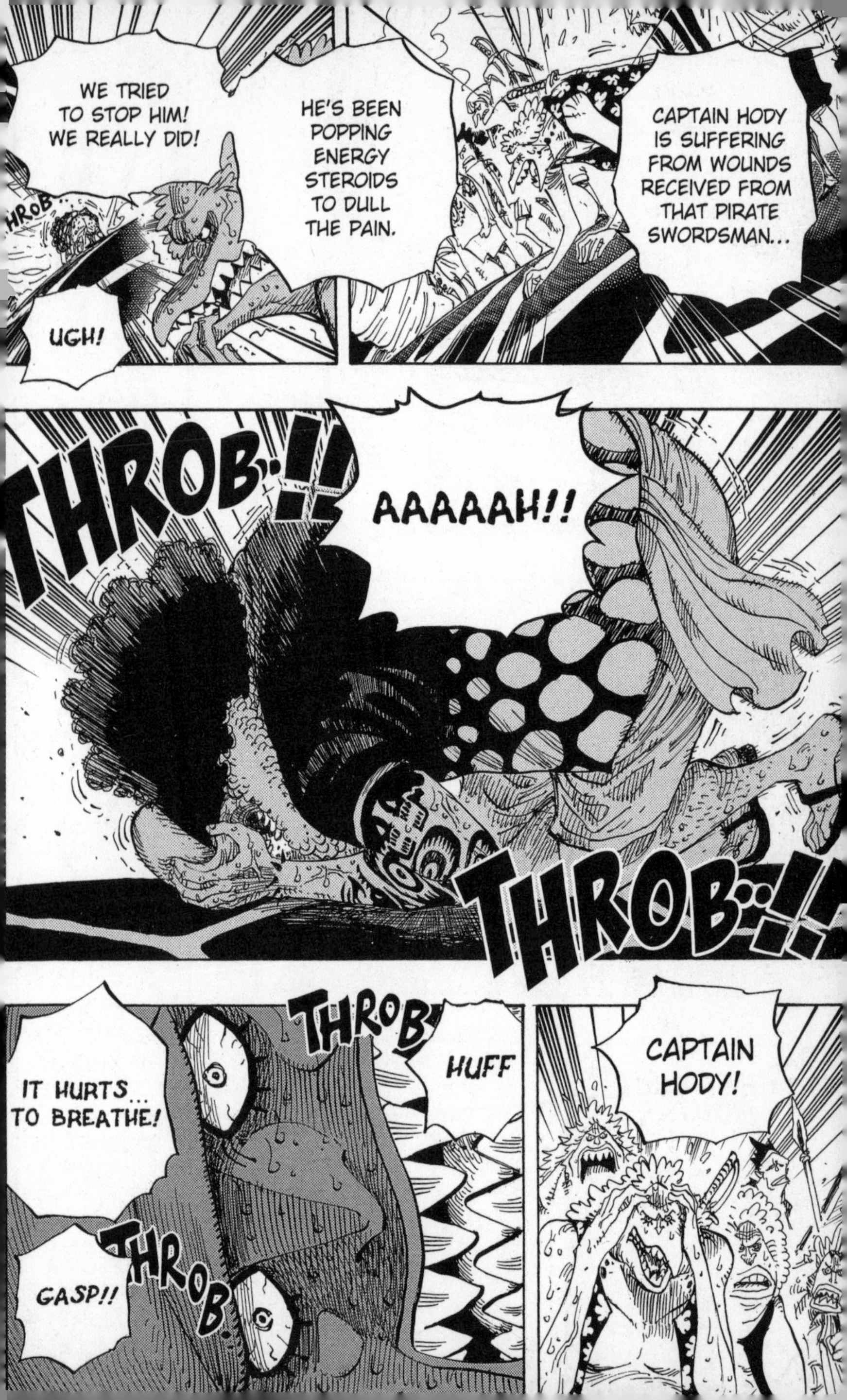
CAPTAIN HODY IS SUFFERING FROM WOUNDS RECEIVED FROM THAT PIRATE SWORDSMAN...
HE'S BEEN POPPING ENERGY STEROIDS TO DULL THE PAIN.
WE TRIED TO STOP HIM! WE REALLY DID!
THROB
UGH!
THROB..!!
AAAAAH!!
THROB..!!
CAPTAIN HODY!
THROB
HUFF
IT HURTS... TO BREATHE!
THROB
GASP!!

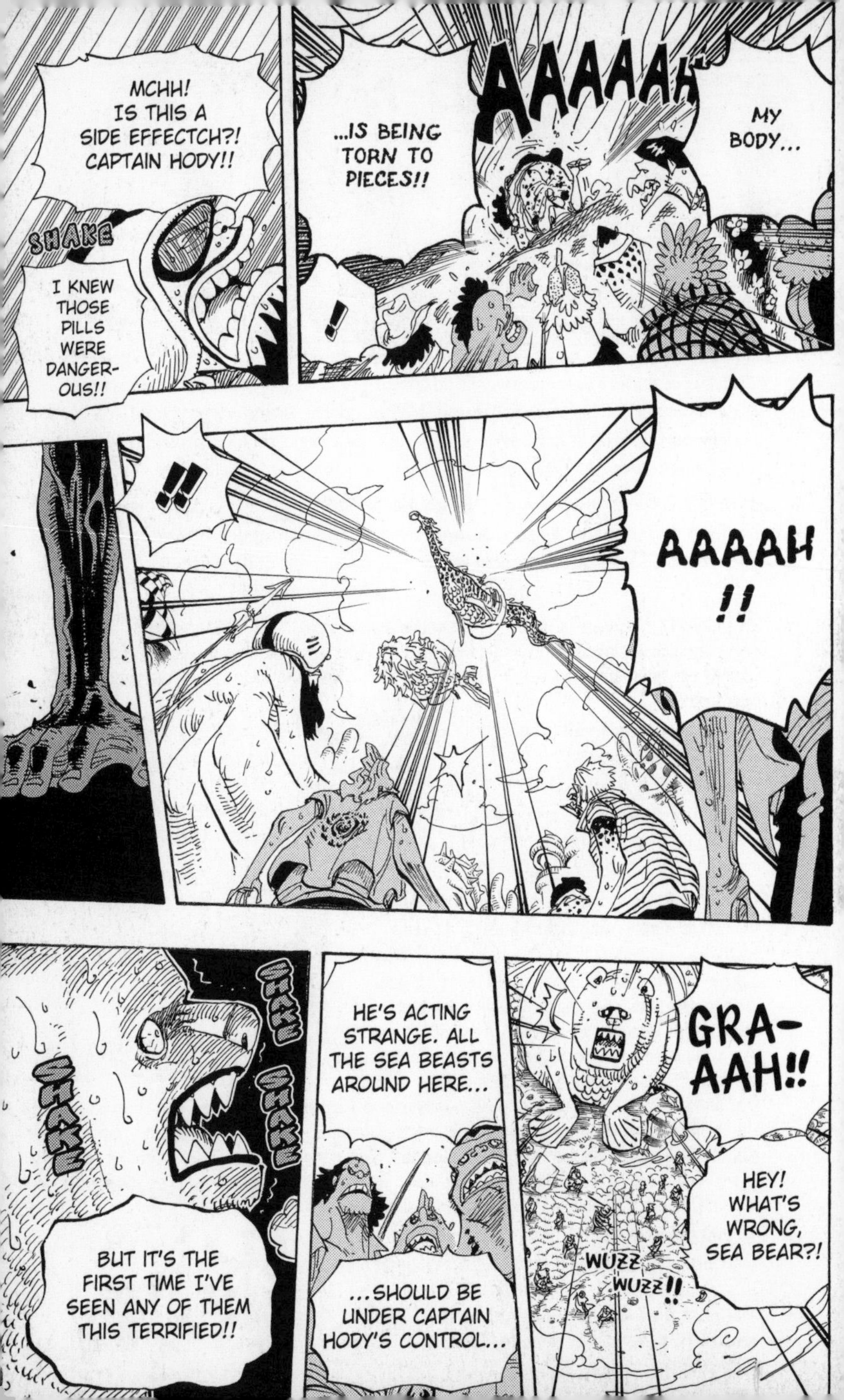
AAAAAH
MY BODY...
...IS BEING TORN TO PIECES!!
MCHH! IS THIS A SIDE EFFECTCH?! CAPTAIN HODY!!
SHAKE
I KNEW THOSE PILLS WERE DANGER-OUS!!
AAAAH !!
!!
GRA-AAH!!
HEY! WHAT'S WRONG, SEA BEAR?!
WUZZ WUZZ!!
HE'S ACTING STRANGE. ALL THE SEA BEASTS AROUND HERE...
...SHOULD BE UNDER CAPTAIN HODY'S CONTROL...
SHAKE
SHAKE
SHAKE
BUT IT'S THE FIRST TIME I'VE SEEN ANY OF THEM THIS TERRIFIED!!

SBS Question Corner

質問コーナー
エスビーエス
いや すっと出せよ!!

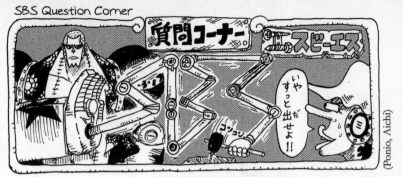

(Ponio, Aichi)

Q: Underwear underwear --Underwear Curse

A: Hey! Wait! Wait! Wait! What happened?!

Q: Underwear underwear underwear underwear underwear underwear underwear underwear underwear underwear underwear underwear underwear --Underwear Curse

A: Stop it! What is this?! The entire postcard has "underwear" written 130 times (I counted) on it. What about underwear? You want to see it? You want to wear it?! This is a question corner, you know?

Q: This is how women all around the world look at you, Odacchi, after reading SBS. No matter how cute they are, they'll still look like this! Good luck! --Yuki

A: What?! Stop it! Ow! Ow! I've been framed, I swear! It's the readers' fault! They're the vulgar ones!

Q: I have a question for (Oda)chinchin! What's going on inside Vice Admiral Strawberry's head? --Shinshu

← Inside this

A: Okay, first off... I'd appreciate it if you didn't call me "chinchin." Ow! I can feel girls shooting daggers at me with their eyes! Anyway, Vice Admiral Strawberry appeared at the Buster Call of Enies Lobby and the Paramount War, but he was wearing a hat at the time. You might have thought it was a long hat, but you see him with an injury to his long head during the flashback of Fish-Man Island. That's right. He just has a long head. It's not his hair in there. His skull is just really long. Oh, he's good at head butting people.

Q: If you tickle Ikaros Much, is it true that he gets four times more tickled than regular people? --Shinshu

A: Hahahahaha! Heeheeheehee! Just thinking about it makes me ticklish! Because he has eight armpits.

Chapter 631:
CONCHCORDE PLAZA

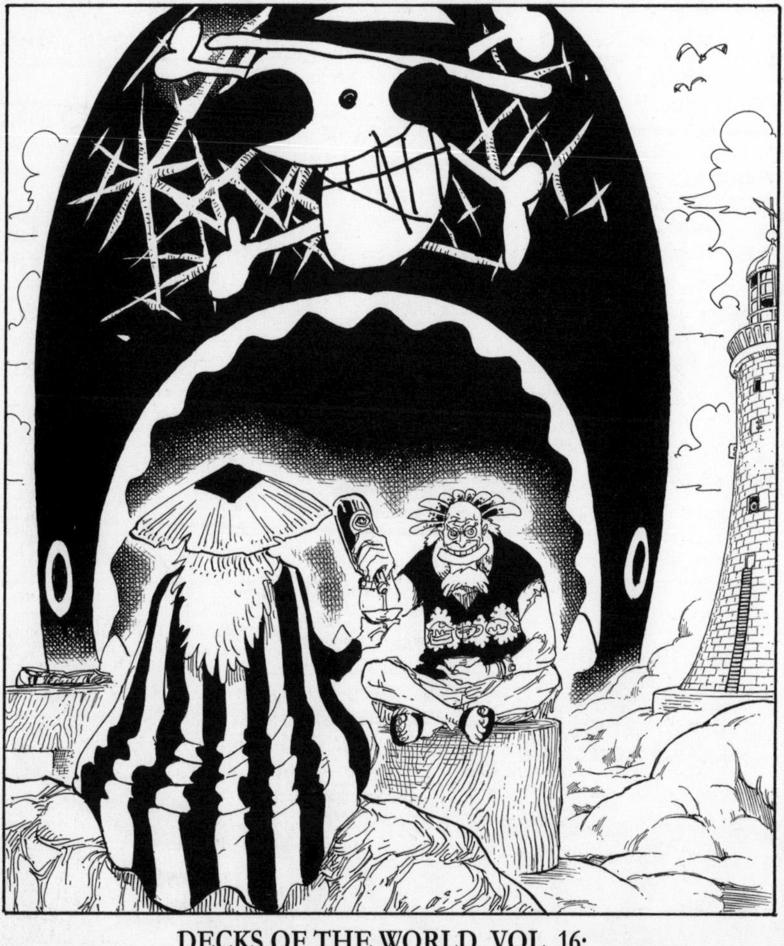

DECKS OF THE WORLD, VOL. 16:
"TWIN CAPE"

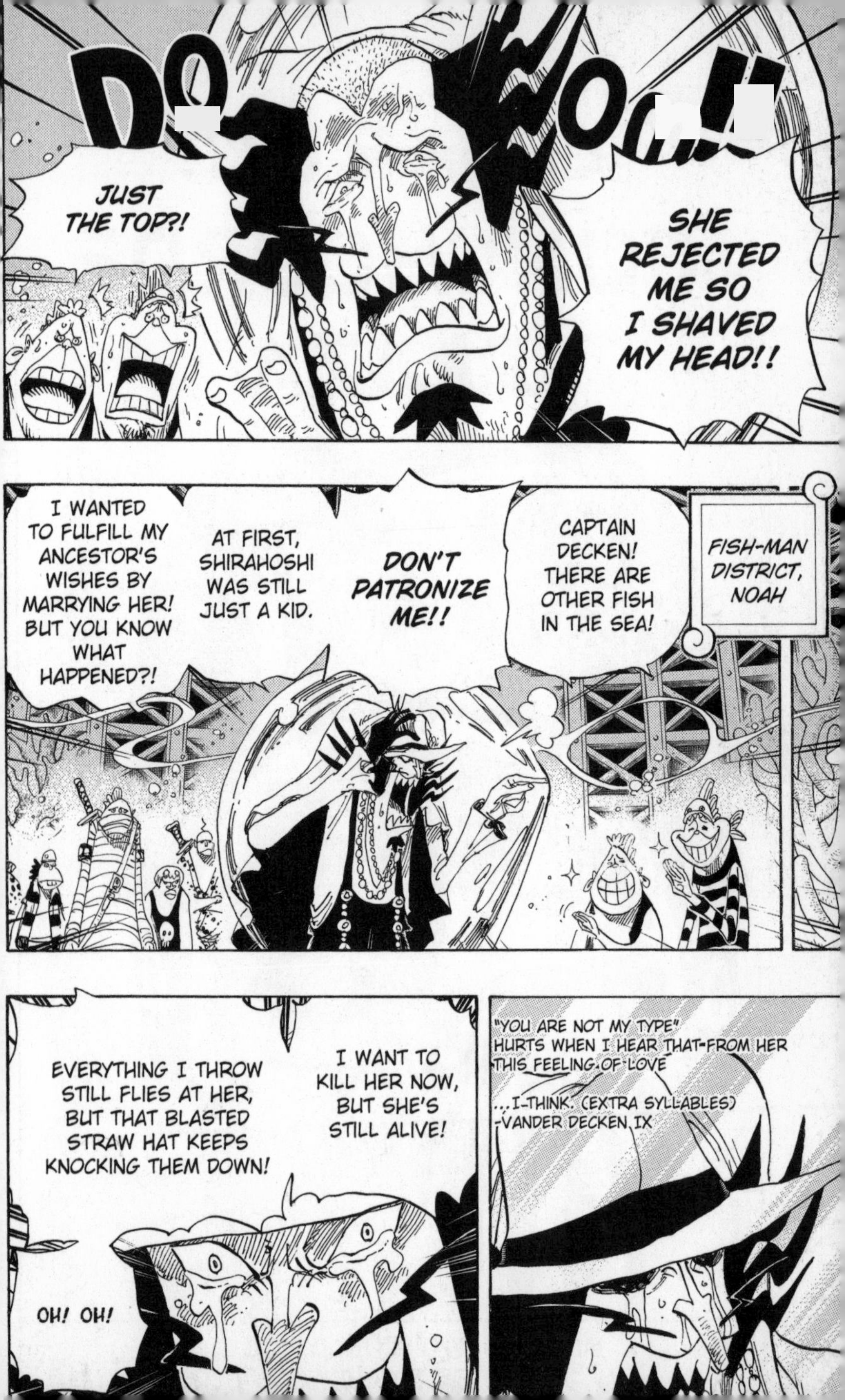
DO
WOO!!
SHE REJECTED ME SO I SHAVED MY HEAD!!
JUST THE TOP?!
FISH-MAN DISTRICT, NOAH
CAPTAIN DECKEN! THERE ARE OTHER FISH IN THE SEA!
DON'T PATRONIZE ME!!
AT FIRST, SHIRAHOSHI WAS STILL JUST A KID.
I WANTED TO FULFILL MY ANCESTOR'S WISHES BY MARRYING HER! BUT YOU KNOW WHAT HAPPENED?!
"YOU ARE NOT MY TYPE"
HURTS WHEN I HEAR THAT FROM HER
THIS FEELING OF LOVE
...I THINK. (EXTRA SYLLABLES)
-VANDER DECKEN IX
I WANT TO KILL HER NOW, BUT SHE'S STILL ALIVE!
EVERYTHING I THROW STILL FLIES AT HER, BUT THAT BLASTED STRAW HAT KEEPS KNOCKING THEM DOWN!
OH! OH!

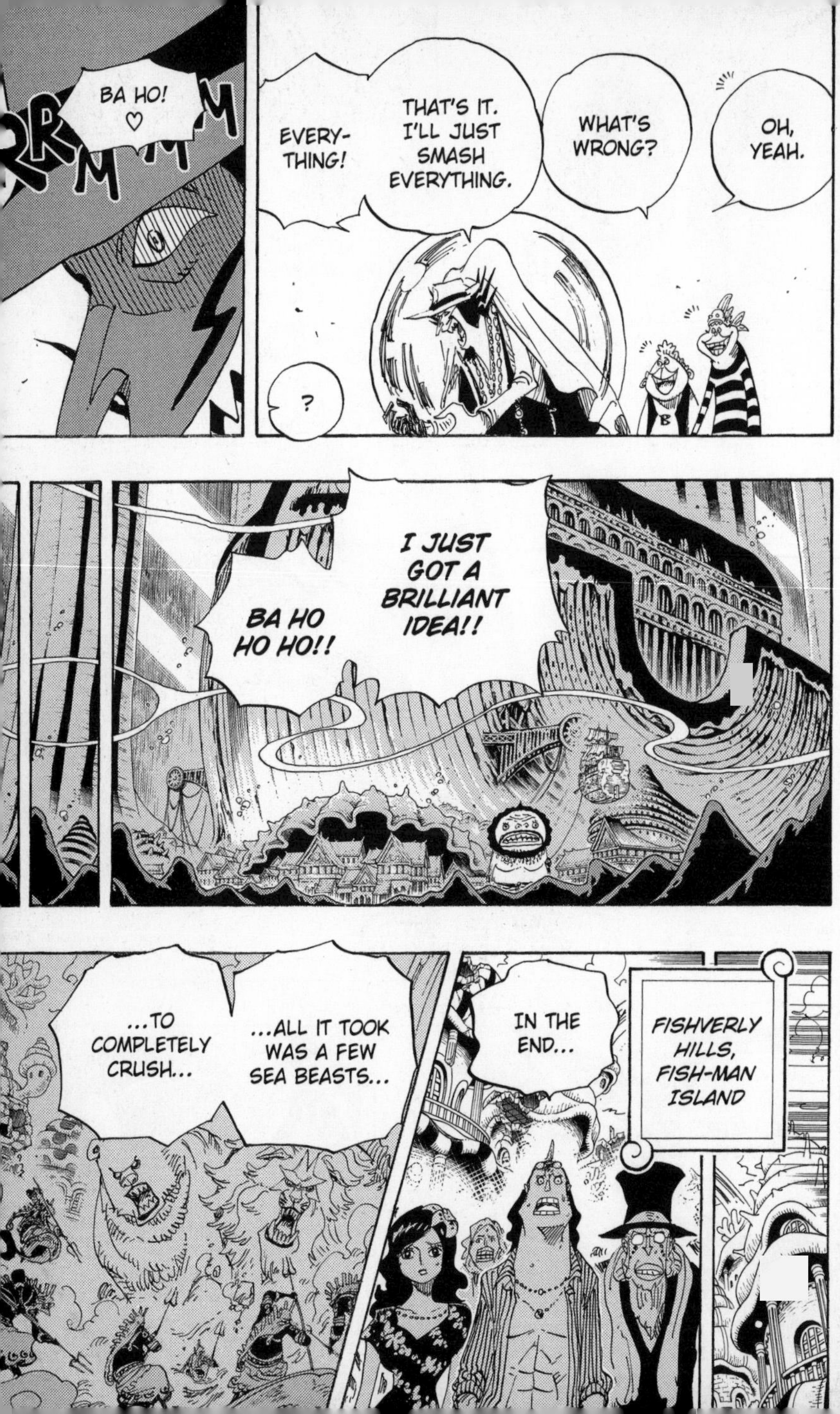
OH, YEAH.
WHAT'S WRONG?
THAT'S IT. I'LL JUST SMASH EVERYTHING.
EVERY-THING!
?
BA HO! ♡
I JUST GOT A BRILLIANT IDEA!!
BA HO HO HO!!
FISHVERLY HILLS, FISH-MAN ISLAND
IN THE END...
...ALL IT TOOK WAS A FEW SEA BEASTS...
...TO COMPLETELY CRUSH...

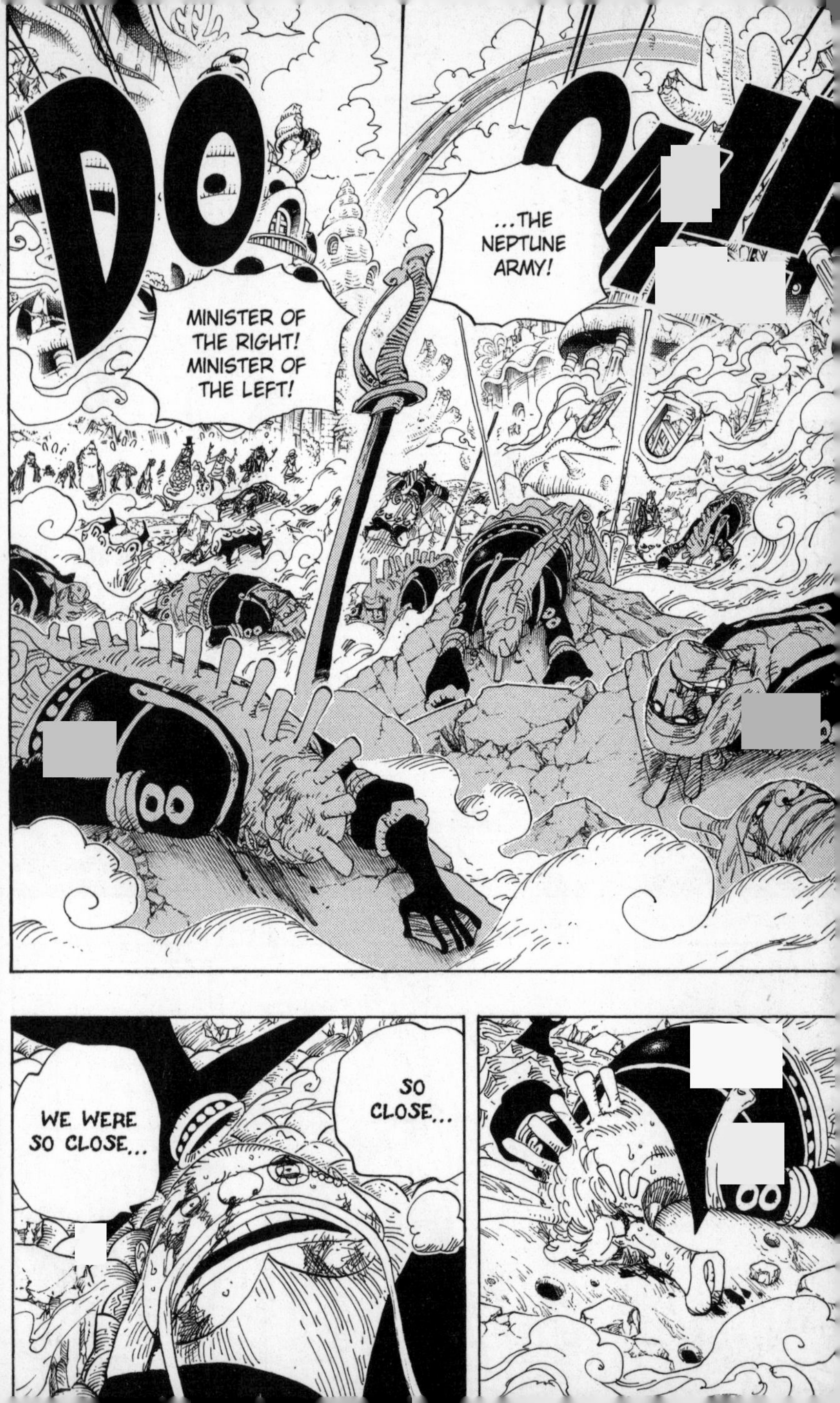
...THE NEPTUNE ARMY!
MINISTER OF THE RIGHT! MINISTER OF THE LEFT!
SO CLOSE...
WE WERE SO CLOSE...

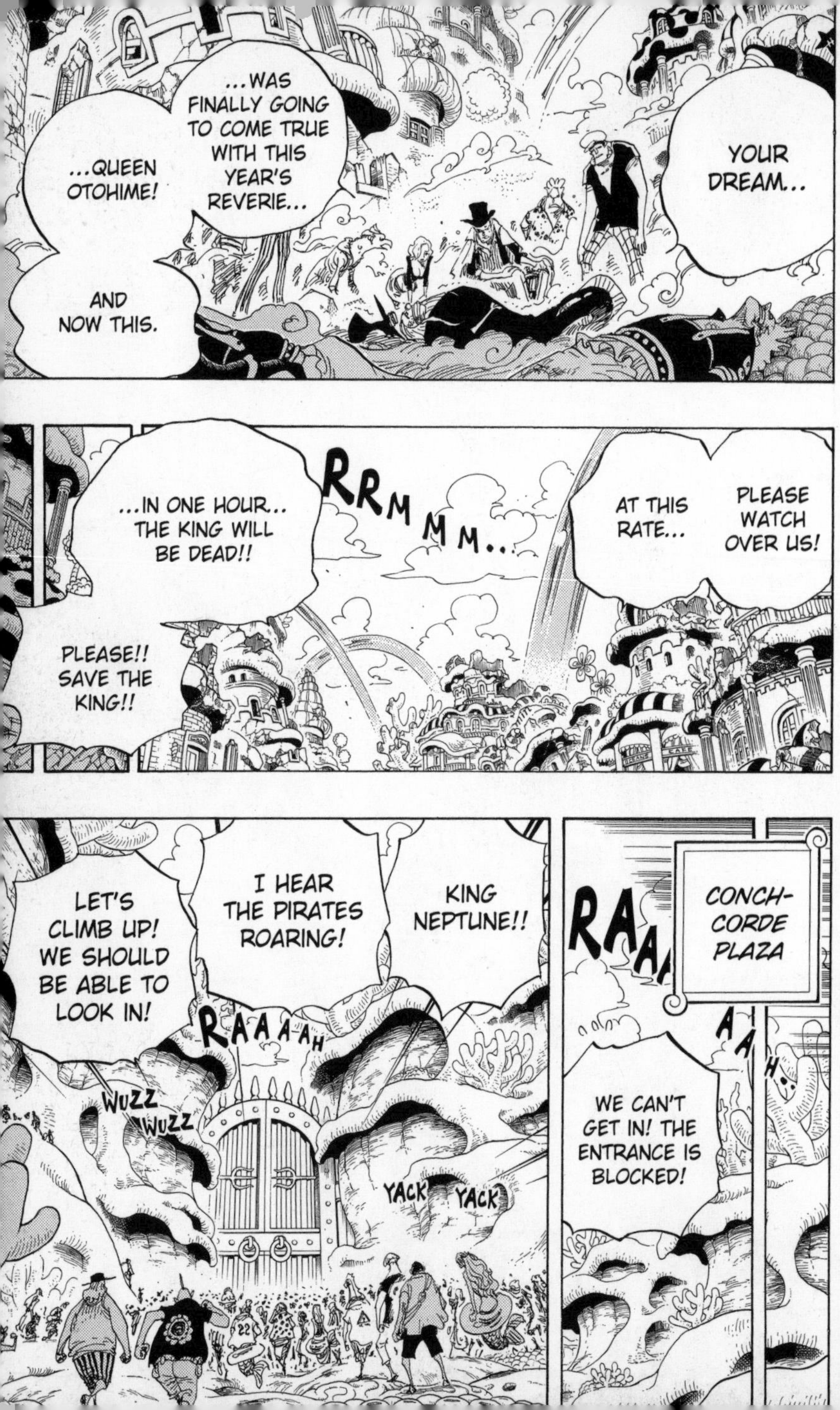
YOUR DREAM...
...WAS FINALLY GOING TO COME TRUE WITH THIS YEAR'S REVERIE...
...QUEEN OTOHIME!
AND NOW THIS.
PLEASE WATCH OVER US!
AT THIS RATE...
RRMMMM...
...IN ONE HOUR... THE KING WILL BE DEAD!!
PLEASE!! SAVE THE KING!!
CONCH-CORDE PLAZA
RAAAAAH
WE CAN'T GET IN! THE ENTRANCE IS BLOCKED!
KING NEPTUNE!!
I HEAR THE PIRATES ROARING!
LET'S CLIMB UP! WE SHOULD BE ABLE TO LOOK IN!
RAAAAAH
WUZZ WUZZ
YACK YACK

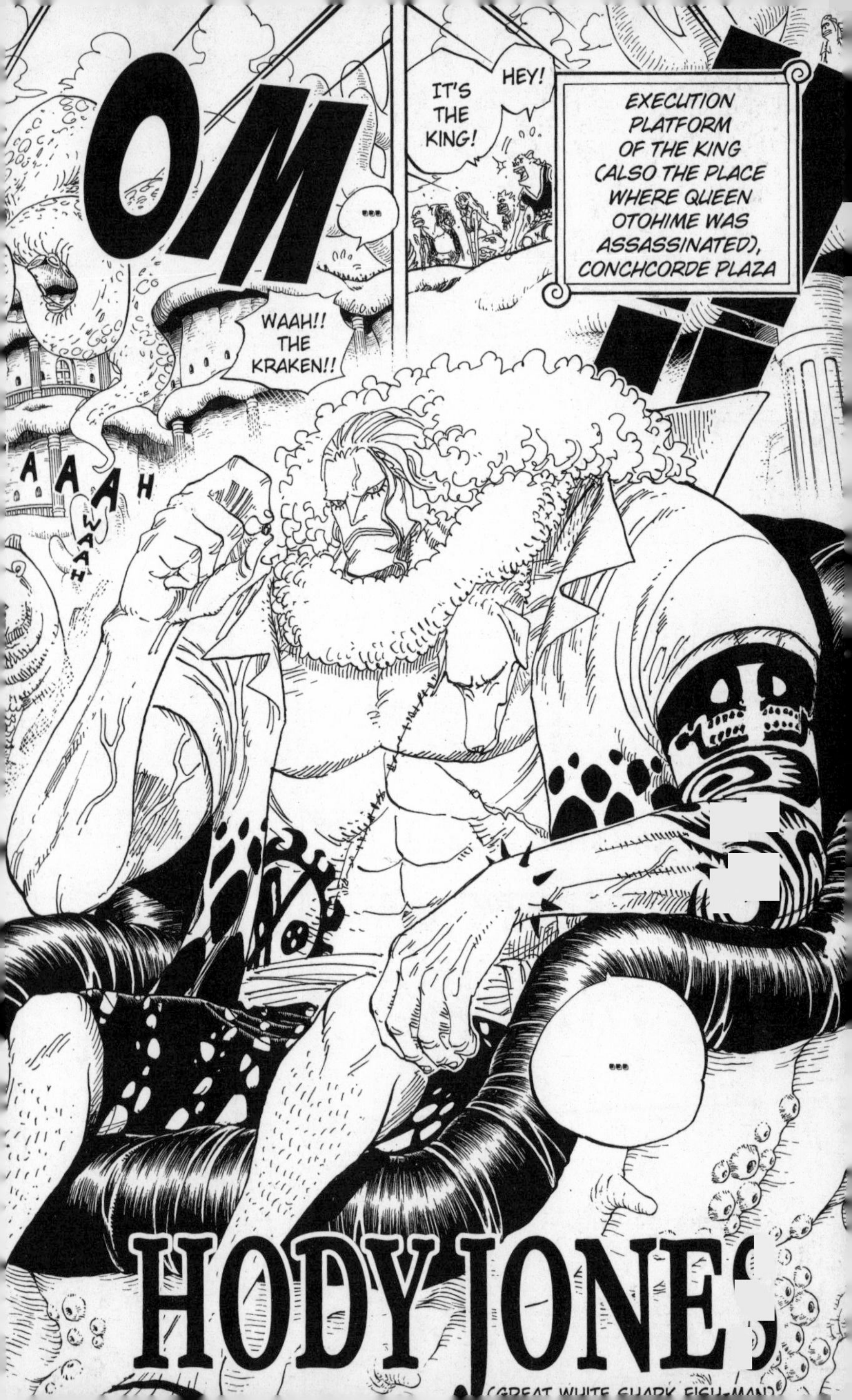
EXECUTION PLATFORM OF THE KING (ALSO THE PLACE WHERE QUEEN OTOHIME WAS ASSASSINATED), CONCHCORDE PLAZA
HEY!
IT'S THE KING!
OM
...
WAAH!! THE KRAKEN!!
AAAAH
WAAAH
...
HODY JONES

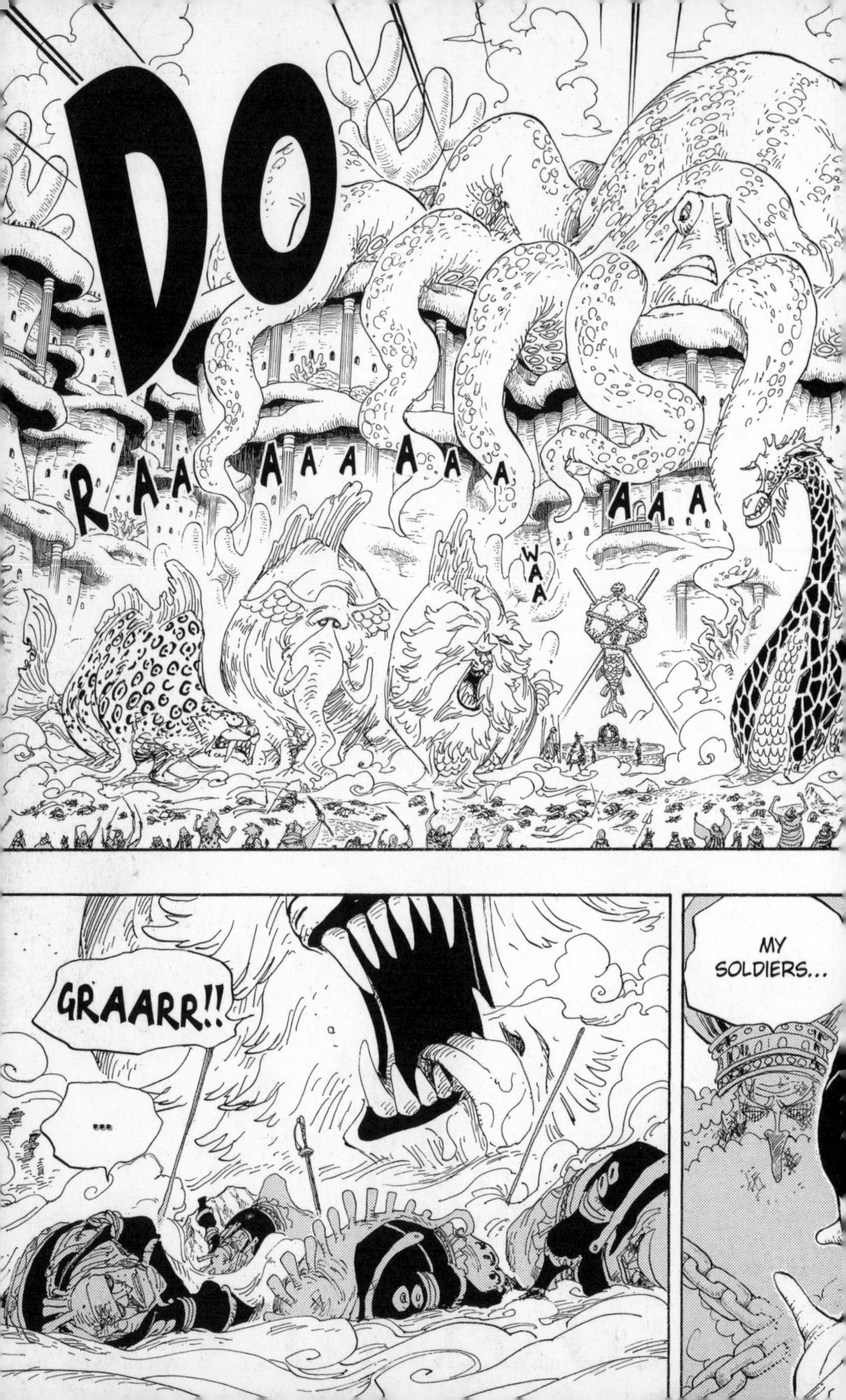
DO
RAAAAAAAAAAA
WAA
MY SOLDIERS...
GRAARR!!
...

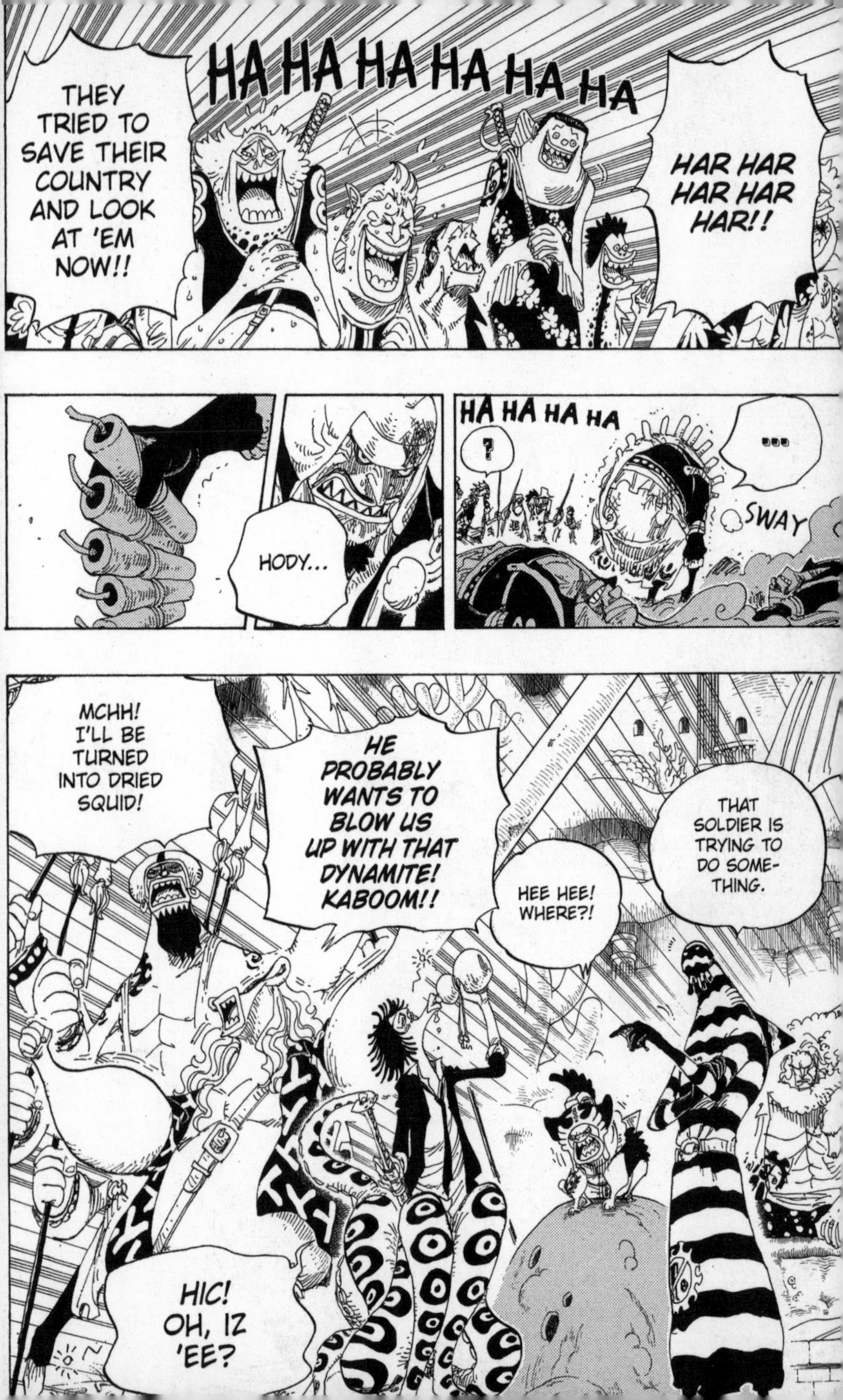
HAR HAR HAR HAR HAR!!
HA HA HA HA HA HA HA
THEY TRIED TO SAVE THEIR COUNTRY AND LOOK AT 'EM NOW!!
...
HA HA HA HA
?
SWAY
HODY...
THAT SOLDIER IS TRYING TO DO SOME-THING.
HEE HEE! WHERE?!
HE PROBABLY WANTS TO BLOW US UP WITH THAT DYNAMITE! KABOOM!!
MCHH! I'LL BE TURNED INTO DRIED SQUID!
HIC! OH, IZ 'EE?

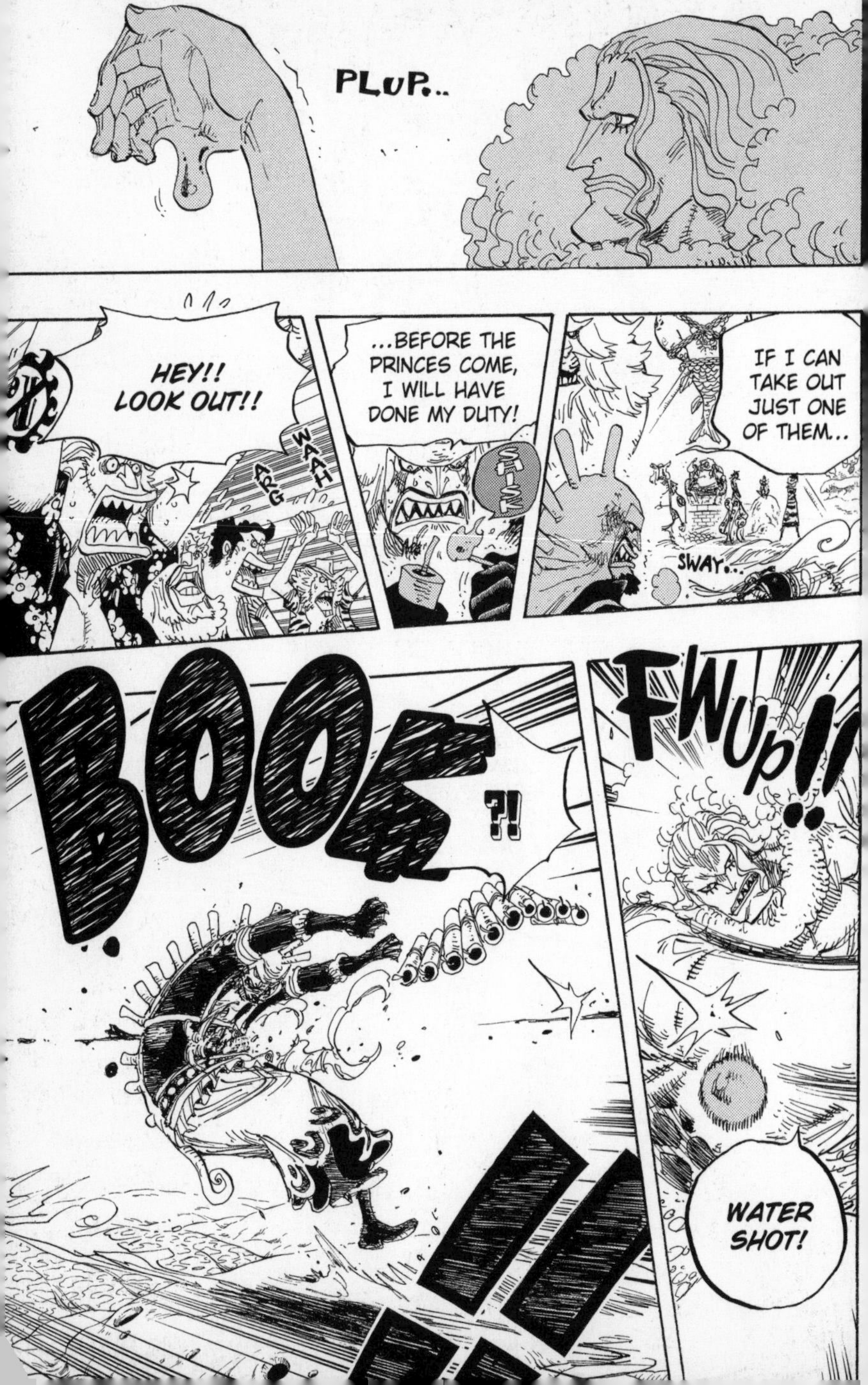
PLUP...
IF I CAN TAKE OUT JUST ONE OF THEM...
SWAY...
...BEFORE THE PRINCES COME, I WILL HAVE DONE MY DUTY!
SHISK
HEY!! LOOK OUT!!
WAAH
ARG
FWUP!!
WATER SHOT!
BOOM
?!

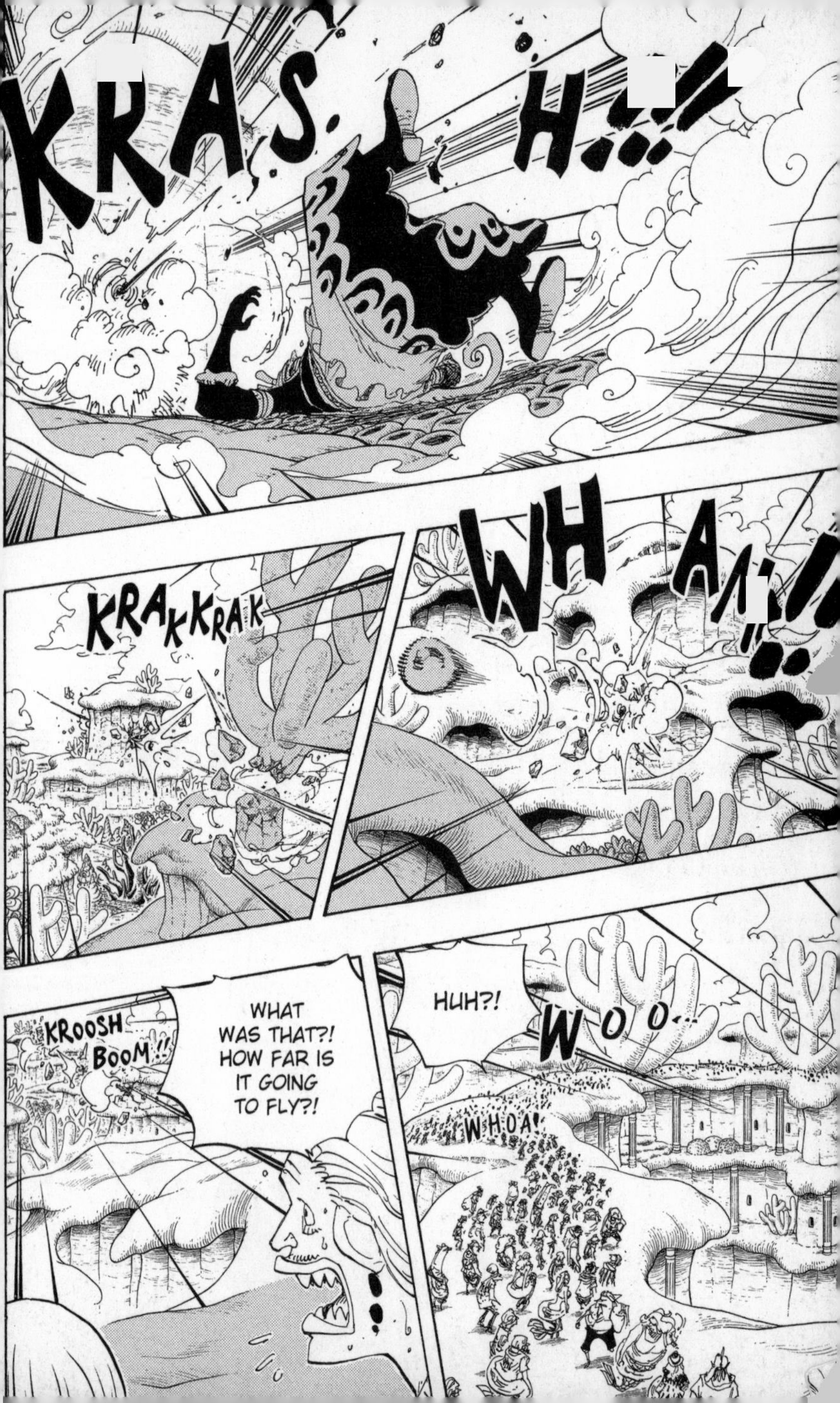
KRASH!!!
WHAM!!
KRAKKRAK
HUH?!
WOOO...
WHOA!
KROOSH BOOM!!
WHAT WAS THAT?! HOW FAR IS IT GOING TO FLY?!

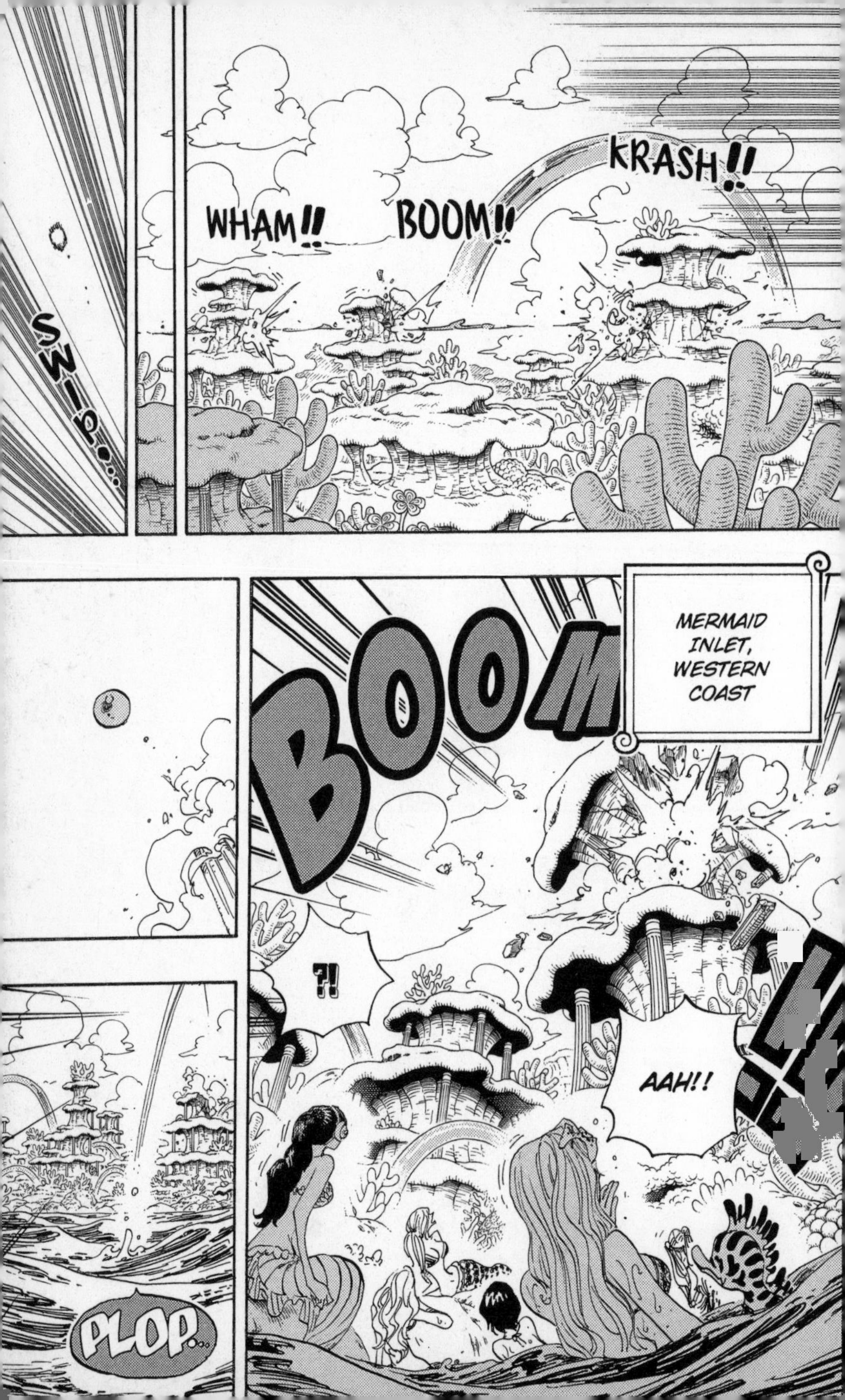
KRASH!!
BOOM!!
WHAM!!
SWIP...
MERMAID INLET, WESTERN COAST
BOOM
AAH!!
?!
PLOP...

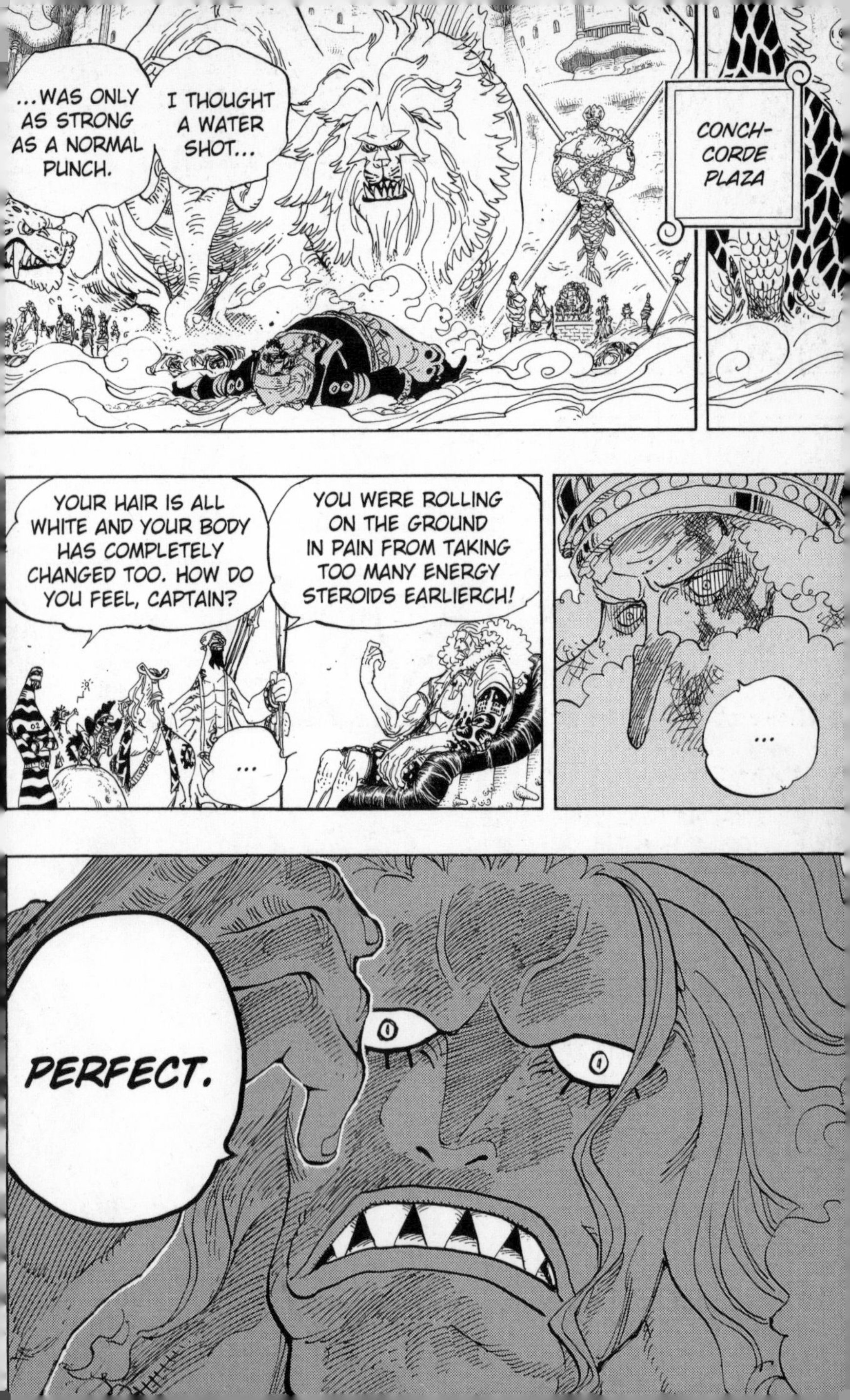
CONCH-CORDE PLAZA
I THOUGHT A WATER SHOT...
...WAS ONLY AS STRONG AS A NORMAL PUNCH.
...
YOU WERE ROLLING ON THE GROUND IN PAIN FROM TAKING TOO MANY ENERGY STEROIDS EARLIERCH!
YOUR HAIR IS ALL WHITE AND YOUR BODY HAS COMPLETELY CHANGED TOO. HOW DO YOU FEEL, CAPTAIN?
...
PERFECT.

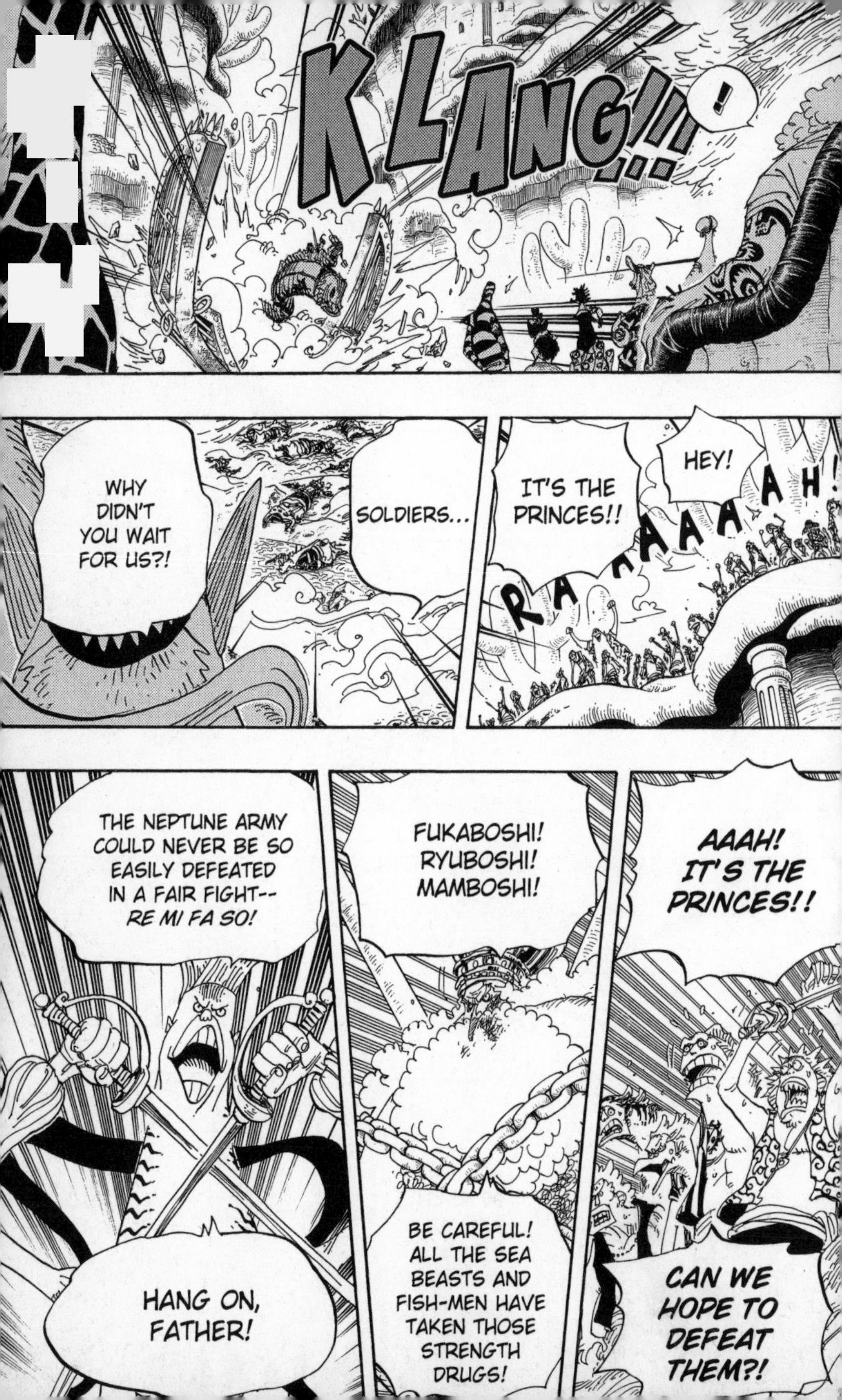
!
KLANG!!!
HEY!
IT'S THE PRINCES!!
RAAAAAAH!
SOLDIERS...
WHY DIDN'T YOU WAIT FOR US?!
AAAH! IT'S THE PRINCES!!
CAN WE HOPE TO DEFEAT THEM?!
FUKABOSHI! RYUBOSHI! MAMBOSHI!
BE CAREFUL! ALL THE SEA BEASTS AND FISH-MEN HAVE TAKEN THOSE STRENGTH DRUGS!
THE NEPTUNE ARMY COULD NEVER BE SO EASILY DEFEATED IN A FAIR FIGHT-- RE MI FA SO!
HANG ON, FATHER!

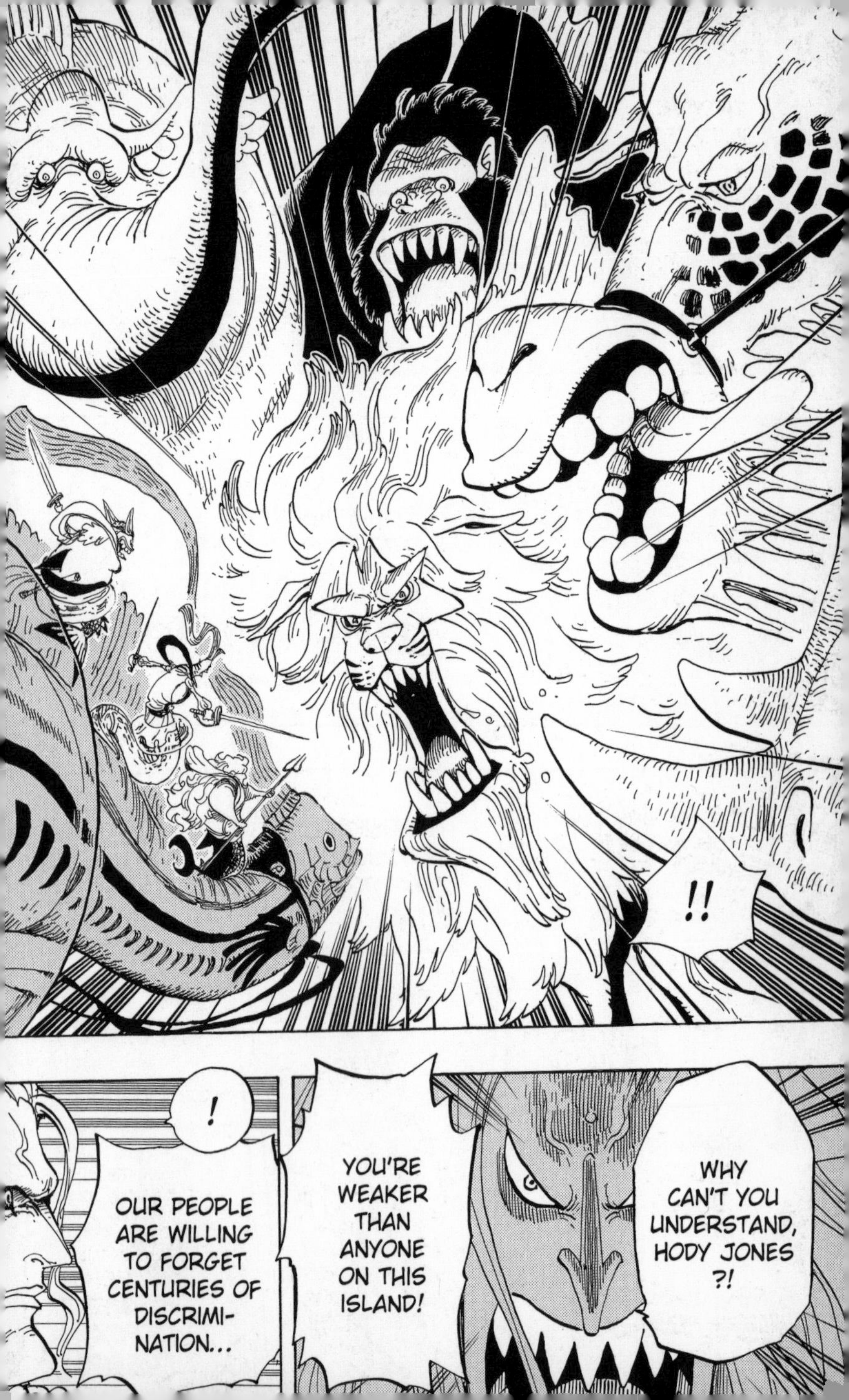
!!
WHY CAN'T YOU UNDERSTAND, HODY JONES ?!
YOU'RE WEAKER THAN ANYONE ON THIS ISLAND!
!
OUR PEOPLE ARE WILLING TO FORGET CENTURIES OF DISCRIMI-NATION...

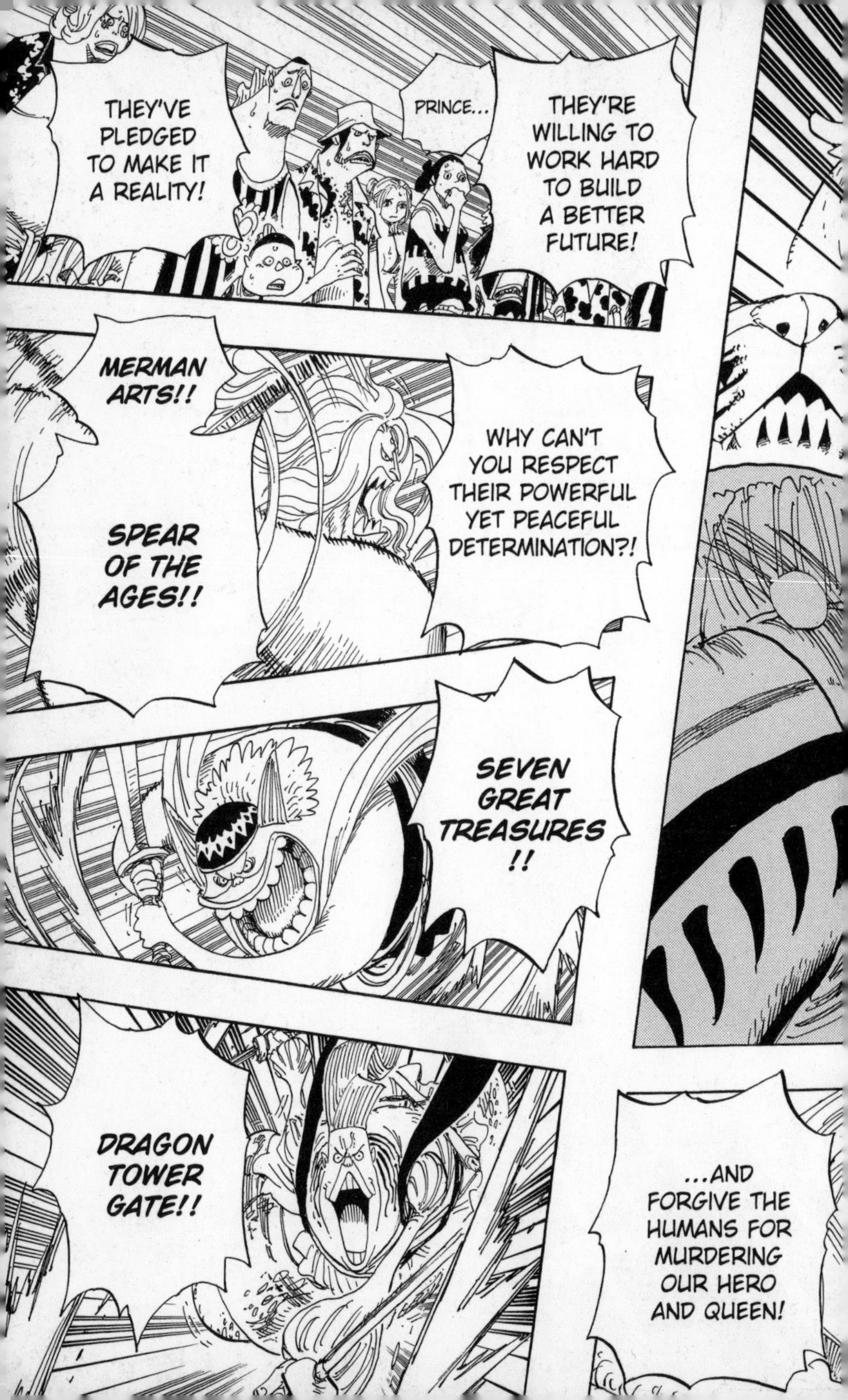
PRINCE...
THEY'RE WILLING TO WORK HARD TO BUILD A BETTER FUTURE!
THEY'VE PLEDGED TO MAKE IT A REALITY!
WHY CAN'T YOU RESPECT THEIR POWERFUL YET PEACEFUL DETERMINATION?!
MERMAN ARTS!!
SPEAR OF THE AGES!!
SEVEN GREAT TREASURES !!
...AND FORGIVE THE HUMANS FOR MURDERING OUR HERO AND QUEEN!
DRAGON TOWER GATE!!

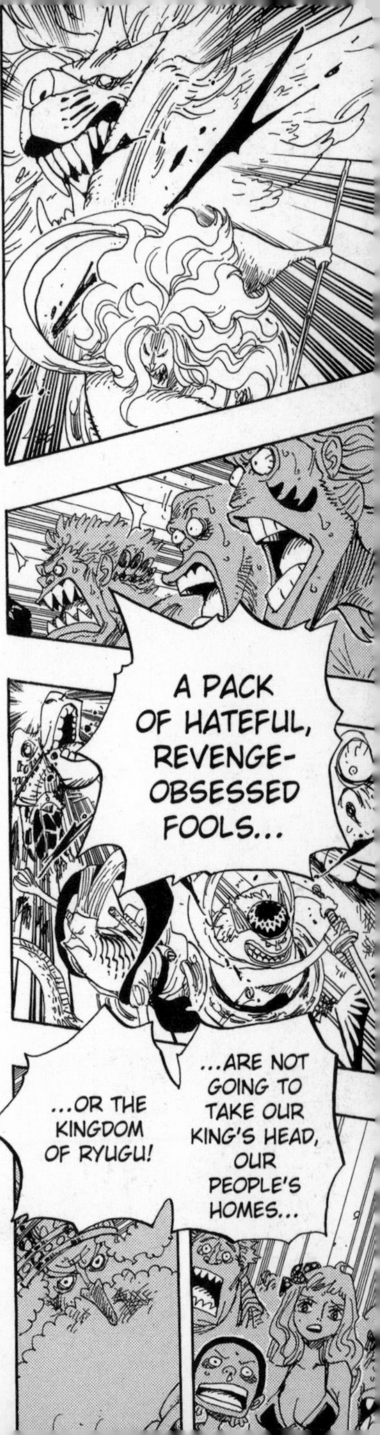
A PACK OF HATEFUL, REVENGE-OBSESSED FOOLS...
...ARE NOT GOING TO TAKE OUR KING'S HEAD, OUR PEOPLE'S HOMES...
...OR THE KINGDOM OF RYUGU!
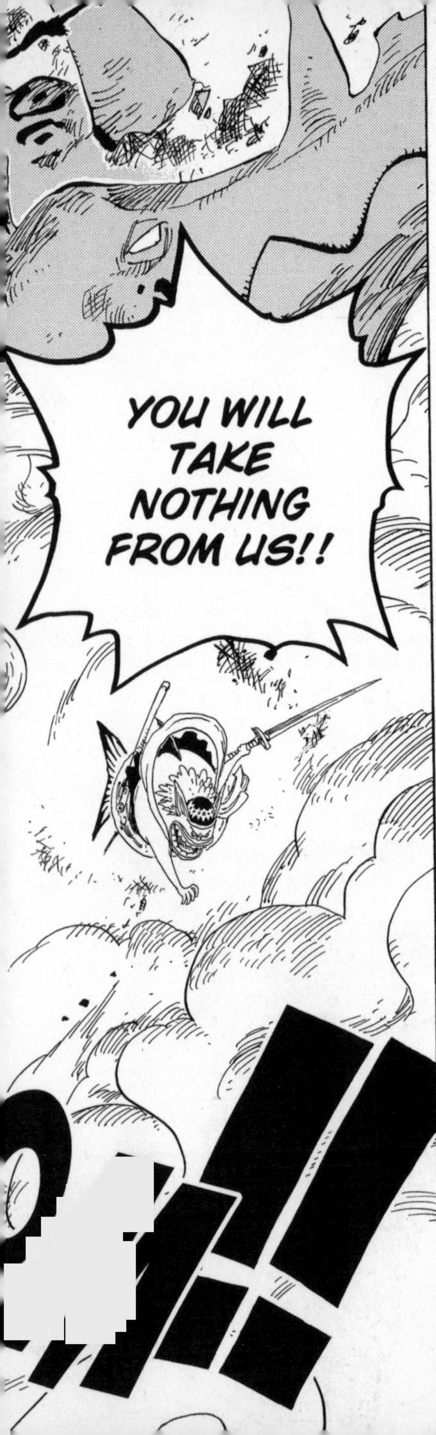
YOU WILL TAKE NOTHING FROM US!!

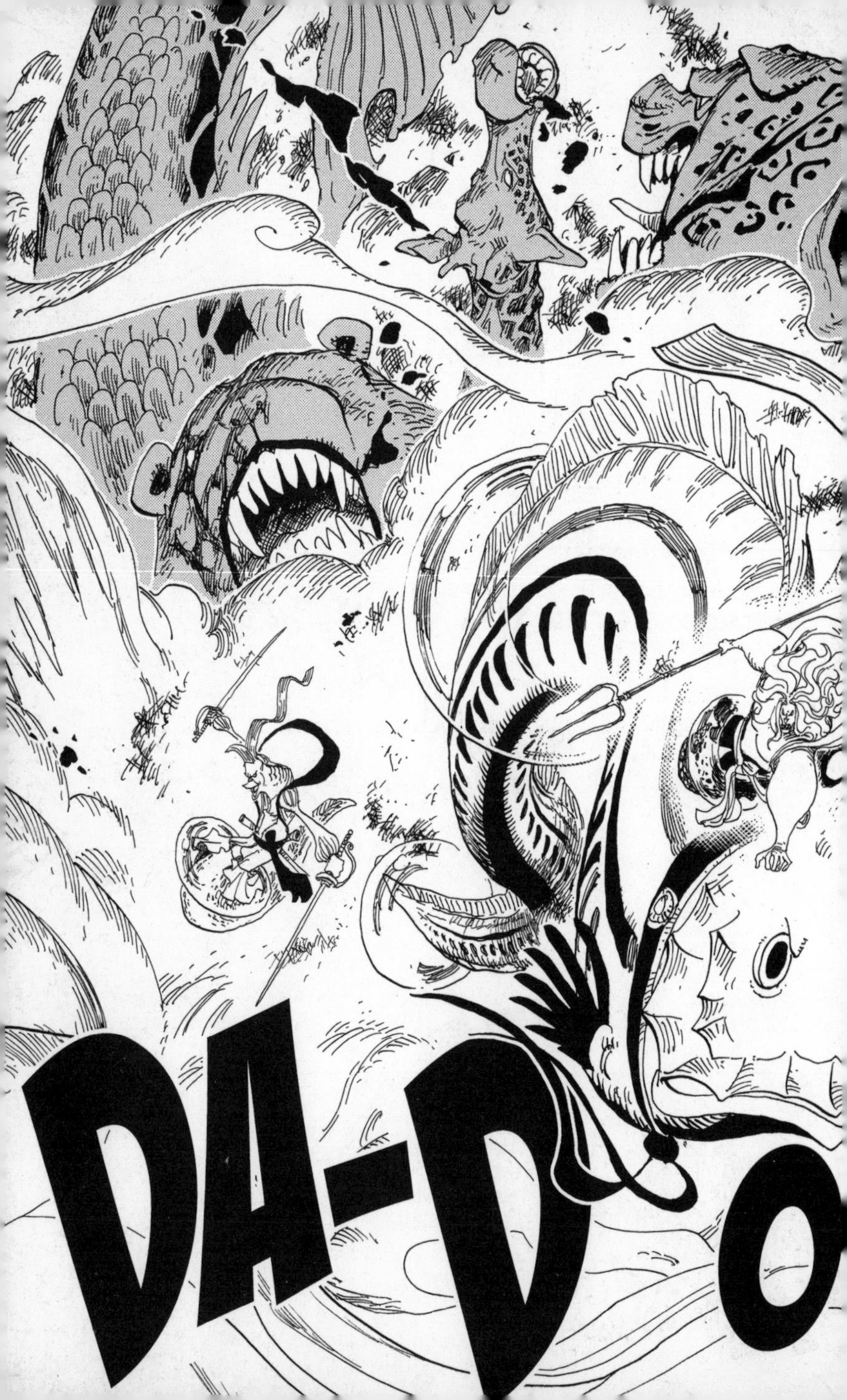
DA-DO

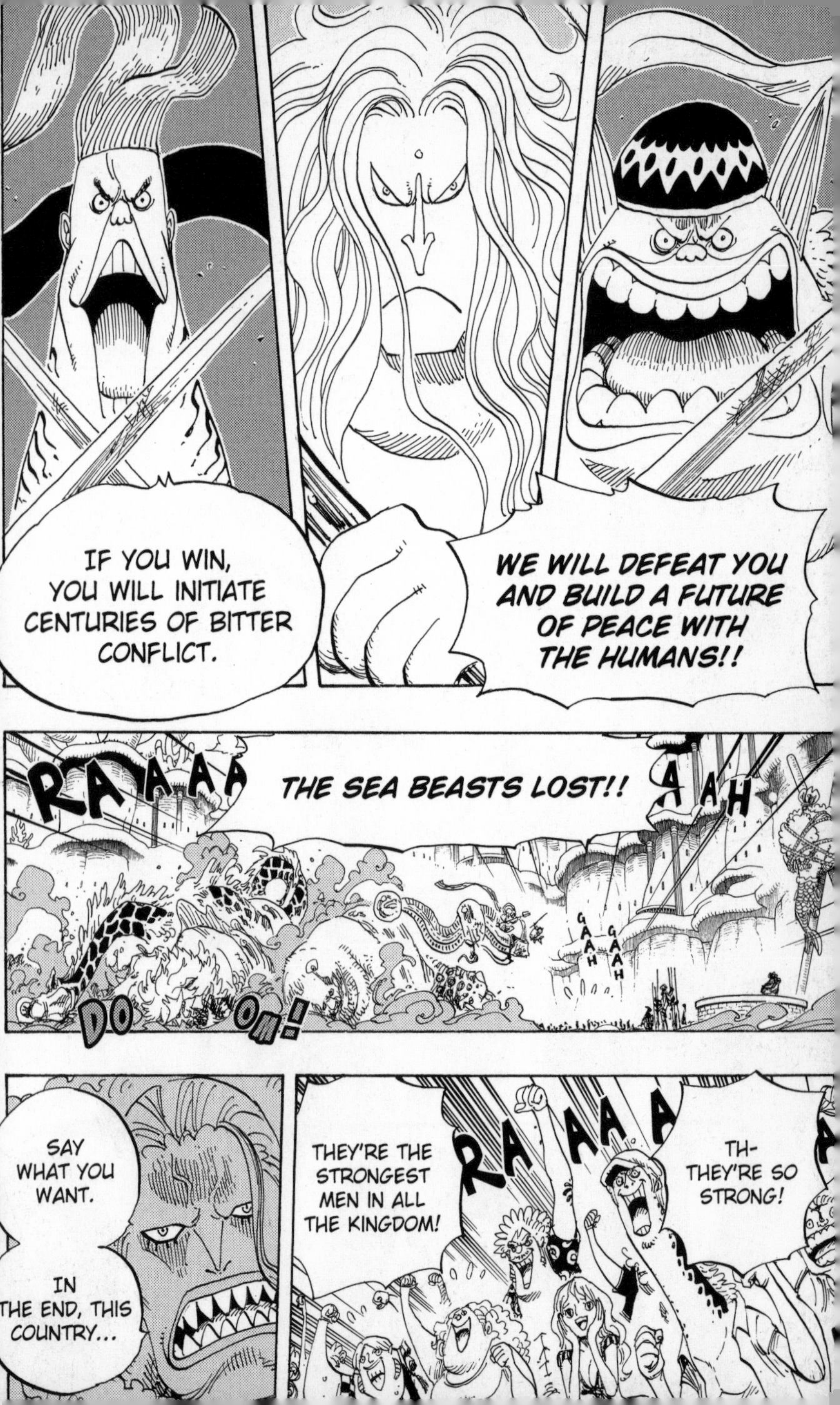
WE WILL DEFEAT YOU AND BUILD A FUTURE OF PEACE WITH THE HUMANS!!
IF YOU WIN, YOU WILL INITIATE CENTURIES OF BITTER CONFLICT.
AAH
THE SEA BEASTS LOST!!
RAAAA
GAAH
GAAAH
DOOM!
TH- THEY'RE SO STRONG!
RAAAA
THEY'RE THE STRONGEST MEN IN ALL THE KINGDOM!
SAY WHAT YOU WANT.
IN THE END, THIS COUNTRY...

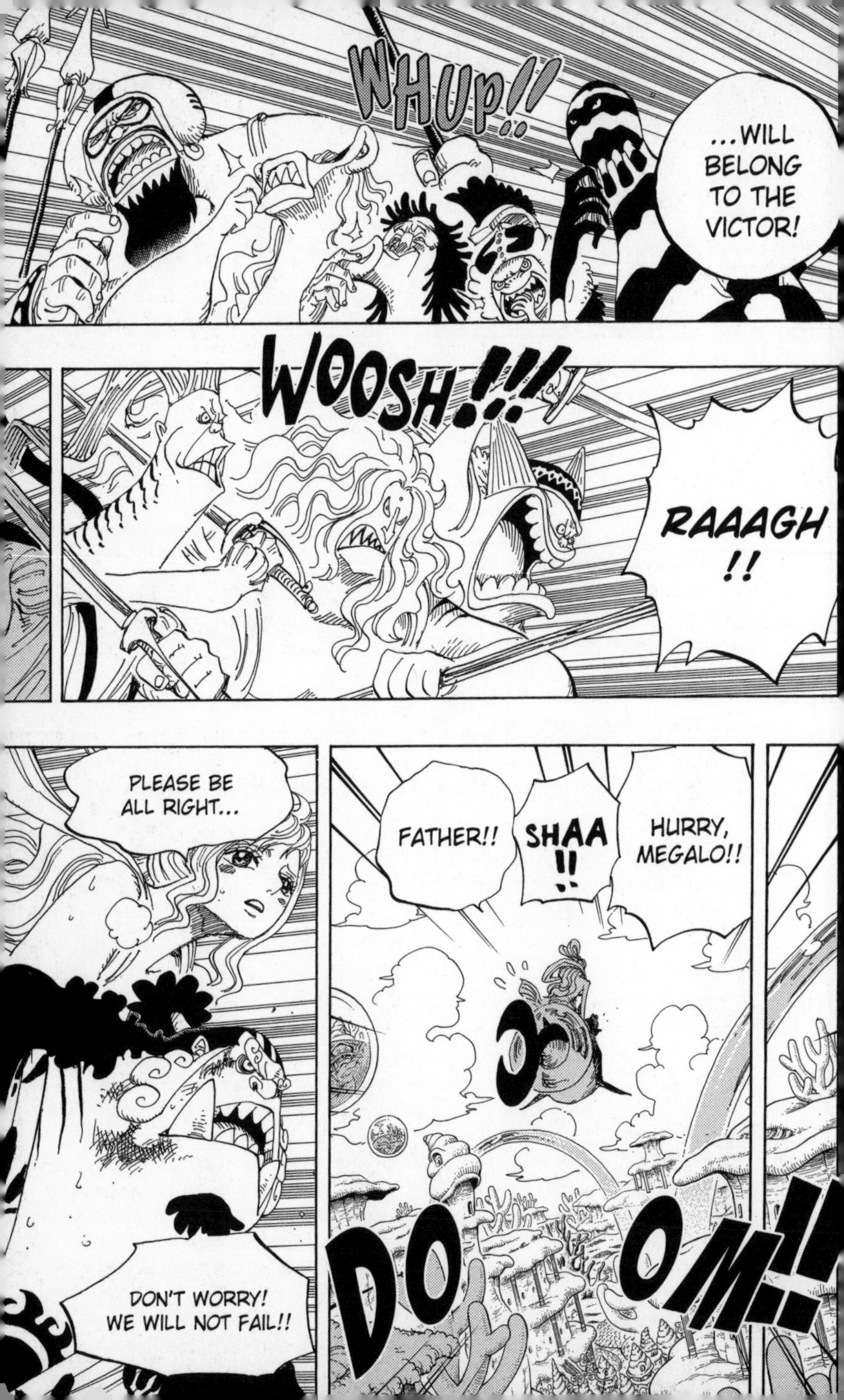
...WILL BELONG TO THE VICTOR!
WHUP!!
RAAAGH!!
WOOSH!!!
HURRY, MEGALO!!
SHAA!!
FATHER!!
DOOM!!
PLEASE BE ALL RIGHT...
DON'T WORRY! WE WILL NOT FAIL!!

エスビーエス
質問コーナ

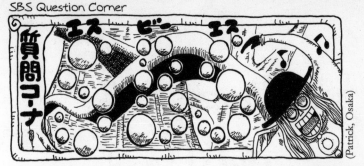

(Patrick, Osaka)

Q: Mr. Oda, hello. I have a question. What exactly are those lifesavers that the mermaids are wearing? Why do they wear them? Please tell me.

--Usoppi

A: They're bubbles. It's similar to what they have in the Sabaody Archipelago. Mermaids have difficulty walking on "foot" so they wear the bubbles and "swim" using their fins in the air. They sit on or push on them. It's pretty versatile. The mermaids always carry their Bubbly Coral around with them.

FWOOF!!
BUBBLY CORAL
BOING!!

Q: And then? --Mercurian

A: Yes, and I would like to hug the mermaids on the bubbles... What?! That was uncalled for!

Q: Mr. Oda! I read a lot of manga, but there are some that have the characters keep their mouths closed while talking and some that do not. To make it seem like the characters are talking, I think it's always better to have their mouths open. In *One Piece*, do you always make sure the characters' mouths are open when they're talking? --Manabi

A: That's a big surprise. You must read a lot of manga. You're right. There are authors who keep their characters' mouths closed even when they are talking. On the other hand, I can't do it. It feels too weird for me. I think it's a difference of what you focus on. Authors that keep the mouths closed are usually people who want to make the characters look cool or make the scene look better. People like me who have to keep the characters' mouths open think of manga as a method of presentation. For us, it's more like, "Even if it looks ugly, it's more important to get the message across!" or "there's no point in it if we don't get our message to the reader!" This is how I think of the "pictures" in my manga. But each author has their own style.

Chapter 632:
I KNEW

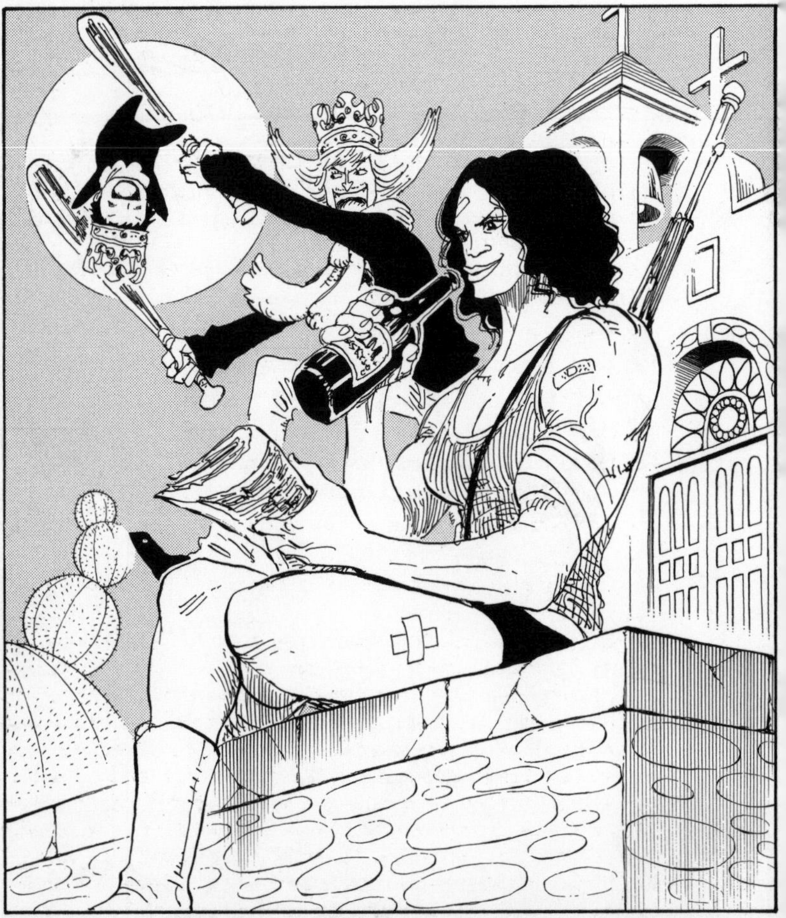

DECKS OF THE WORLD, VOL. 17:
"WHISKY PEAK AND THE BOUNTY HUNTERS"

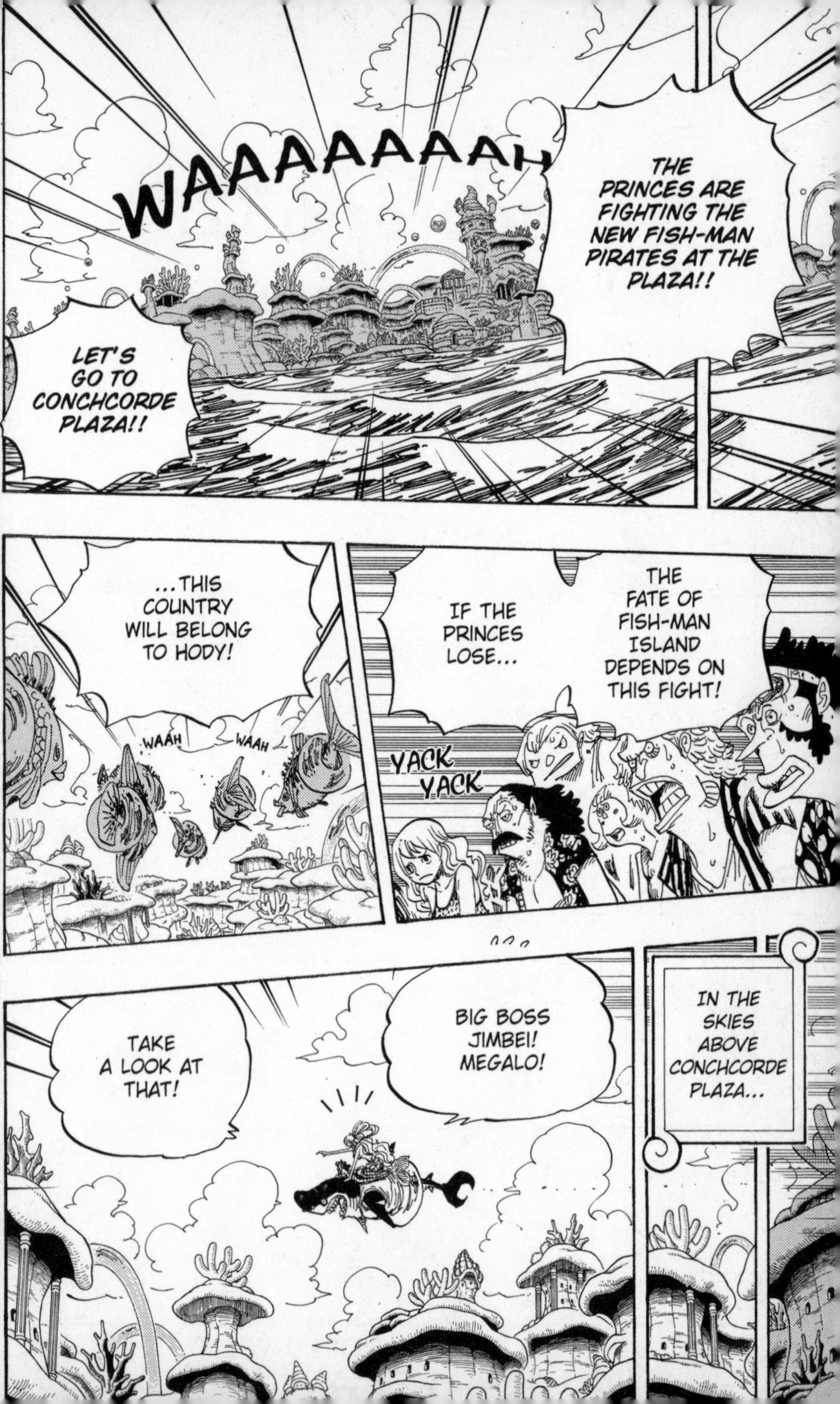
THE PRINCES ARE FIGHTING THE NEW FISH-MAN PIRATES AT THE PLAZA!!
WAAAAAAAAH
LET'S GO TO CONCHCORDE PLAZA!!
THE FATE OF FISH-MAN ISLAND DEPENDS ON THIS FIGHT!
IF THE PRINCES LOSE...
YACK YACK
...THIS COUNTRY WILL BELONG TO HODY!
WAAH
WAAH
IN THE SKIES ABOVE CONCHCORDE PLAZA...
BIG BOSS JIMBEI! MEGALO!
TAKE A LOOK AT THAT!

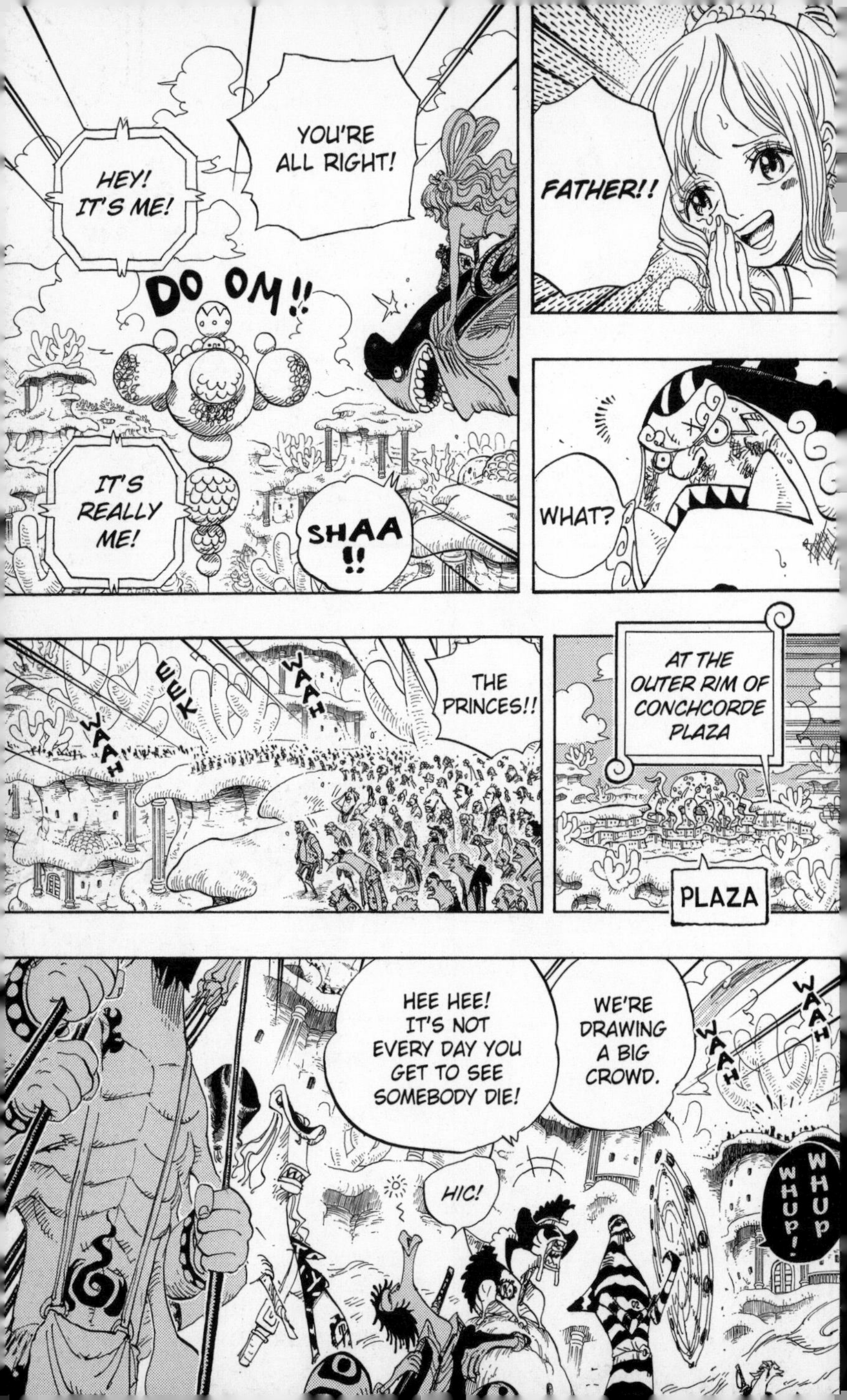
FATHER!!
WHAT?
YOU'RE ALL RIGHT!
HEY! IT'S ME!
DO OM!!
SHAA!!
IT'S REALLY ME!
AT THE OUTER RIM OF CONCHCORDE PLAZA
PLAZA
THE PRINCES!!
WAAH
EEK
WAAH
WAAH
WAAH
WE'RE DRAWING A BIG CROWD.
HEE HEE! IT'S NOT EVERY DAY YOU GET TO SEE SOMEBODY DIE!
WHUP WHUP!
HIC!

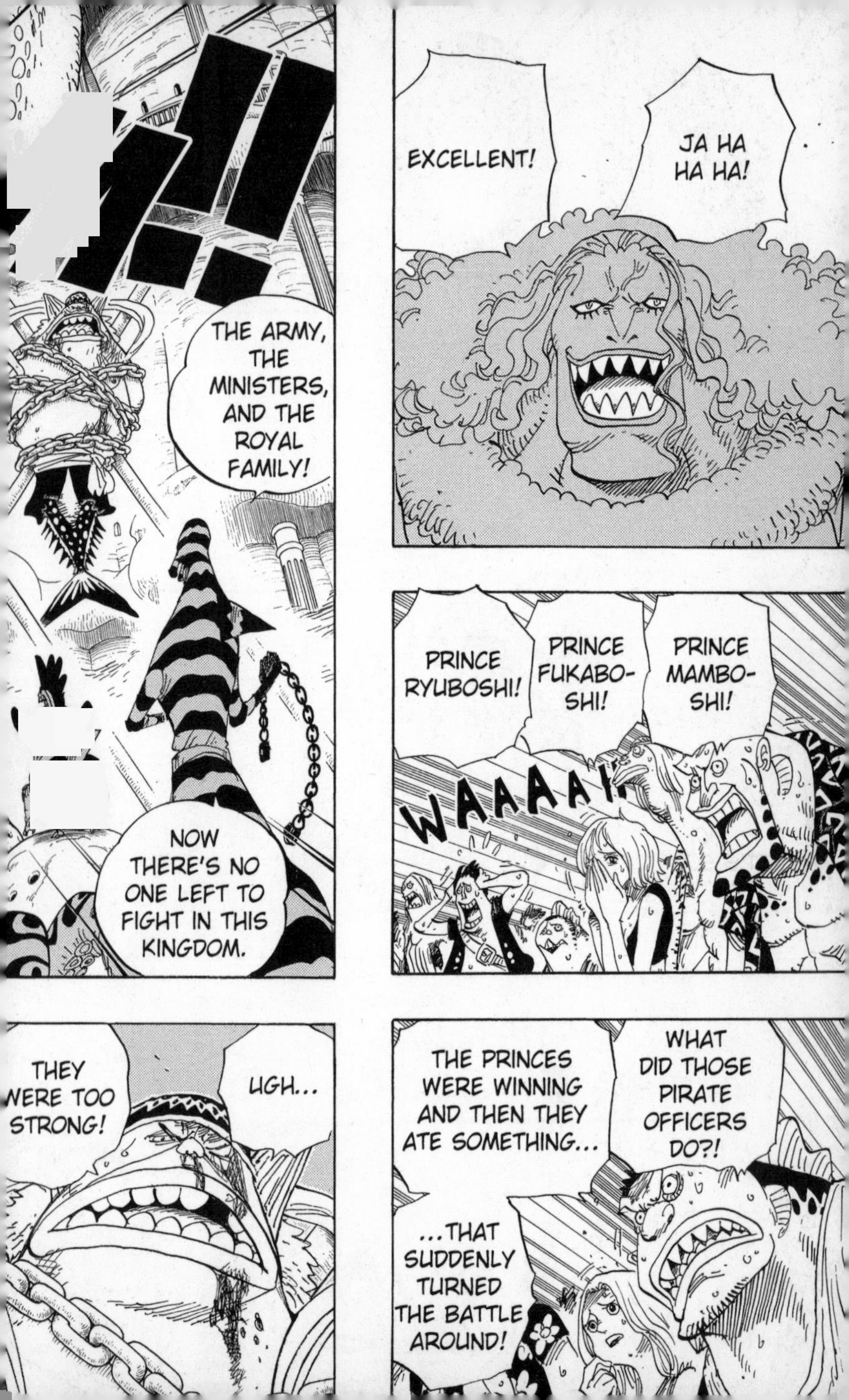
JA HA HA HA!
EXCELLENT!
PRINCE MAMBO-SHI!
PRINCE FUKABO-SHI!
PRINCE RYUBOSHI!
WAAAA
THE ARMY, THE MINISTERS, AND THE ROYAL FAMILY!
NOW THERE'S NO ONE LEFT TO FIGHT IN THIS KINGDOM.
WHAT DID THOSE PIRATE OFFICERS DO?!
THE PRINCES WERE WINNING AND THEN THEY ATE SOMETHING...
...THAT SUDDENLY TURNED THE BATTLE AROUND!
UGH...
THEY WERE TOO STRONG!

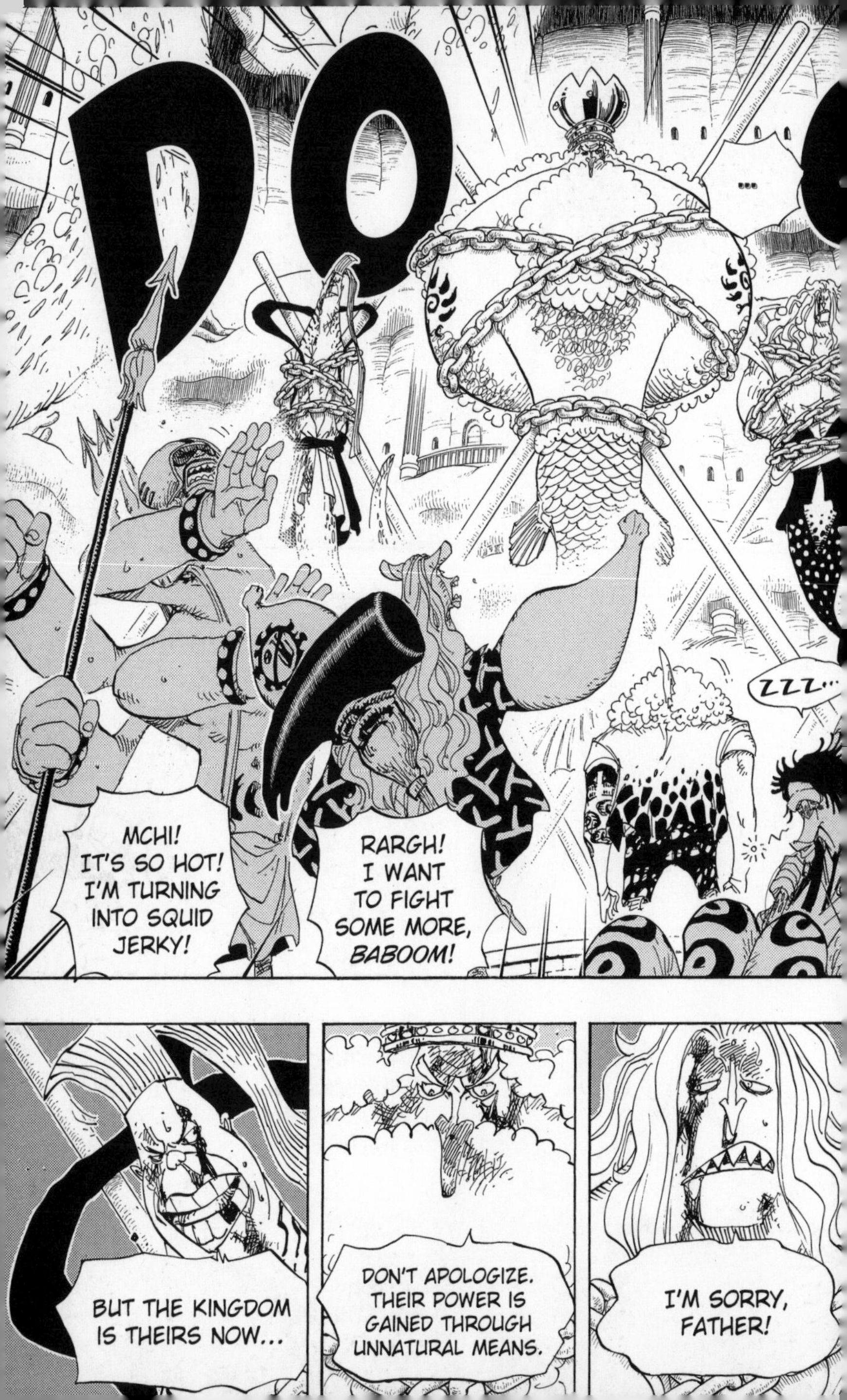
...
DO
ZZZ...
RARGH! I WANT TO FIGHT SOME MORE, BABOOM!
MCHI! IT'S SO HOT! I'M TURNING INTO SQUID JERKY!
I'M SORRY, FATHER!
DON'T APOLOGIZE. THEIR POWER IS GAINED THROUGH UNNATURAL MEANS.
BUT THE KINGDOM IS THEIRS NOW...

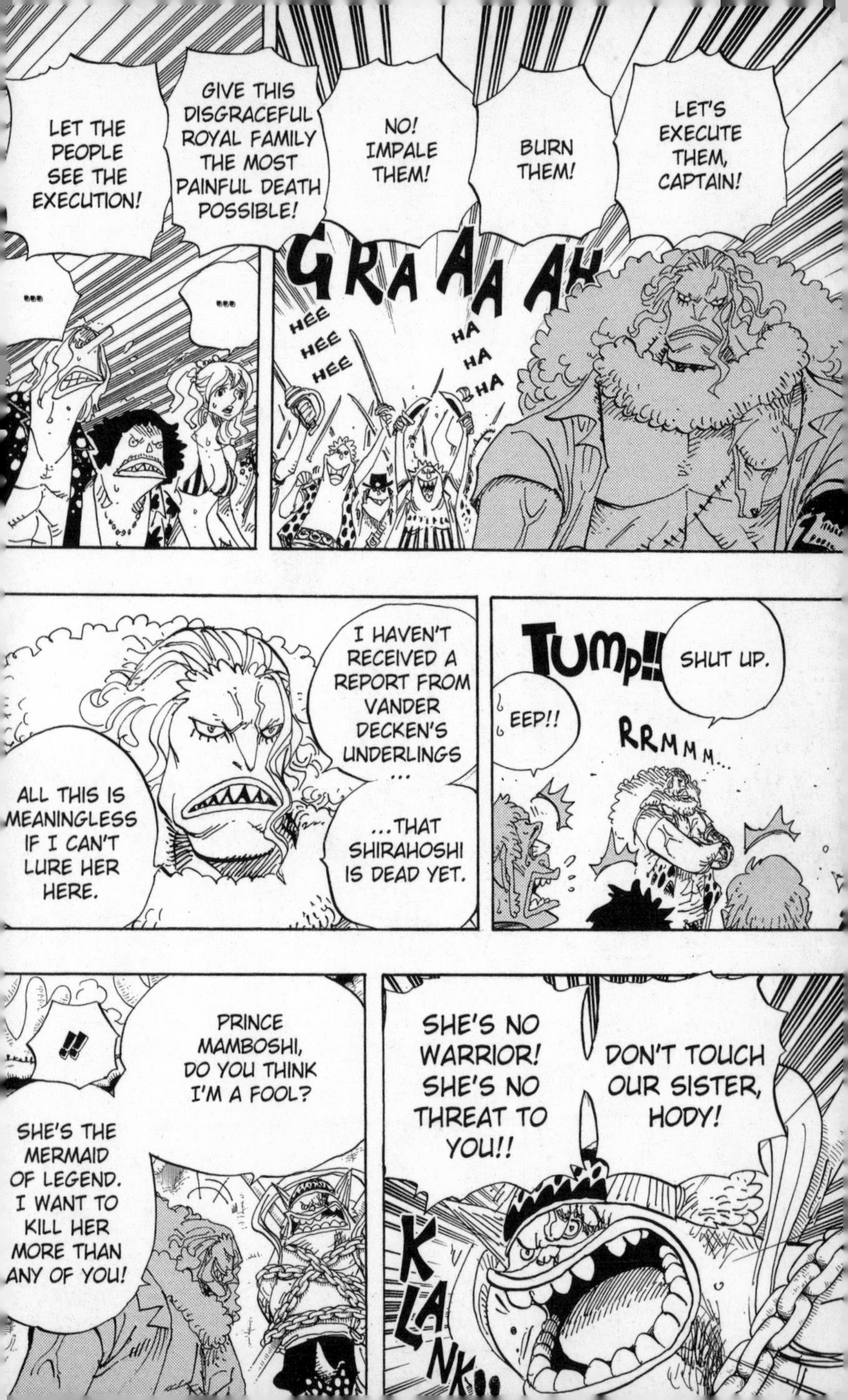
LET'S EXECUTE THEM, CAPTAIN!
BURN THEM!
NO! IMPALE THEM!
GIVE THIS DISGRACEFUL ROYAL FAMILY THE MOST PAINFUL DEATH POSSIBLE!
LET THE PEOPLE SEE THE EXECUTION!
GRAAAAH
HEE HEE HEE
HA HA HA
...
...
TUMP!!
SHUT UP.
EEP!!
RRMMMM...
I HAVEN'T RECEIVED A REPORT FROM VANDER DECKEN'S UNDERLINGS...
...THAT SHIRAHOSHI IS DEAD YET.
ALL THIS IS MEANINGLESS IF I CAN'T LURE HER HERE.
DON'T TOUCH OUR SISTER, HODY!
SHE'S NO WARRIOR! SHE'S NO THREAT TO YOU!!
KLANK...
!!
PRINCE MAMBOSHI, DO YOU THINK I'M A FOOL?
SHE'S THE MERMAID OF LEGEND. I WANT TO KILL HER MORE THAN ANY OF YOU!

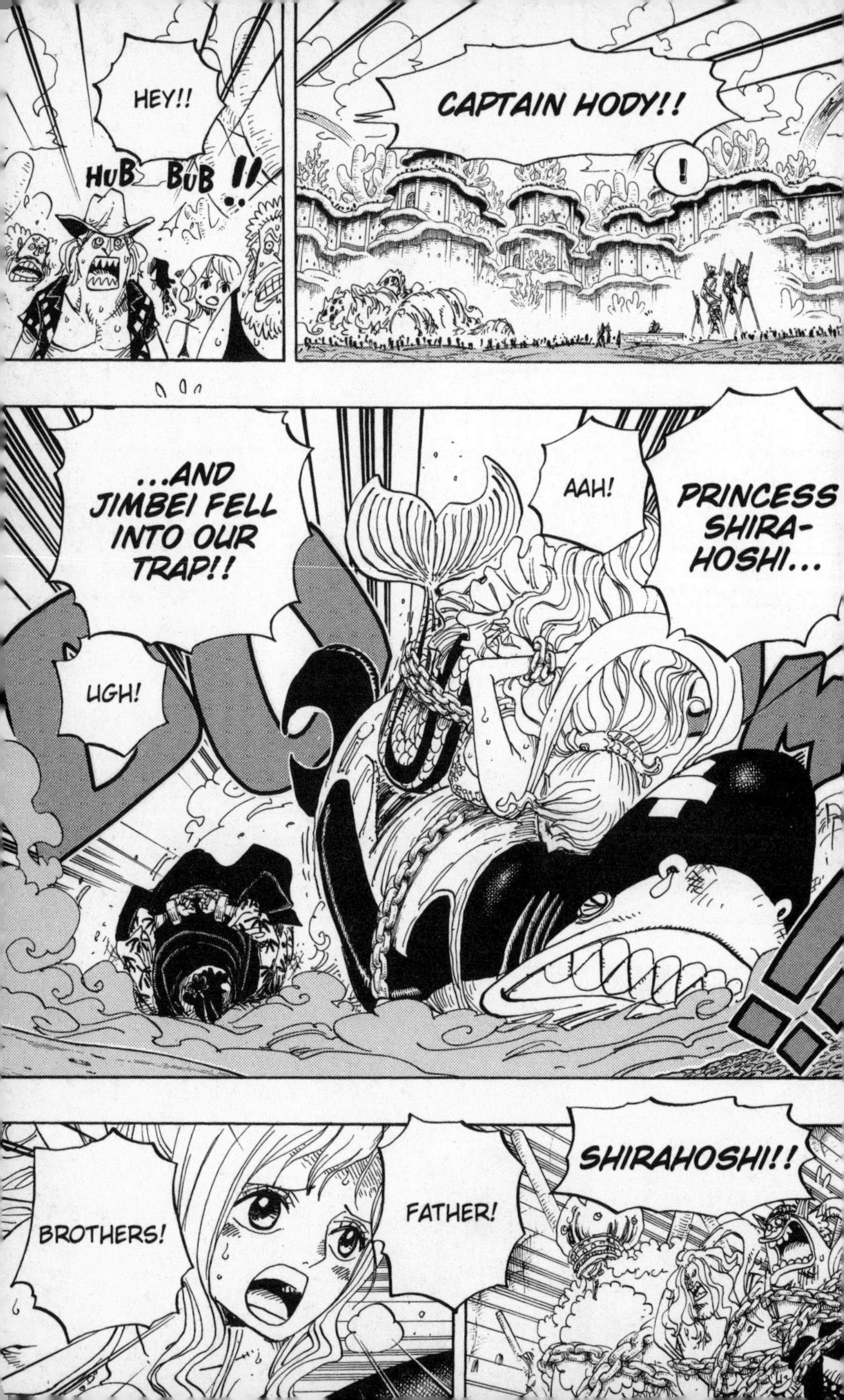
CAPTAIN HODY!!
!
HEY!!
HUB BUB !!
PRINCESS SHIRA-HOSHI...
AAH!
...AND JIMBEI FELL INTO OUR TRAP!!
UGH!
SHIRAHOSHI!!
FATHER!
BROTHERS!

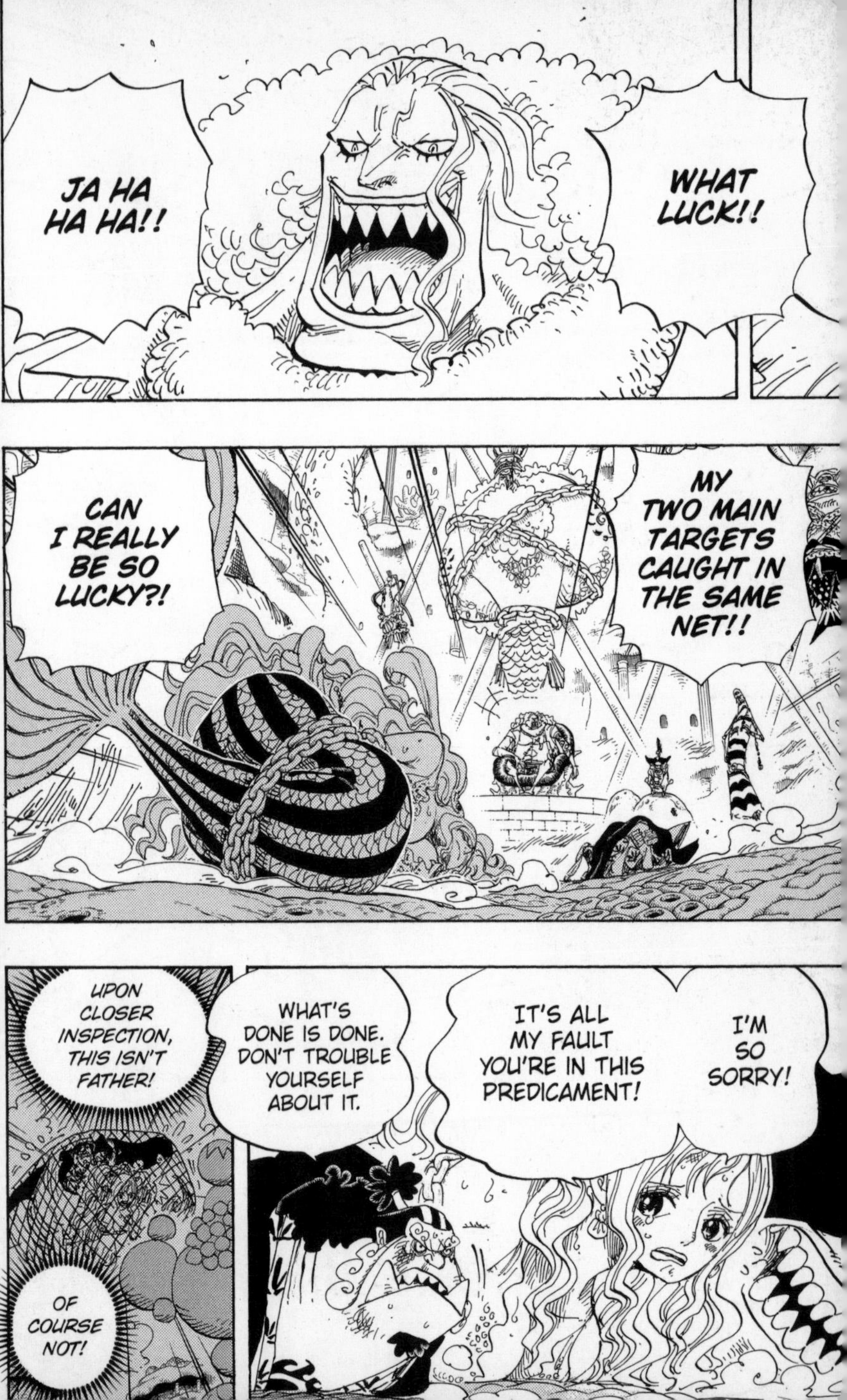
WHAT LUCK!!
JA HA HA HA!!
MY TWO MAIN TARGETS CAUGHT IN THE SAME NET!!
CAN I REALLY BE SO LUCKY?!
I'M SO SORRY!
IT'S ALL MY FAULT YOU'RE IN THIS PREDICAMENT!
WHAT'S DONE IS DONE. DON'T TROUBLE YOURSELF ABOUT IT.
UPON CLOSER INSPECTION, THIS ISN'T FATHER!
OF COURSE NOT!

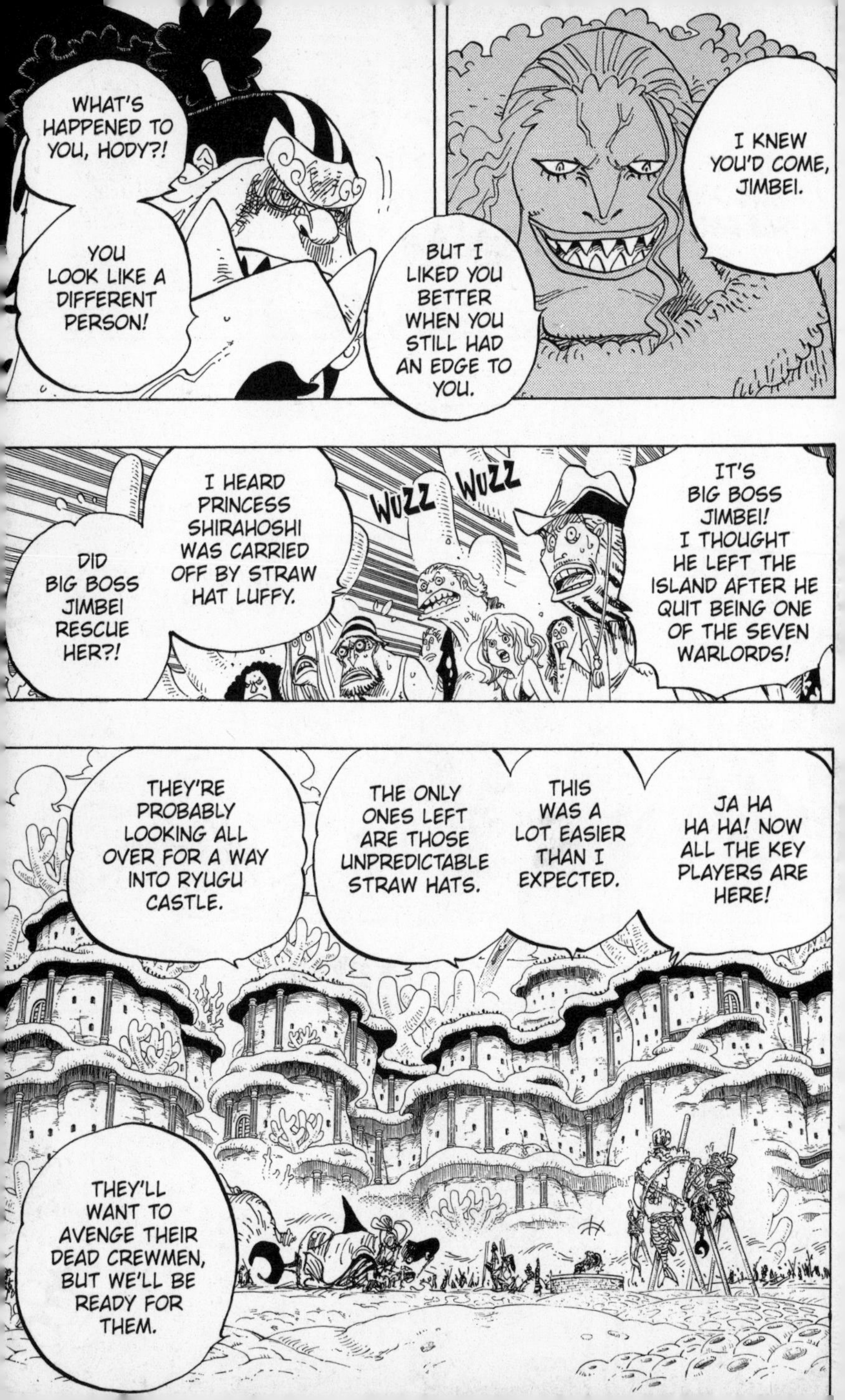
I KNEW YOU'D COME, JIMBEI.
WHAT'S HAPPENED TO YOU, HODY?!
YOU LOOK LIKE A DIFFERENT PERSON!
BUT I LIKED YOU BETTER WHEN YOU STILL HAD AN EDGE TO YOU.
IT'S BIG BOSS JIMBEI! I THOUGHT HE LEFT THE ISLAND AFTER HE QUIT BEING ONE OF THE SEVEN WARLORDS!
WUZZ WUZZ
I HEARD PRINCESS SHIRAHOSHI WAS CARRIED OFF BY STRAW HAT LUFFY.
DID BIG BOSS JIMBEI RESCUE HER?!
JA HA HA HA! NOW ALL THE KEY PLAYERS ARE HERE!
THIS WAS A LOT EASIER THAN I EXPECTED.
THE ONLY ONES LEFT ARE THOSE UNPREDICTABLE STRAW HATS.
THEY'RE PROBABLY LOOKING ALL OVER FOR A WAY INTO RYUGU CASTLE.
THEY'LL WANT TO AVENGE THEIR DEAD CREWMEN, BUT WE'LL BE READY FOR THEM.

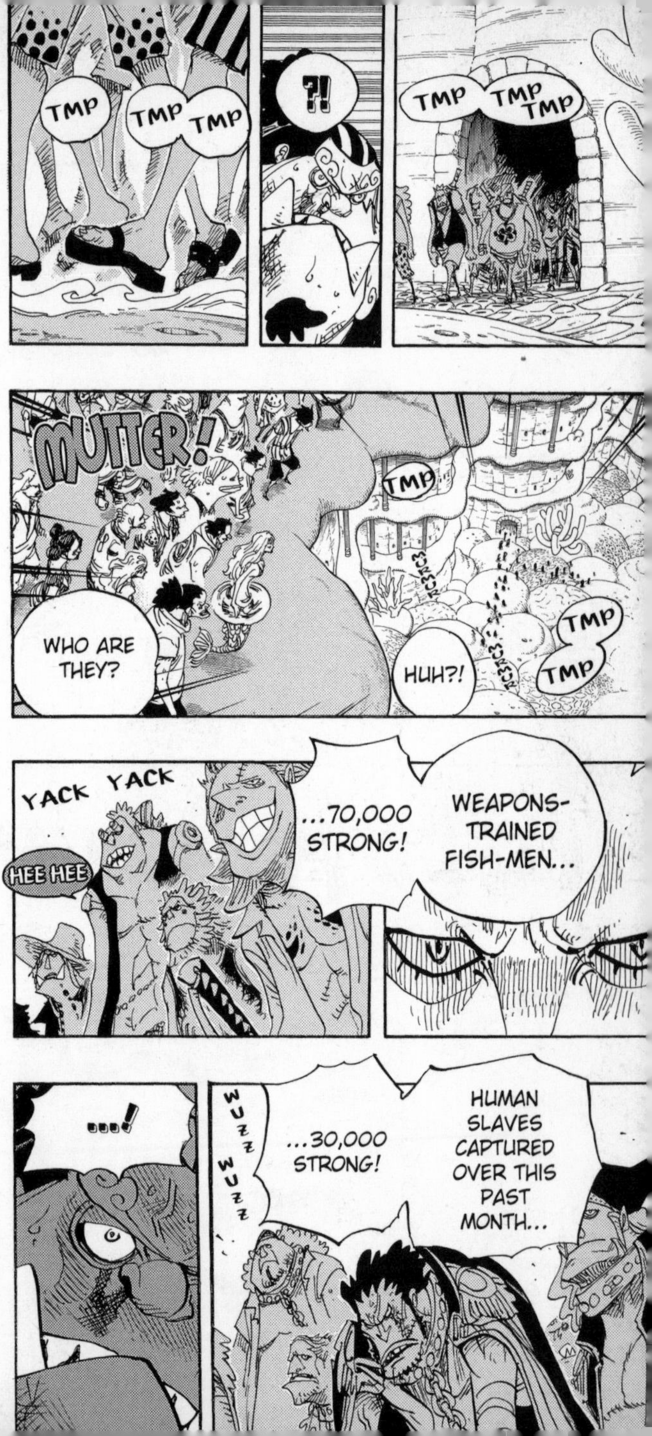
TMP
TMP TMP
?!
TMP TMP TMP
TMP
TMP TMP
HUH?!
MUTTER!
WHO ARE THEY?
WEAPONS-TRAINED FISH-MEN...
...70,000 STRONG!
YACK YACK
HEE HEE
HUMAN SLAVES CAPTURED OVER THIS PAST MONTH...
...30,000 STRONG!
WUZZ WUZZ
...!
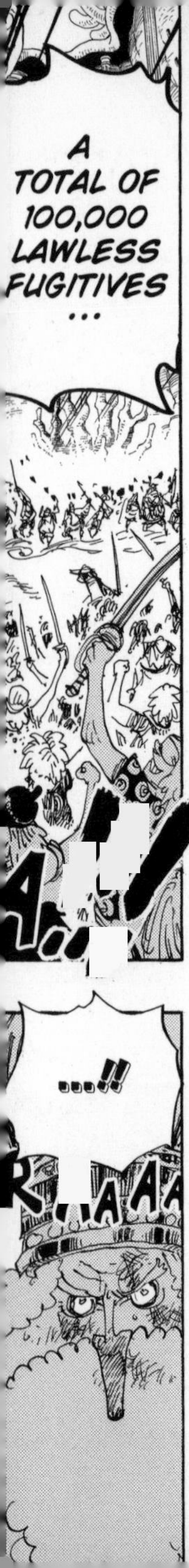
A TOTAL OF 100,000 LAWLESS FUGITIVES...
...!!

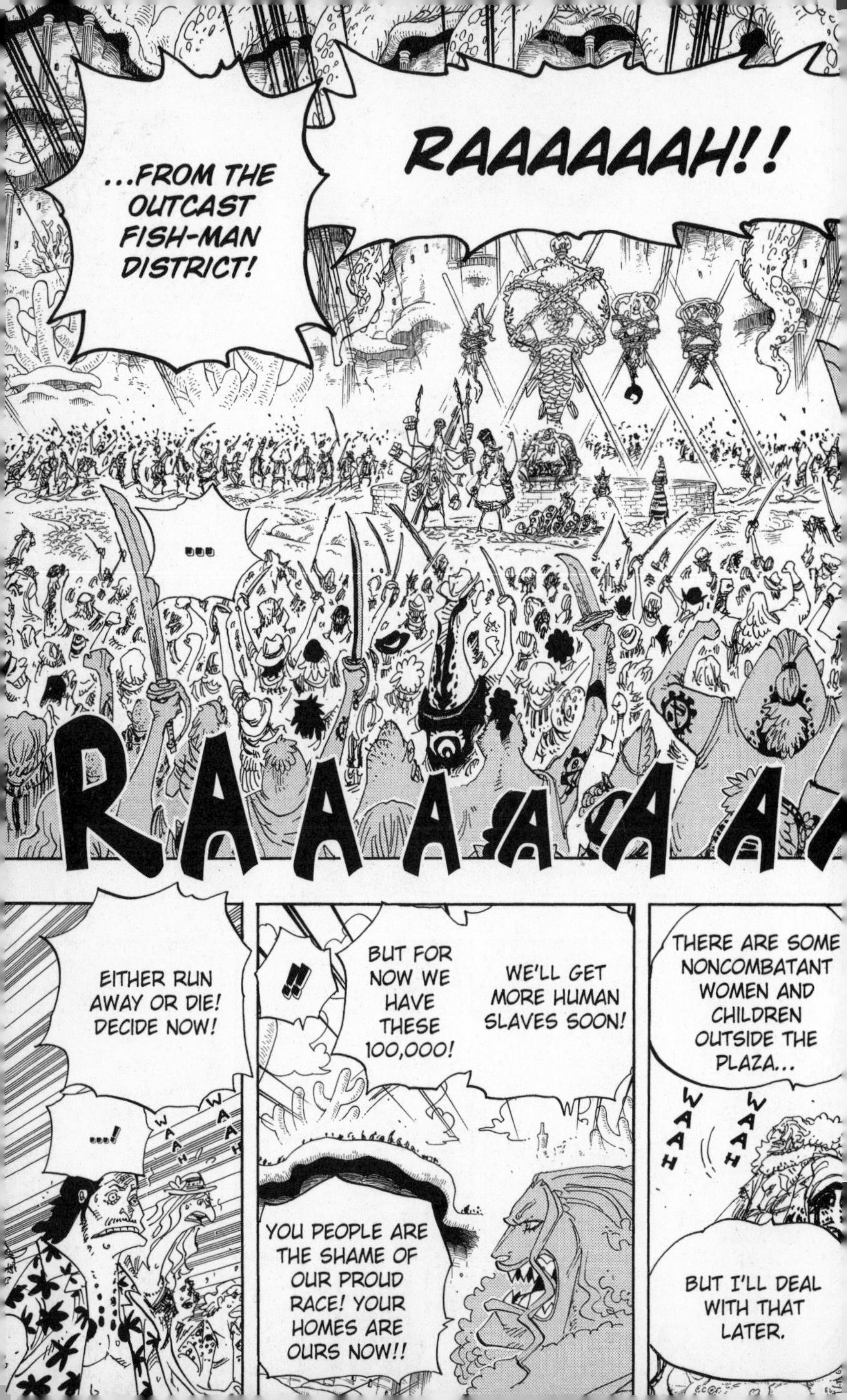
...FROM THE OUTCAST FISH-MAN DISTRICT!
RAAAAAAH!!
...
RAAAAAAA
THERE ARE SOME NONCOMBATANT WOMEN AND CHILDREN OUTSIDE THE PLAZA...
WAAH
WAAH
BUT I'LL DEAL WITH THAT LATER.
WE'LL GET MORE HUMAN SLAVES SOON!
BUT FOR NOW WE HAVE THESE 100,000!
!!
YOU PEOPLE ARE THE SHAME OF OUR PROUD RACE! YOUR HOMES ARE OURS NOW!!
EITHER RUN AWAY OR DIE! DECIDE NOW!
WAAH
WAAH
...!

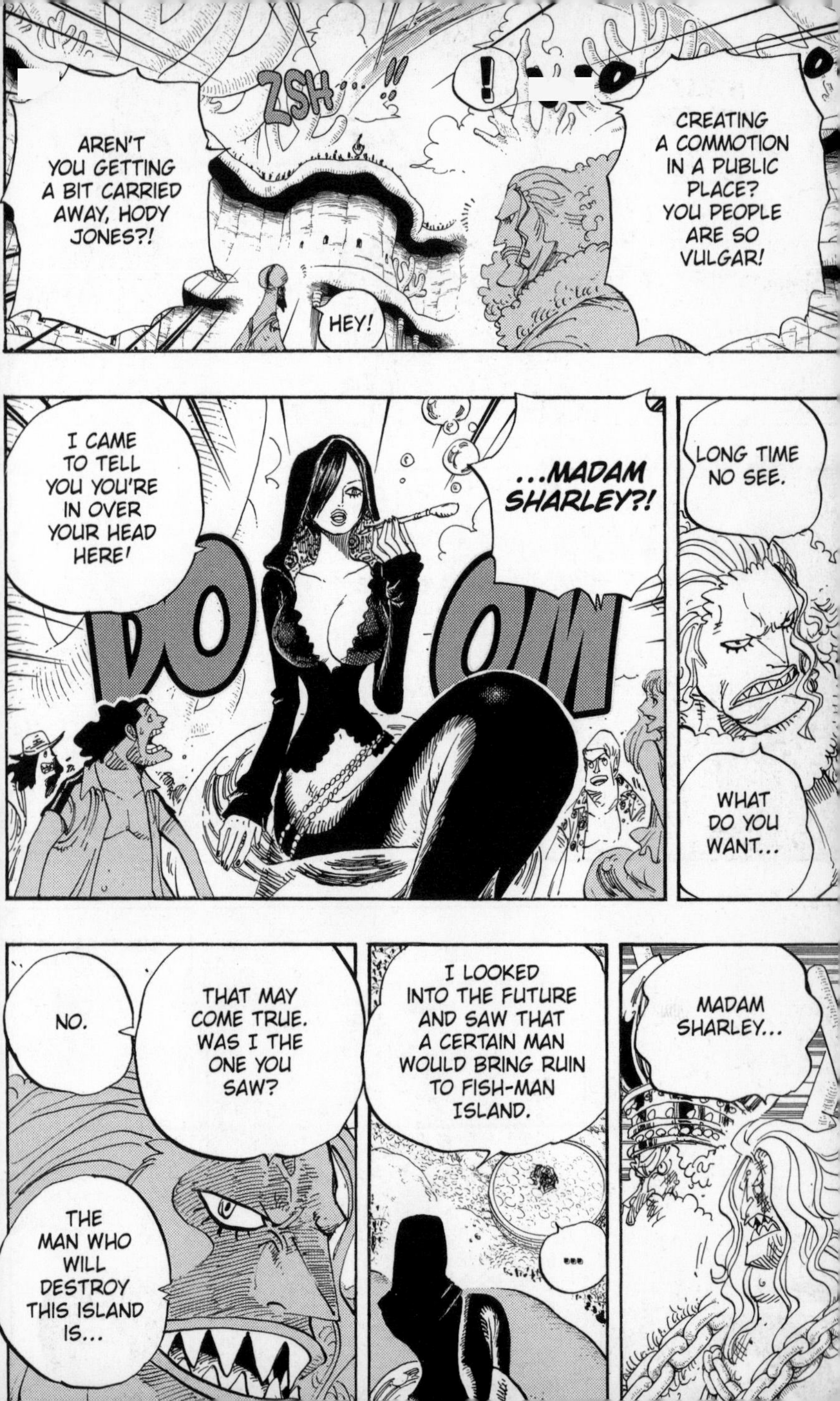
CREATING A COMMOTION IN A PUBLIC PLACE? YOU PEOPLE ARE SO VULGAR!
!
ZSH..!!
HEY!
AREN'T YOU GETTING A BIT CARRIED AWAY, HODY JONES?!
LONG TIME NO SEE.
WHAT DO YOU WANT...
...MADAM SHARLEY?!
DOOM
I CAME TO TELL YOU YOU'RE IN OVER YOUR HEAD HERE!
MADAM SHARLEY...
I LOOKED INTO THE FUTURE AND SAW THAT A CERTAIN MAN WOULD BRING RUIN TO FISH-MAN ISLAND.
...
THAT MAY COME TRUE. WAS I THE ONE YOU SAW?
NO.
THE MAN WHO WILL DESTROY THIS ISLAND IS...

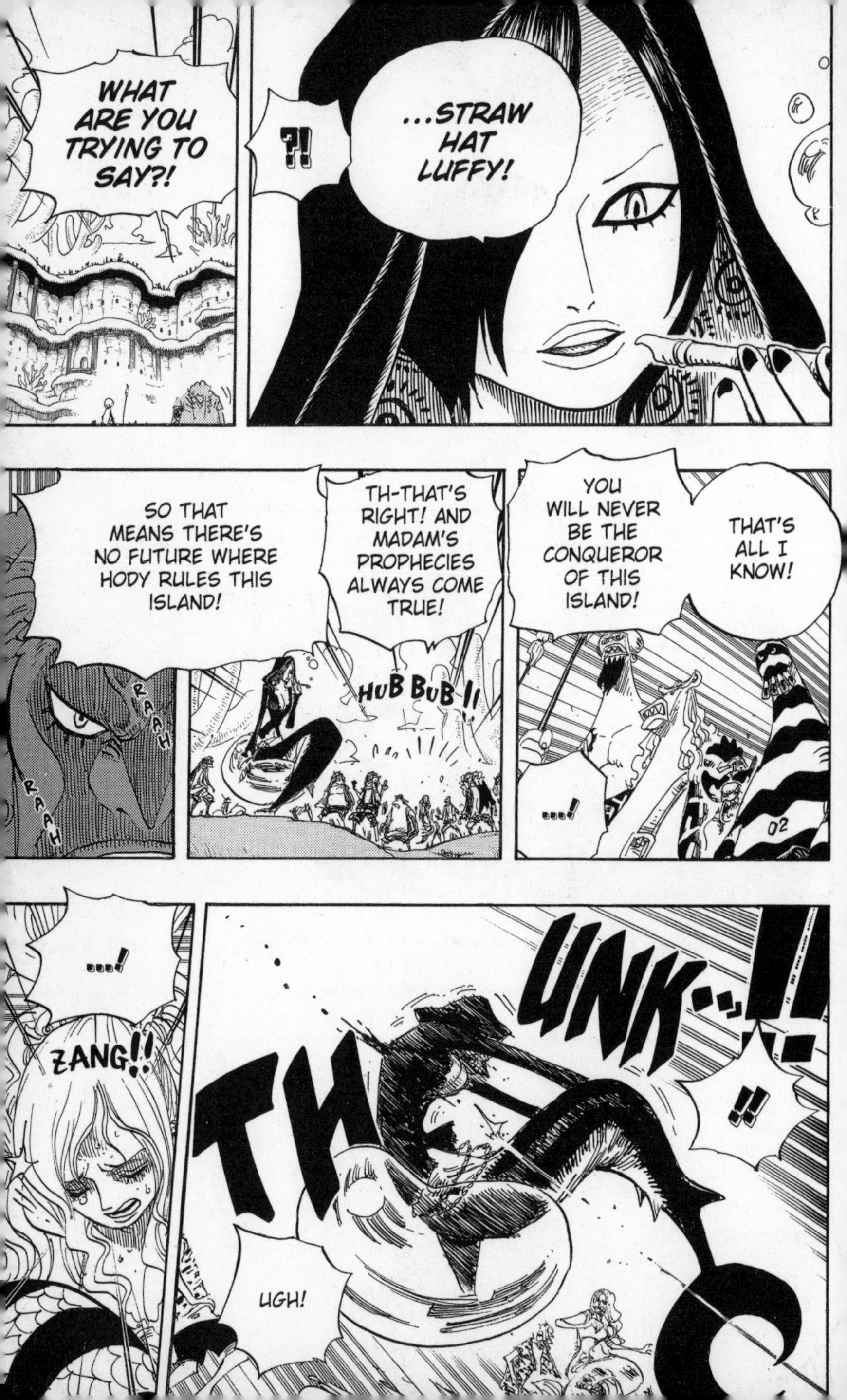
...STRAW HAT LUFFY!
?!
WHAT ARE YOU TRYING TO SAY?!
YOU WILL NEVER BE THE CONQUEROR OF THIS ISLAND!
THAT'S ALL I KNOW!
...!
TH-THAT'S RIGHT! AND MADAM'S PROPHECIES ALWAYS COME TRUE!
HUB BUB!!
SO THAT MEANS THERE'S NO FUTURE WHERE HODY RULES THIS ISLAND!
RAAAH
RAAAH
THUNK..!!
!!
UGH!
...!
ZANG!!

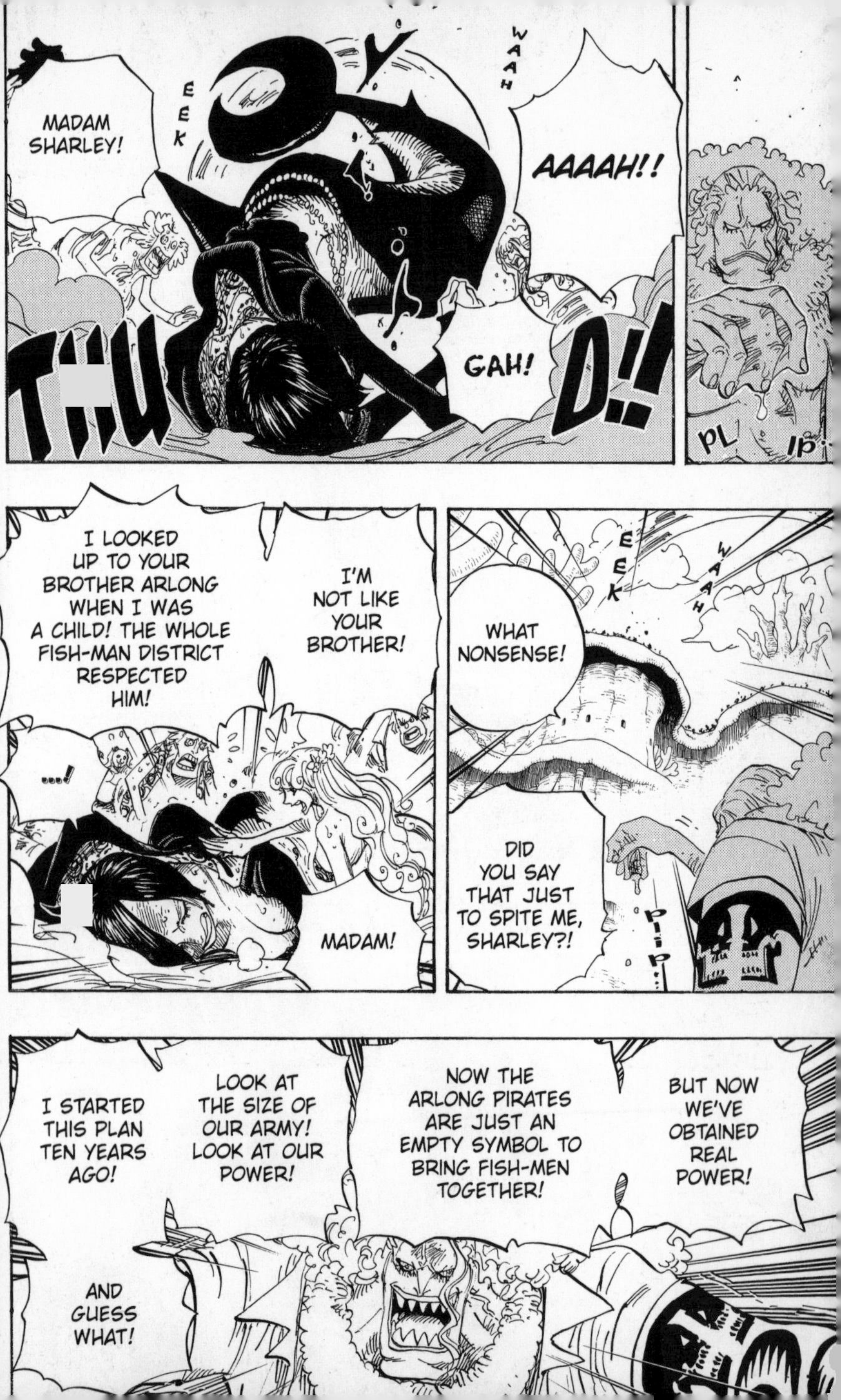
PL
IP
WAAAH
AAAAH!!
EEK
MADAM SHARLEY!
D!!
GAH!
THU
EEK
WAAAH
WHAT NONSENSE!
DID YOU SAY THAT JUST TO SPITE ME, SHARLEY?!
PLIP...
I'M NOT LIKE YOUR BROTHER!
I LOOKED UP TO YOUR BROTHER ARLONG WHEN I WAS A CHILD! THE WHOLE FISH-MAN DISTRICT RESPECTED HIM!
...!
MADAM!
BUT NOW WE'VE OBTAINED REAL POWER!
NOW THE ARLONG PIRATES ARE JUST AN EMPTY SYMBOL TO BRING FISH-MEN TOGETHER!
LOOK AT THE SIZE OF OUR ARMY! LOOK AT OUR POWER!
I STARTED THIS PLAN TEN YEARS AGO!
AND GUESS WHAT!

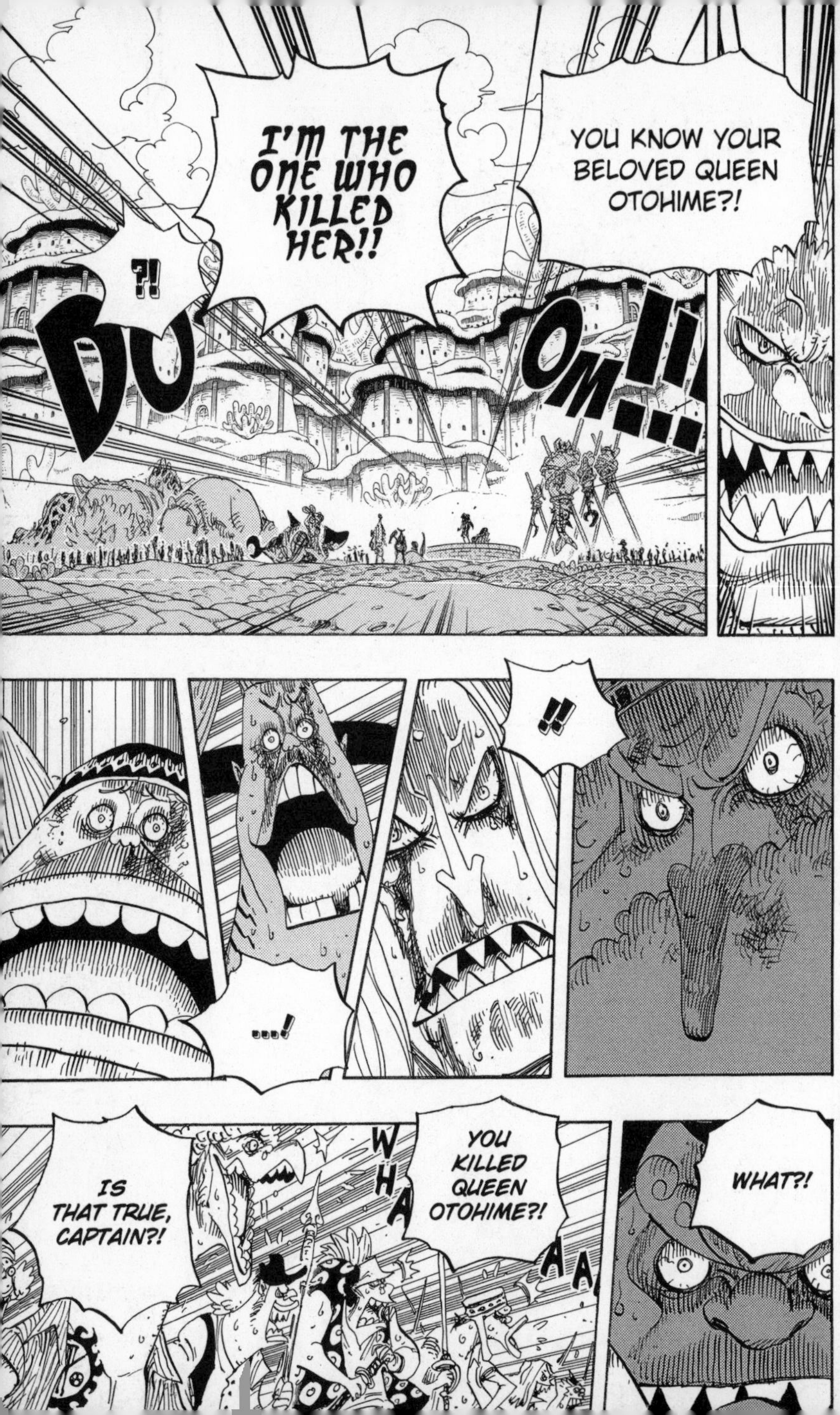
YOU KNOW YOUR BELOVED QUEEN OTOHIME?!
I'M THE ONE WHO KILLED HER!!
?!
BOOM!!
!!
...!
WHAT?!
YOU KILLED QUEEN OTOHIME?!
WHAAA
IS THAT TRUE, CAPTAIN?!

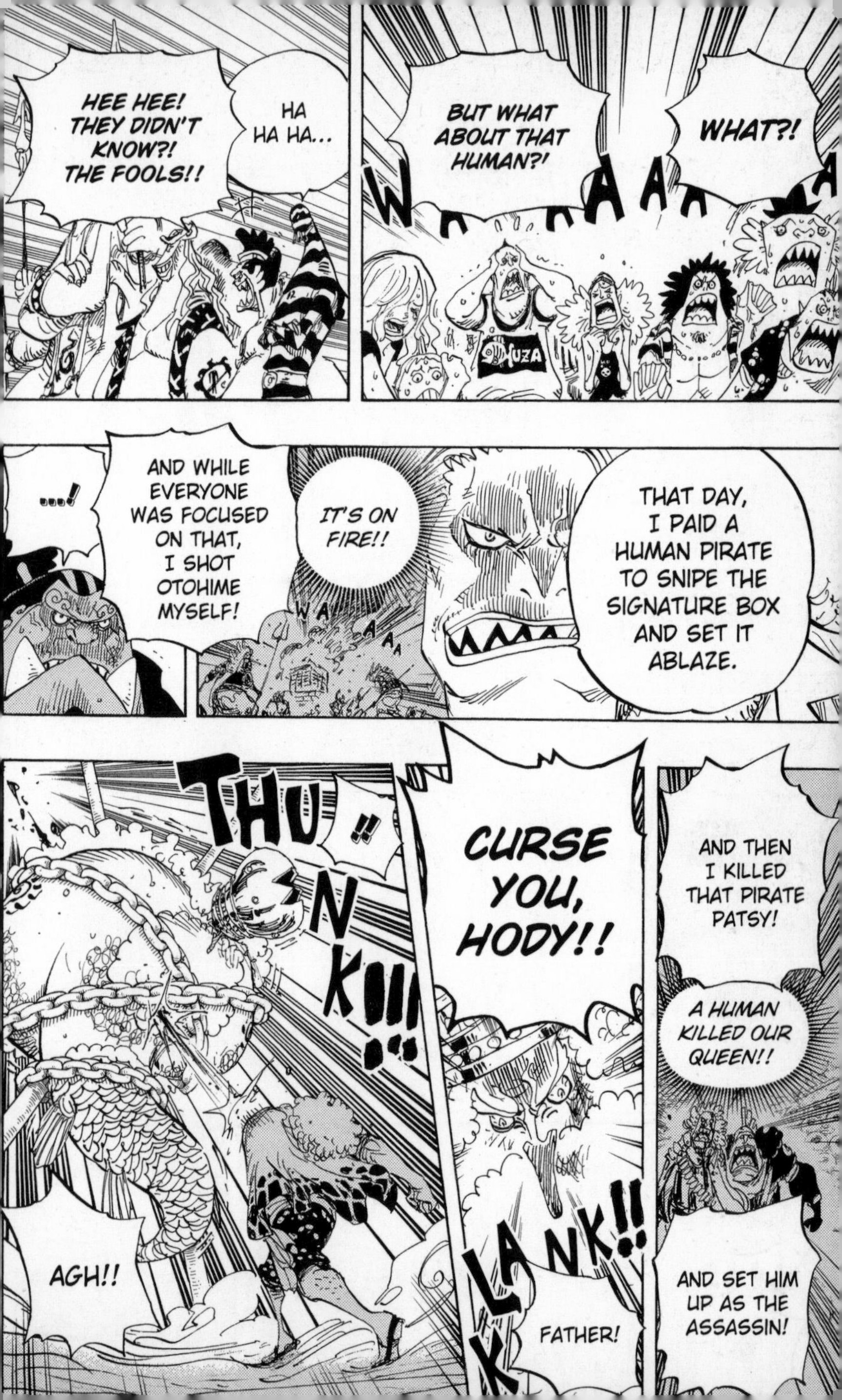
WHAT?!
BUT WHAT ABOUT THAT HUMAN?!
HA HA HA...
HEE HEE! THEY DIDN'T KNOW?! THE FOOLS!!
THAT DAY, I PAID A HUMAN PIRATE TO SNIPE THE SIGNATURE BOX AND SET IT ABLAZE.
IT'S ON FIRE!!
AND WHILE EVERYONE WAS FOCUSED ON THAT, I SHOT OTOHIME MYSELF!
...!
AND THEN I KILLED THAT PIRATE PATSY!
A HUMAN KILLED OUR QUEEN!!
AND SET HIM UP AS THE ASSASSIN!
CURSE YOU, HODY!!
KLANK!!
FATHER!
THUNK!!
AGH!!

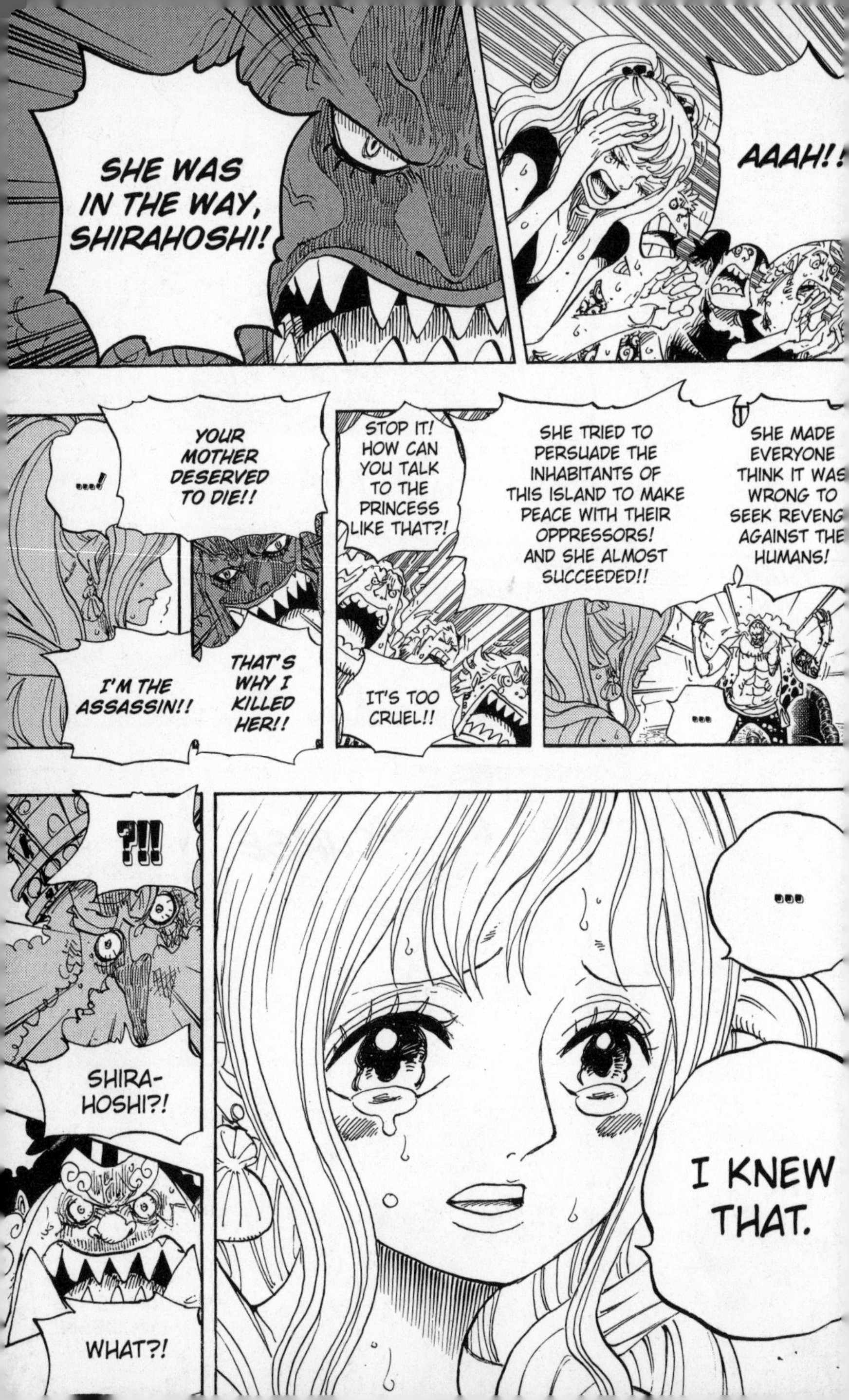
AAAH!!
SHE WAS IN THE WAY, SHIRAHOSHI!!
SHE MADE EVERYONE THINK IT WAS WRONG TO SEEK REVENG AGAINST THE HUMANS!
SHE TRIED TO PERSUADE THE INHABITANTS OF THIS ISLAND TO MAKE PEACE WITH THEIR OPPRESSORS! AND SHE ALMOST SUCCEEDED!!
...
STOP IT! HOW CAN YOU TALK TO THE PRINCESS LIKE THAT?!
IT'S TOO CRUEL!!
YOUR MOTHER DESERVED TO DIE!!
...!
THAT'S WHY I KILLED HER!!
I'M THE ASSASSIN!!
...
I KNEW THAT.
?!!
SHIRA-HOSHI?!
WHAT?!

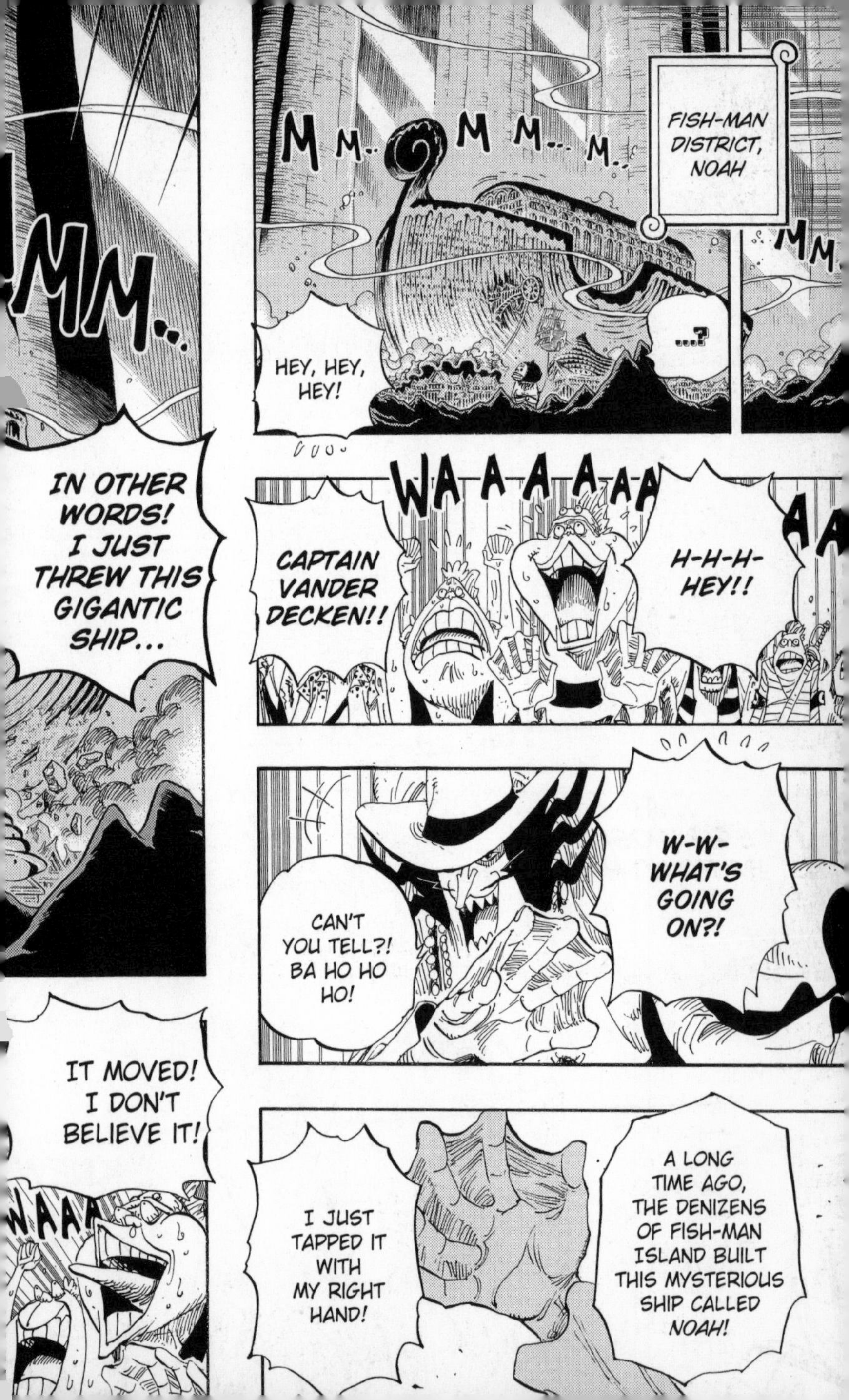

FISH-MAN DISTRICT, NOAH
MM..
MM.. M M.. M.. M..
...?
HEY, HEY, HEY!
H-H-H-HEY!!
AA
WAAAAA
CAPTAIN VANDER DECKEN!!
W-W-WHAT'S GOING ON?!
CAN'T YOU TELL?! BA HO HO HO!
A LONG TIME AGO, THE DENIZENS OF FISH-MAN ISLAND BUILT THIS MYSTERIOUS SHIP CALLED NOAH!
I JUST TAPPED IT WITH MY RIGHT HAND!
MMM...
IN OTHER WORDS! I JUST THREW THIS GIGANTIC SHIP...
IT MOVED! I DON'T BELIEVE IT!
WAAA

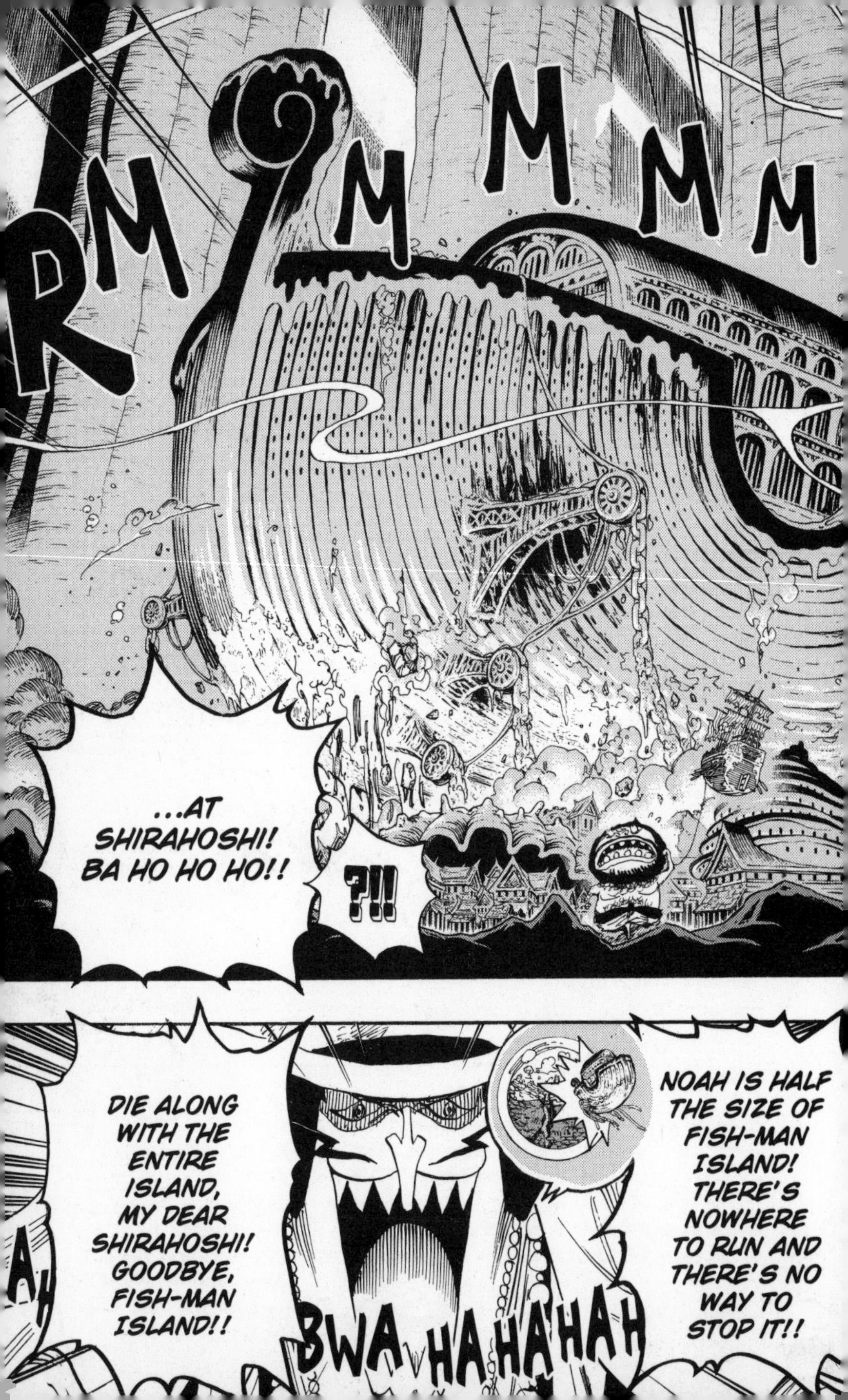
RRMMMMMM
?!!
...AT SHIRAHOSHI! BA HO HO HO!!
NOAH IS HALF THE SIZE OF FISH-MAN ISLAND! THERE'S NOWHERE TO RUN AND THERE'S NO WAY TO STOP IT!!
DIE ALONG WITH THE ENTIRE ISLAND, MY DEAR SHIRAHOSHI! GOODBYE, FISH-MAN ISLAND!!
BWA HA HA HA HAH
AH

質問コーナー

(SKY☆, Ibaraki)

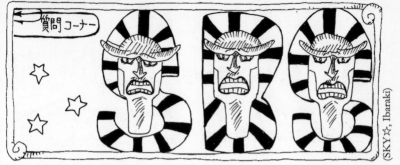

Q: Heeeey! Hey hey hey hey hey, Odacchi, Odacchi who flew in from somewhere. I got somethin' to say to you! You know the scene in volume 63, chapter 626 where Otohime cried about the signatures? There's someone that looks identical to the Nami Mermaid that Luffy drew in volume 8, chapter 69. What's going on?! If you don't tell me, I'll… Well, I don't know.

--King of Gedatsu

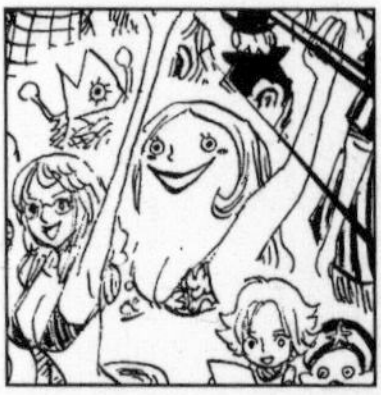

A: I got lots of letters about this. I'm surprised you found it. Moreover, I'm surprised that what Luffy imagined actually existed.

なみ

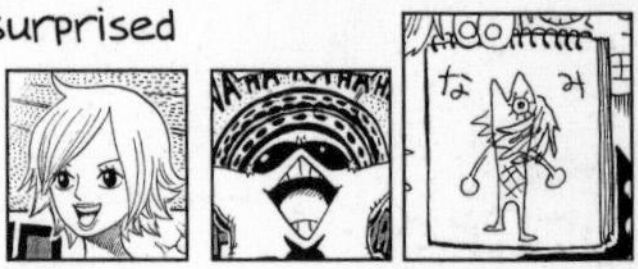

Q: Earwax, boogers, or eye boogers. Which one do you prefer?

--Hatamori

A: Earwax, I guess.

BA—DUMP!

Q: Mr. Oda. You're not my type.

--Match and Takeshi

A: What?! But you read One Piece so I like you.

Q: Odacchi! This is my first letter to you and it's a serious question. In chapter 598, it mentioned something about Soul King's TD sales or whatnot. What is this "TD" thing? Is it like a CD in that world? I want to know.

--Toruman

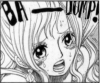

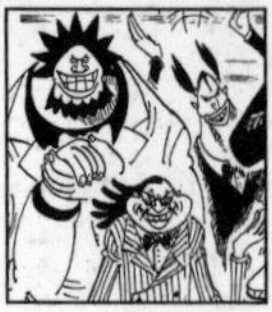

A: That's right. You can assume that that's what it is. A lot of things changed over the past two years including much of the technology. TD stands for "tone dial." It's a shell that can store sound like the ones in sky island. They managed to farm and improve upon that technology. They are sold in pieces of two and they can be enjoyed in headphone and stereo.

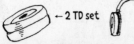

← 2 TD set

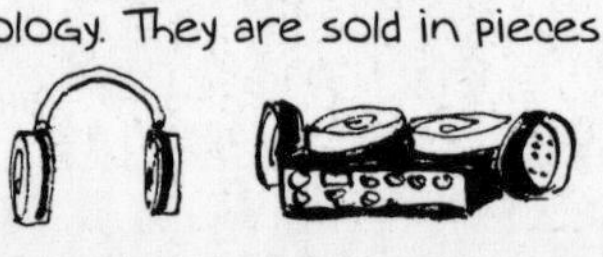

Chapter 633:
FRIEND OR FOE

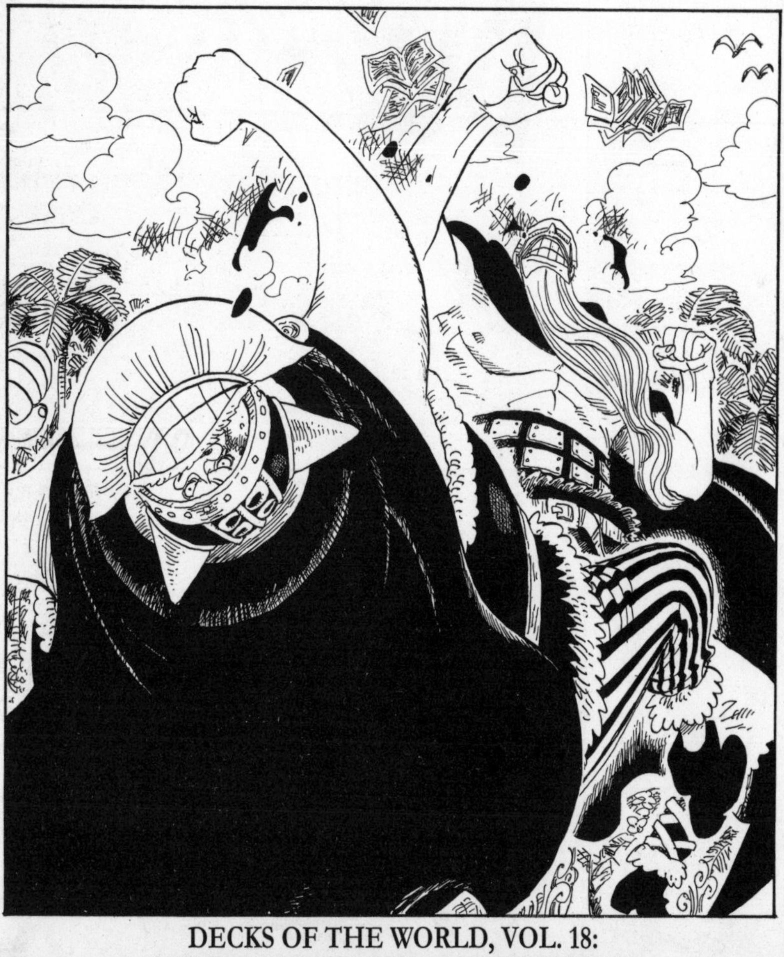

DECKS OF THE WORLD, VOL. 18:
"LITTLE GARDEN, ISLAND OF GIANTS"

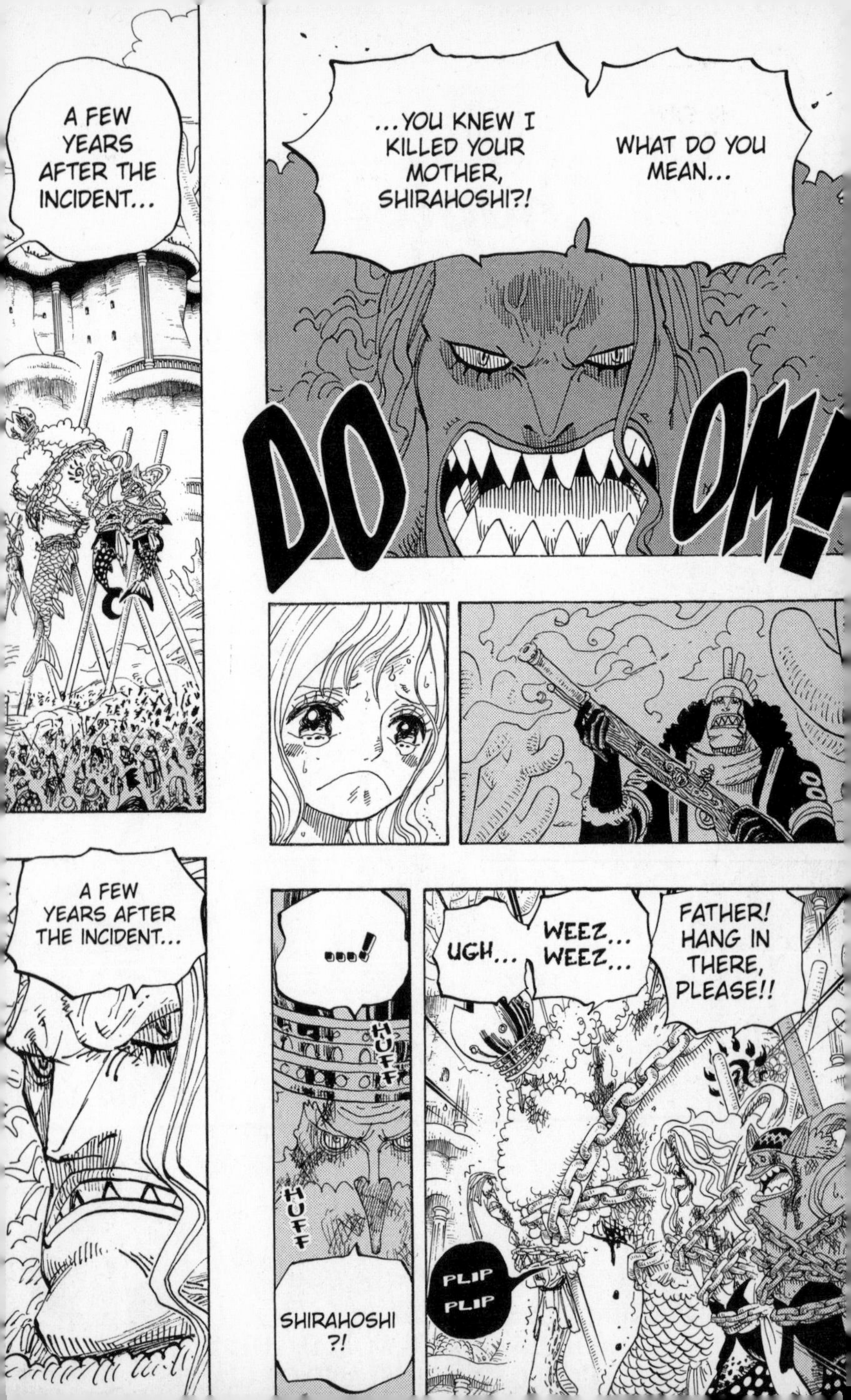
WHAT DO YOU MEAN...
...YOU KNEW I KILLED YOUR MOTHER, SHIRAHOSHI?!
DOOM!!
FATHER! HANG IN THERE, PLEASE!!
WEEZ... WEEZ...
UGH...
PLIP PLIP
...!
HUFF
HUFF
SHIRAHOSHI ?!
A FEW YEARS AFTER THE INCIDENT...
A FEW YEARS AFTER THE INCIDENT...

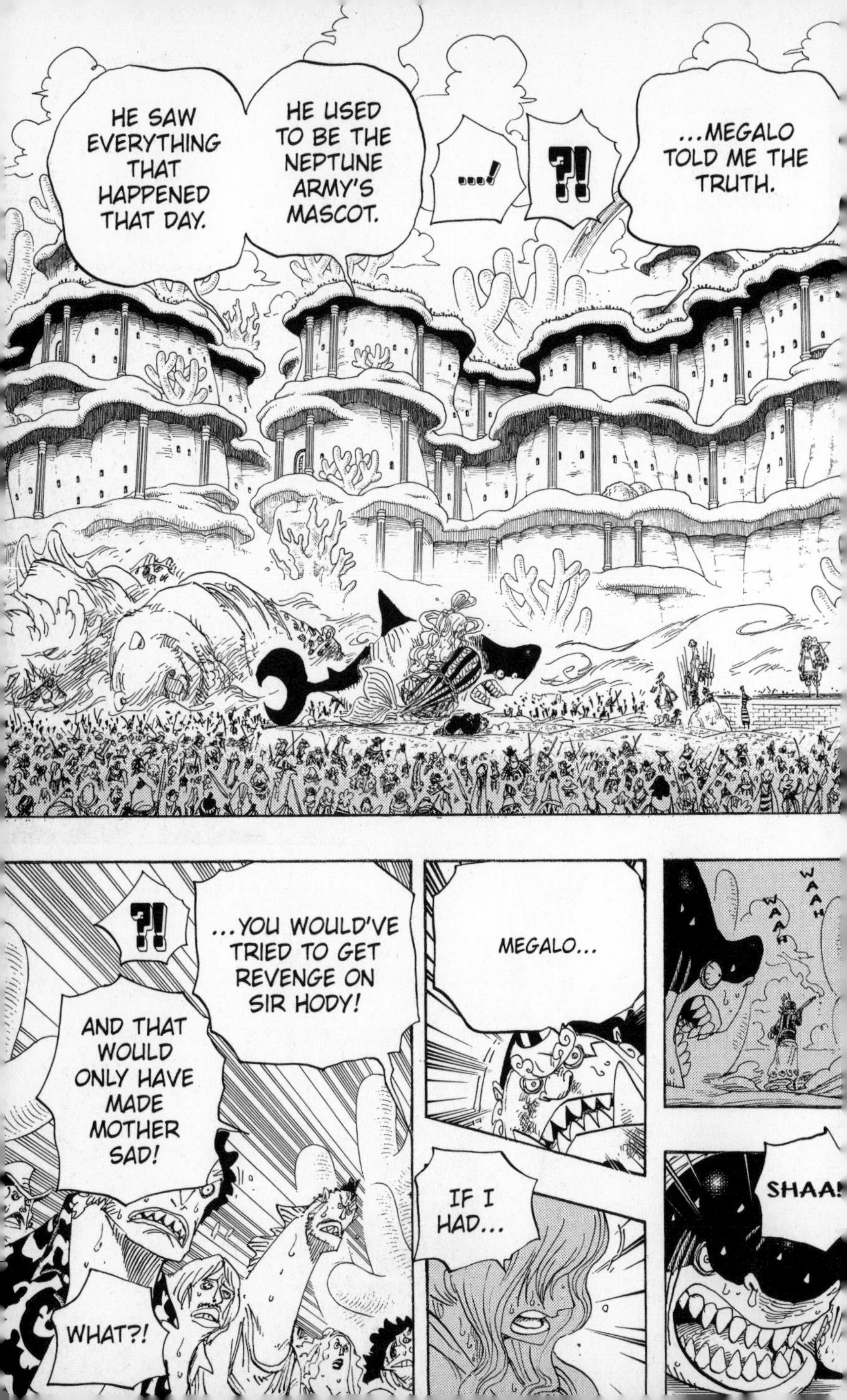
...MEGALO TOLD ME THE TRUTH.
?!
...!
HE USED TO BE THE NEPTUNE ARMY'S MASCOT.
HE SAW EVERYTHING THAT HAPPENED THAT DAY.
WAAH
WAAH
SHAA!
MEGALO...
IF I HAD...
...YOU WOULD'VE TRIED TO GET REVENGE ON SIR HODY!
?!
AND THAT WOULD ONLY HAVE MADE MOTHER SAD!
WHAT?!

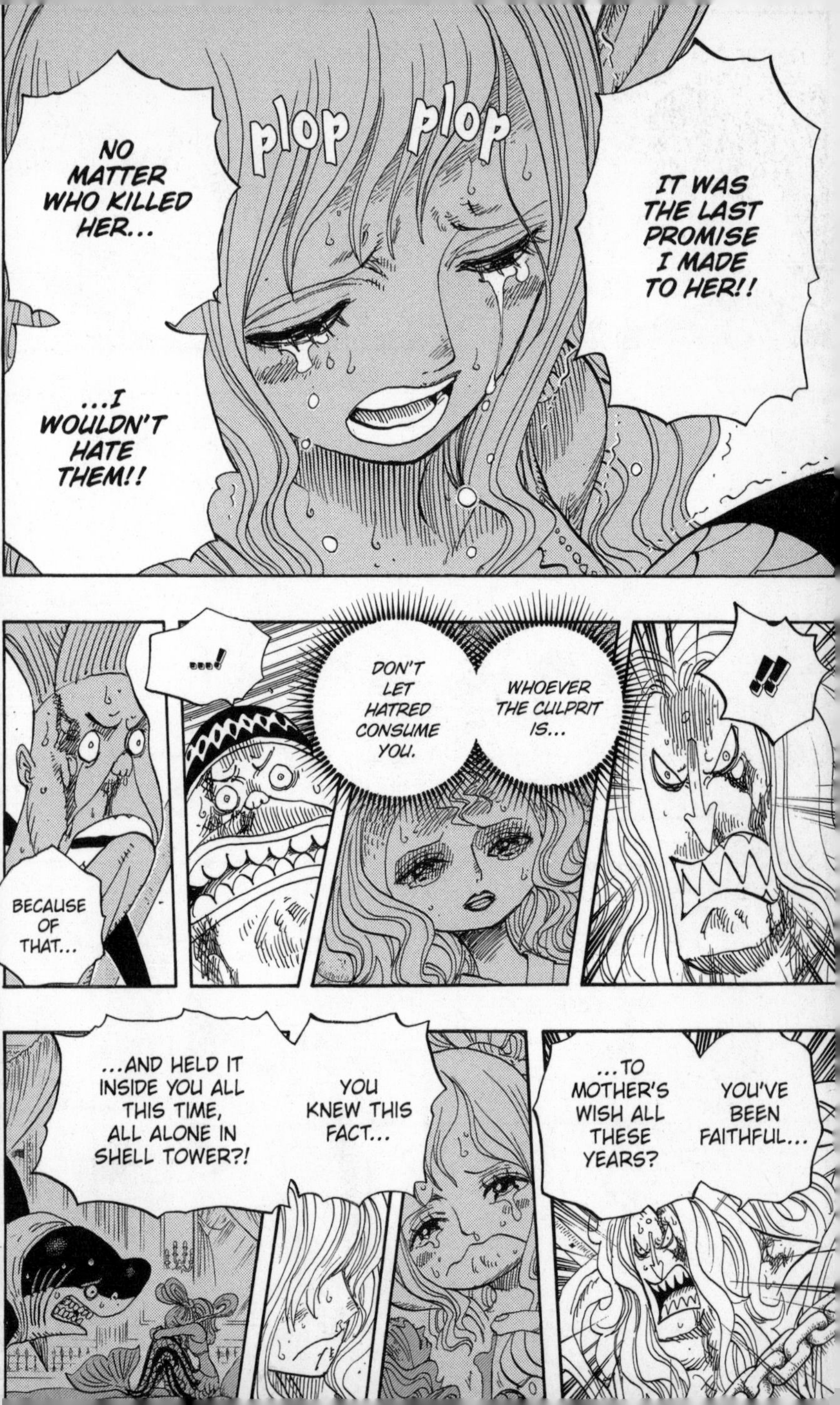
IT WAS THE LAST PROMISE I MADE TO HER!!
plop plop
NO MATTER WHO KILLED HER...
...I WOULDN'T HATE THEM!!
!!
WHOEVER THE CULPRIT IS...
DON'T LET HATRED CONSUME YOU.
...!
BECAUSE OF THAT...
YOU'VE BEEN FAITHFUL...
...TO MOTHER'S WISH ALL THESE YEARS?
YOU KNEW THIS FACT...
...AND HELD IT INSIDE YOU ALL THIS TIME, ALL ALONE IN SHELL TOWER?!

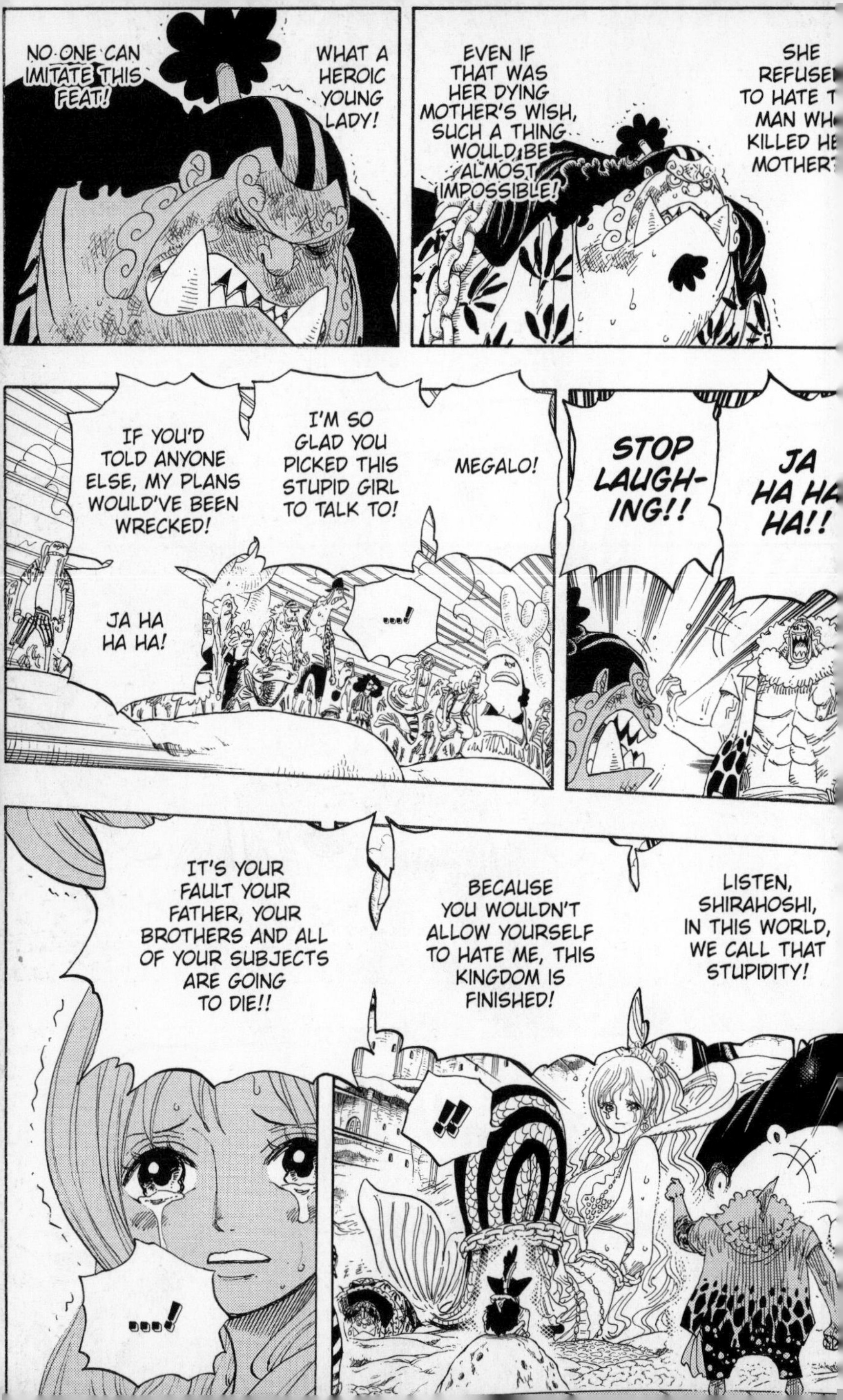
SHE REFUSE TO HATE T MAN WH KILLED HE MOTHER
EVEN IF THAT WAS HER DYING MOTHER'S WISH, SUCH A THING WOULD BE ALMOST IMPOSSIBLE!
WHAT A HEROIC YOUNG LADY!
NO ONE CAN IMITATE THIS FEAT!
JA HA HA HA!!
STOP LAUGHING!!
MEGALO!
I'M SO GLAD YOU PICKED THIS STUPID GIRL TO TALK TO!
IF YOU'D TOLD ANYONE ELSE, MY PLANS WOULD'VE BEEN WRECKED!
...!
JA HA HA HA!
LISTEN, SHIRAHOSHI, IN THIS WORLD, WE CALL THAT STUPIDITY!
BECAUSE YOU WOULDN'T ALLOW YOURSELF TO HATE ME, THIS KINGDOM IS FINISHED!
IT'S YOUR FAULT YOUR FATHER, YOUR BROTHERS AND ALL OF YOUR SUBJECTS ARE GOING TO DIE!!
!!
...!

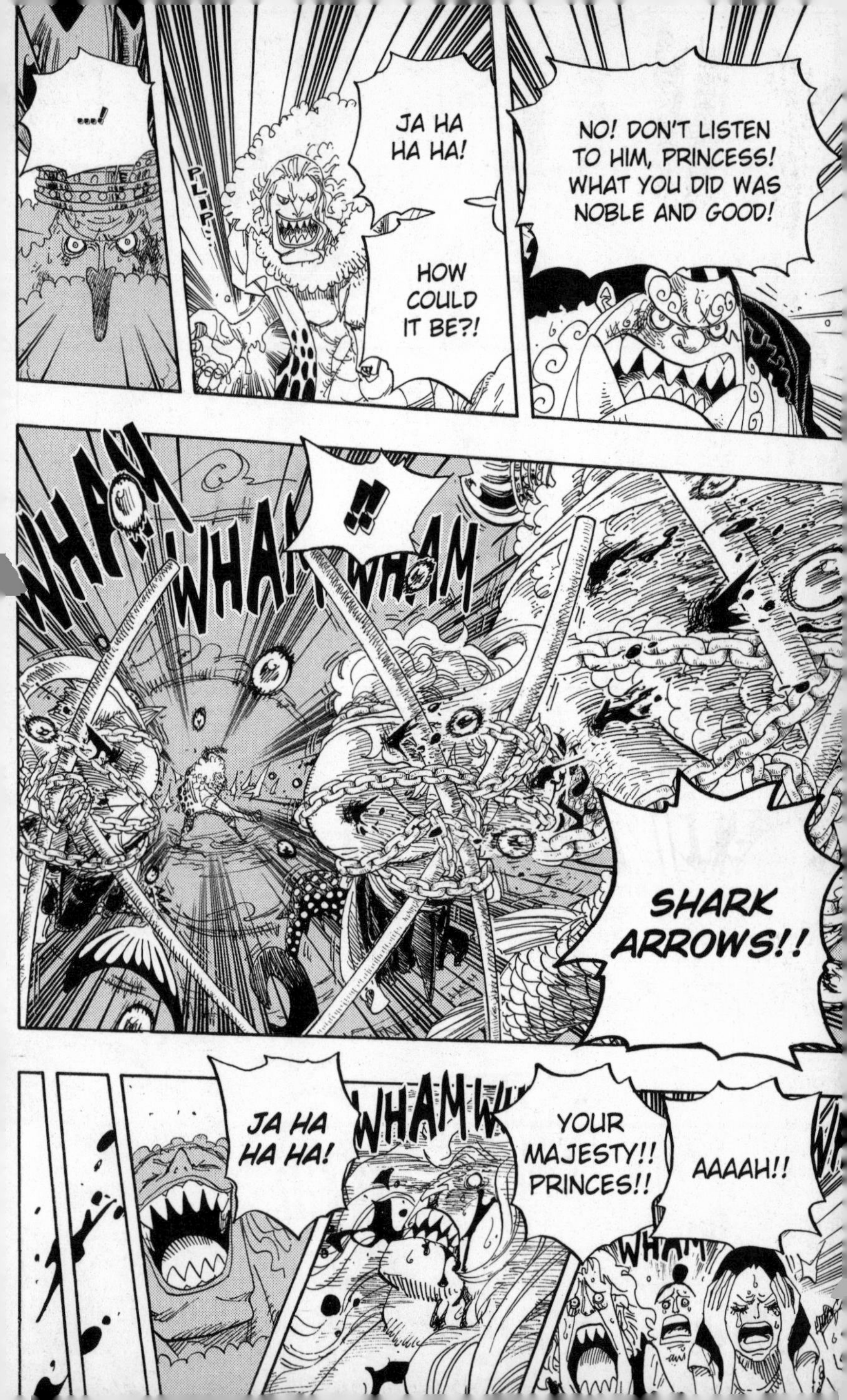
NO! DON'T LISTEN TO HIM, PRINCESS! WHAT YOU DID WAS NOBLE AND GOOD!
JA HA HA HA!
HOW COULD IT BE?!
PLIP
...!
!!
WHAM
WHAM
WHAM
SHARK ARROWS!!
AAAAH!!
WHAM
YOUR MAJESTY!! PRINCES!!
WHAM
JA HA HA HA!

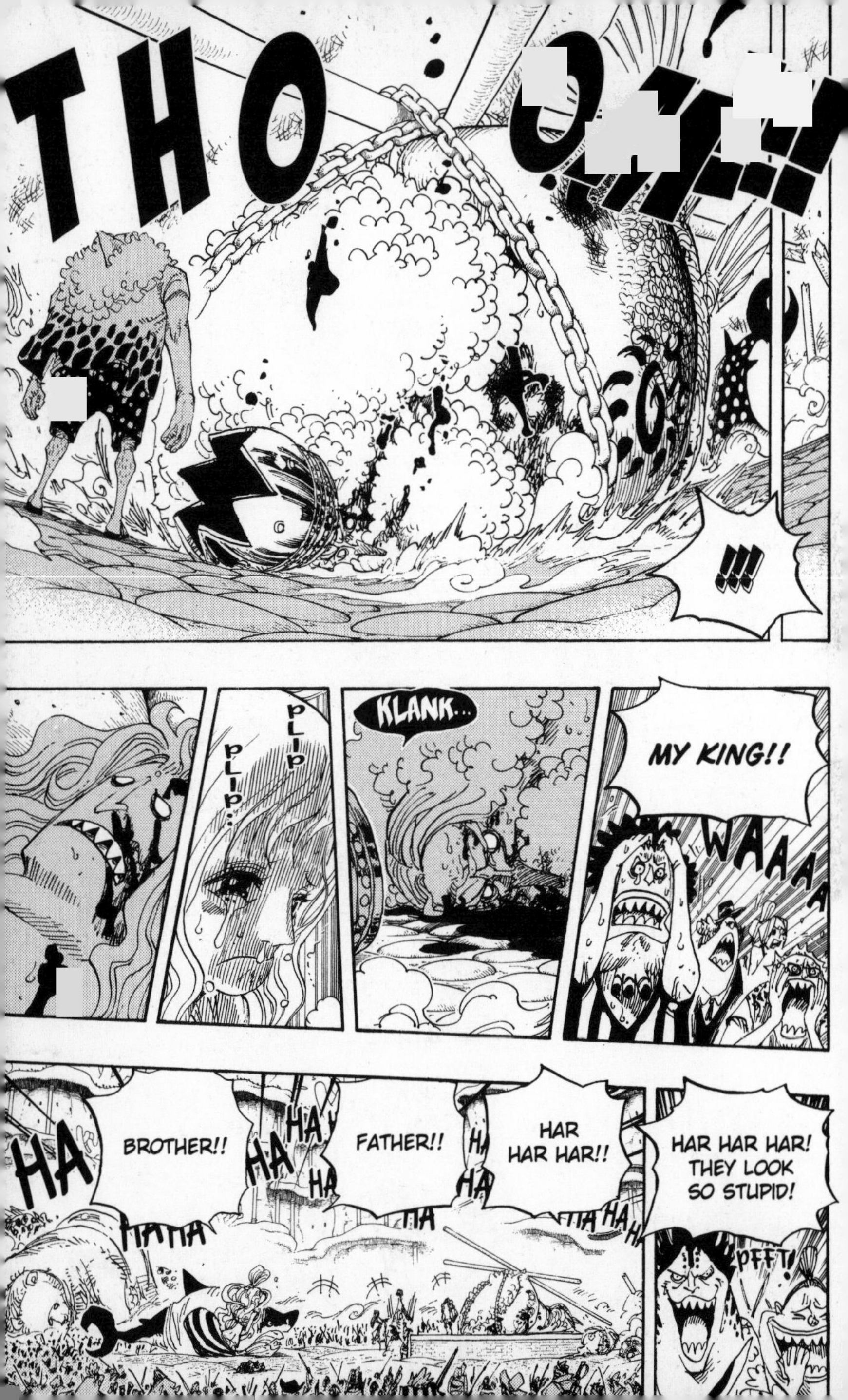

THO
!!!
MY KING!!
WAAAA
KLANK...
plip plip
HAR HAR HAR! THEY LOOK SO STUPID!
PFFT!
HAR HAR HAR!!
FATHER!!
BROTHER!!
HA HA HA HA HA

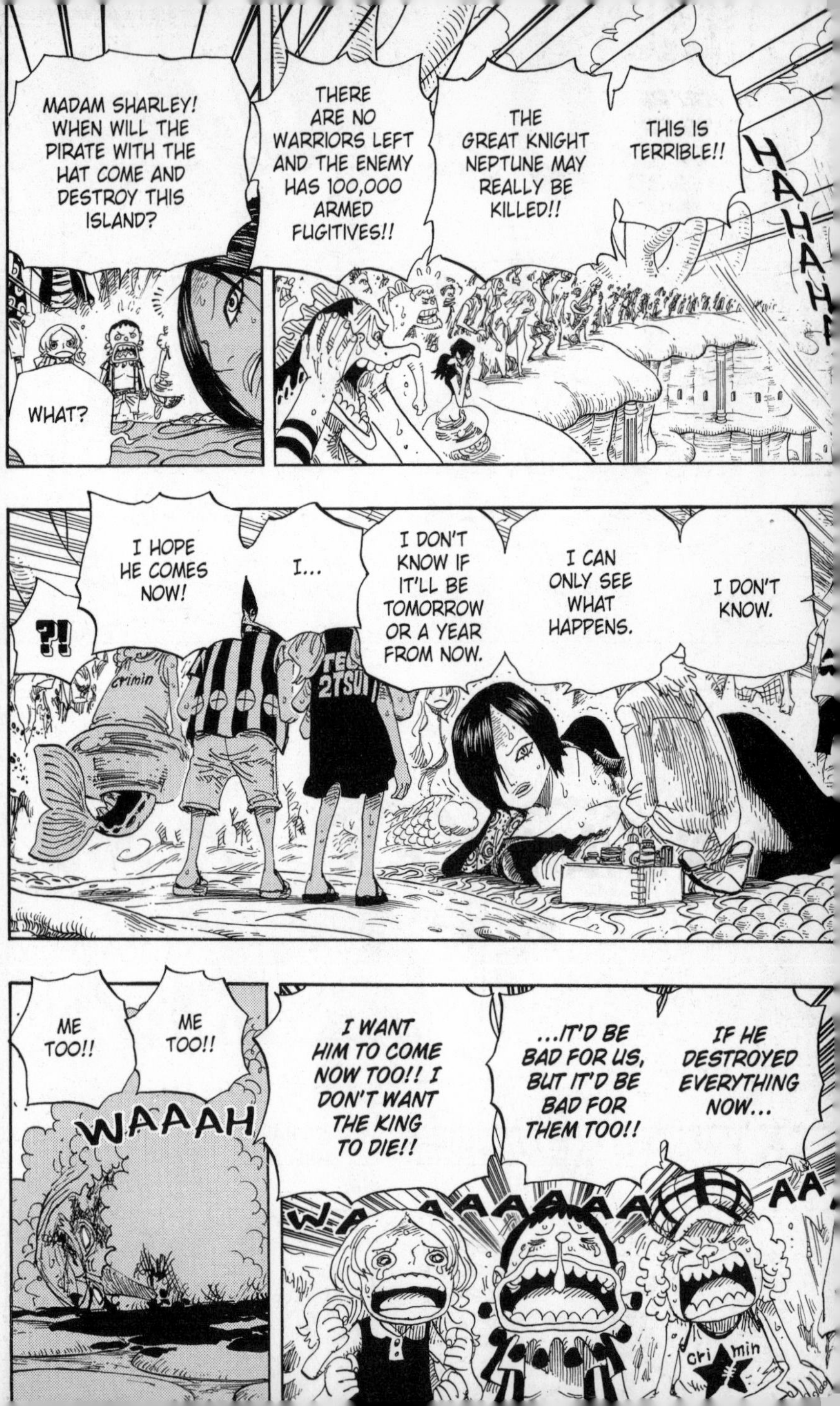
HAHAH
THIS IS TERRIBLE!!
THE GREAT KNIGHT NEPTUNE MAY REALLY BE KILLED!!
THERE ARE NO WARRIORS LEFT AND THE ENEMY HAS 100,000 ARMED FUGITIVES!!
MADAM SHARLEY! WHEN WILL THE PIRATE WITH THE HAT COME AND DESTROY THIS ISLAND?
WHAT?
I DON'T KNOW.
I CAN ONLY SEE WHAT HAPPENS.
I DON'T KNOW IF IT'LL BE TOMORROW OR A YEAR FROM NOW.
I...
I HOPE HE COMES NOW!
?!
crimin
IF HE DESTROYED EVERYTHING NOW...
...IT'D BE BAD FOR US, BUT IT'D BE BAD FOR THEM TOO!!
I WANT HIM TO COME NOW TOO!! I DON'T WANT THE KING TO DIE!!
WAAAAAAAAAA
AA
cri min
ME TOO!!
ME TOO!!
WAAAH

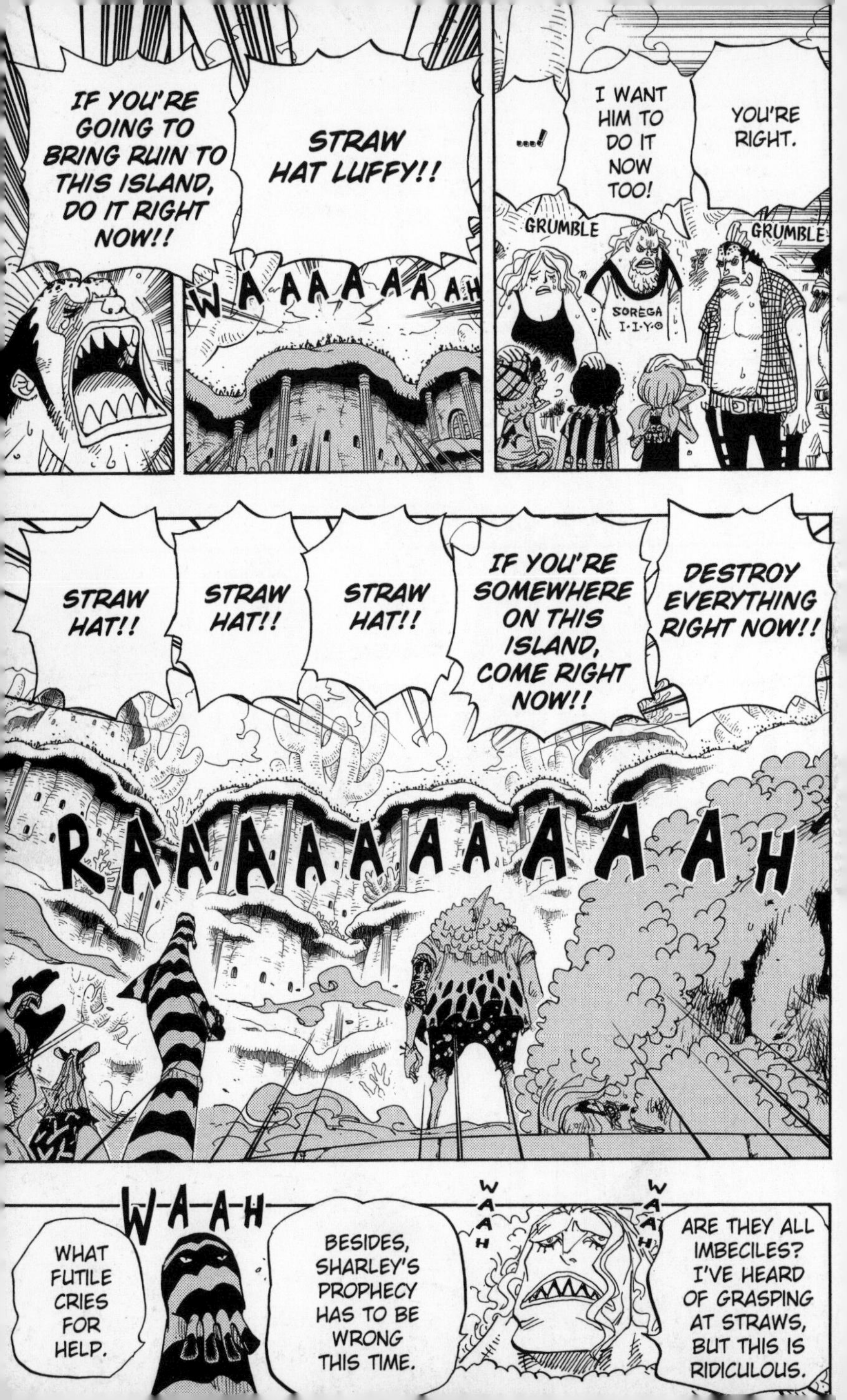
YOU'RE RIGHT.
I WANT HIM TO DO IT NOW TOO!
...!
GRUMBLE
GRUMBLE
SOREGA I·I·Y·O
STRAW HAT LUFFY!!
WAAAAAAAH
IF YOU'RE GOING TO BRING RUIN TO THIS ISLAND, DO IT RIGHT NOW!!
DESTROY EVERYTHING RIGHT NOW!!
IF YOU'RE SOMEWHERE ON THIS ISLAND, COME RIGHT NOW!!
STRAW HAT!!
STRAW HAT!!
STRAW HAT!!
RAAAAAAAAAAH
ARE THEY ALL IMBECILES? I'VE HEARD OF GRASPING AT STRAWS, BUT THIS IS RIDICULOUS.
WAAH
WAAH
BESIDES, SHARLEY'S PROPHECY HAS TO BE WRONG THIS TIME.
WAAH
WHAT FUTILE CRIES FOR HELP.

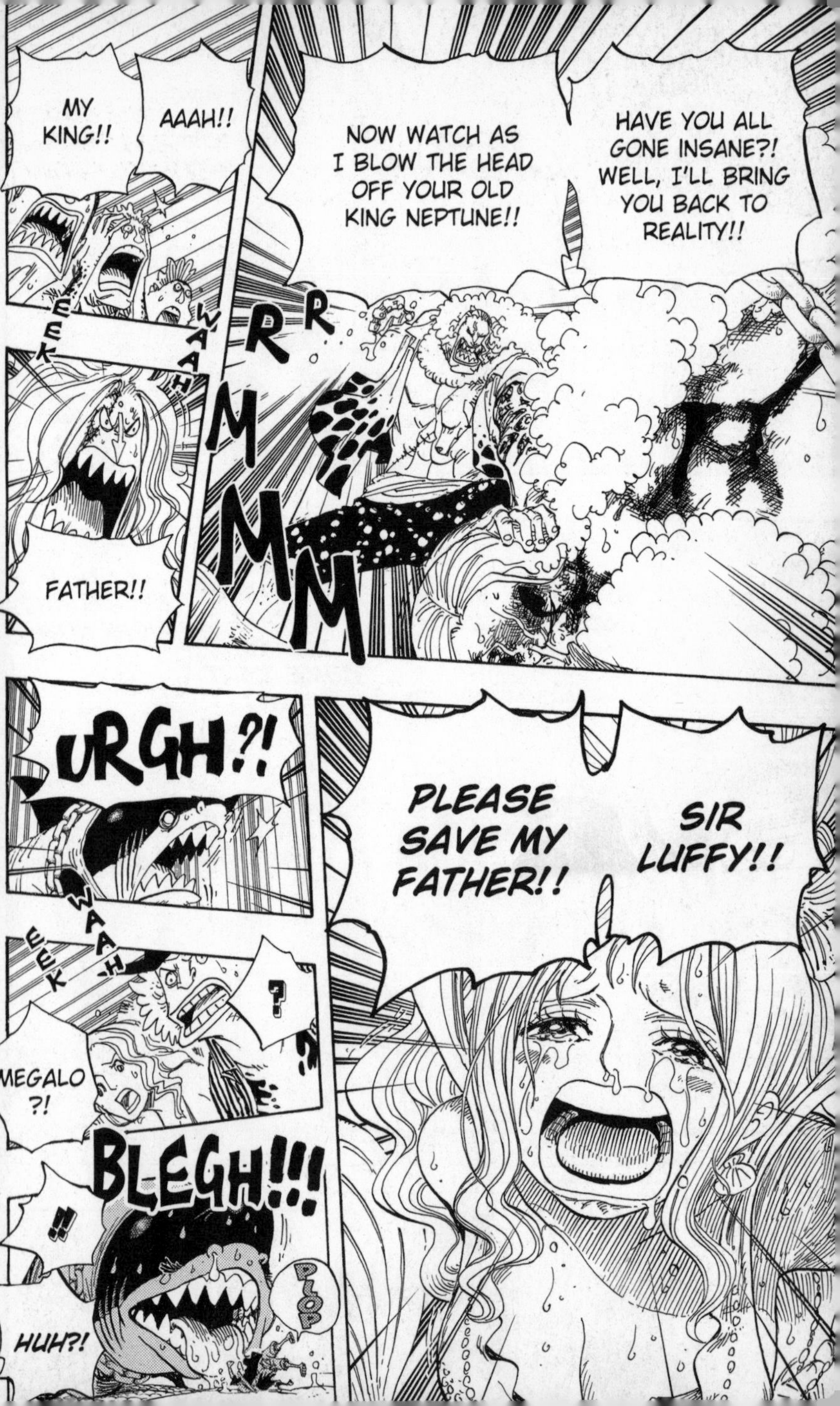
HAVE YOU ALL GONE INSANE?! WELL, I'LL BRING YOU BACK TO REALITY!!
NOW WATCH AS I BLOW THE HEAD OFF YOUR OLD KING NEPTUNE!!
RRMMMM
AAAH!!
MY KING!!
WAAAH
EEEK
FATHER!!
SIR LUFFY!!
PLEASE SAVE MY FATHER!!
URGH?!
WAAAH
EEEK
?
MEGALO ?!
BLEGH!!!
!!
PLOP
HUH?!

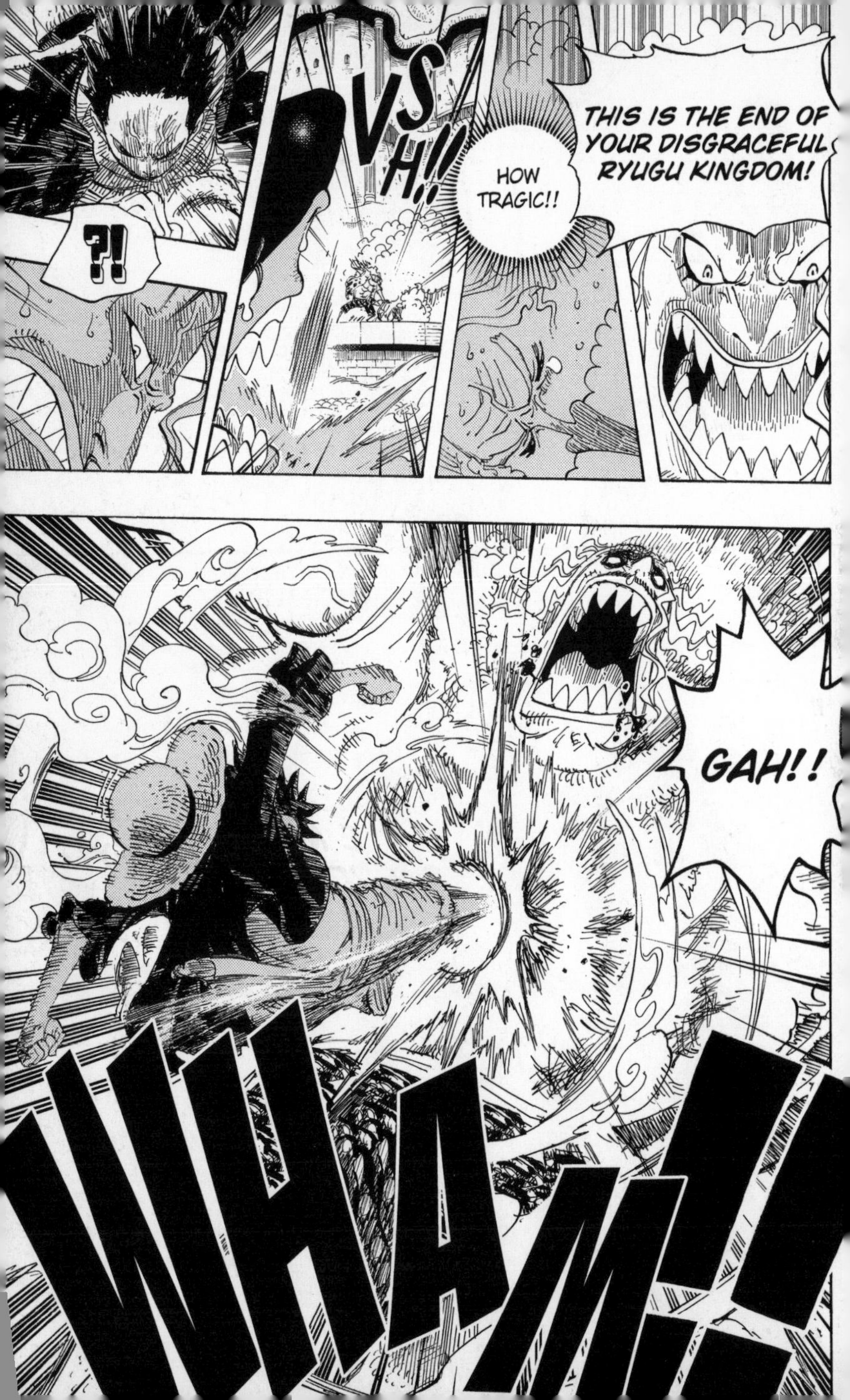
THIS IS THE END OF YOUR DISGRACEFUL RYUGU KINGDOM!
HOW TRAGIC!!
VSH!!
?!
GAH!!
WHAM!!

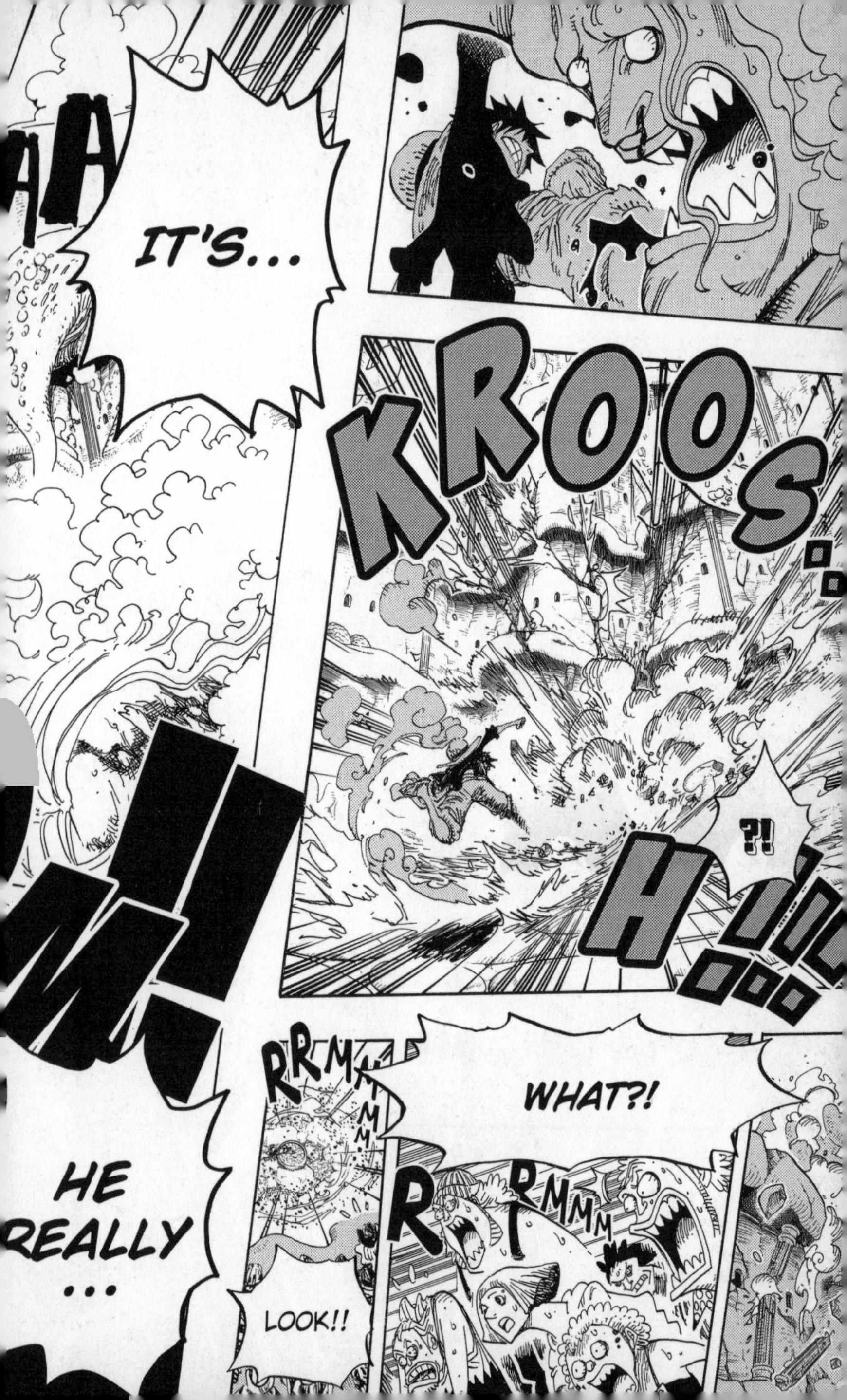
KROOSH!!!...
?!
AA
IT'S...
HE REALLY...
WHAT?!
RRMMMM
RRMMMM
RRMMMM
LOOK!!

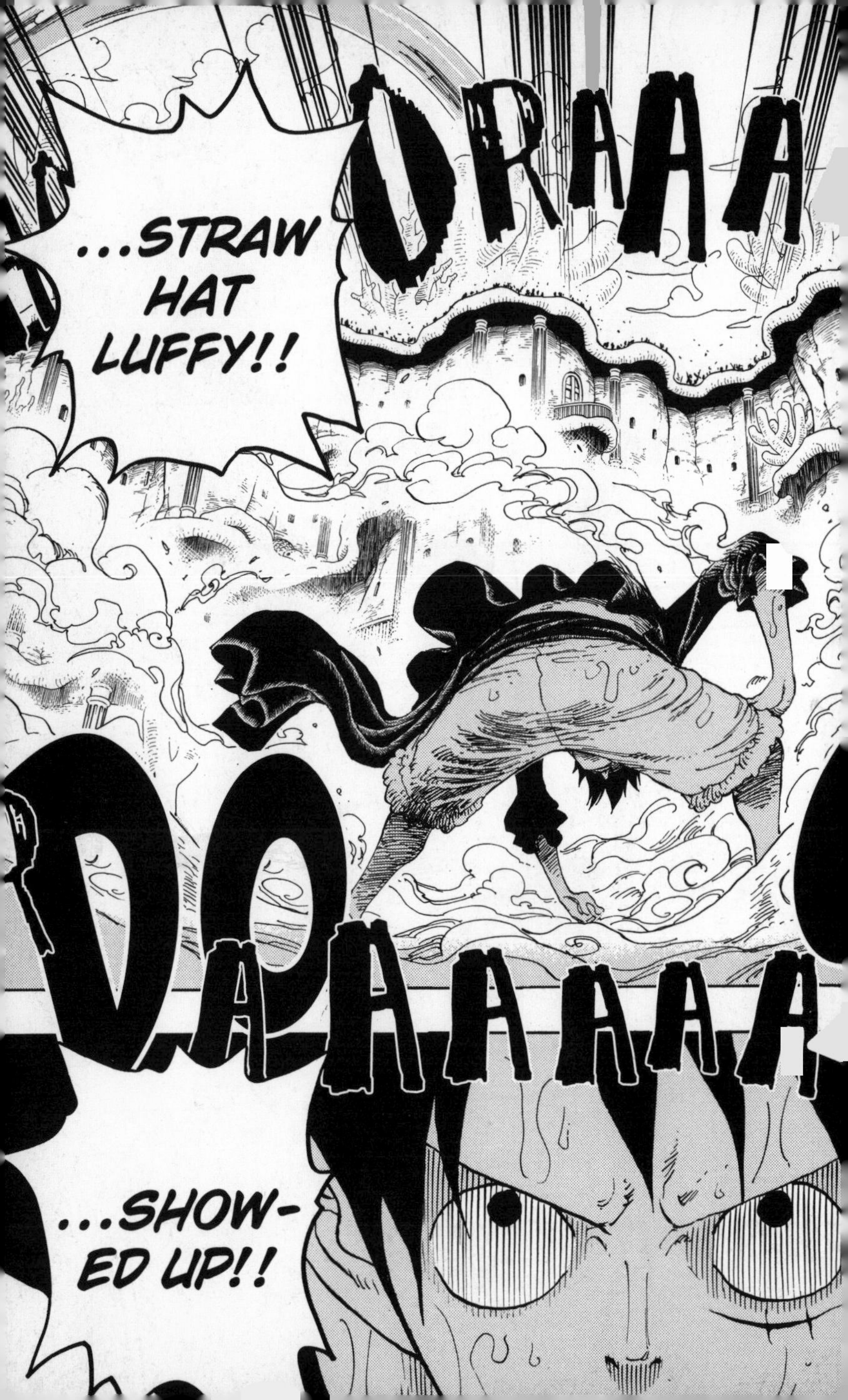
...STRAW HAT LUFFY!!
DORAAA
DODAAAAAA
...SHOW-ED UP!!

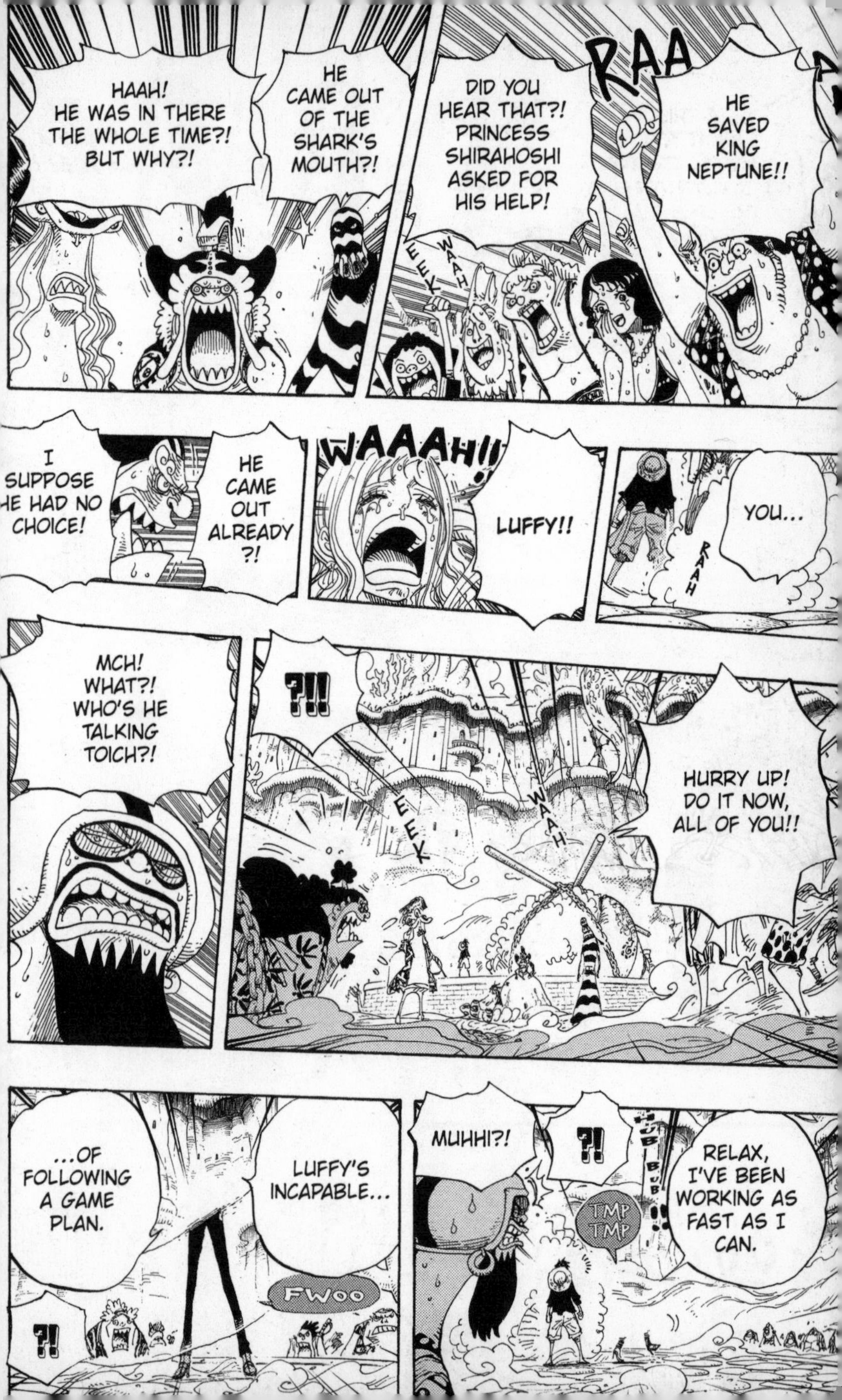
RAA
HE SAVED KING NEPTUNE!!
DID YOU HEAR THAT?! PRINCESS SHIRAHOSHI ASKED FOR HIS HELP!
WAAH
EEEK
HE CAME OUT OF THE SHARK'S MOUTH?!
HAAH! HE WAS IN THERE THE WHOLE TIME?! BUT WHY?!
YOU...
RAAH
LUFFY!!
WAAAH!!
HE CAME OUT ALREADY?!
I SUPPOSE HE HAD NO CHOICE!
HURRY UP! DO IT NOW, ALL OF YOU!!
WAAH
EEEK
?!!
MCH! WHAT?! WHO'S HE TALKING TOICH?!
RELAX, I'VE BEEN WORKING AS FAST AS I CAN.
BUB BUB
TMP TMP
?!
MUHHI?!
LUFFY'S INCAPABLE...
...OF FOLLOWING A GAME PLAN.
FWOO
?!

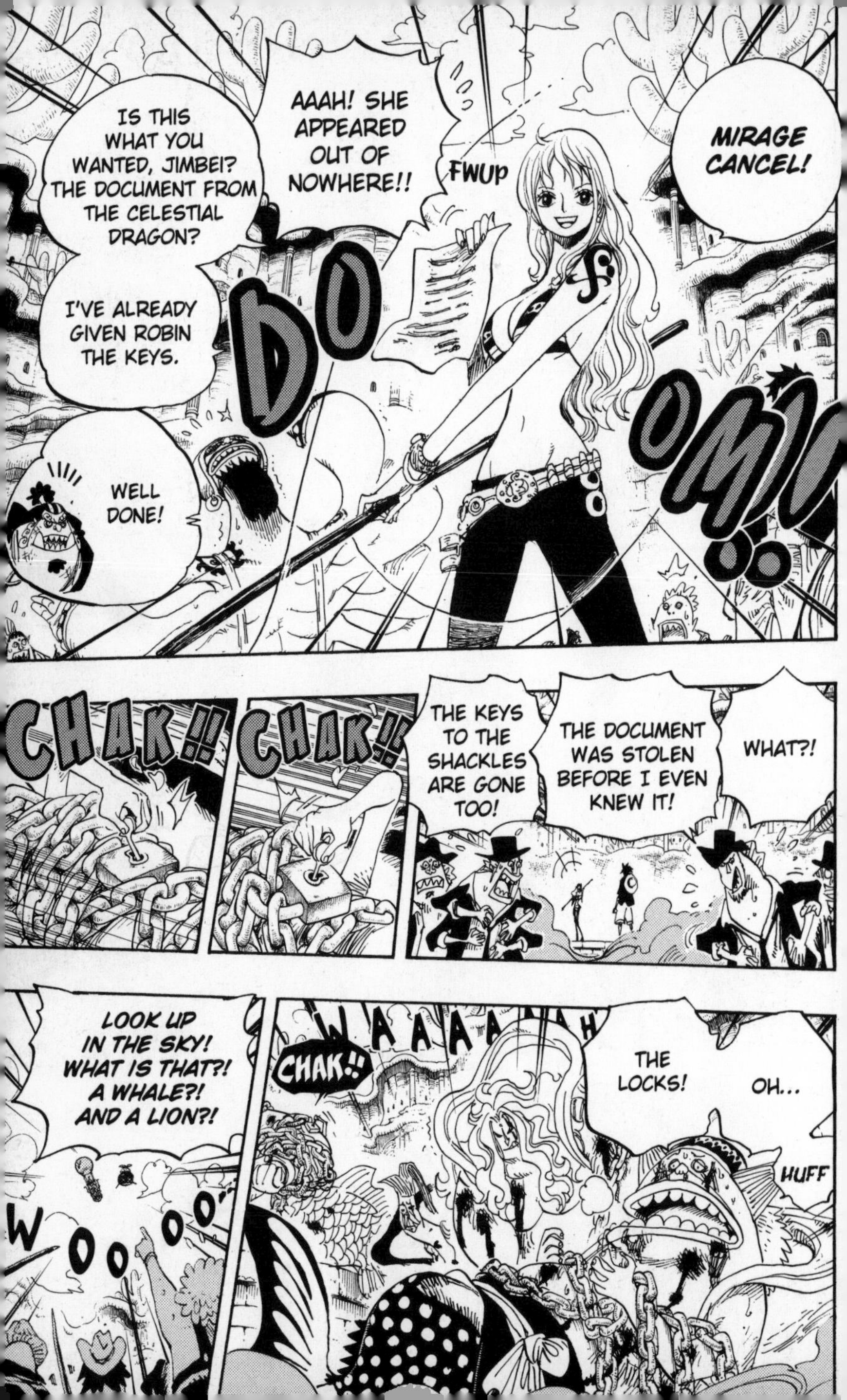
MIRAGE CANCEL!
FWUP
AAAH! SHE APPEARED OUT OF NOWHERE!!
IS THIS WHAT YOU WANTED, JIMBEI? THE DOCUMENT FROM THE CELESTIAL DRAGON?
I'VE ALREADY GIVEN ROBIN THE KEYS.
DOOM!!
WELL DONE!
WHAT?!
THE DOCUMENT WAS STOLEN BEFORE I EVEN KNEW IT!
THE KEYS TO THE SHACKLES ARE GONE TOO!
CHAK!!
CHAK!!
OH...
THE LOCKS!
HUFF
WAAAAAAH
CHAK!!
LOOK UP IN THE SKY! WHAT IS THAT?! A WHALE?! AND A LION?!
WOOOO

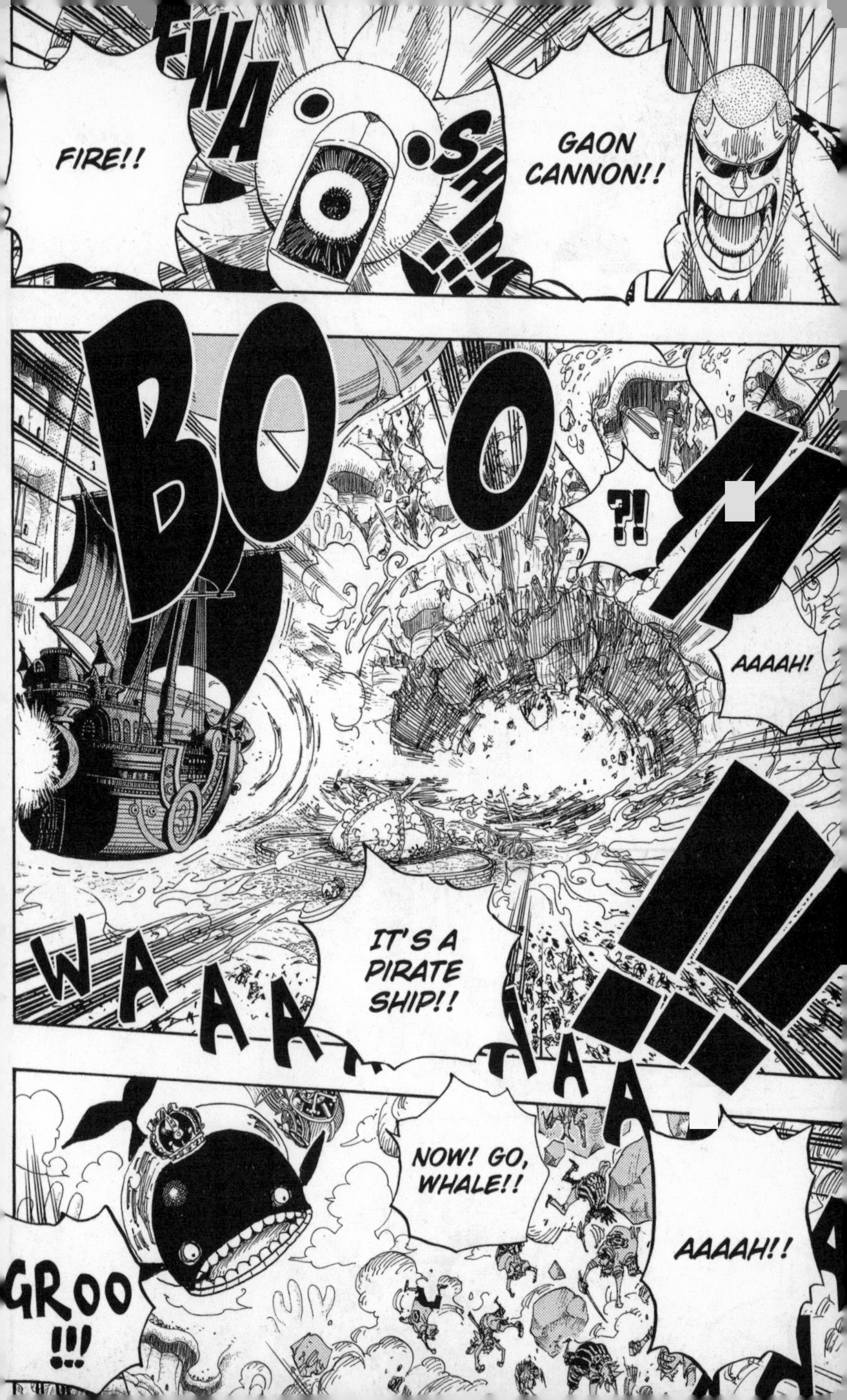
GAON CANNON!!
FIRE!!
?!
AAAAH!
IT'S A PIRATE SHIP!!
AAAAH!!
NOW! GO, WHALE!!
GROO !!!

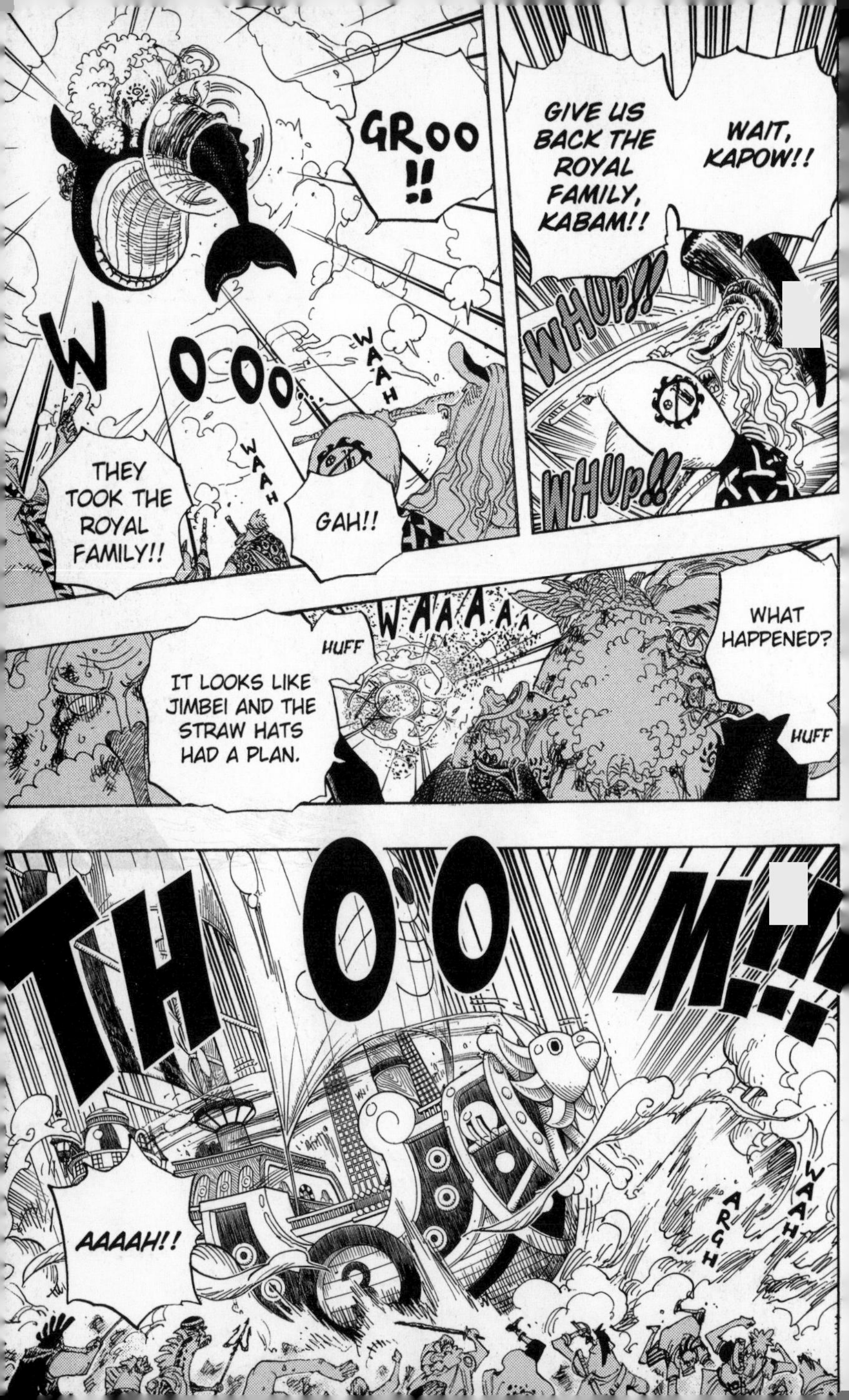
WAIT, KAPOW!!
GIVE US BACK THE ROYAL FAMILY, KABAM!!
WHUP!!
WHUP!!
GROO!!
WOOO...
WAAH
WAAH
GAH!!
THEY TOOK THE ROYAL FAMILY!!
WHAT HAPPENED?
HUFF
WAAAAA
HUFF
IT LOOKS LIKE JIMBEI AND THE STRAW HATS HAD A PLAN.
THOOOM!!
WAAAH
ARGH
AAAAH!!

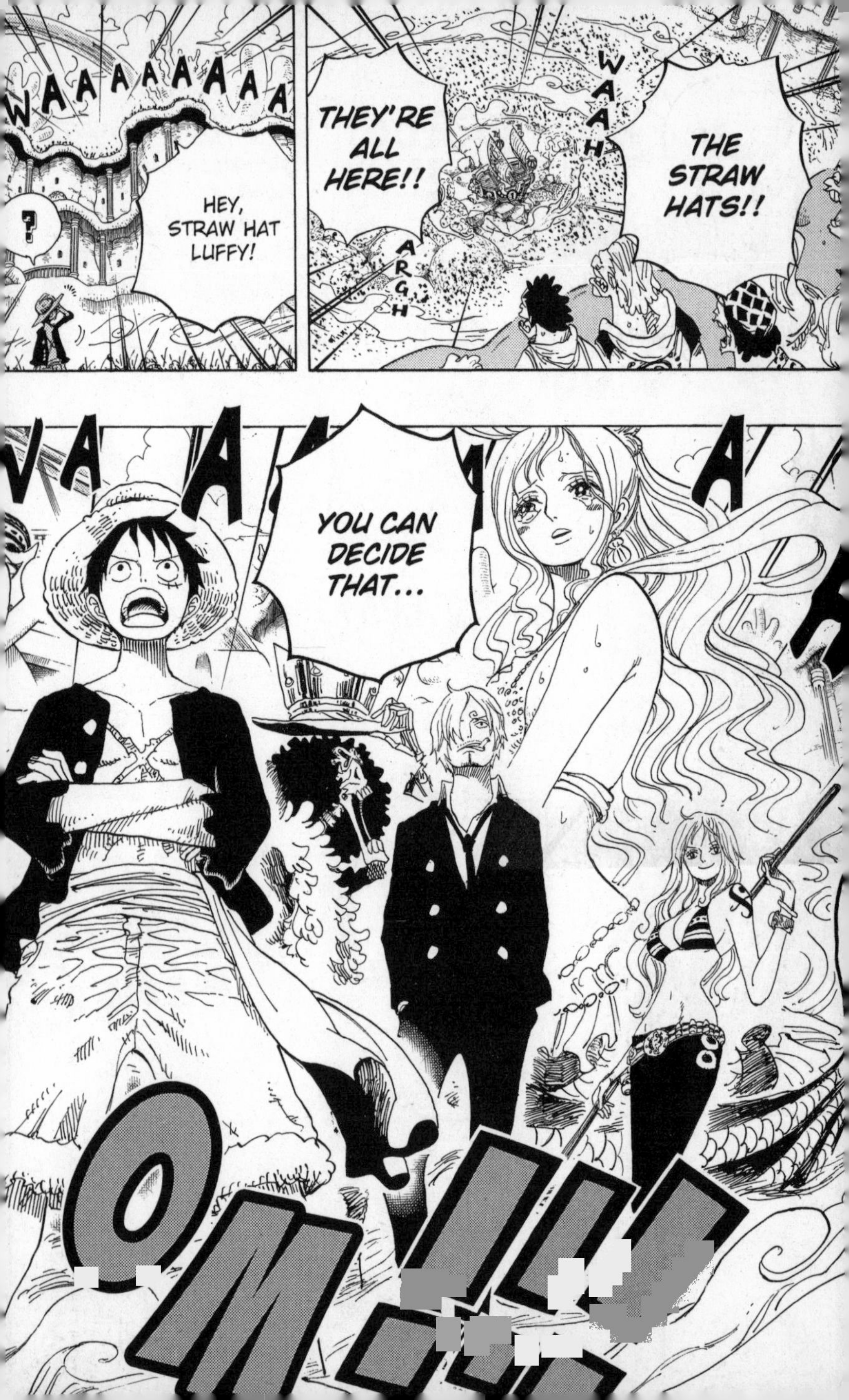
THE STRAW HATS!!
WAAH
THEY'RE ALL HERE!!
ARGH
WAAAAAAAA
HEY, STRAW HAT LUFFY!
?
YOU CAN DECIDE THAT...

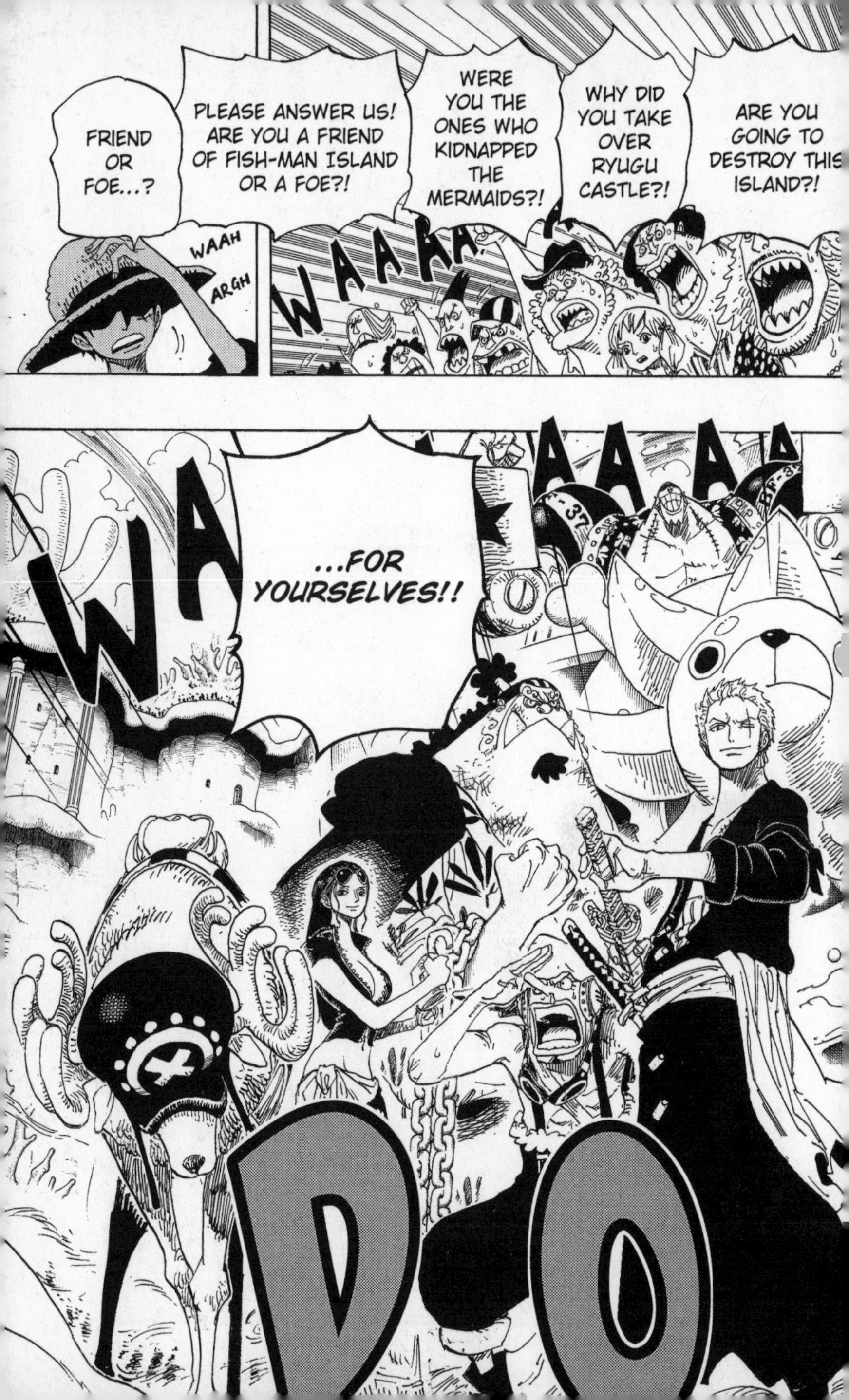
ARE YOU GOING TO DESTROY THIS ISLAND?!
WHY DID YOU TAKE OVER RYUGU CASTLE?!
WERE YOU THE ONES WHO KIDNAPPED THE MERMAIDS?!
PLEASE ANSWER US! ARE YOU A FRIEND OF FISH-MAN ISLAND OR A FOE?!
WAAAA
FRIEND OR FOE...?
WAAH
ARGH
WAAAAA
...FOR YOURSELVES!!
DO

100,000 VS. 10

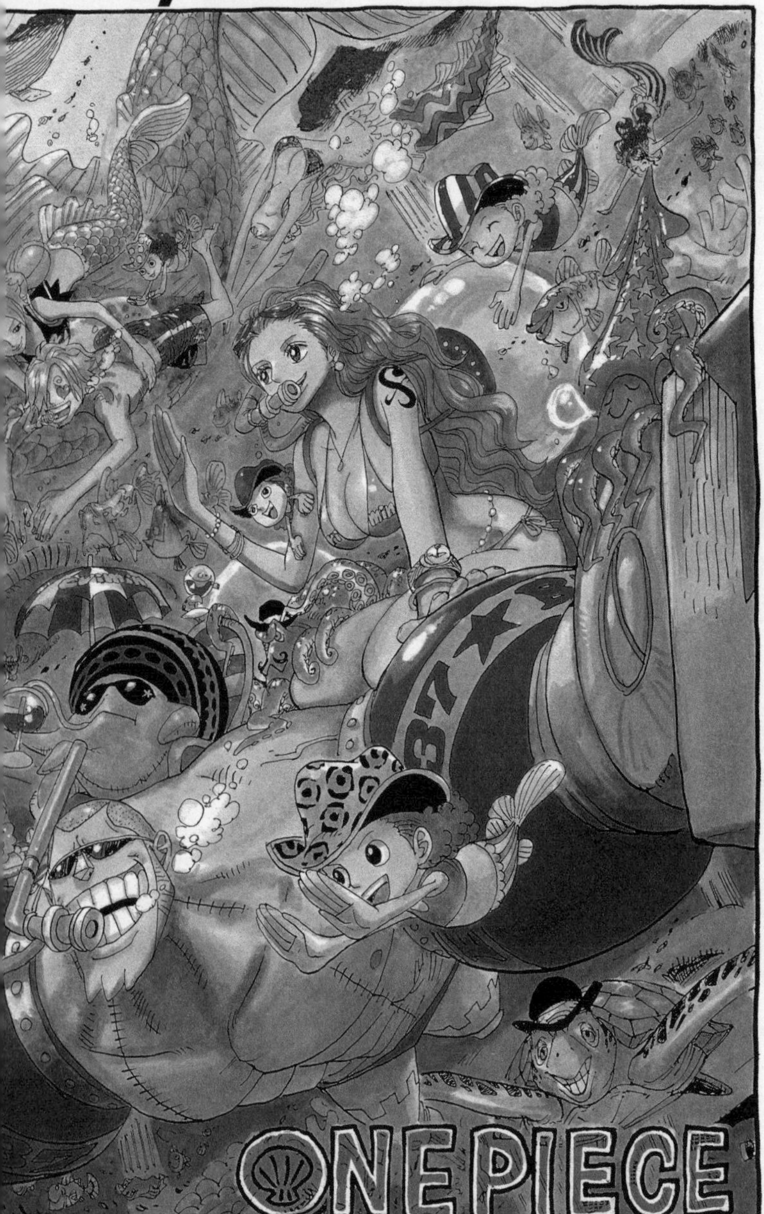

ONE PIECE

Chapter 634:

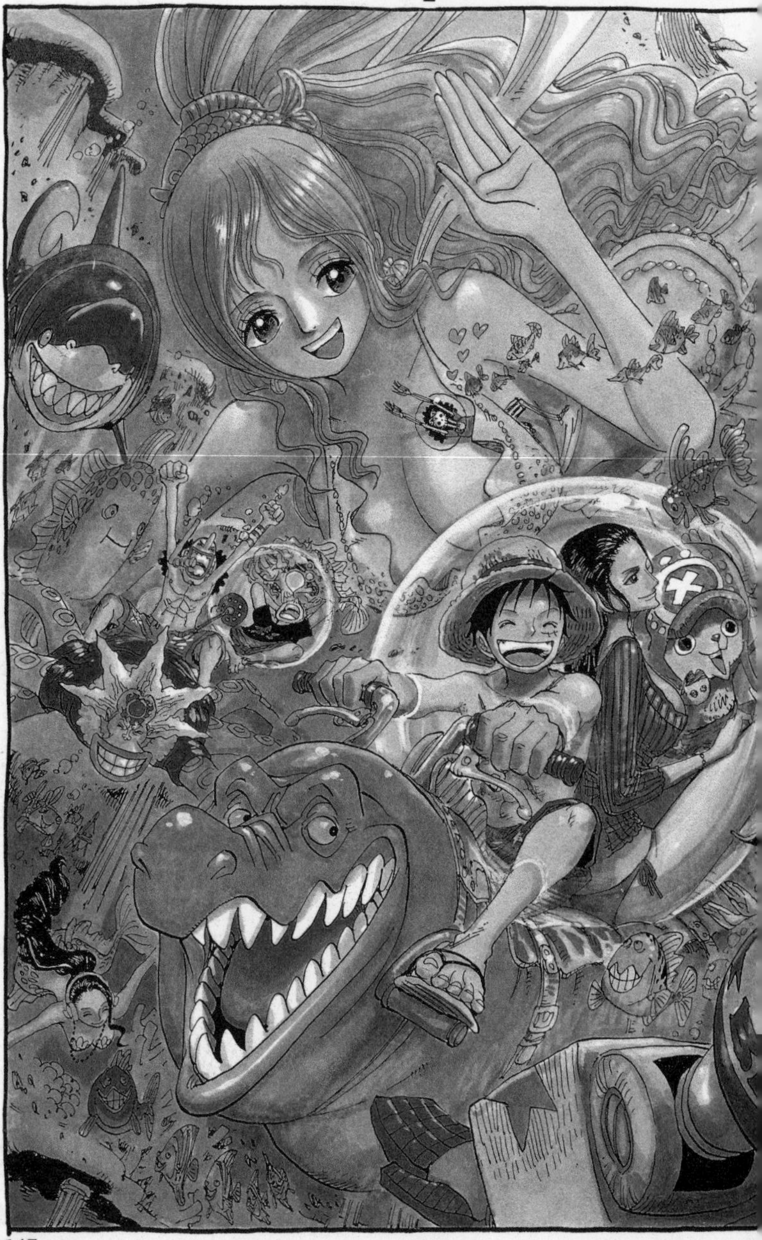

vol.64
ONE PIECE

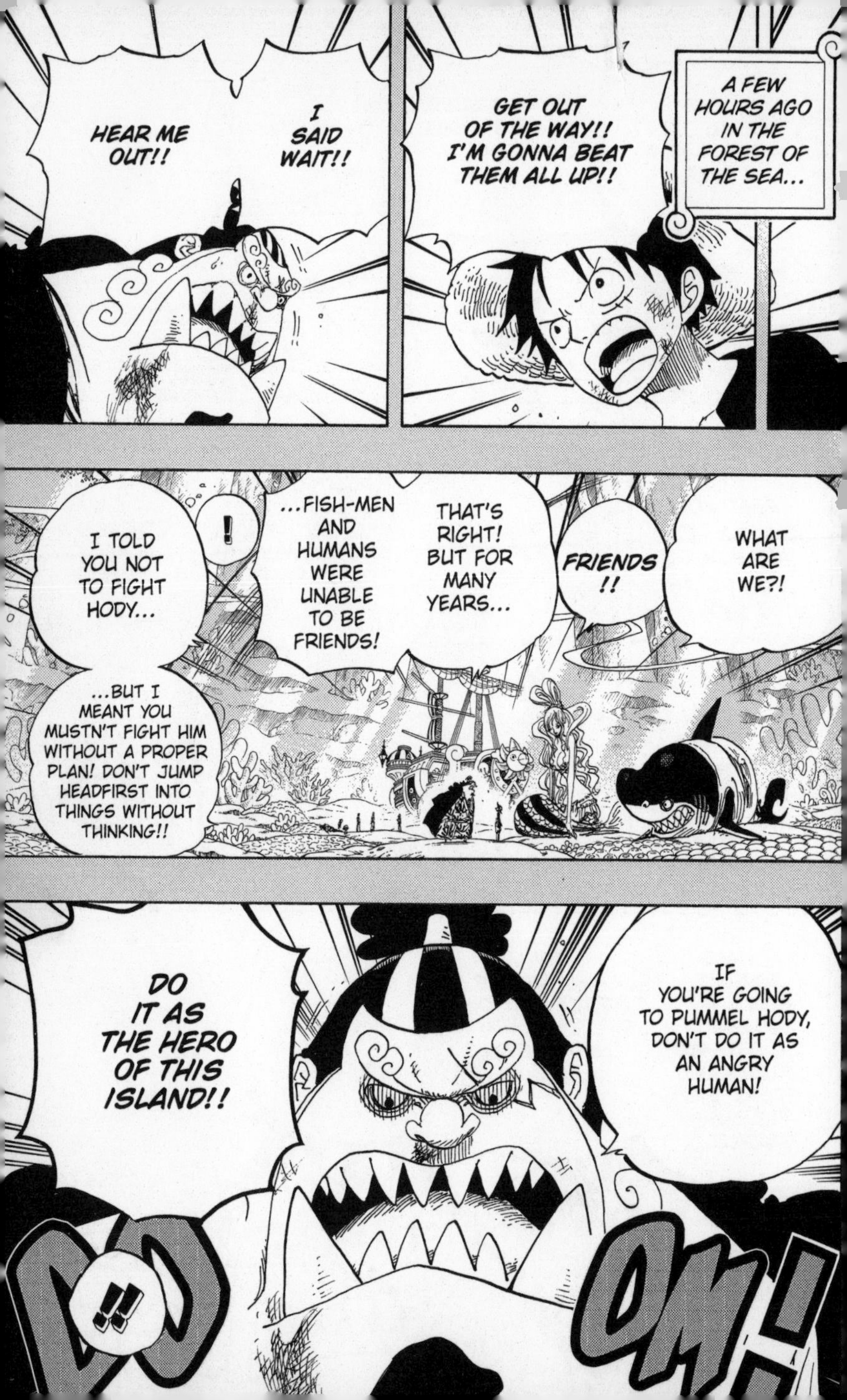

A FEW HOURS AGO IN THE FOREST OF THE SEA...
GET OUT OF THE WAY!! I'M GONNA BEAT THEM ALL UP!!
I SAID WAIT!!
HEAR ME OUT!!
WHAT ARE WE?!
FRIENDS !!
THAT'S RIGHT! BUT FOR MANY YEARS...
...FISH-MEN AND HUMANS WERE UNABLE TO BE FRIENDS!
!
I TOLD YOU NOT TO FIGHT HODY...
...BUT I MEANT YOU MUSTN'T FIGHT HIM WITHOUT A PROPER PLAN! DON'T JUMP HEADFIRST INTO THINGS WITHOUT THINKING!!
IF YOU'RE GOING TO PUMMEL HODY, DON'T DO IT AS AN ANGRY HUMAN!
DO IT AS THE HERO OF THIS ISLAND!!
!!
GOOM!

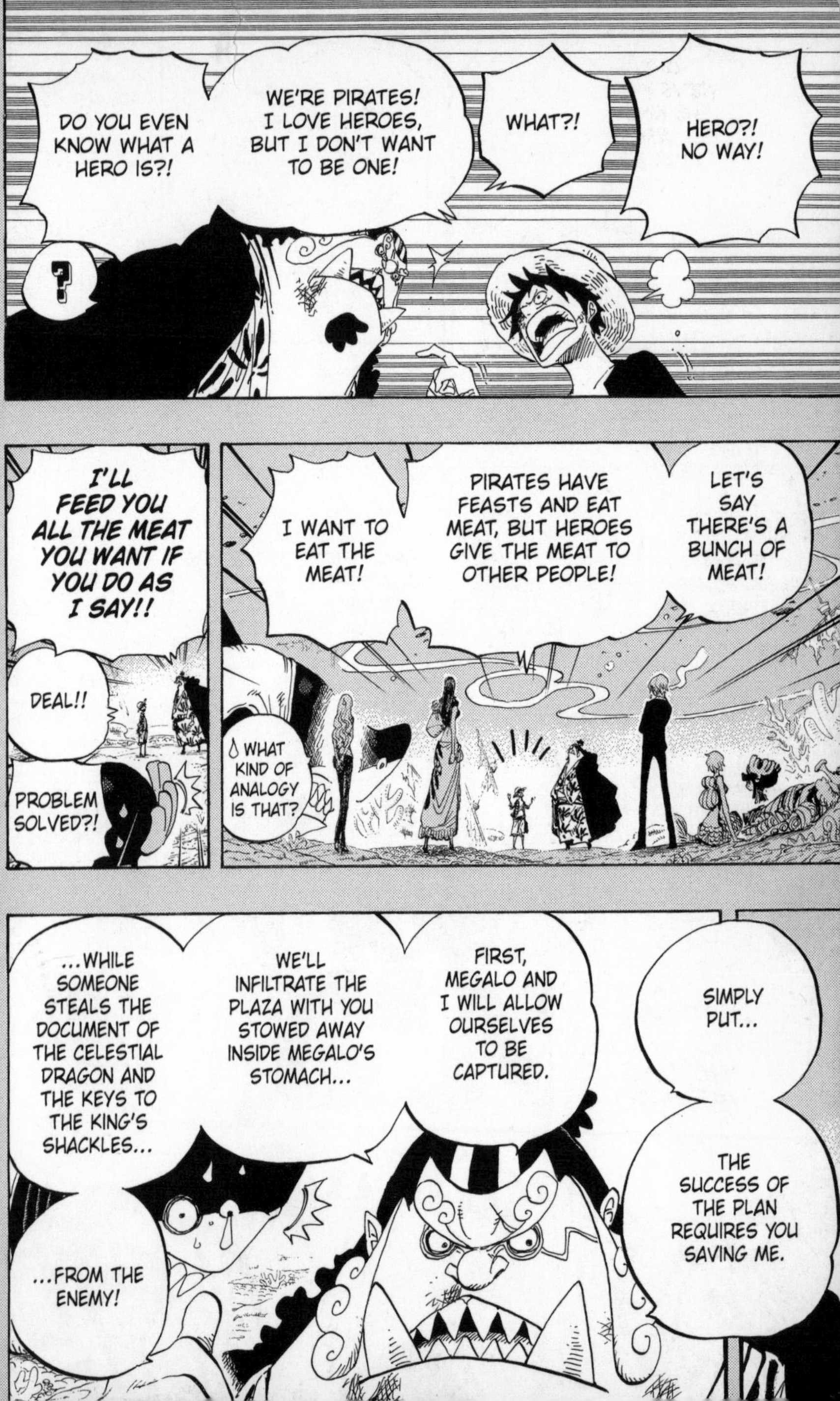
HERO?! NO WAY!
WHAT?!
WE'RE PIRATES! I LOVE HEROES, BUT I DON'T WANT TO BE ONE!
DO YOU EVEN KNOW WHAT A HERO IS?!
?
LET'S SAY THERE'S A BUNCH OF MEAT!
PIRATES HAVE FEASTS AND EAT MEAT, BUT HEROES GIVE THE MEAT TO OTHER PEOPLE!
I WANT TO EAT THE MEAT!
WHAT KIND OF ANALOGY IS THAT?
I'LL FEED YOU ALL THE MEAT YOU WANT IF YOU DO AS I SAY!!
DEAL!!
PROBLEM SOLVED?!
SIMPLY PUT...
FIRST, MEGALO AND I WILL ALLOW OURSELVES TO BE CAPTURED.
WE'LL INFILTRATE THE PLAZA WITH YOU STOWED AWAY INSIDE MEGALO'S STOMACH...
...WHILE SOMEONE STEALS THE DOCUMENT OF THE CELESTIAL DRAGON AND THE KEYS TO THE KING'S SHACKLES...
THE SUCCESS OF THE PLAN REQUIRES YOU SAVING ME.
...FROM THE ENEMY!

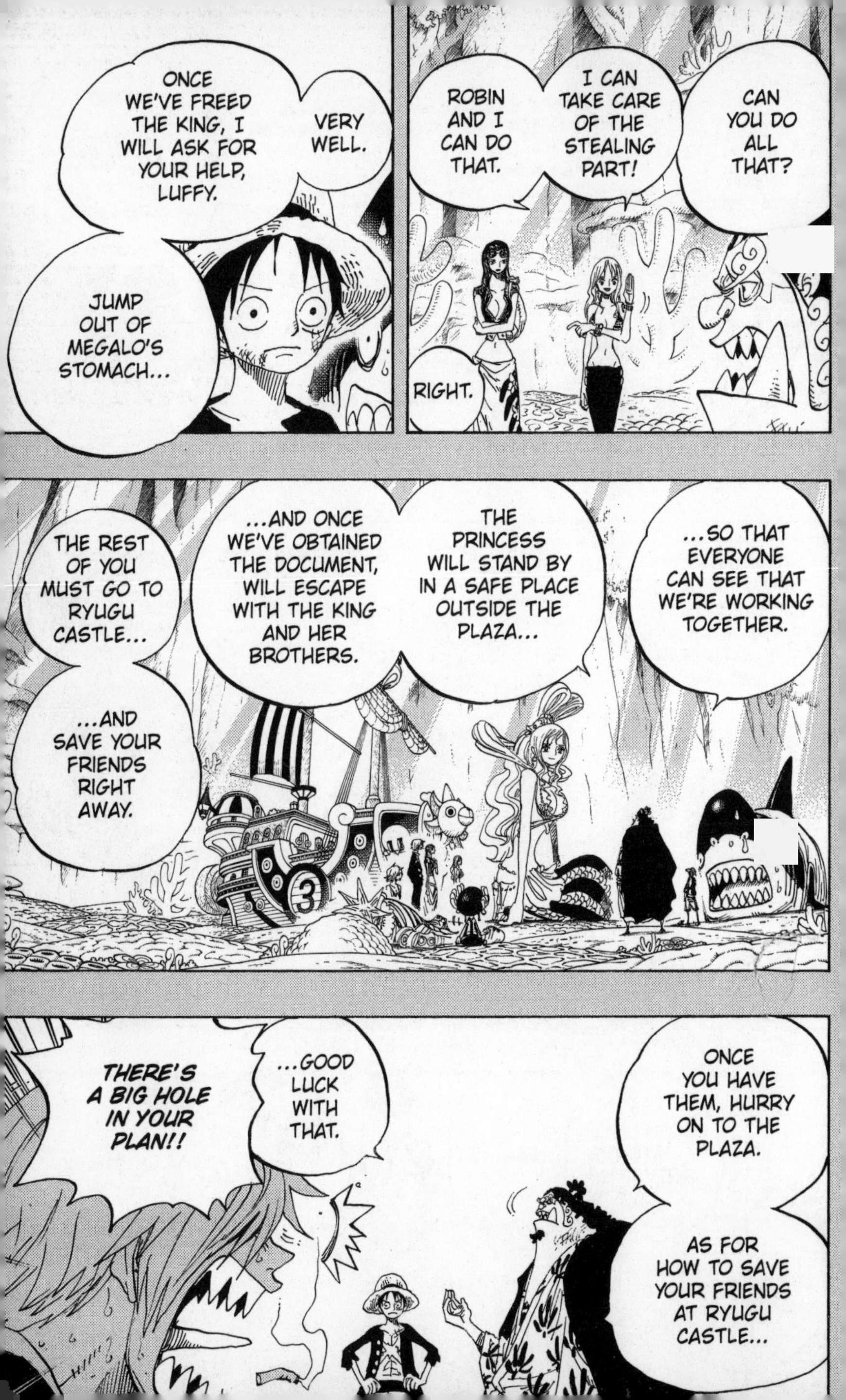
CAN YOU DO ALL THAT?
I CAN TAKE CARE OF THE STEALING PART!
ROBIN AND I CAN DO THAT.
RIGHT.
VERY WELL.
ONCE WE'VE FREED THE KING, I WILL ASK FOR YOUR HELP, LUFFY.
JUMP OUT OF MEGALO'S STOMACH...
THE PRINCESS WILL STAND BY IN A SAFE PLACE OUTSIDE THE PLAZA...
...SO THAT EVERYONE CAN SEE THAT WE'RE WORKING TOGETHER.
...AND ONCE WE'VE OBTAINED THE DOCUMENT, WILL ESCAPE WITH THE KING AND HER BROTHERS.
THE REST OF YOU MUST GO TO RYUGU CASTLE...
...AND SAVE YOUR FRIENDS RIGHT AWAY.
ONCE YOU HAVE THEM, HURRY ON TO THE PLAZA.
AS FOR HOW TO SAVE YOUR FRIENDS AT RYUGU CASTLE...
...GOOD LUCK WITH THAT.
THERE'S A BIG HOLE IN YOUR PLAN!!

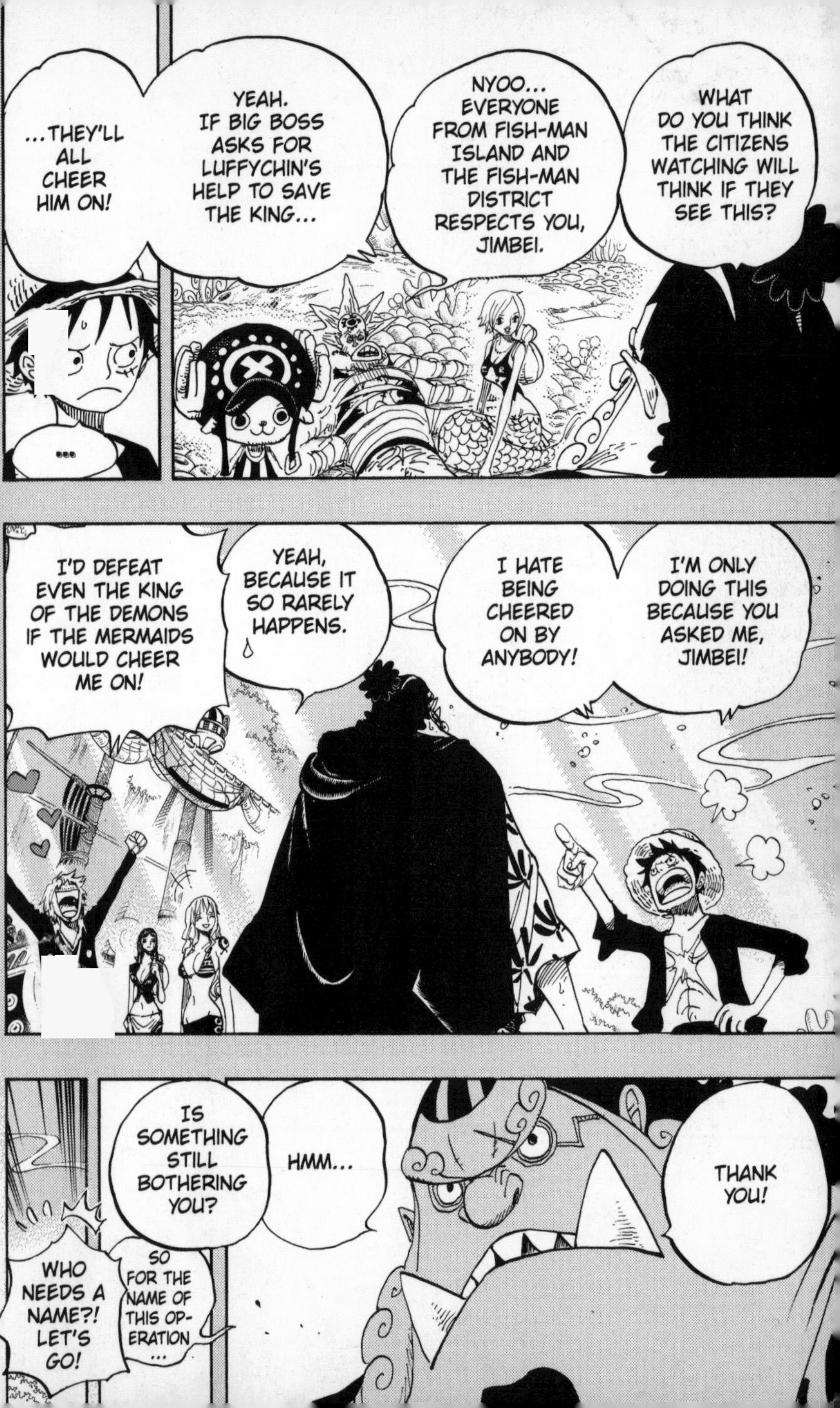
WHAT DO YOU THINK THE CITIZENS WATCHING WILL THINK IF THEY SEE THIS?
NYOO... EVERYONE FROM FISH-MAN ISLAND AND THE FISH-MAN DISTRICT RESPECTS YOU, JIMBEI.
YEAH. IF BIG BOSS ASKS FOR LUFFYCHIN'S HELP TO SAVE THE KING...
...THEY'LL ALL CHEER HIM ON!
...
I'M ONLY DOING THIS BECAUSE YOU ASKED ME, JIMBEI!
I HATE BEING CHEERED ON BY ANYBODY!
YEAH, BECAUSE IT SO RARELY HAPPENS.
I'D DEFEAT EVEN THE KING OF THE DEMONS IF THE MERMAIDS WOULD CHEER ME ON!
THANK YOU!
HMM...
IS SOMETHING STILL BOTHERING YOU?
SO FOR THE NAME OF THIS OPERATION...
WHO NEEDS A NAME?! LET'S GO!

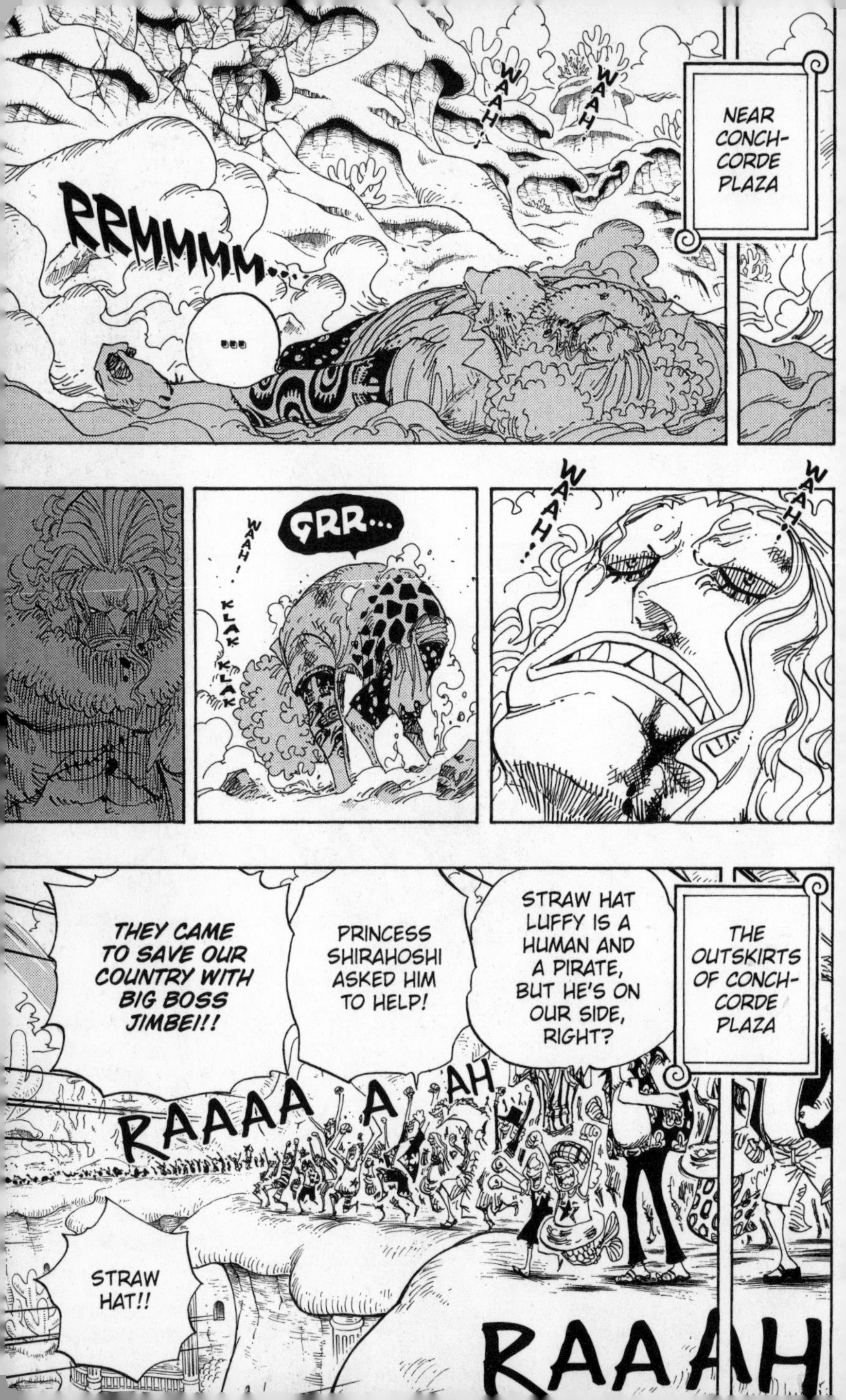
NEAR CONCH-CORDE PLAZA
WAAH!
WAAH!
RRMMMM...
...
WAAH!
WAAH!...
GRR...
WAAH!
KLAK KLAK
THE OUTSKIRTS OF CONCH-CORDE PLAZA
STRAW HAT LUFFY IS A HUMAN AND A PIRATE, BUT HE'S ON OUR SIDE, RIGHT?
PRINCESS SHIRAHOSHI ASKED HIM TO HELP!
THEY CAME TO SAVE OUR COUNTRY WITH BIG BOSS JIMBEI!!
RAAAAA A AH
STRAW HAT!!
RAAAH

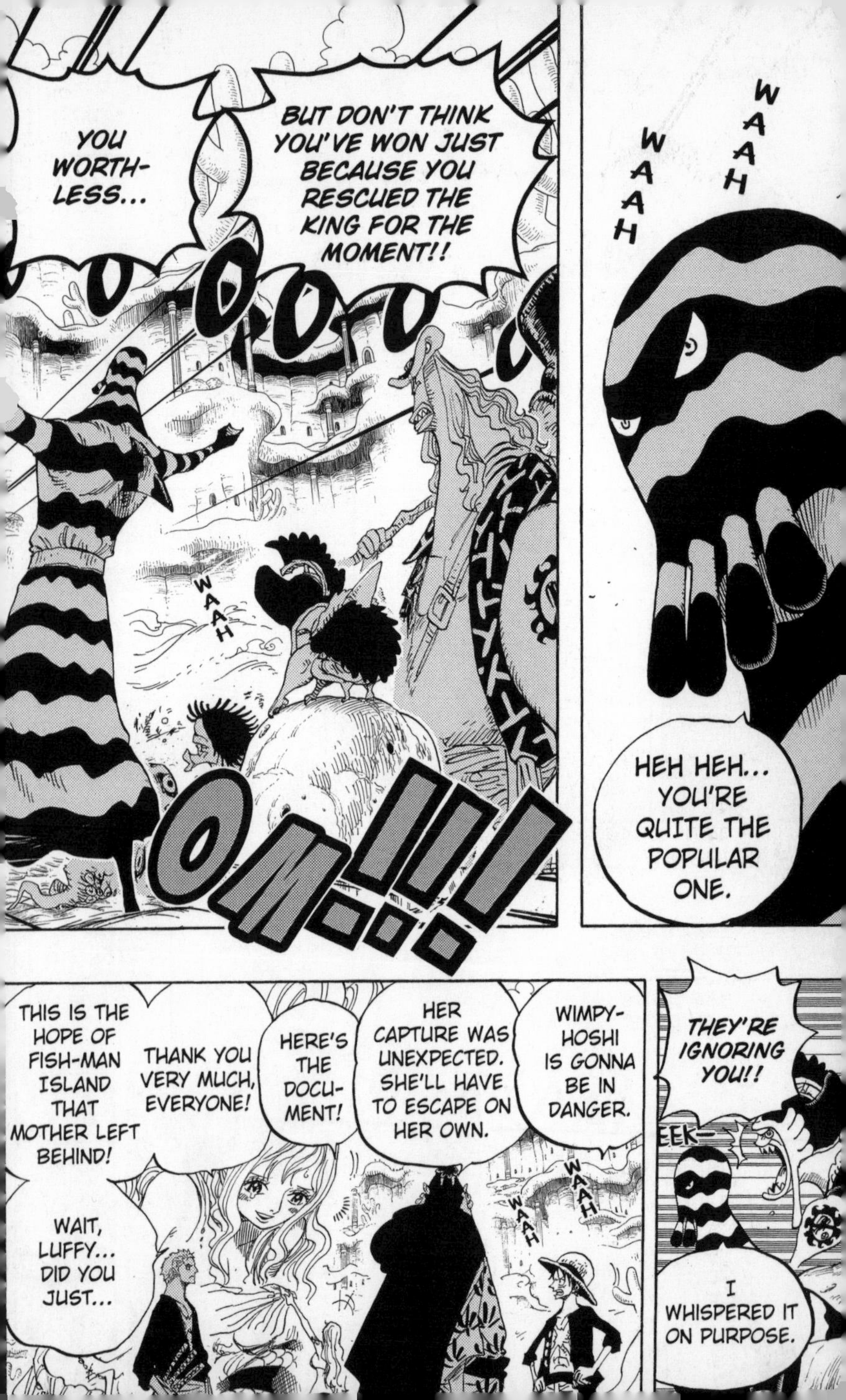
WAAH
WAAH
HEH HEH... YOU'RE QUITE THE POPULAR ONE.
YOU WORTHLESS...
BUT DON'T THINK YOU'VE WON JUST BECAUSE YOU RESCUED THE KING FOR THE MOMENT!!
WAAH
OH...!!!
THEY'RE IGNORING YOU!!
EEK—
I WHISPERED IT ON PURPOSE.
WIMPY-HOSHI IS GONNA BE IN DANGER.
HER CAPTURE WAS UNEXPECTED. SHE'LL HAVE TO ESCAPE ON HER OWN.
HERE'S THE DOCUMENT!
THANK YOU VERY MUCH, EVERYONE!
THIS IS THE HOPE OF FISH-MAN ISLAND THAT MOTHER LEFT BEHIND!
WAAH
WAAH
WAIT, LUFFY... DID YOU JUST...

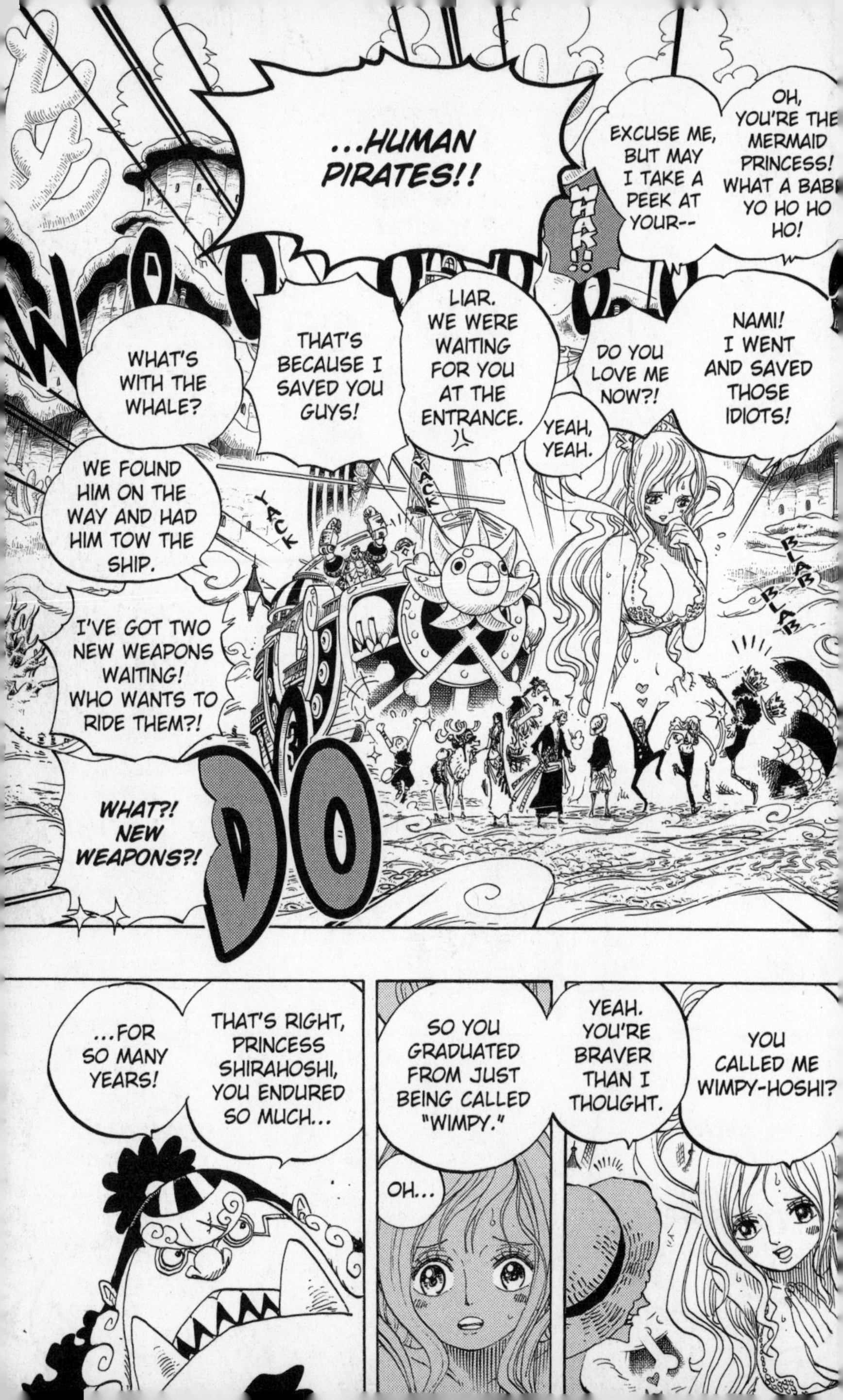
OH, YOU'RE THE MERMAID PRINCESS! WHAT A BAB YO HO HO HO!
EXCUSE ME, BUT MAY I TAKE A PEEK AT YOUR--
WHAK!!
...HUMAN PIRATES!!
NAMI! I WENT AND SAVED THOSE IDIOTS!
DO YOU LOVE ME NOW?!
YEAH, YEAH.
LIAR. WE WERE WAITING FOR YOU AT THE ENTRANCE.
THAT'S BECAUSE I SAVED YOU GUYS!
WHAT'S WITH THE WHALE?
WE FOUND HIM ON THE WAY AND HAD HIM TOW THE SHIP.
YACK
YACK
BLAB BLAB
I'VE GOT TWO NEW WEAPONS WAITING! WHO WANTS TO RIDE THEM?!
WHAT?! NEW WEAPONS?!
DO
YOU CALLED ME WIMPY-HOSHI?
YEAH. YOU'RE BRAVER THAN I THOUGHT.
SO YOU GRADUATED FROM JUST BEING CALLED "WIMPY."
OH...
THAT'S RIGHT, PRINCESS SHIRAHOSHI, YOU ENDURED SO MUCH...
...FOR SO MANY YEARS!

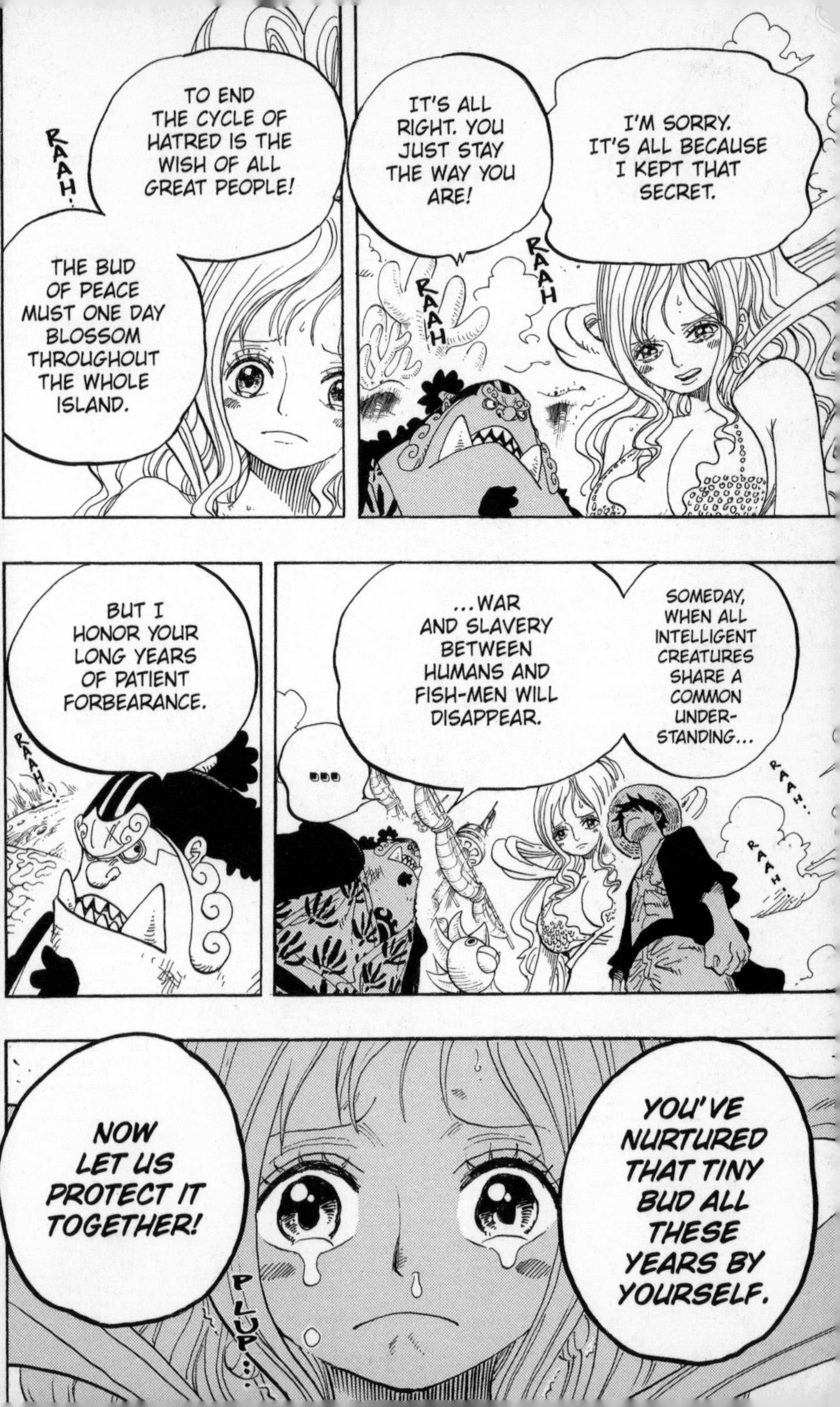
I'M SORRY. IT'S ALL BECAUSE I KEPT THAT SECRET.
RAAH
IT'S ALL RIGHT. YOU JUST STAY THE WAY YOU ARE!
RAAH
TO END THE CYCLE OF HATRED IS THE WISH OF ALL GREAT PEOPLE!
RAAH!
THE BUD OF PEACE MUST ONE DAY BLOSSOM THROUGHOUT THE WHOLE ISLAND.
SOMEDAY, WHEN ALL INTELLIGENT CREATURES SHARE A COMMON UNDER-STANDING...
...WAR AND SLAVERY BETWEEN HUMANS AND FISH-MEN WILL DISAPPEAR.
RAAH...
RAAH...
...
RAAH...
BUT I HONOR YOUR LONG YEARS OF PATIENT FORBEARANCE.
YOU'VE NURTURED THAT TINY BUD ALL THESE YEARS BY YOURSELF.
NOW LET US PROTECT IT TOGETHER!
PLUP...

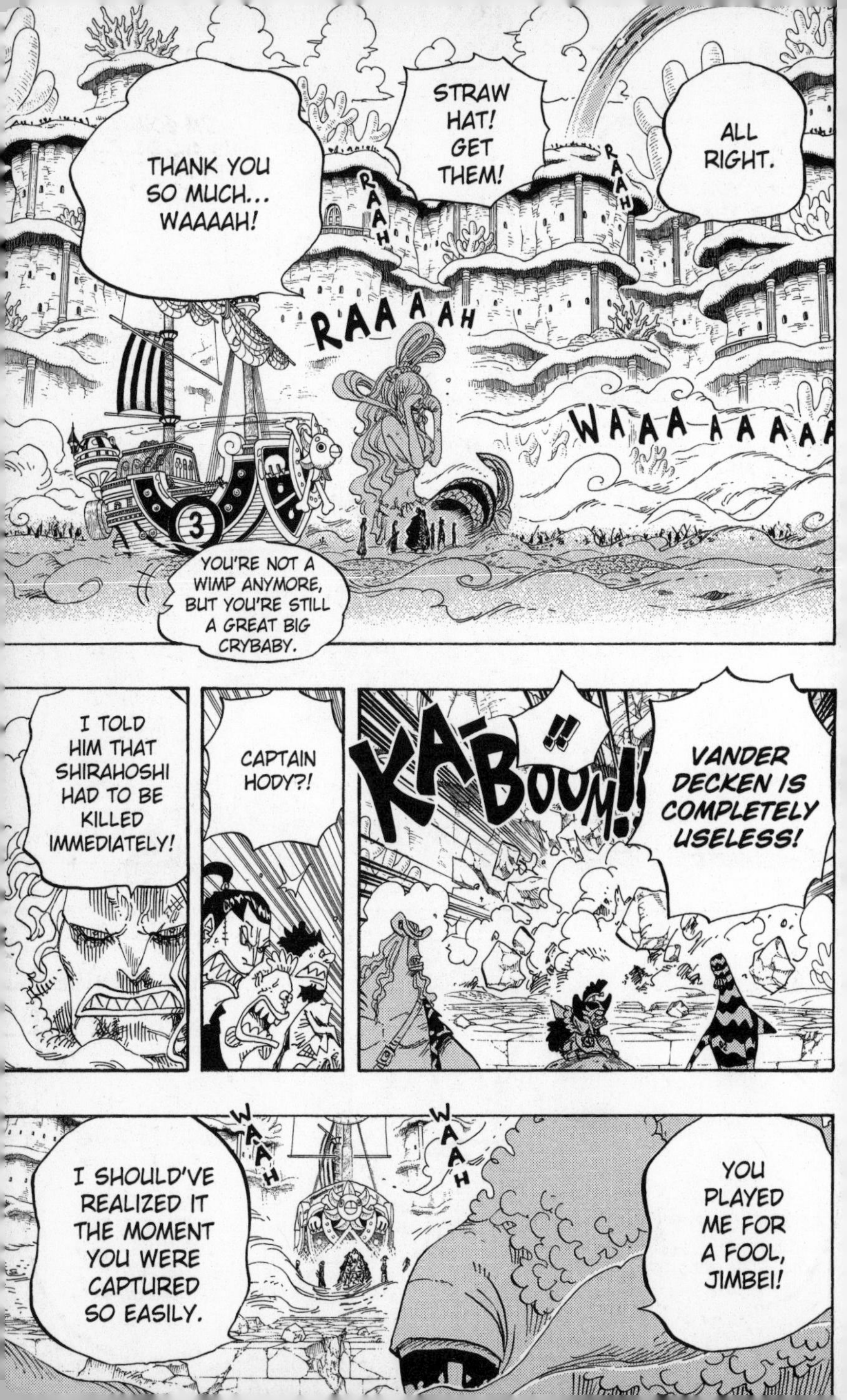
ALL RIGHT.
RAAH
STRAW HAT! GET THEM!
RAAH
THANK YOU SO MUCH... WAAAAH!
WAAAAAAAAA
RAAAAH
YOU'RE NOT A WIMP ANYMORE, BUT YOU'RE STILL A GREAT BIG CRYBABY.
!!
VANDER DECKEN IS COMPLETELY USELESS!
KA-BOOM!!
CAPTAIN HODY?!
I TOLD HIM THAT SHIRAHOSHI HAD TO BE KILLED IMMEDIATELY!
YOU PLAYED ME FOR A FOOL, JIMBEI!
WAAH
WAAH
I SHOULD'VE REALIZED IT THE MOMENT YOU WERE CAPTURED SO EASILY.

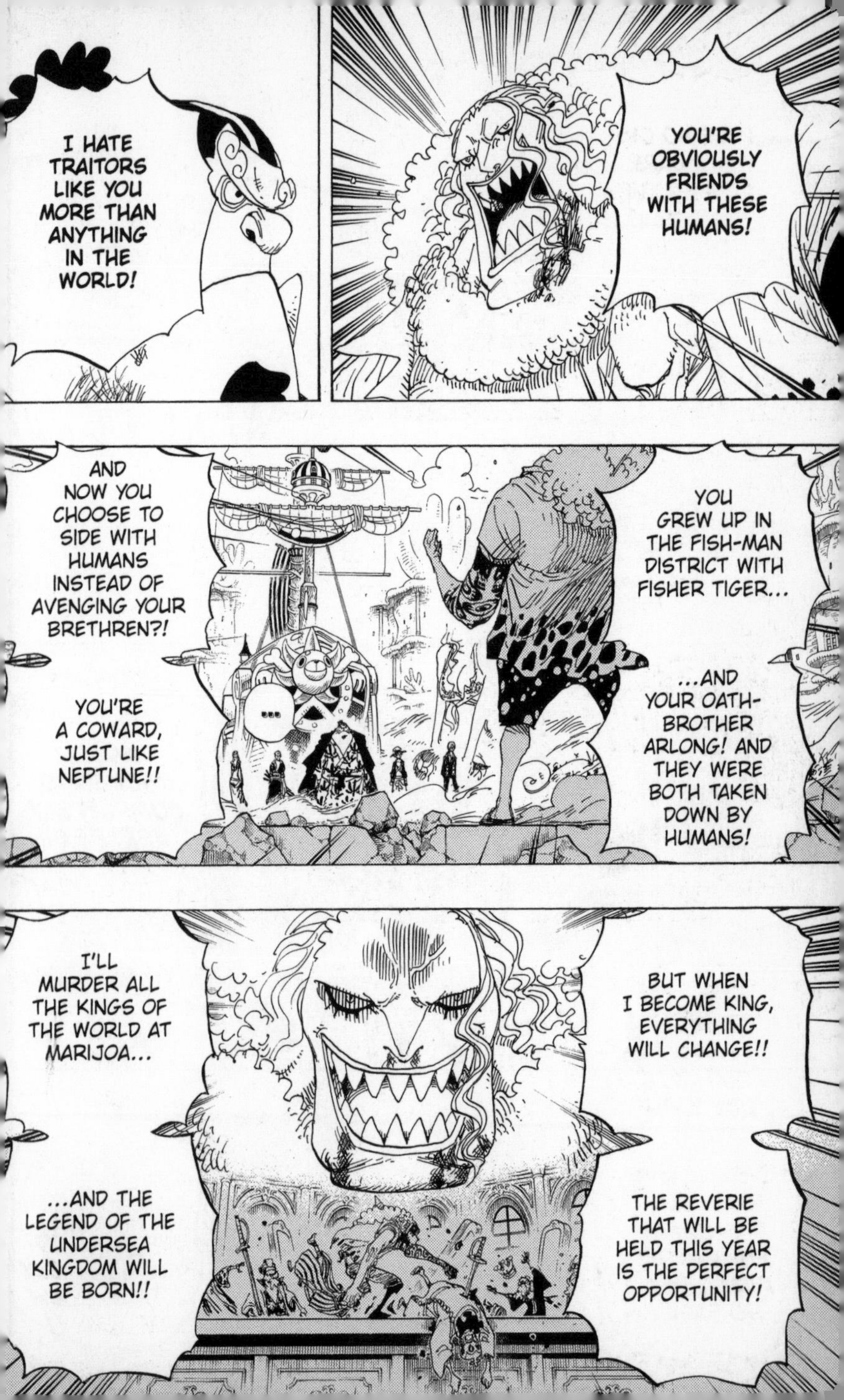
YOU'RE OBVIOUSLY FRIENDS WITH THESE HUMANS!
I HATE TRAITORS LIKE YOU MORE THAN ANYTHING IN THE WORLD!
YOU GREW UP IN THE FISH-MAN DISTRICT WITH FISHER TIGER...
...AND YOUR OATH-BROTHER ARLONG! AND THEY WERE BOTH TAKEN DOWN BY HUMANS!
AND NOW YOU CHOOSE TO SIDE WITH HUMANS INSTEAD OF AVENGING YOUR BRETHREN?!
YOU'RE A COWARD, JUST LIKE NEPTUNE!!
...
BUT WHEN I BECOME KING, EVERYTHING WILL CHANGE!!
THE REVERIE THAT WILL BE HELD THIS YEAR IS THE PERFECT OPPORTUNITY!
I'LL MURDER ALL THE KINGS OF THE WORLD AT MARIJOA...
...AND THE LEGEND OF THE UNDERSEA KINGDOM WILL BE BORN!!

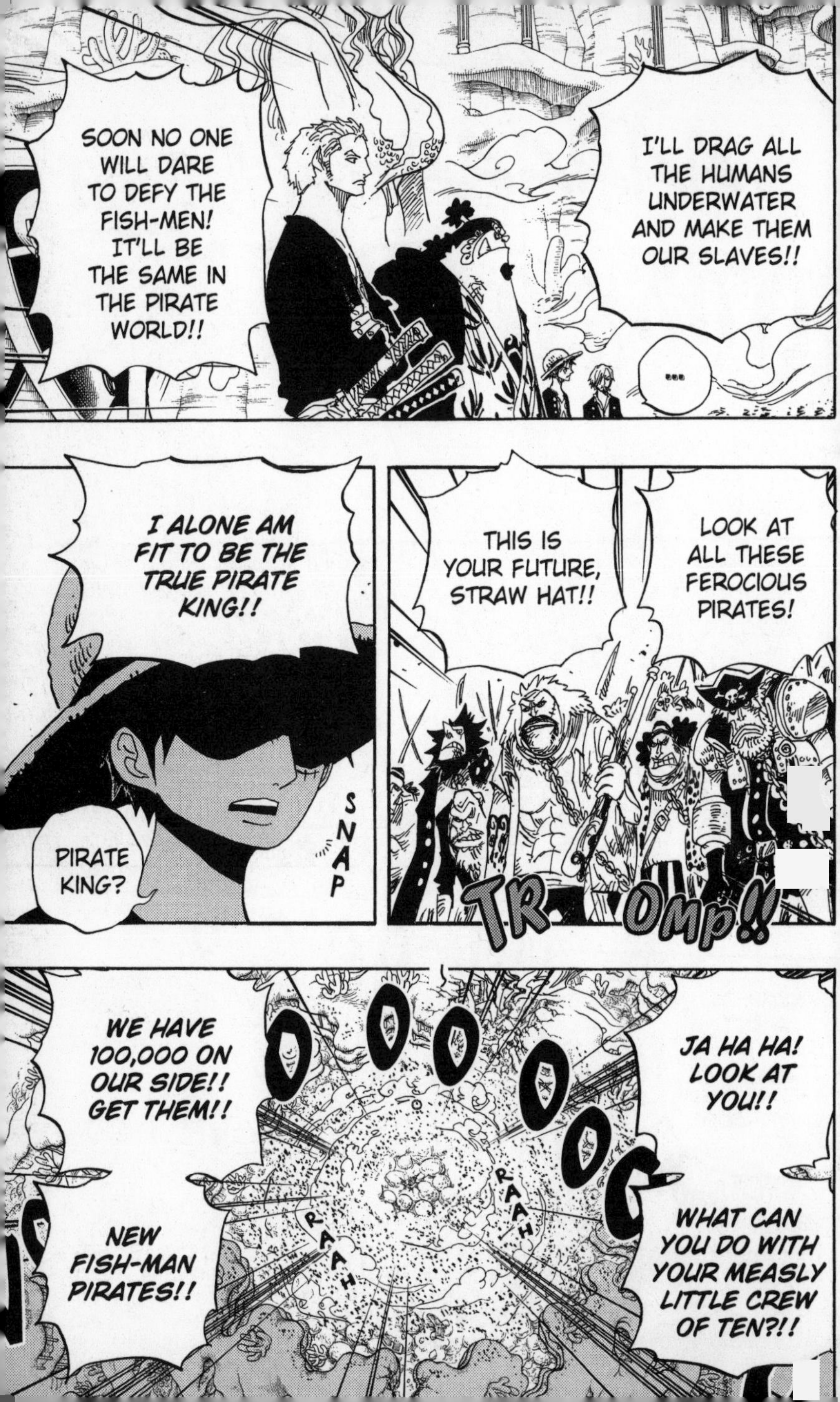
I'LL DRAG ALL THE HUMANS UNDERWATER AND MAKE THEM OUR SLAVES!!
SOON NO ONE WILL DARE TO DEFY THE FISH-MEN! IT'LL BE THE SAME IN THE PIRATE WORLD!!
...
LOOK AT ALL THESE FEROCIOUS PIRATES!
THIS IS YOUR FUTURE, STRAW HAT!!
TROMP!!
I ALONE AM FIT TO BE THE TRUE PIRATE KING!!
SNAP
PIRATE KING?
JA HA HA! LOOK AT YOU!!
WE HAVE 100,000 ON OUR SIDE!! GET THEM!!
RAAH
RAAAH
WHAT CAN YOU DO WITH YOUR MEASLY LITTLE CREW OF TEN?!!
NEW FISH-MAN PIRATES!!

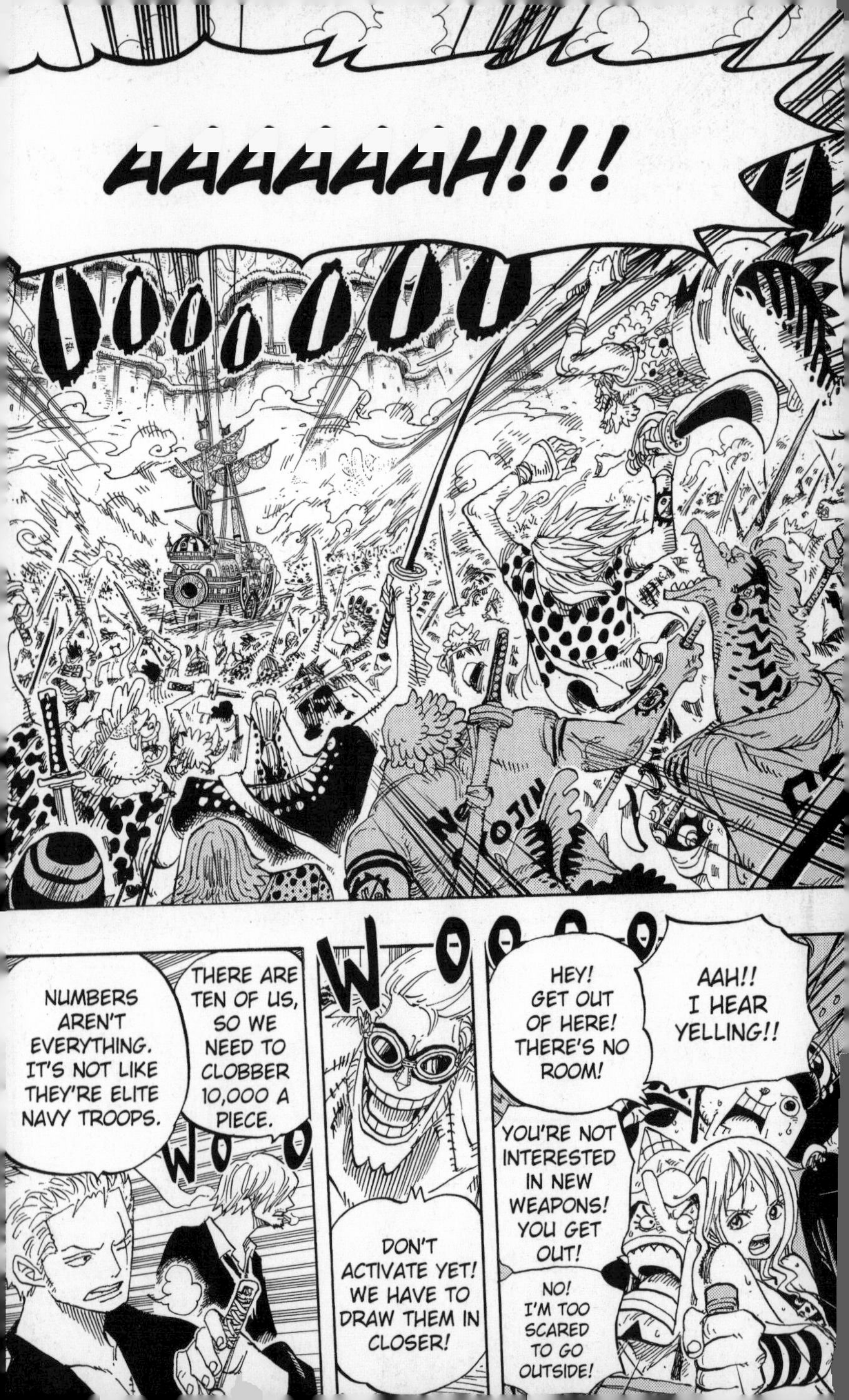
AAAAAAAH!!!
OOOOOOO
WOOOO
AAH!! I HEAR YELLING!!
HEY! GET OUT OF HERE! THERE'S NO ROOM!
YOU'RE NOT INTERESTED IN NEW WEAPONS! YOU GET OUT!
NO! I'M TOO SCARED TO GO OUTSIDE!
DON'T ACTIVATE YET! WE HAVE TO DRAW THEM IN CLOSER!
THERE ARE TEN OF US, SO WE NEED TO CLOBBER 10,000 A PIECE.
NUMBERS AREN'T EVERYTHING. IT'S NOT LIKE THEY'RE ELITE NAVY TROOPS.
WOO

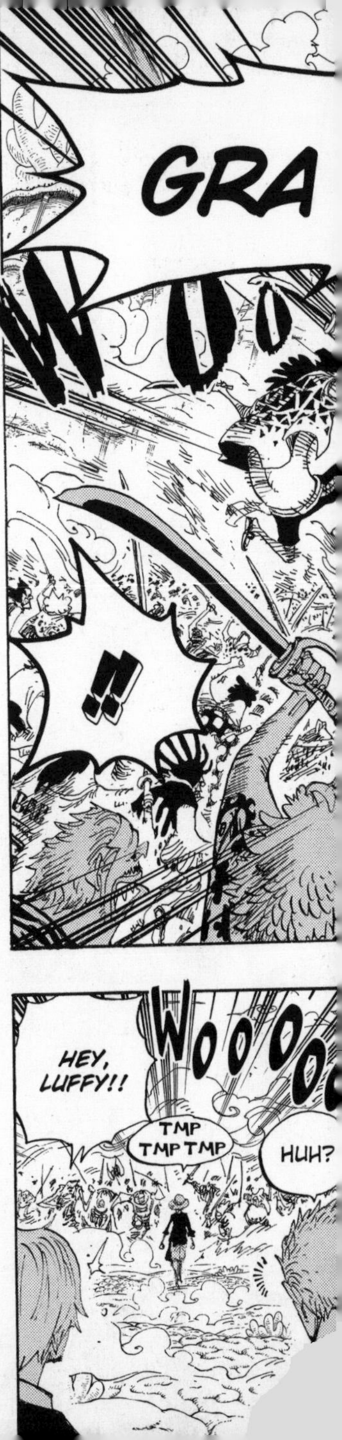
GRA
WOO
!!
WOOOO
HEY, LUFFY!!
TMP TMP TMP
HUH?
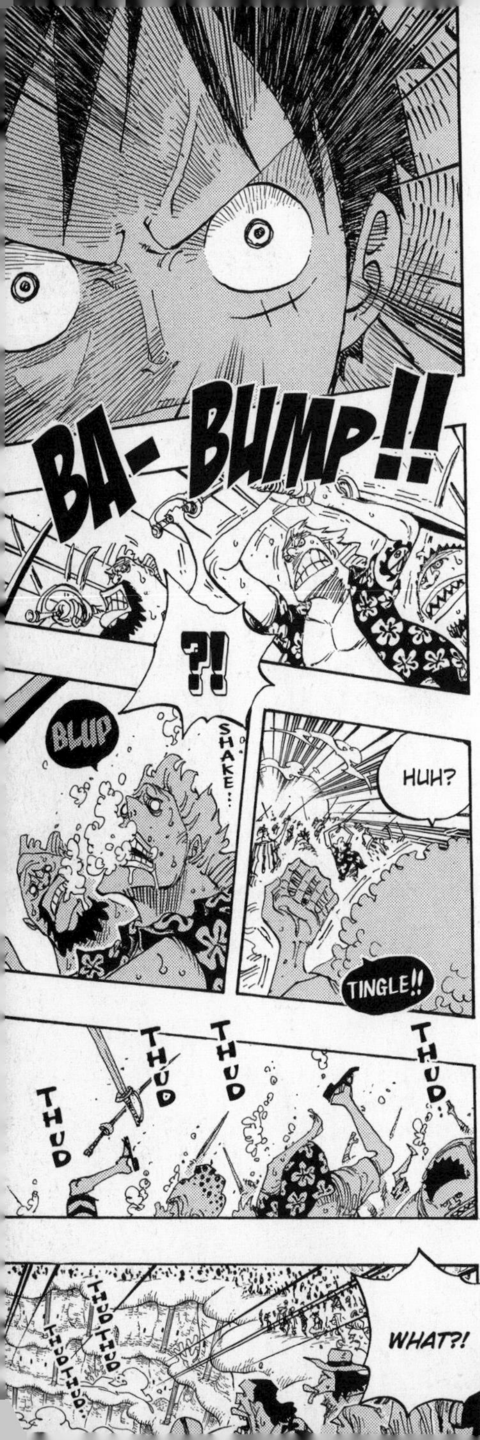
BA- BUMP!!
?!
HUH?
TINGLE!!
SHAKE...
BLUP
THUD
THUD
THUD
THUD
WHAT?!
THUDTHUD
THUDTHUD...

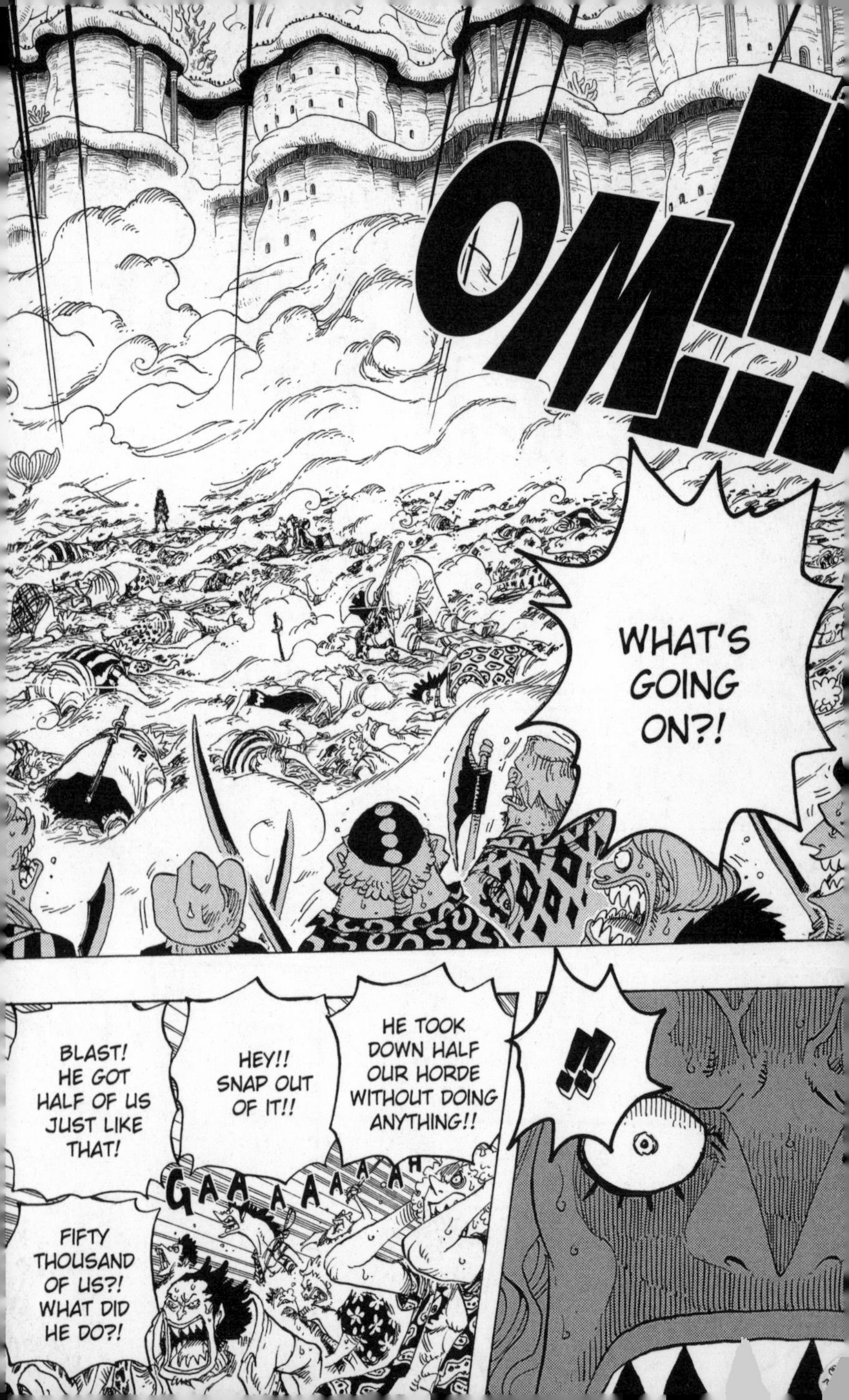
OM!!!
WHAT'S GOING ON?!
!!
HE TOOK DOWN HALF OUR HORDE WITHOUT DOING ANYTHING!!
HEY!! SNAP OUT OF IT!!
BLAST! HE GOT HALF OF US JUST LIKE THAT!
GAAAAAAAH
FIFTY THOUSAND OF US?! WHAT DID HE DO?!

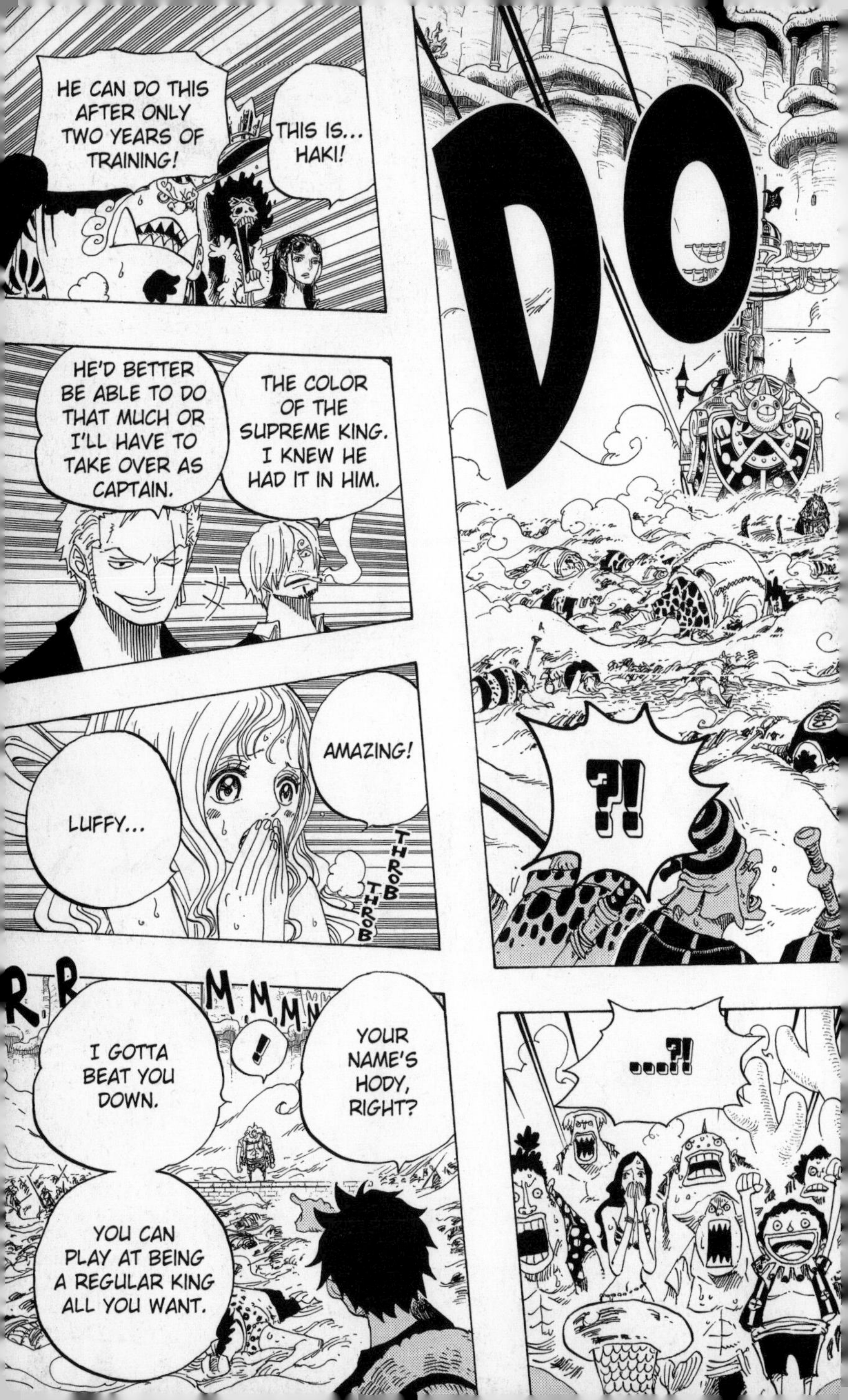
DO
?!
THIS IS... HAKI!
HE CAN DO THIS AFTER ONLY TWO YEARS OF TRAINING!
THE COLOR OF THE SUPREME KING. I KNEW HE HAD IT IN HIM.
HE'D BETTER BE ABLE TO DO THAT MUCH OR I'LL HAVE TO TAKE OVER AS CAPTAIN.
AMAZING!
THROB THROB
LUFFY...
...?!
RR MMMN
YOUR NAME'S HODY, RIGHT?
!
I GOTTA BEAT YOU DOWN.
YOU CAN PLAY AT BEING A REGULAR KING ALL YOU WANT.

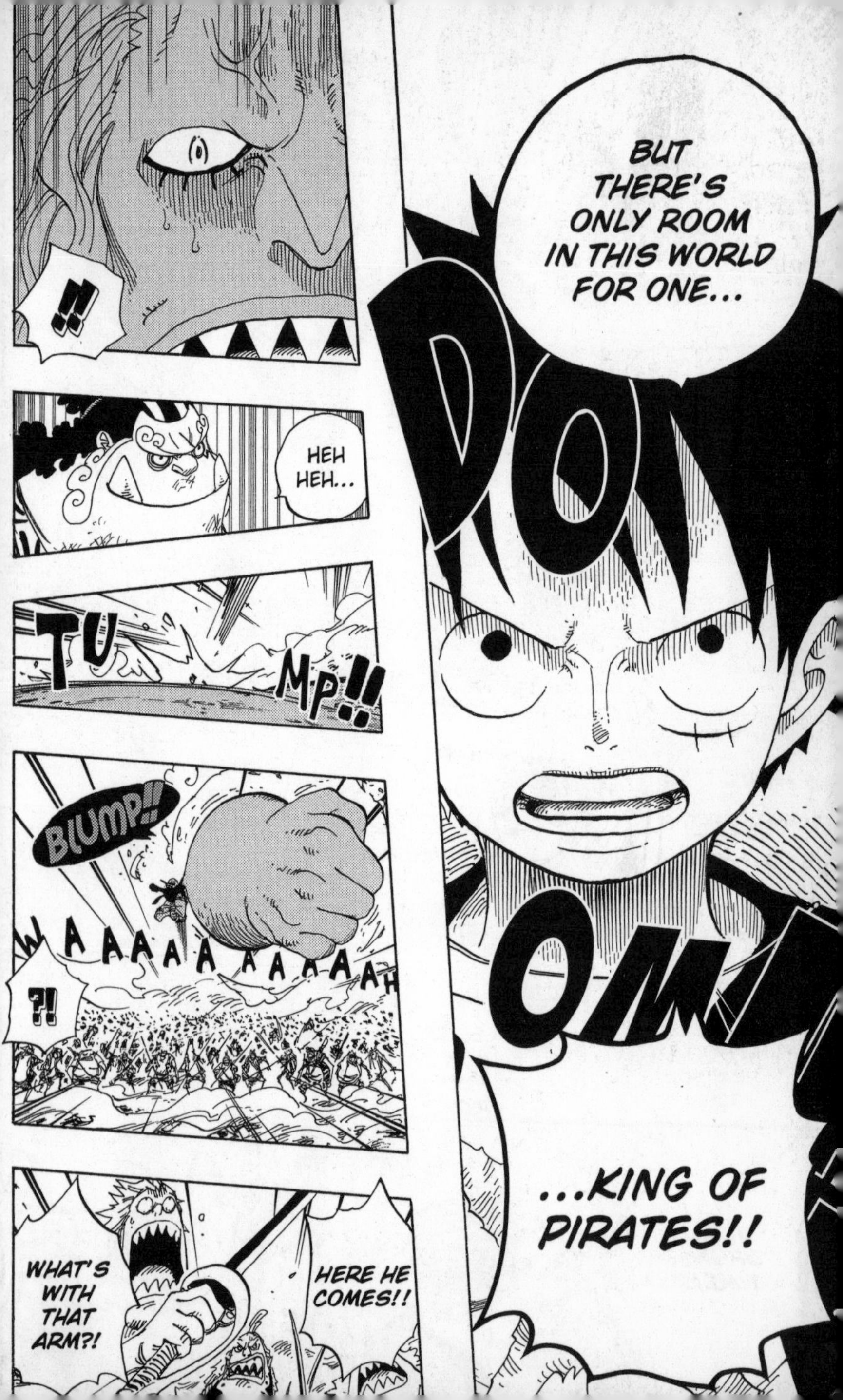
BUT THERE'S ONLY ROOM IN THIS WORLD FOR ONE...
DOOM
...KING OF PIRATES!!
!!
HEH HEH...
TUMP!!
BLUMP!!
WAAAAAAAAAAAH
?!
HERE HE COMES!!
WHAT'S WITH THAT ARM?!

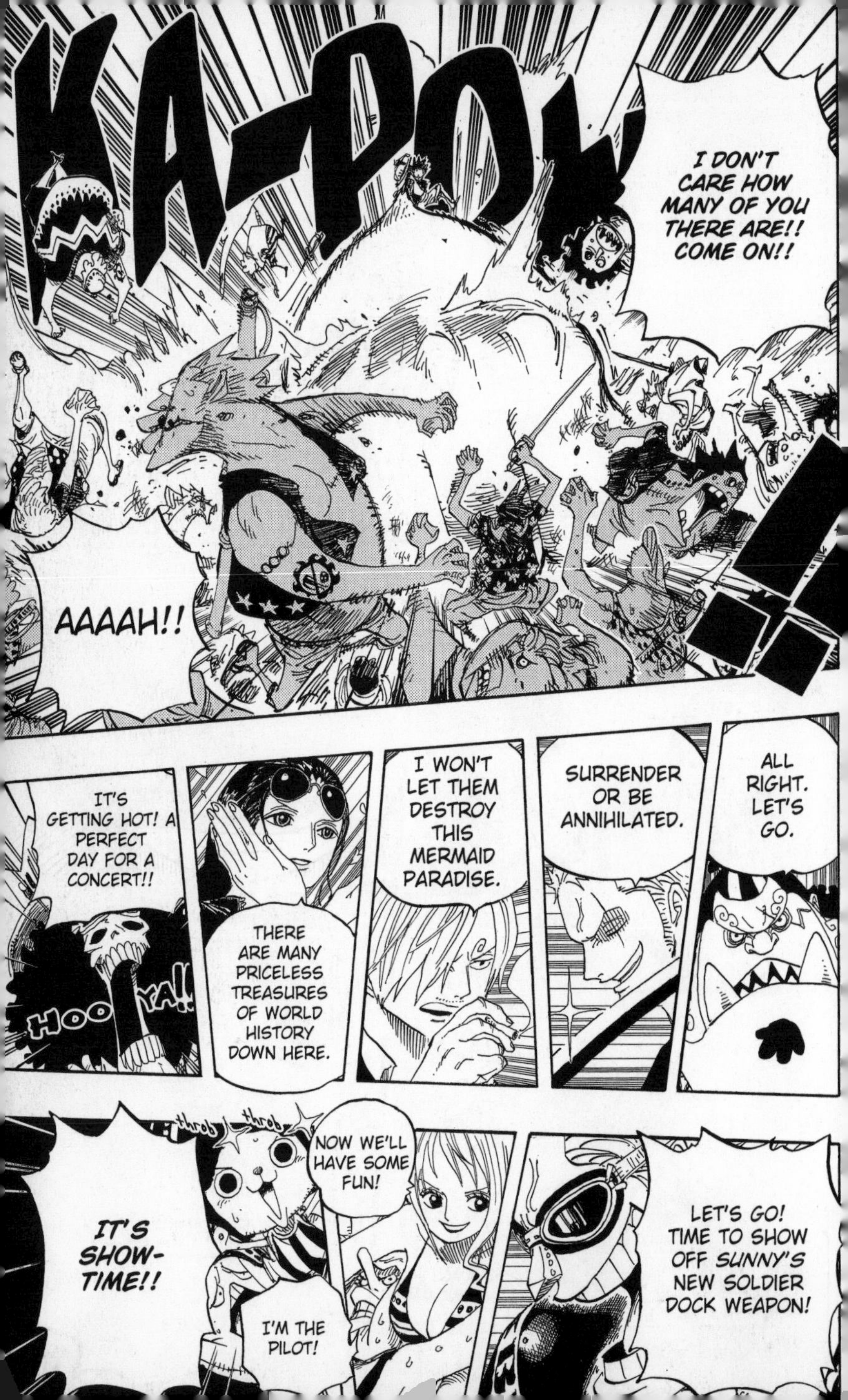
I DON'T CARE HOW MANY OF YOU THERE ARE!! COME ON!!
KA-POW
AAAAH!!
ALL RIGHT. LET'S GO.
SURRENDER OR BE ANNIHILATED.
I WON'T LET THEM DESTROY THIS MERMAID PARADISE.
THERE ARE MANY PRICELESS TREASURES OF WORLD HISTORY DOWN HERE.
IT'S GETTING HOT! A PERFECT DAY FOR A CONCERT!!
HOO YA!!
LET'S GO! TIME TO SHOW OFF SUNNY'S NEW SOLDIER DOCK WEAPON!
NOW WE'LL HAVE SOME FUN!
I'M THE PILOT!
throb throb
IT'S SHOW-TIME!!

SBS Question Corner

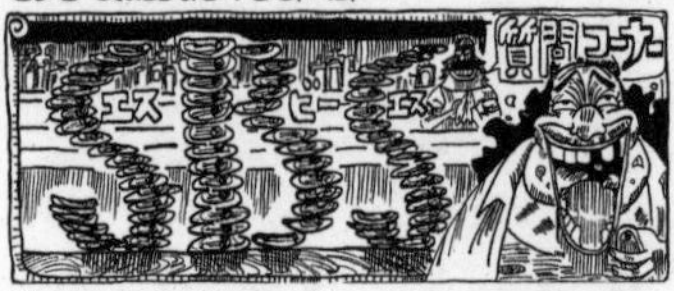

(Tomoya Sato, Yamanashi)

Q: Mr. Oda, I have a question. Will you please draw all the Supernovas when they were kids?

--Yutaka Harada

A: Sure. My SBS is going to end here. Starting on page 186 is the voice actor SBS!

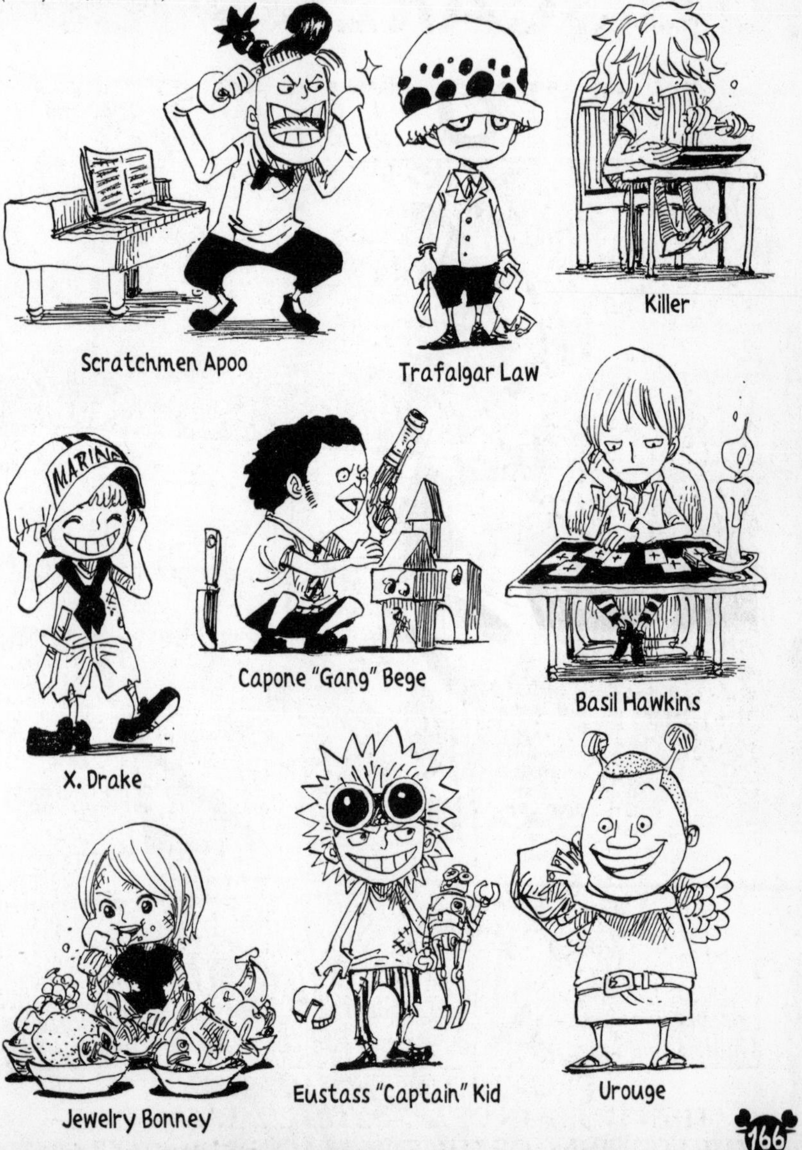
Scratchmen Apoo
Trafalgar Law
Killer
MARINE
X. Drake
Capone "Gang" Bege
Basil Hawkins
Jewelry Bonney
Eustass "Captain" Kid
Urouge

Chapter 635:
SO SCARED I RAN UP TO THE SKY

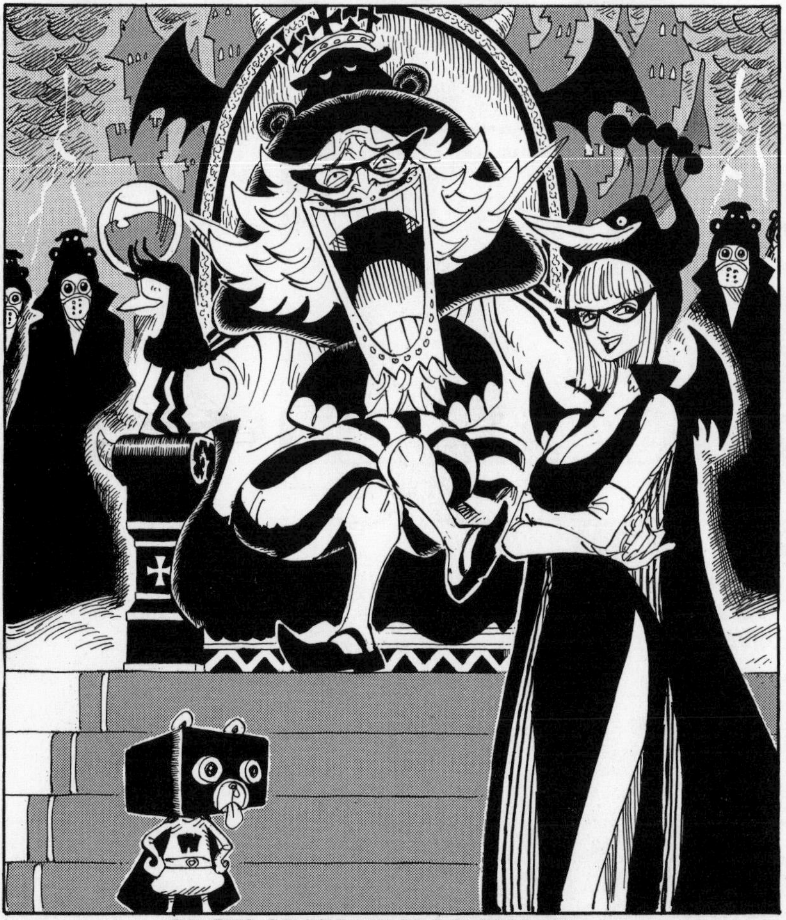

DECKS OF THE WORLD, VOL. 19:
"THE CHAIRMAN OF A CERTAIN CONGLOMERATE–
THE FOUNDING OF THE EVIL BLACK DRUM KINGDOM"

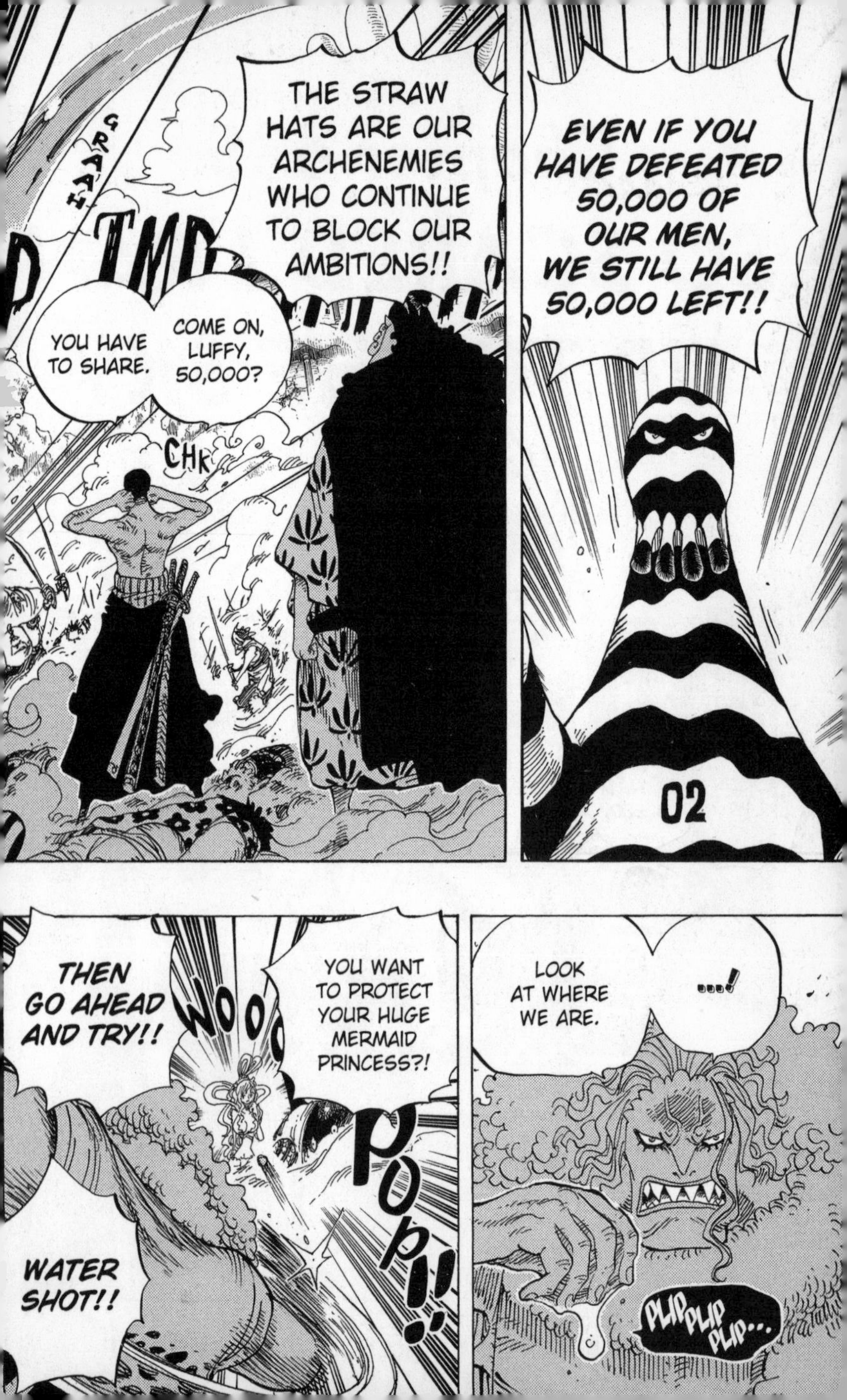
EVEN IF YOU HAVE DEFEATED 50,000 OF OUR MEN, WE STILL HAVE 50,000 LEFT!!
02
THE STRAW HATS ARE OUR ARCHENEMIES WHO CONTINUE TO BLOCK OUR AMBITIONS!!
GRAAAH
COME ON, LUFFY, 50,000?
YOU HAVE TO SHARE.
CHK
...!
LOOK AT WHERE WE ARE.
PLIP PLIP PLIP...
YOU WANT TO PROTECT YOUR HUGE MERMAID PRINCESS?!
THEN GO AHEAD AND TRY!!
WOOO
POP!!
WATER SHOT!!

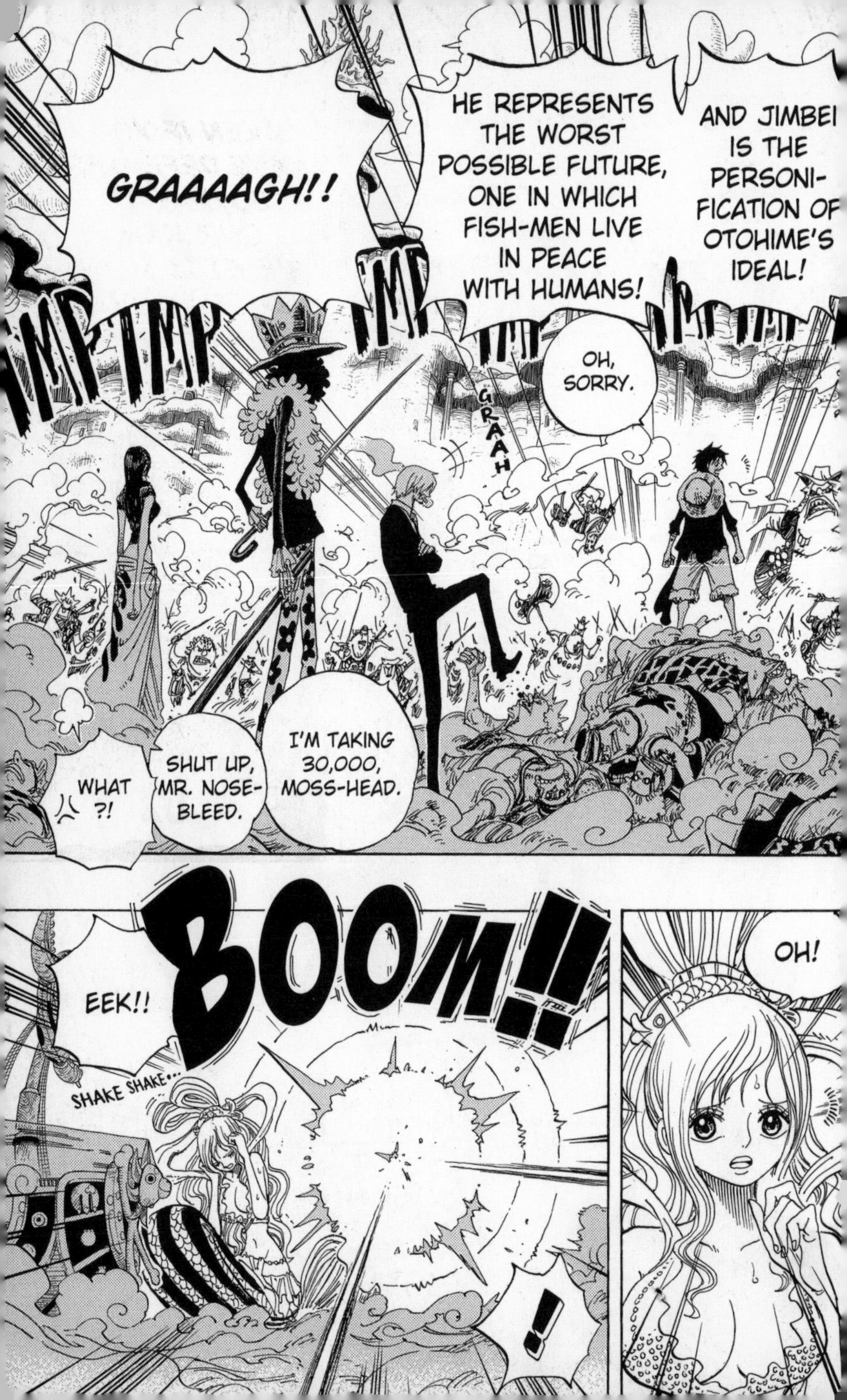
AND JIMBEI IS THE PERSONIFICATION OF OTOHIME'S IDEAL!
HE REPRESENTS THE WORST POSSIBLE FUTURE, ONE IN WHICH FISH-MEN LIVE IN PEACE WITH HUMANS!
GRAAAAGH!!
OH, SORRY.
GRAAH
I'M TAKING 30,000, MOSS-HEAD.
SHUT UP, MR. NOSE-BLEED.
WHAT ?!
OH!
BOOM!!
EEK!!
SHAKE SHAKE...
!

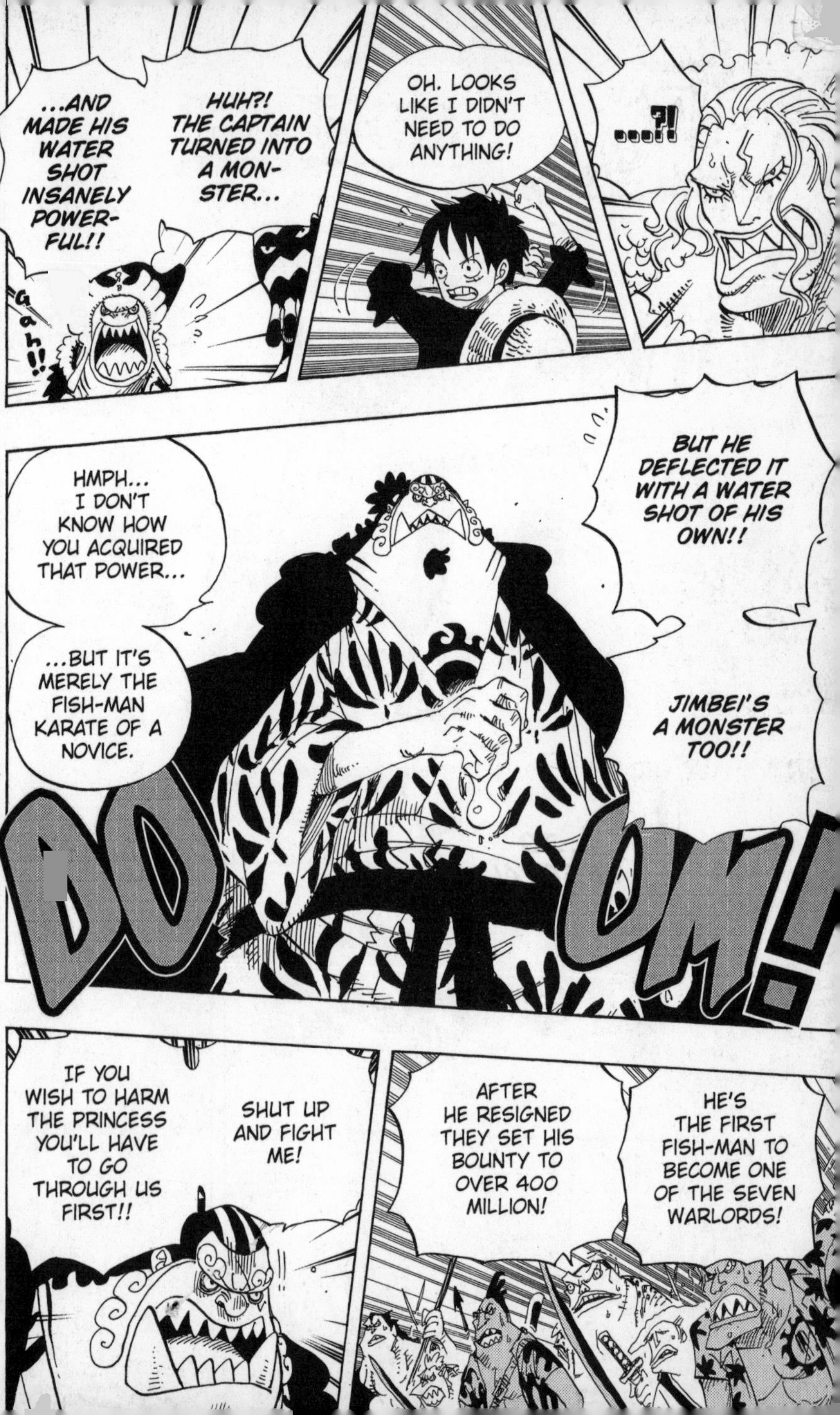
...?!
OH. LOOKS LIKE I DIDN'T NEED TO DO ANYTHING!
HUH?! THE CAPTAIN TURNED INTO A MONSTER...
...AND MADE HIS WATER SHOT INSANELY POWERFUL!!
Gah!!
BUT HE DEFLECTED IT WITH A WATER SHOT OF HIS OWN!!
JIMBEI'S A MONSTER TOO!!
HMPH... I DON'T KNOW HOW YOU ACQUIRED THAT POWER...
...BUT IT'S MERELY THE FISH-MAN KARATE OF A NOVICE.
DOOM!
HE'S THE FIRST FISH-MAN TO BECOME ONE OF THE SEVEN WARLORDS!
AFTER HE RESIGNED THEY SET HIS BOUNTY TO OVER 400 MILLION!
SHUT UP AND FIGHT ME!
IF YOU WISH TO HARM THE PRINCESS YOU'LL HAVE TO GO THROUGH US FIRST!!

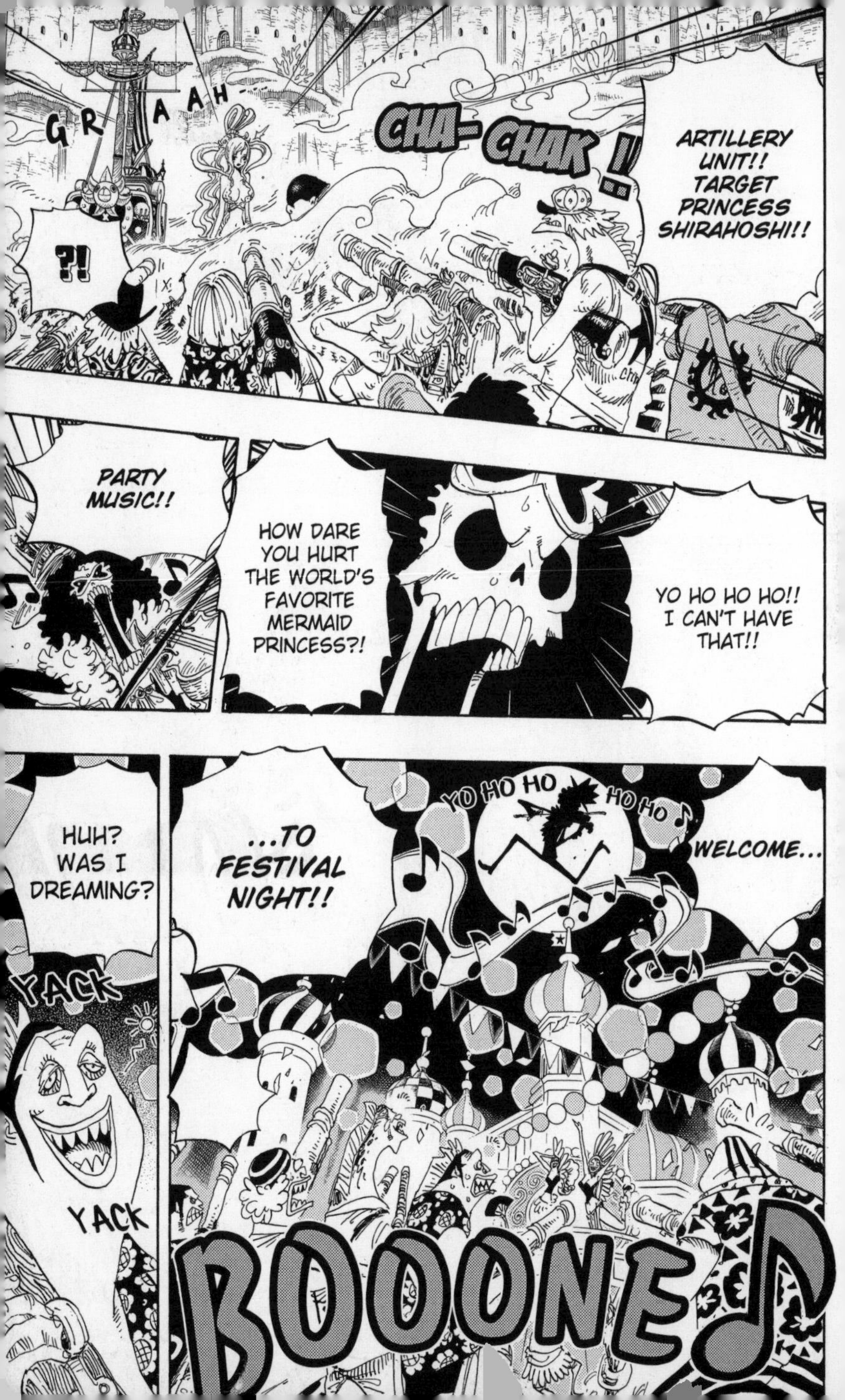
ARTILLERY UNIT!! TARGET PRINCESS SHIRAHOSHI!!
CHA-CHAK!!
GRAAH
?!
YO HO HO HO!! I CAN'T HAVE THAT!!
HOW DARE YOU HURT THE WORLD'S FAVORITE MERMAID PRINCESS?!
PARTY MUSIC!!
WELCOME...
YO HO HO HO HO
...TO FESTIVAL NIGHT!!
BOOONE
HUH? WAS I DREAMING?
YACK
YACK

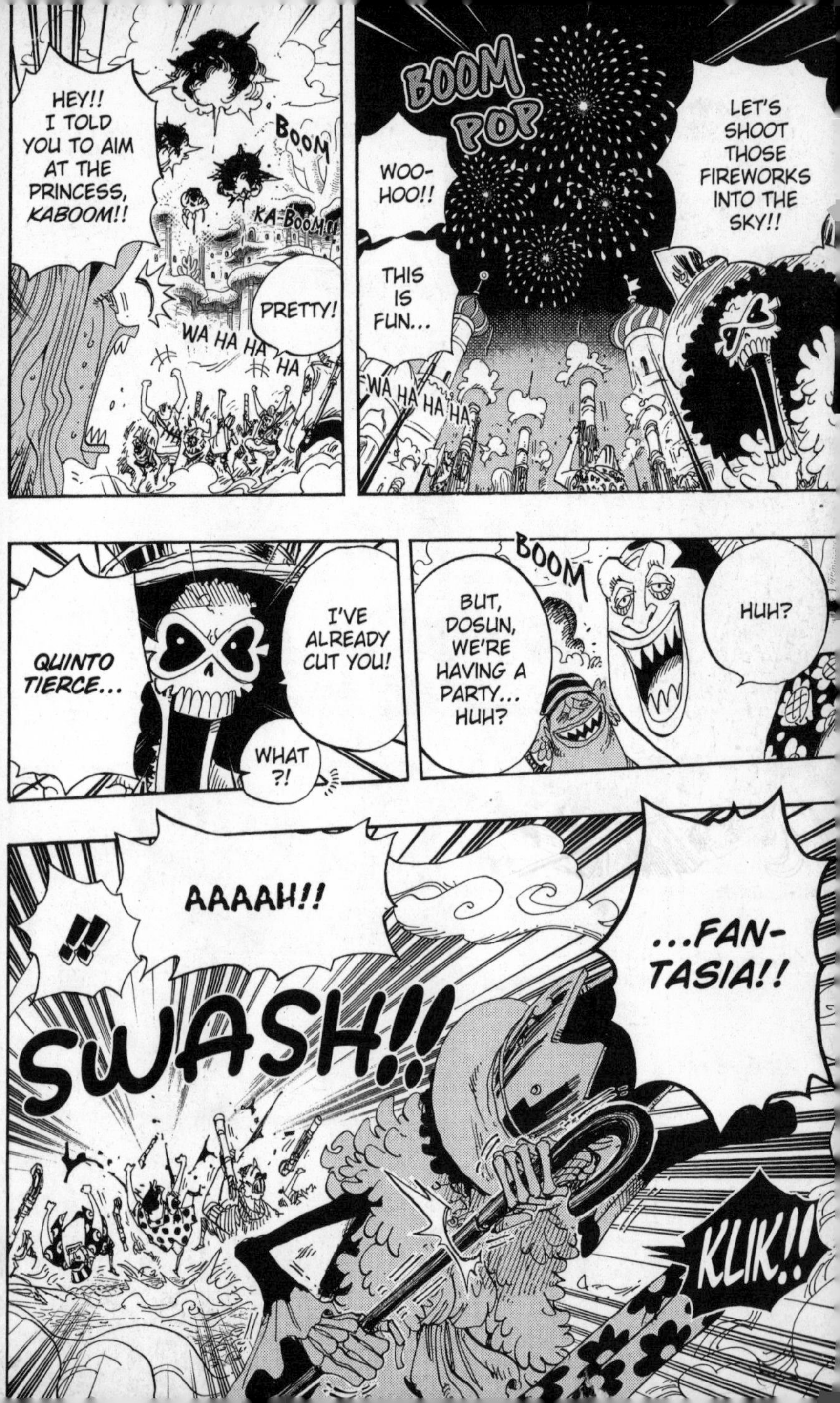
LET'S SHOOT THOSE FIREWORKS INTO THE SKY!!
BOOM
POP
WOO-HOO!!
THIS IS FUN...
WA HA HA HA
HEY!! I TOLD YOU TO AIM AT THE PRINCESS, KABOOM!!
BOOM
KA-BOOM!!
PRETTY!
WA HA HA HA
BOOM
HUH?
BUT, DOSUN, WE'RE HAVING A PARTY... HUH?
I'VE ALREADY CUT YOU!
QUINTO TIERCE...
WHAT ?!
...FAN-TASIA!!
AAAAH!!
!!
SWASH!!
KLIK!!

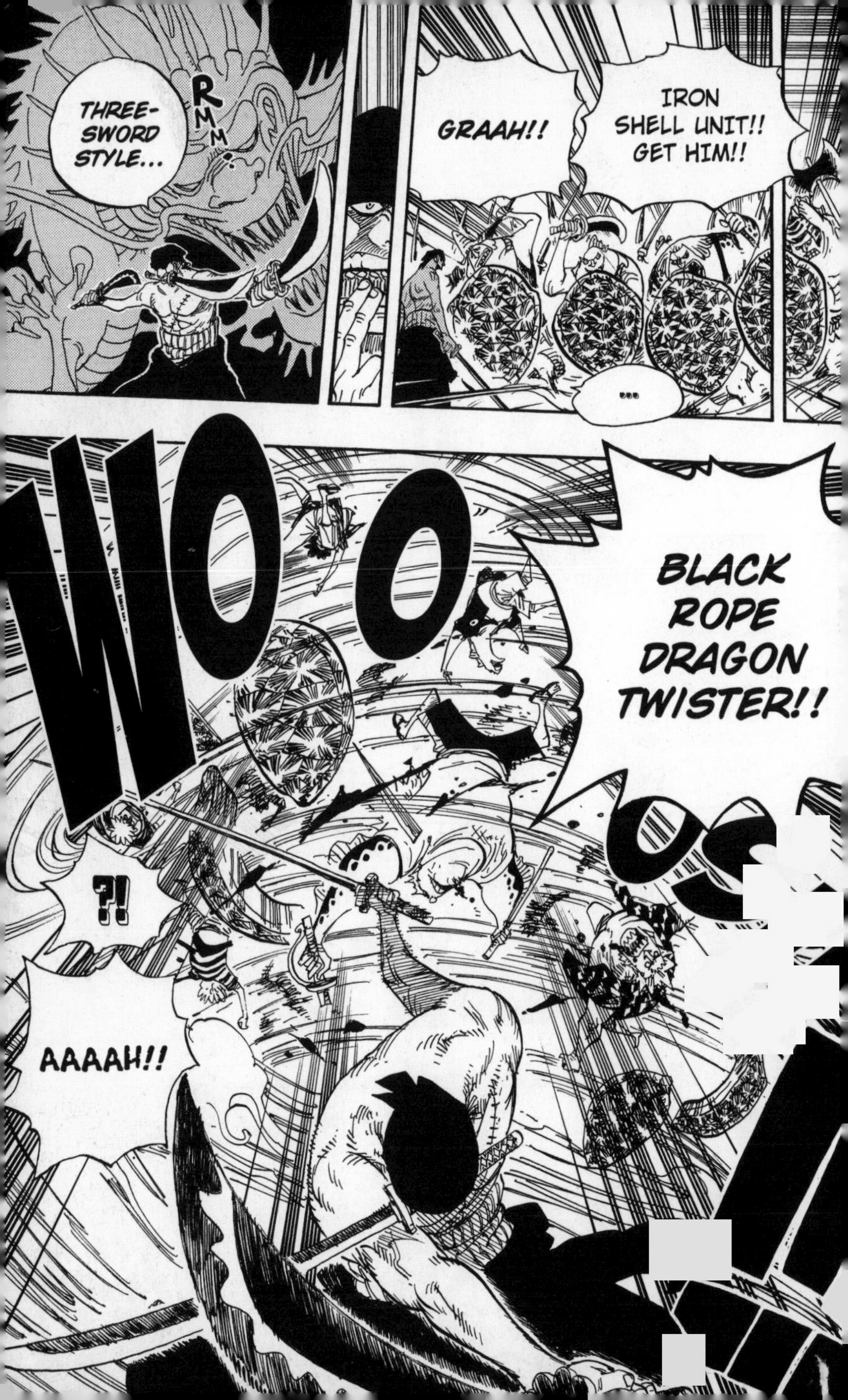
IRON SHELL UNIT!! GET HIM!!
GRAAH!!
...
RMM
THREE-SWORD STYLE...
BLACK ROPE DRAGON TWISTER!!
?!
AAAAH!!

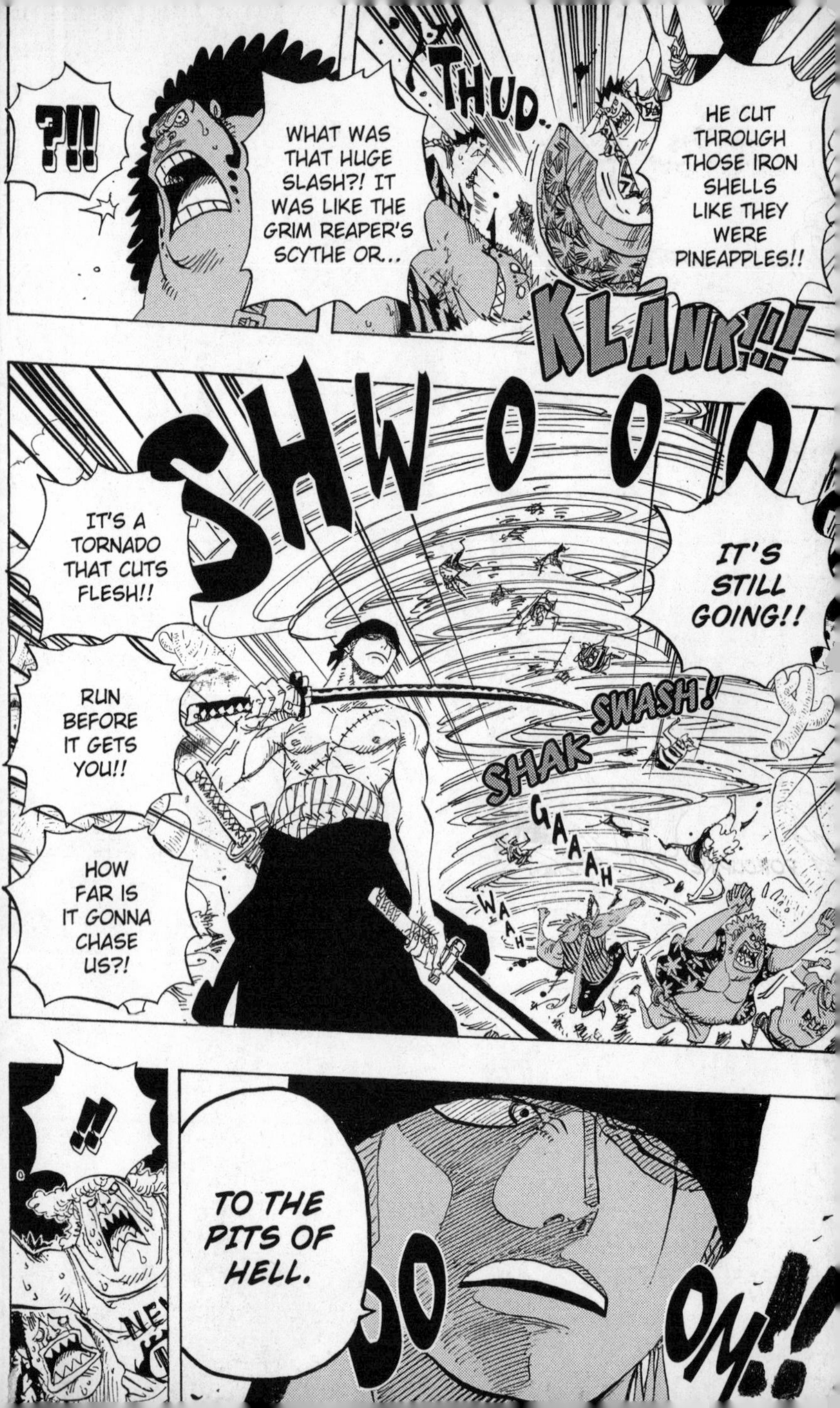
THUD..
HE CUT THROUGH THOSE IRON SHELLS LIKE THEY WERE PINEAPPLES!!
WHAT WAS THAT HUGE SLASH?! IT WAS LIKE THE GRIM REAPER'S SCYTHE OR...
?!!
KLANK!!!
SHWOOO
IT'S STILL GOING!!
SWASH!
SHAK
IT'S A TORNADO THAT CUTS FLESH!!
RUN BEFORE IT GETS YOU!!
GAAAAH
HOW FAR IS IT GONNA CHASE US?!
WAAH
TO THE PITS OF HELL.
DOOOM!!
!!

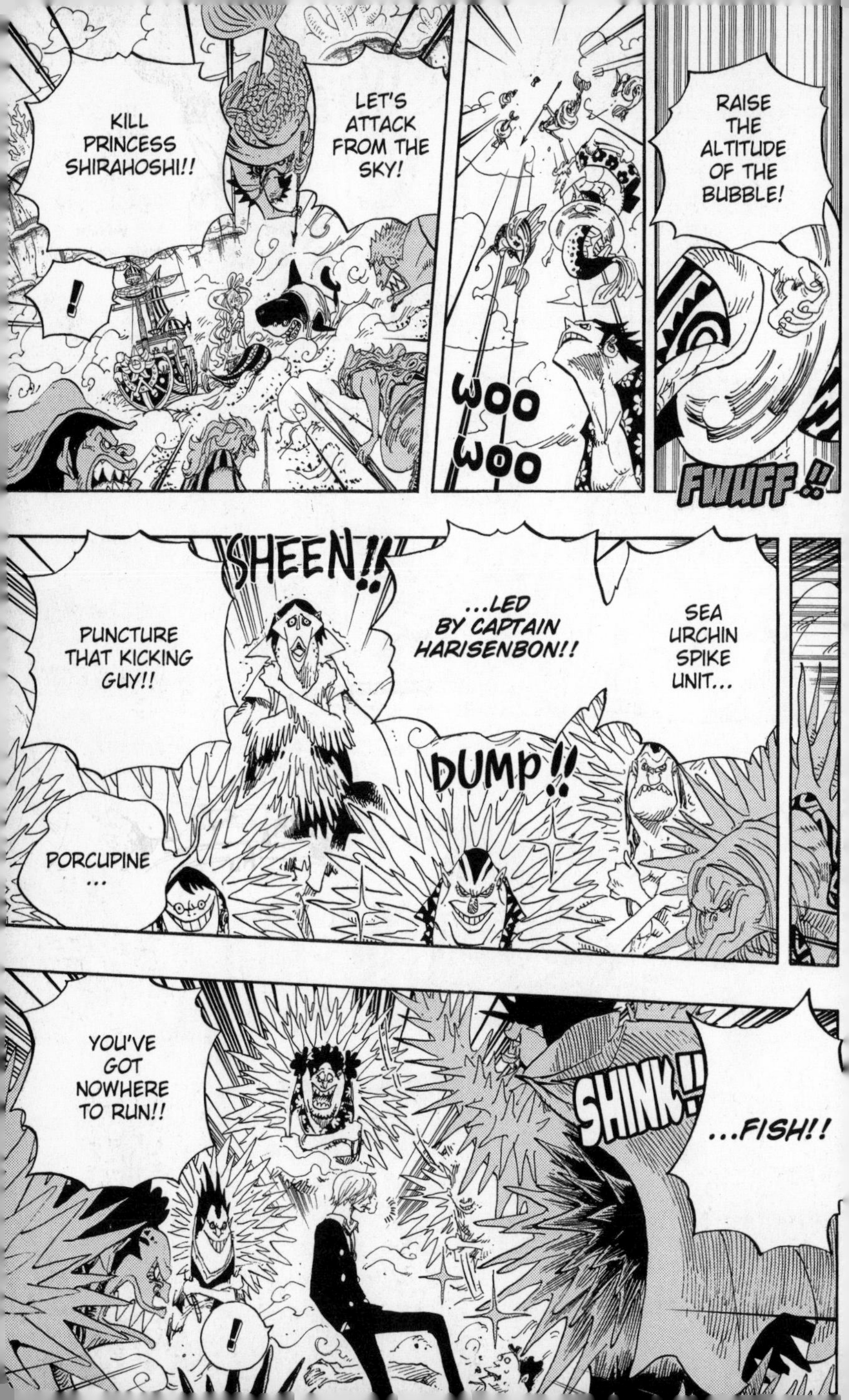
RAISE THE ALTITUDE OF THE BUBBLE!
FWUFF!!
WOO WOO
LET'S ATTACK FROM THE SKY!
KILL PRINCESS SHIRAHOSHI!!
!
SEA URCHIN SPIKE UNIT...
...LED BY CAPTAIN HARISENBON!!
SHEEN!!
PUNCTURE THAT KICKING GUY!!
DUMP!!
PORCUPINE ...
...FISH!!
SHINK!!
YOU'VE GOT NOWHERE TO RUN!!
!

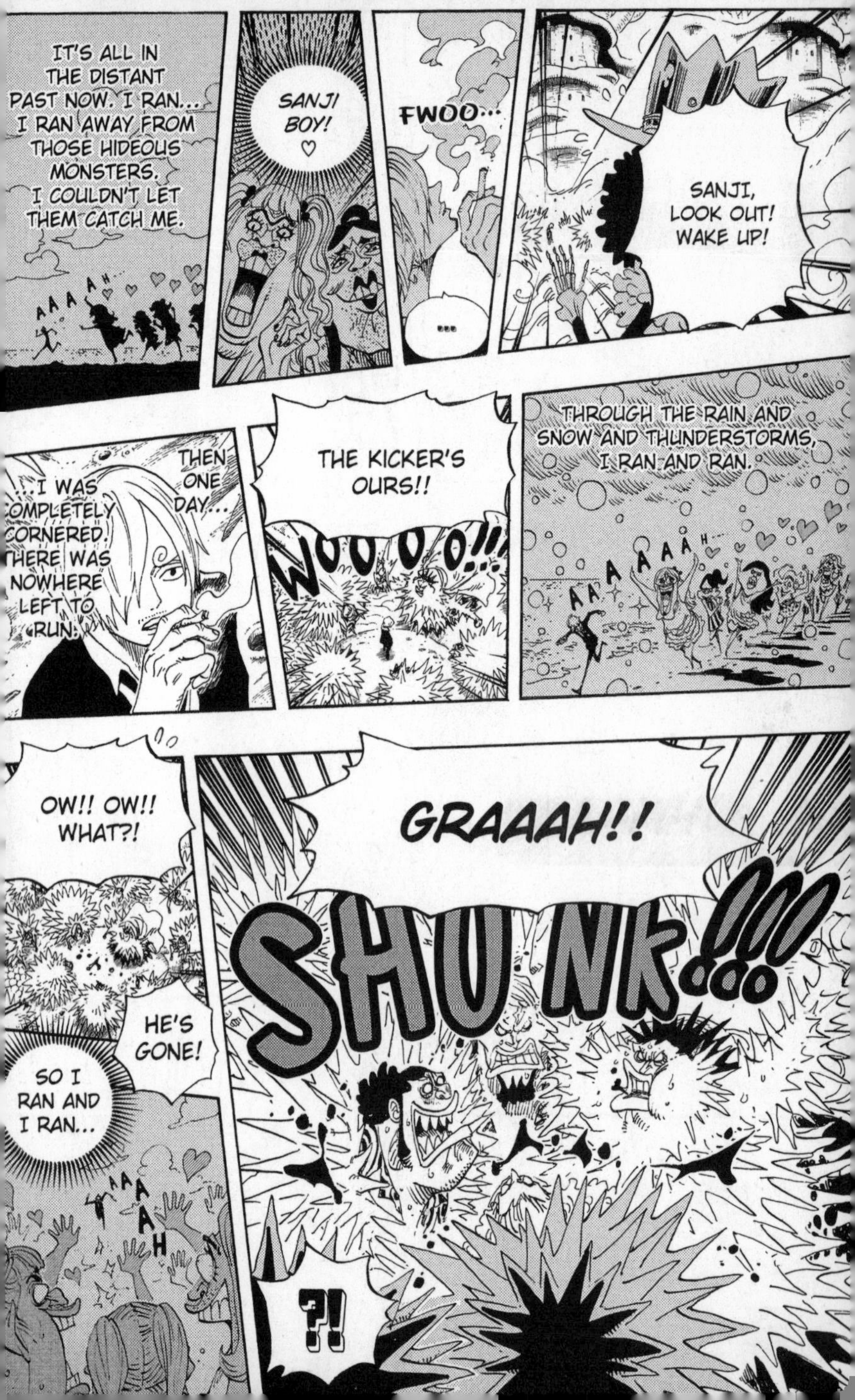
SANJI, LOOK OUT! WAKE UP!
FWOO...
...
SANJI BOY! ♥
IT'S ALL IN THE DISTANT PAST NOW. I RAN... I RAN AWAY FROM THOSE HIDEOUS MONSTERS. I COULDN'T LET THEM CATCH ME.
AAAAH
THROUGH THE RAIN AND SNOW AND THUNDERSTORMS, I RAN AND RAN.
AAAAAAH
THE KICKER'S OURS!!
WOOOO!!!
THEN ONE DAY...
...I WAS COMPLETELY CORNERED. THERE WAS NOWHERE LEFT TO RUN.
GRAAAH!!
SHUNK!!!
SANJI...!
?!
OW!! OW!! WHAT?!
HE'S GONE!
SO I RAN AND I RAN...
AAAAH

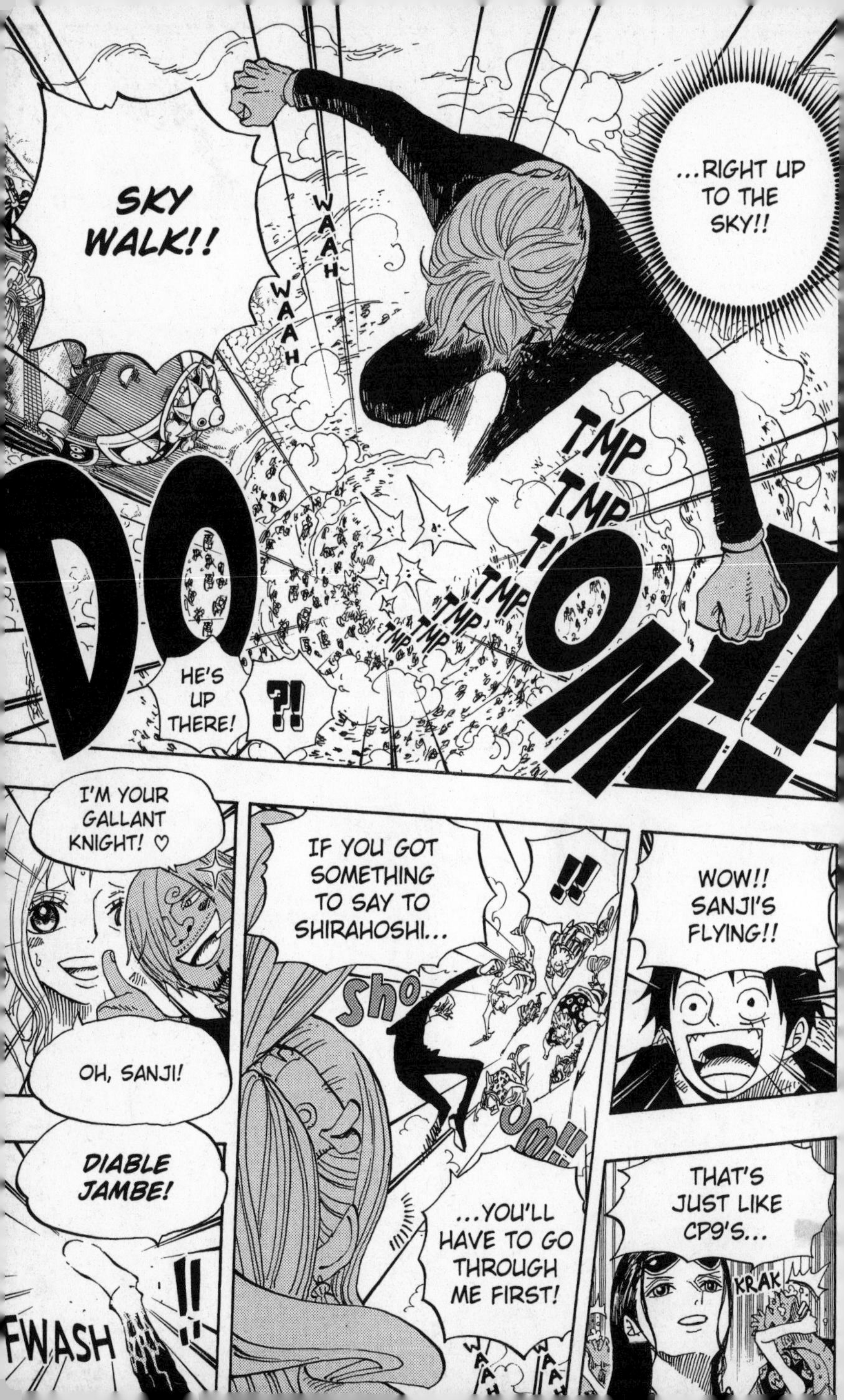
...RIGHT UP TO THE SKY!!
SKY WALK!!
WAAH
WAAH
TMP TMP TMP TMP TMP TMP TMP
DOOM!!
HE'S UP THERE!
?!
WOW!! SANJI'S FLYING!!
THAT'S JUST LIKE CP9'S...
KRAK
IF YOU GOT SOMETHING TO SAY TO SHIRAHOSHI...
!!
SHOOM!!
...YOU'LL HAVE TO GO THROUGH ME FIRST!
I'M YOUR GALLANT KNIGHT! ♡
OH, SANJI!
DIABLE JAMBE!
!!
FWASH

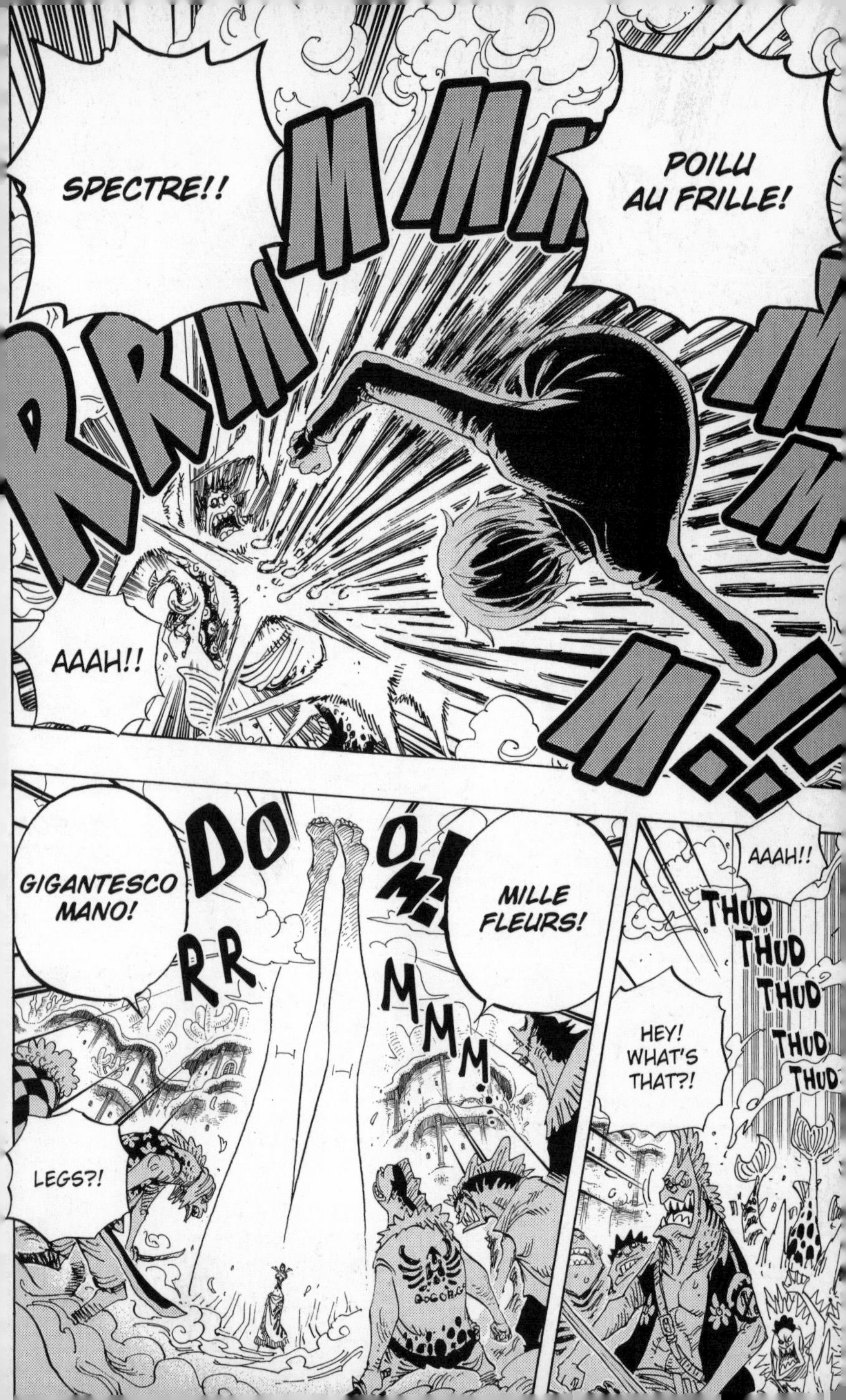
POILU AU FRILLE!
SPECTRE!!
AAAH!!
AAAH!!
THUD THUD THUD THUD THUD
HEY! WHAT'S THAT?!
MILLE FLEURS!
GIGANTESCO MANO!
LEGS?!

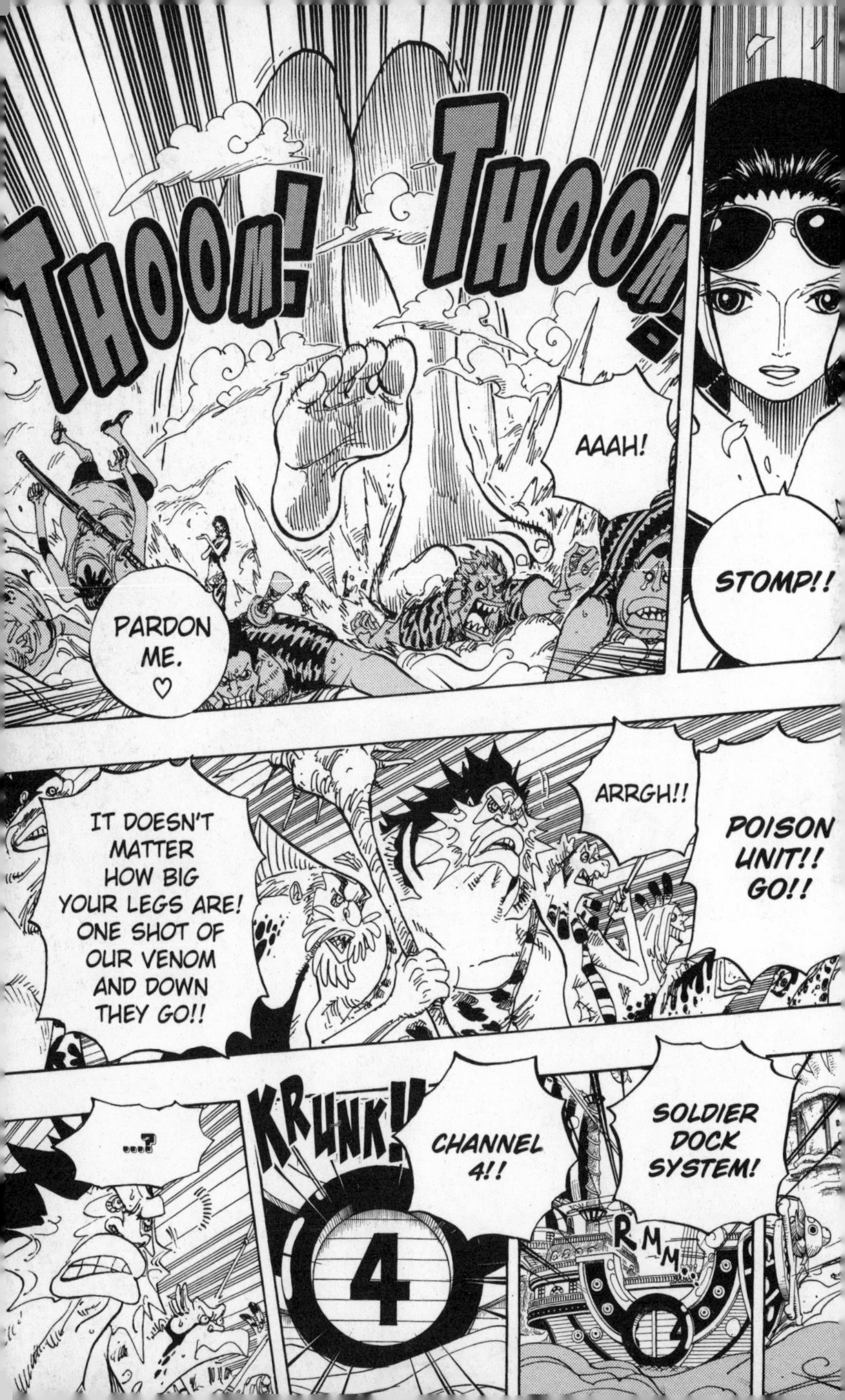
STOMP!!
THOOM!
THOOM!
AAAH!
PARDON ME. ♡
POISON UNIT!! GO!!
ARRGH!!
IT DOESN'T MATTER HOW BIG YOUR LEGS ARE! ONE SHOT OF OUR VENOM AND DOWN THEY GO!!
SOLDIER DOCK SYSTEM!
RMM
CHANNEL 4!!
KRUNK!
4
...?

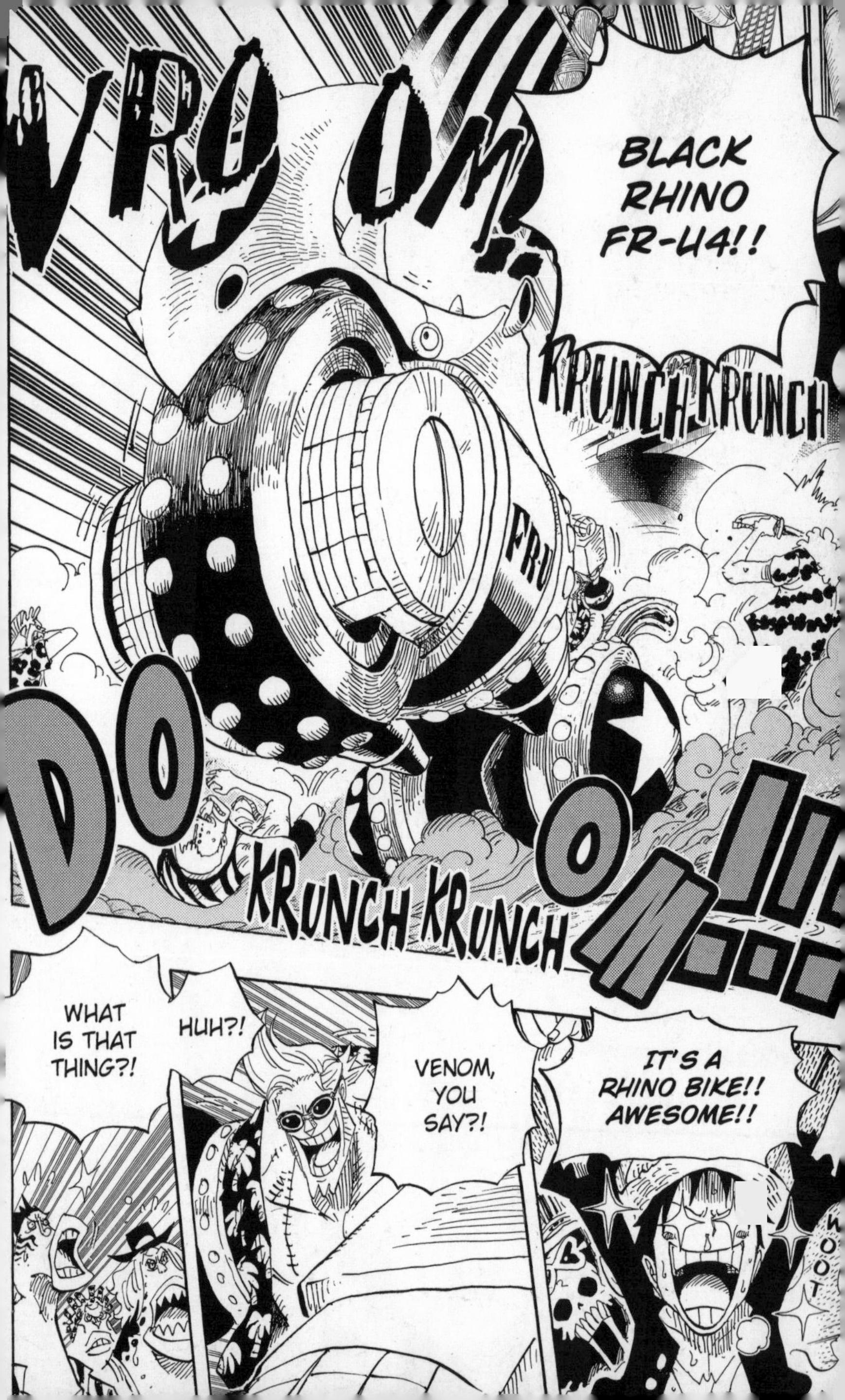
VROOM
BLACK RHINO FR-U4!!
KRUNCH KRUNCH
FRU
DOOM!!
KRUNCH KRUNCH
IT'S A RHINO BIKE!! AWESOME!!
WOOT
VENOM, YOU SAY?!
HUH?!
WHAT IS THAT THING?!

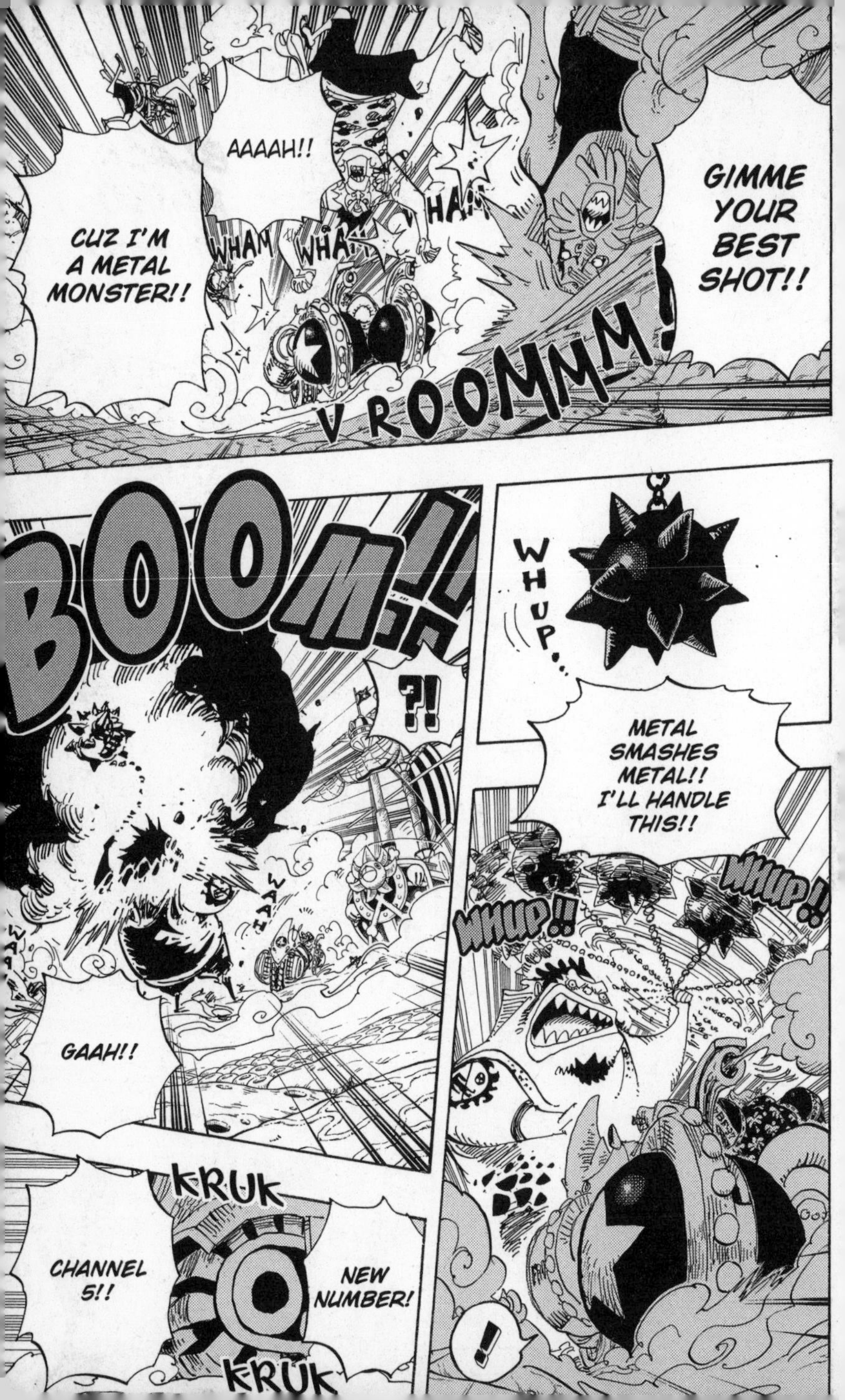
GIMME YOUR BEST SHOT!!
VROOMMM!
WHAM
WHAM
AAAAH!!
CUZ I'M A METAL MONSTER!!
WHUP...
METAL SMASHES METAL!! I'LL HANDLE THIS!!
WHUP!!
WHUP!!
!
BOOM!!
?!
WAAH
GAAH!!
KRUK
NEW NUMBER!
CHANNEL 5!!
KRUK

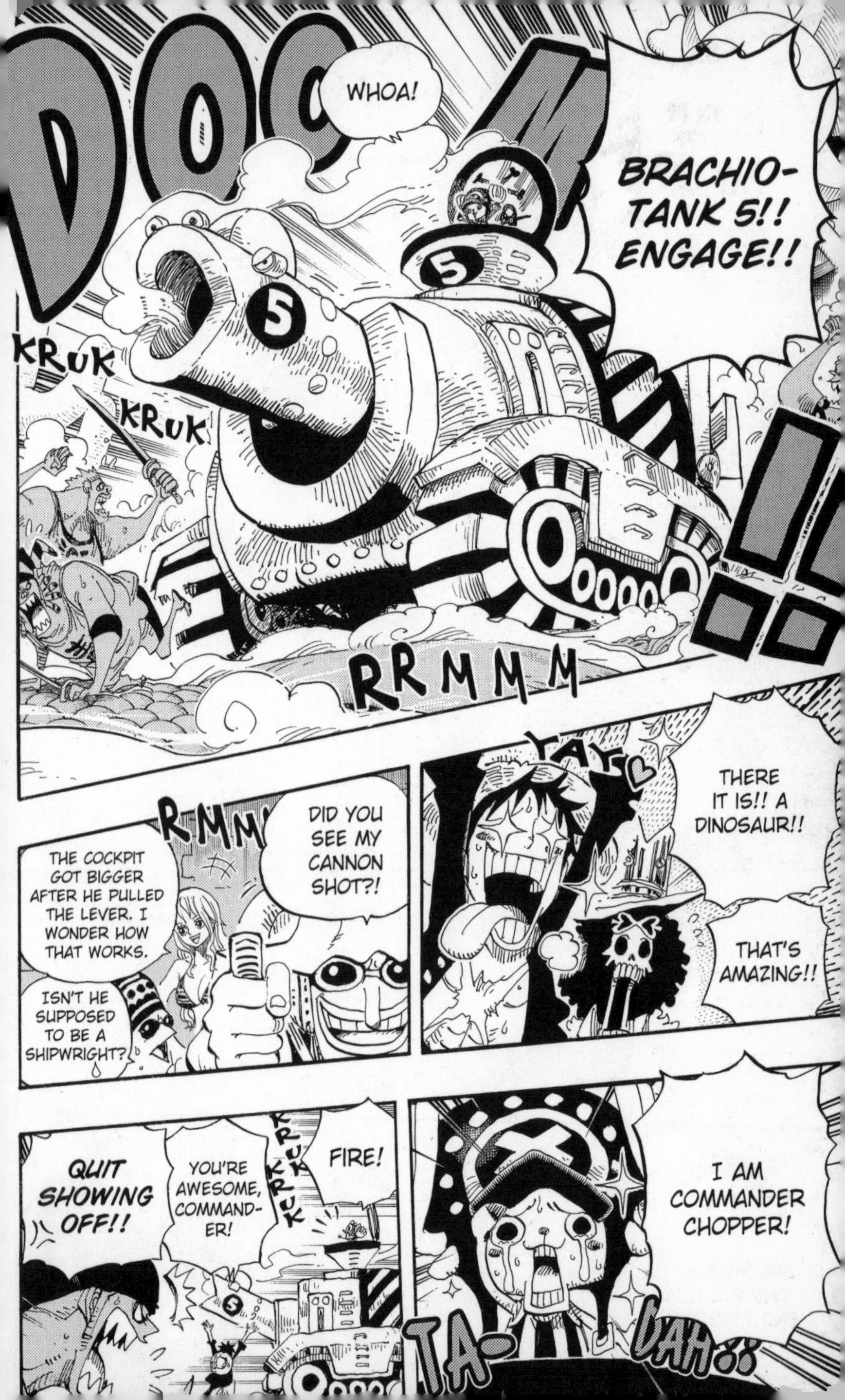
BRACHIO-TANK 5!! ENGAGE!!
WHOA!
DOOM
!!
KRUK
KRUK
RRMMM
YAY
THERE IT IS!! A DINOSAUR!!
THAT'S AMAZING!!
DID YOU SEE MY CANNON SHOT?!
RMM
THE COCKPIT GOT BIGGER AFTER HE PULLED THE LEVER. I WONDER HOW THAT WORKS.
ISN'T HE SUPPOSED TO BE A SHIPWRIGHT?
I AM COMMANDER CHOPPER!
TA-DAH
FIRE!
KRUK KRUK KRUK
YOU'RE AWESOME, COMMANDER!
QUIT SHOWING OFF!!

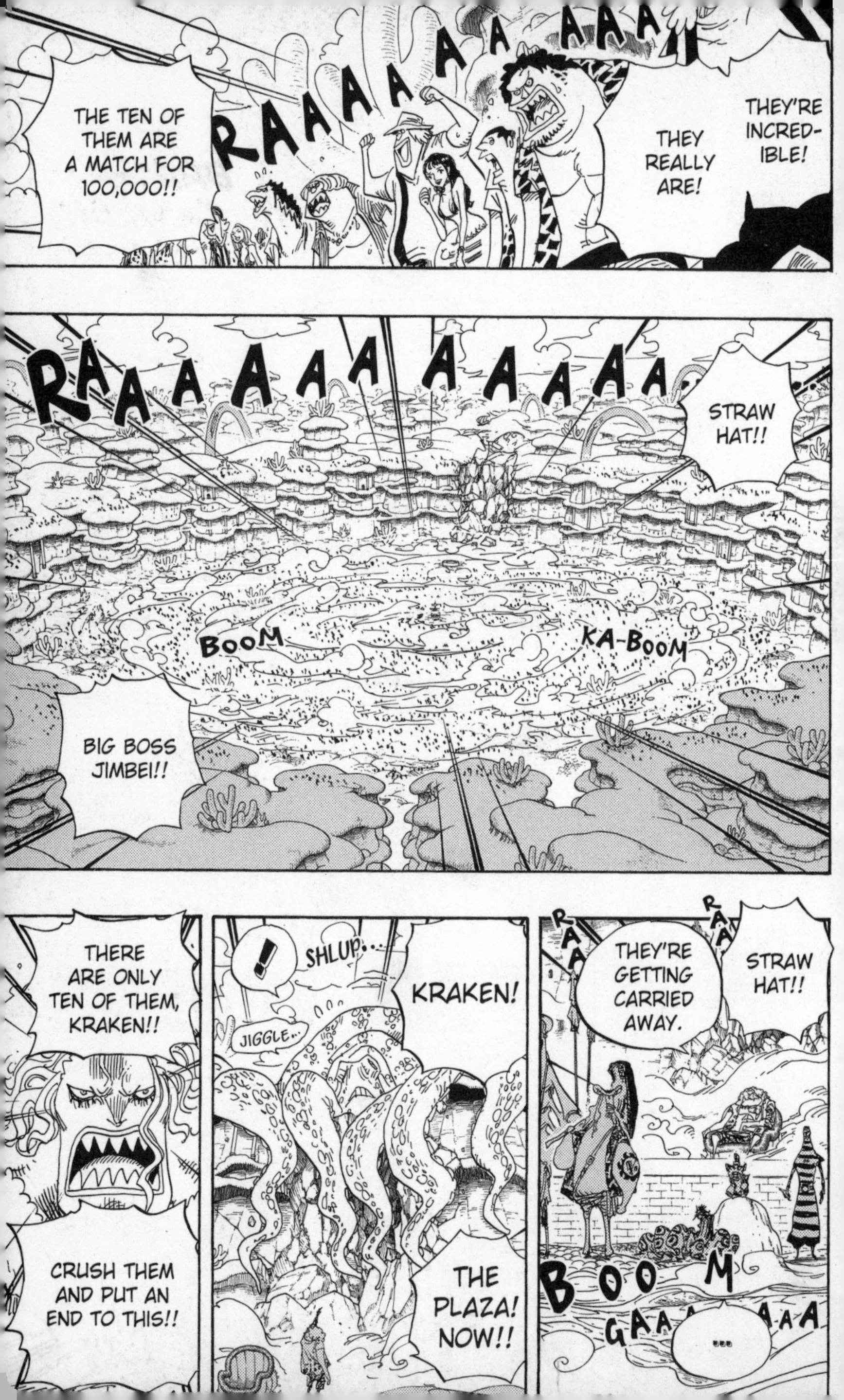
THEY'RE INCREDIBLE!
THEY REALLY ARE!
RAAAAAAAAAA
THE TEN OF THEM ARE A MATCH FOR 100,000!!
STRAW HAT!!
RAAAAAAAAAAA
KA-BOOM
BOOM
BIG BOSS JIMBEI!!
RAA
STRAW HAT!!
THEY'RE GETTING CARRIED AWAY.
RAA
BOOM
GAAA AAA
...
KRAKEN!
SHLUP...
!
JIGGLE...
THE PLAZA! NOW!!
THERE ARE ONLY TEN OF THEM, KRAKEN!!
CRUSH THEM AND PUT AN END TO THIS!!

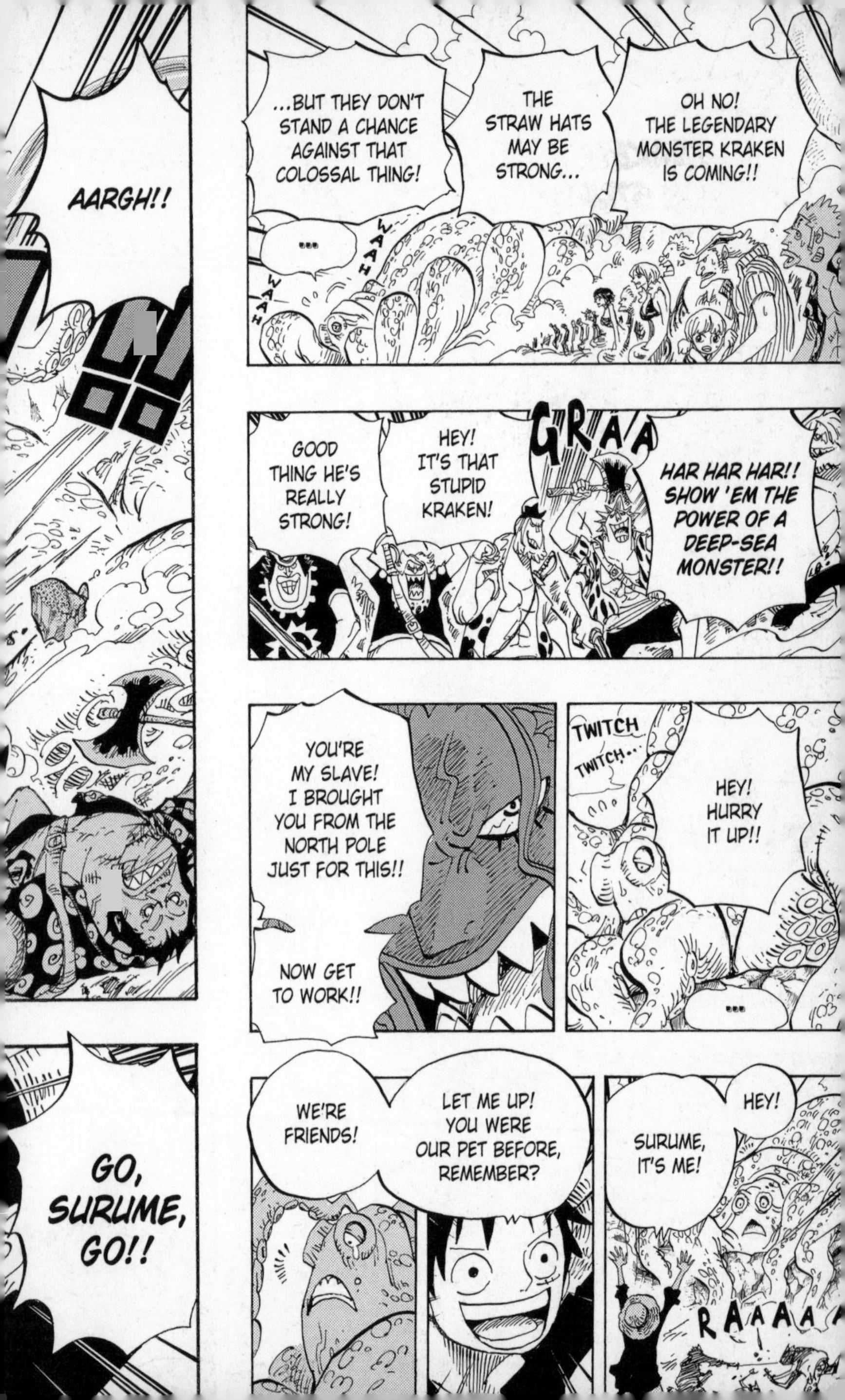
OH NO! THE LEGENDARY MONSTER KRAKEN IS COMING!!
THE STRAW HATS MAY BE STRONG...
...BUT THEY DON'T STAND A CHANCE AGAINST THAT COLOSSAL THING!
WAAH
WAAH
...
HAR HAR HAR!! SHOW 'EM THE POWER OF A DEEP-SEA MONSTER!!
GRAA
HEY! IT'S THAT STUPID KRAKEN!
GOOD THING HE'S REALLY STRONG!
TWITCH
TWITCH...
HEY! HURRY IT UP!!
...
YOU'RE MY SLAVE! I BROUGHT YOU FROM THE NORTH POLE JUST FOR THIS!!
NOW GET TO WORK!!
AARGH!!
HEY!
SURUME, IT'S ME!
RAAAA
LET ME UP! YOU WERE OUR PET BEFORE, REMEMBER?
WE'RE FRIENDS!
GO, SURUME, GO!!

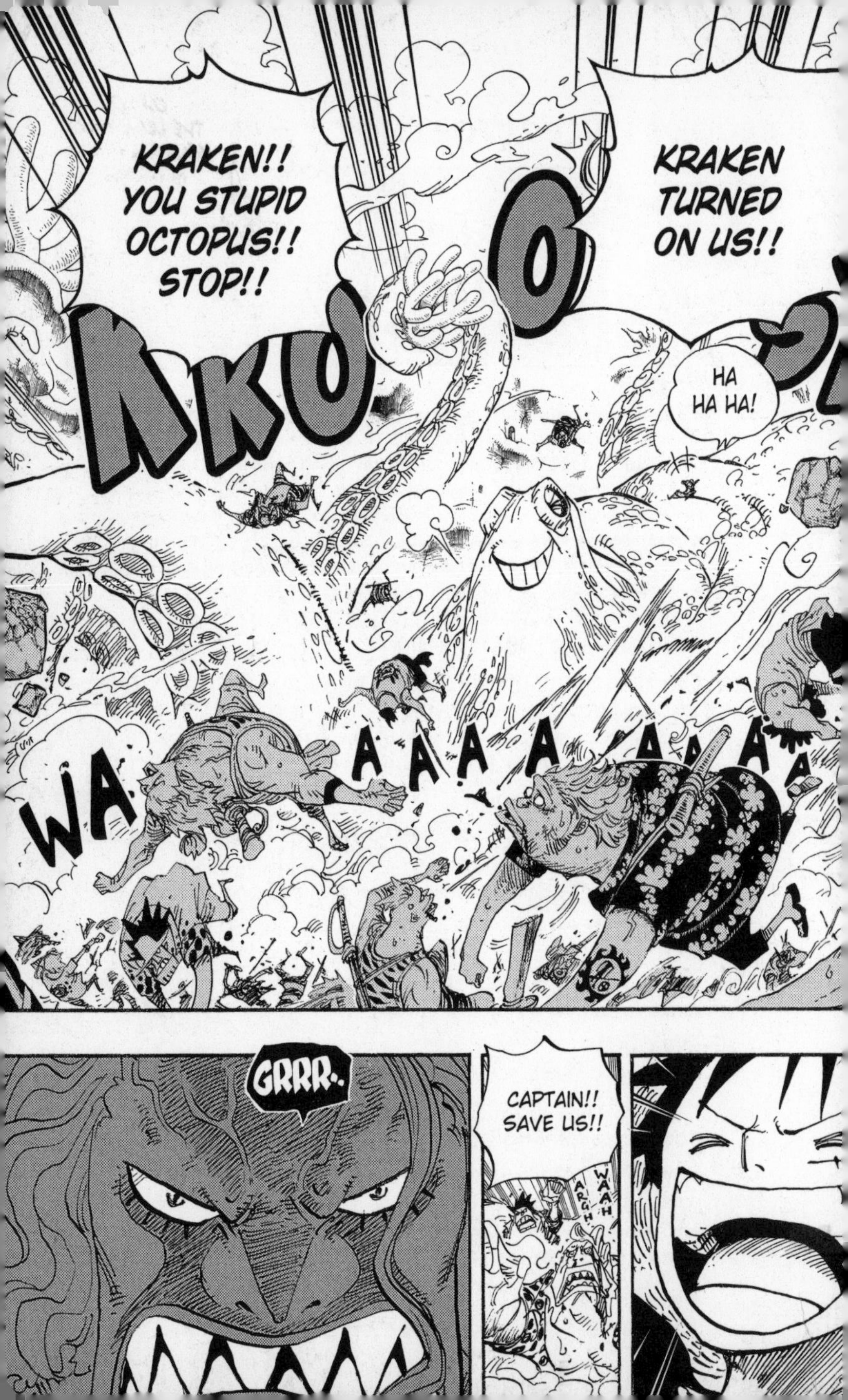
KRAKEN TURNED ON US!!
KRAKEN!! YOU STUPID OCTOPUS!! STOP!!
HA HA HA!
CAPTAIN!! SAVE US!!
WAAH
ARGH
GRRR..

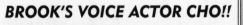

BROOK'S VOICE ACTOR CHO!!

Five Old Star no Himatsubushi
SBS

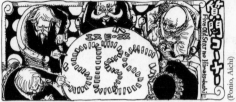

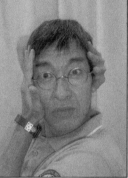

(Ponio, Aichi)

SBS Question Corner

Hey, how do you do?! This is going to be the ninth one. Thank you all for waiting! This is the final Voice Actor SBS! For our guest this time, depending on what generation you are, he's really, really famous! A long time ago, he used to host a children's show on NHK, called "Tanken Boku no machi." Now, he's playing "Wanwan" on another program on NHK called "Inai Inai Ba"! He puts on a stuffed animal suit and talks in the show. He is a true thespian! It's Brook's voice actor Cho in the house!

Oda(O): Please come on down! It's Cho!

Cho(C): Oh, I'm so glad you didn't forget about me! *Cries*

O: Oh, look! You just came here and you're crying already. I preemptively apologized by plugging your shows on NHK. Please wipe your tears. Oh, yeah, I have some candy for...

C: 45 degrees!

O: He's not listening! And he ran off! Hey! Cho!

C: Oh, Odacchi. It was time for my jog!

O: Huh?! Wait! I know you have your daily routine, but can you just...

C: Sure.

O: That's it?! Well, before you run off again, do you know what SBS stands for?

C: (S)uper!

O: Okay, okay. That's your "S," but the whole thing is "SBS."

C: Oh, right. Then how about... (S)uper (B)oy (S)uper!

O: You people have no intention of getting it right, huh?! Shoot! This is going to be the last SBS I do with these uncontrollable people! (One trouble after another... Sheesh). Okay, Cho! Here are the letters!

C: Okay, I'm off! *Runs*

O: What?! You're going to do the SBS while jogging?! Oh, do whatever you want!

Cho's SBS continues on Page 206 ☞

Chapter 636:
GENERAL FROM FUTURELAND

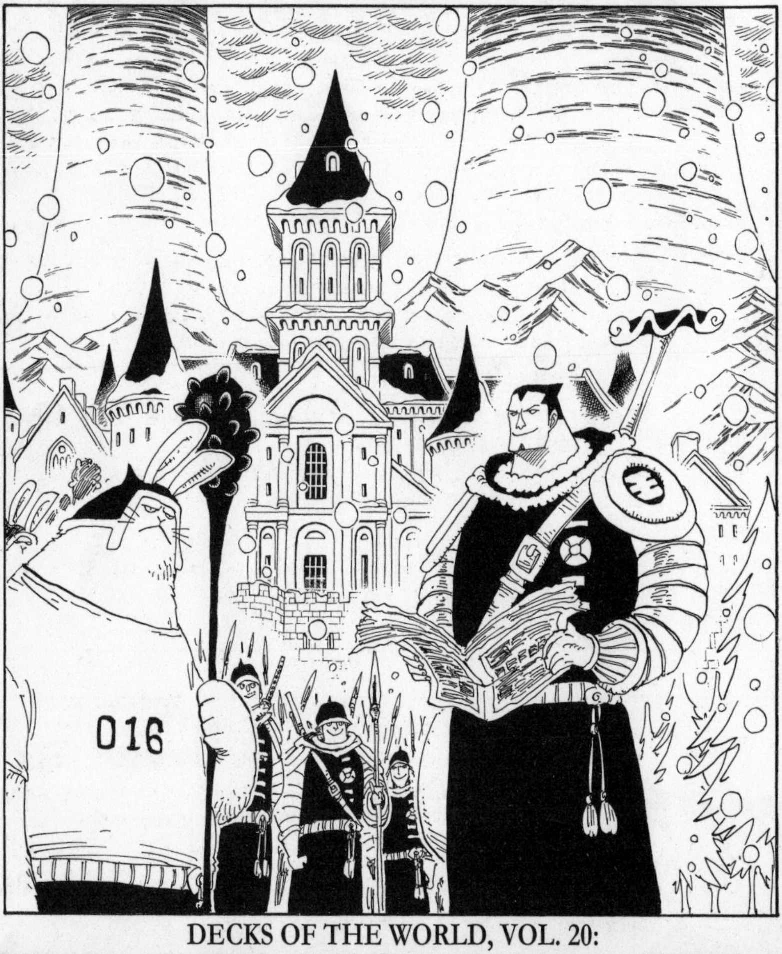
016

DECKS OF THE WORLD, VOL. 20:
"DRUM ISLAND–CHERRY BLOSSOM KINGDOM PEACEKEEPERS

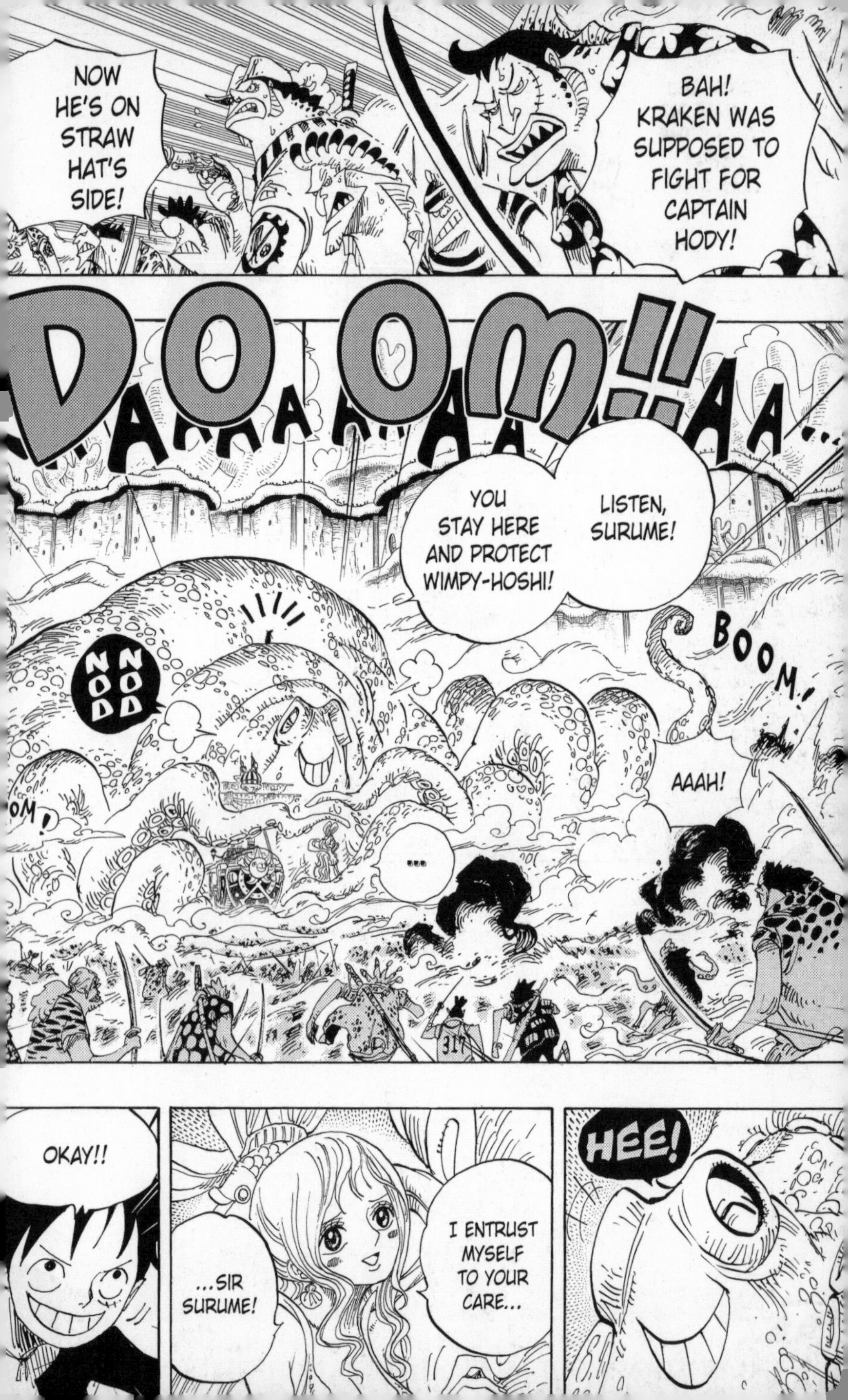
BAH! KRAKEN WAS SUPPOSED TO FIGHT FOR CAPTAIN HODY!
NOW HE'S ON STRAW HAT'S SIDE!
DOOM!!
AAAAAAA...
LISTEN, SURUME!
YOU STAY HERE AND PROTECT WIMPY-HOSHI!
BOOM!
AAAH!
NOD NOD
...
OM!
HEE!
I ENTRUST MYSELF TO YOUR CARE...
...SIR SURUME!
OKAY!!

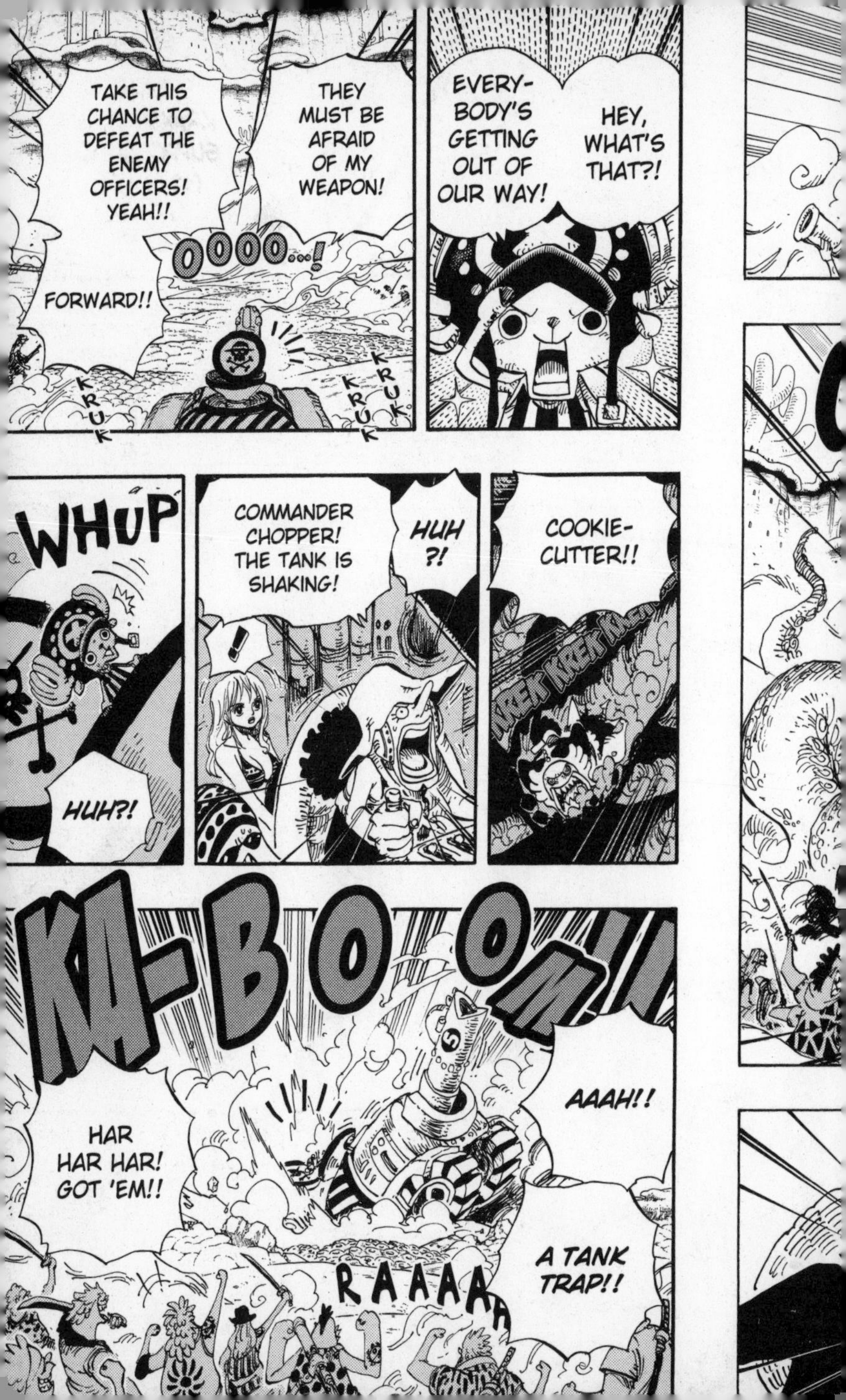
HEY, WHAT'S THAT?!
EVERY-BODY'S GETTING OUT OF OUR WAY!
THEY MUST BE AFRAID OF MY WEAPON!
TAKE THIS CHANCE TO DEFEAT THE ENEMY OFFICERS! YEAH!!
OOOO...!
FORWARD!!
KRUK KRUK
KRUK
COOKIE-CUTTER!!
KREK KREK KREK
HUH ?!
COMMANDER CHOPPER! THE TANK IS SHAKING!
!
WHUP
HUH?!
KA-BOOM
AAAH!!
HAR HAR HAR! GOT 'EM!!
A TANK TRAP!!
RAAAAH

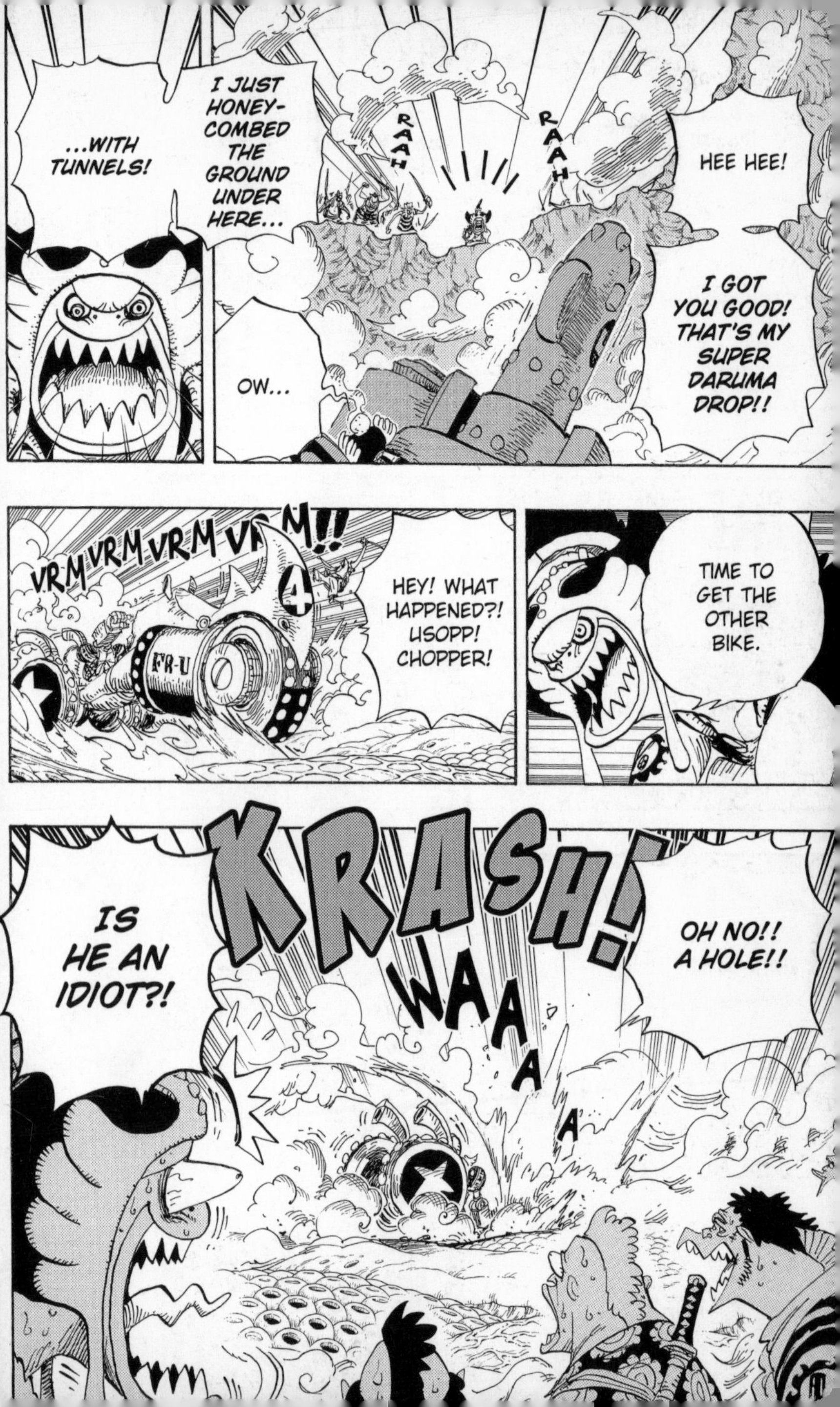
HEE HEE!
I GOT YOU GOOD! THAT'S MY SUPER DARUMA DROP!!
RAAH
RAAH
OW...
I JUST HONEY-COMBED THE GROUND UNDER HERE...
...WITH TUNNELS!
TIME TO GET THE OTHER BIKE.
VRM VRM VRM VR M!!
4
FR-U
HEY! WHAT HAPPENED?! USOPP! CHOPPER!
OH NO!! A HOLE!!
KRASH!
WAAAAA
IS HE AN IDIOT?!

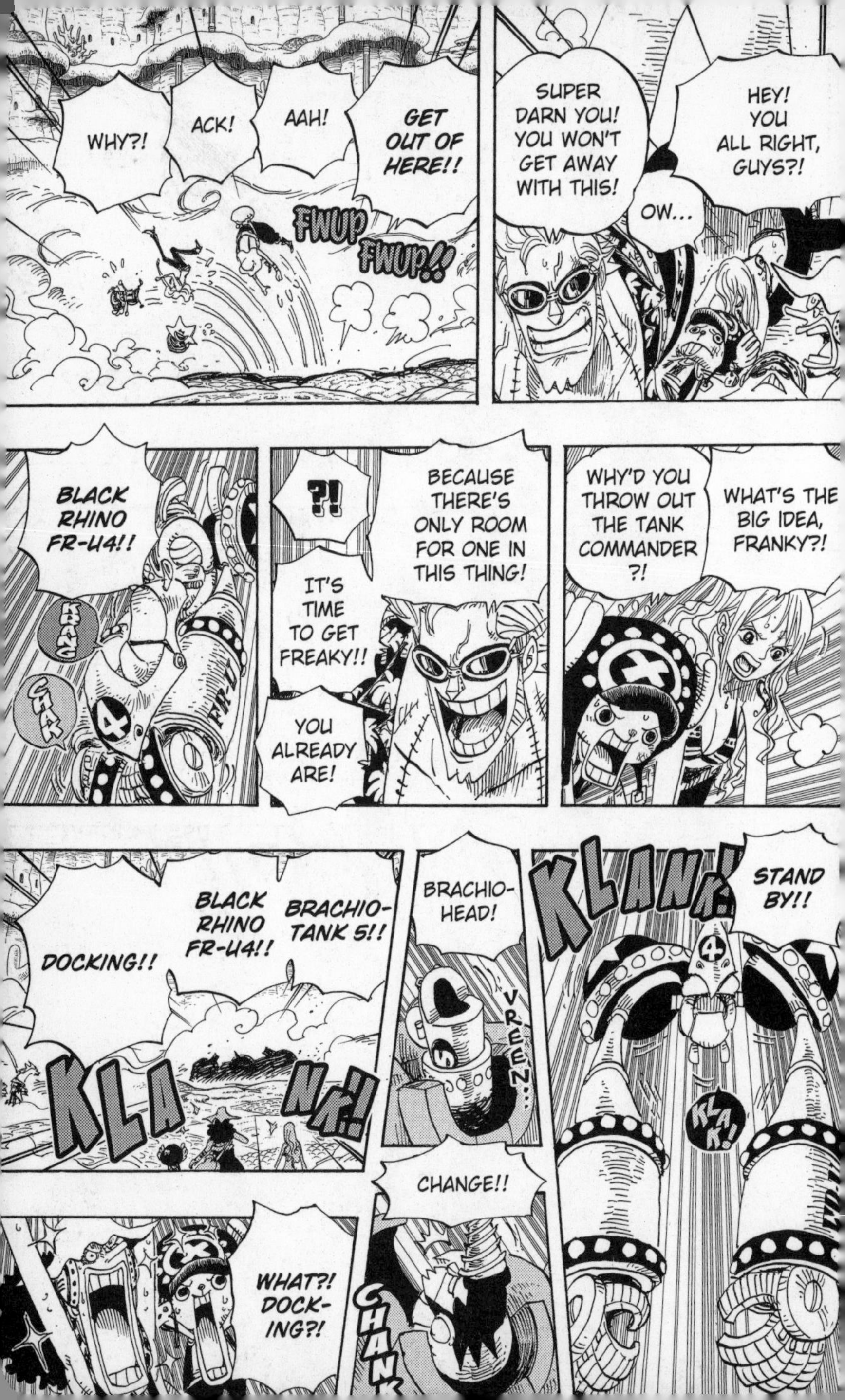
HEY! YOU ALL RIGHT, GUYS?!
OW...
SUPER DARN YOU! YOU WON'T GET AWAY WITH THIS!
GET OUT OF HERE!!
AAH!
ACK!
WHY?!
FWUP FWUP!!
WHAT'S THE BIG IDEA, FRANKY?!
WHY'D YOU THROW OUT THE TANK COMMANDER ?!
BECAUSE THERE'S ONLY ROOM FOR ONE IN THIS THING!
?!
IT'S TIME TO GET FREAKY!!
YOU ALREADY ARE!
BLACK RHINO FR-U4!!
KRANG
CHAK
STAND BY!!
KLANK!
KLAK!
BRACHIO-HEAD!
VREEN...
CHANGE!!
CHANK
BRACHIO-TANK 5!!
BLACK RHINO FR-U4!!
DOCKING!!
KLANK!!
WHAT?! DOCKING?!

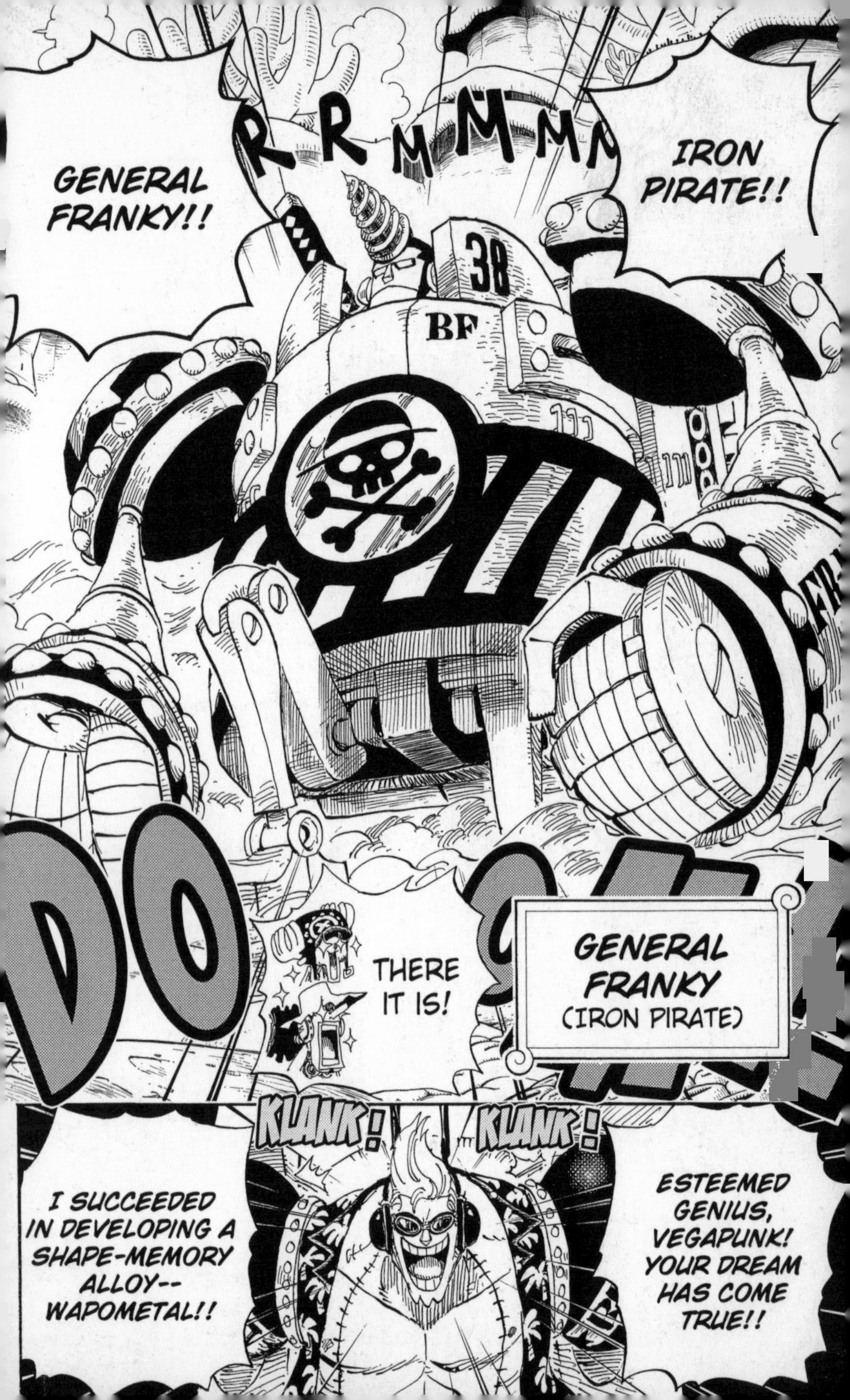
RRMMMM
IRON PIRATE!!
GENERAL FRANKY!!
38
BF
DO
GENERAL FRANKY (IRON PIRATE)
THERE IT IS!
KLANK! KLANK!
ESTEEMED GENIUS, VEGAPUNK! YOUR DREAM HAS COME TRUE!!
I SUCCEEDED IN DEVELOPING A SHAPE-MEMORY ALLOY-- WAPOMETAL!!

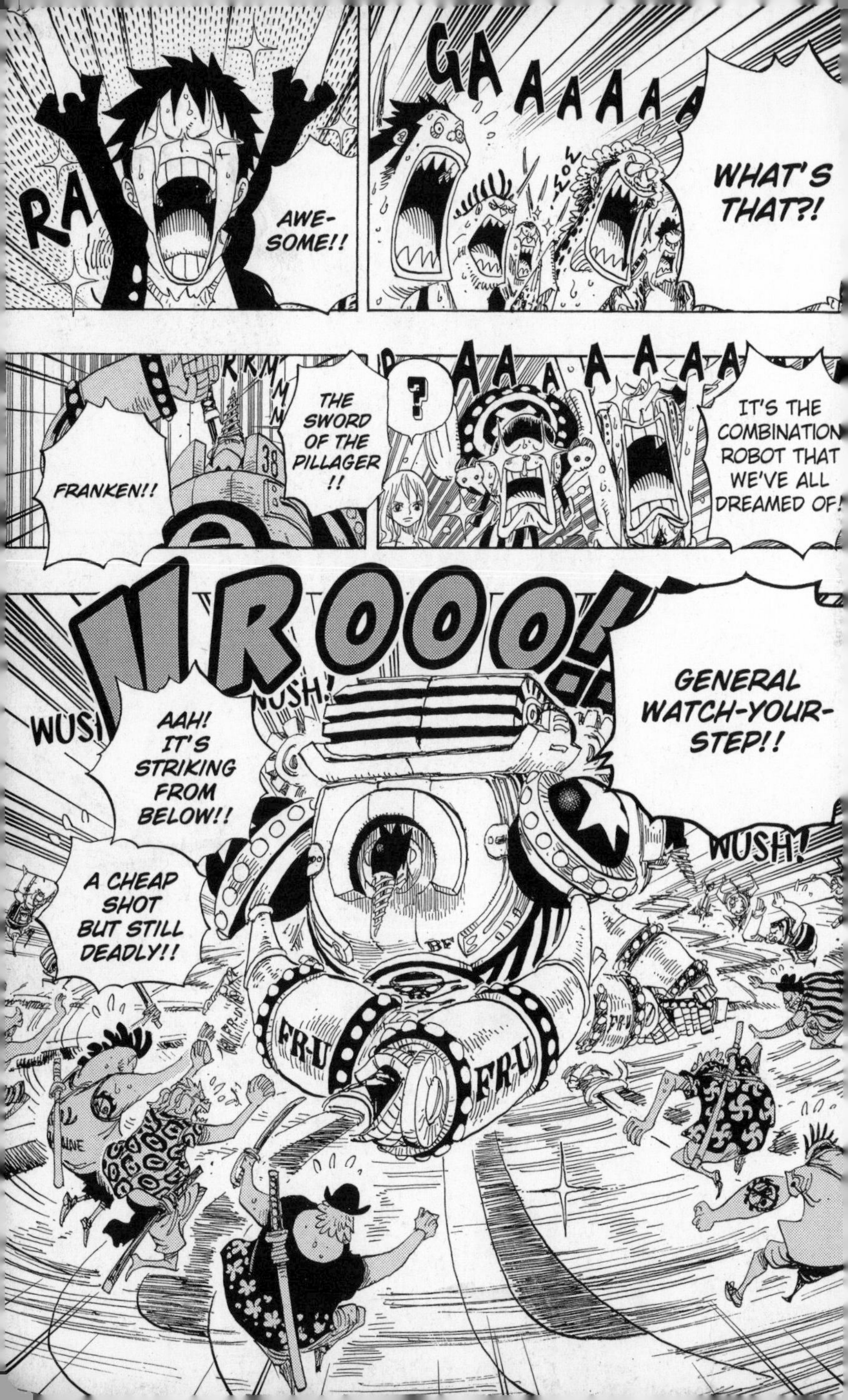
GAAAAAA
WOW
WHAT'S THAT?!
RA
AWE-SOME!!
AAAAAAA
?
IT'S THE COMBINATION ROBOT THAT WE'VE ALL DREAMED OF!
RRMMM
THE SWORD OF THE PILLAGER!!
FRANKEN!!
VROOO!!
GENERAL WATCH-YOUR-STEP!!
WUSH!
WUSH!
WUSH
AAH! IT'S STRIKING FROM BELOW!!
A CHEAP SHOT BUT STILL DEADLY!!
FR-U
FR-U

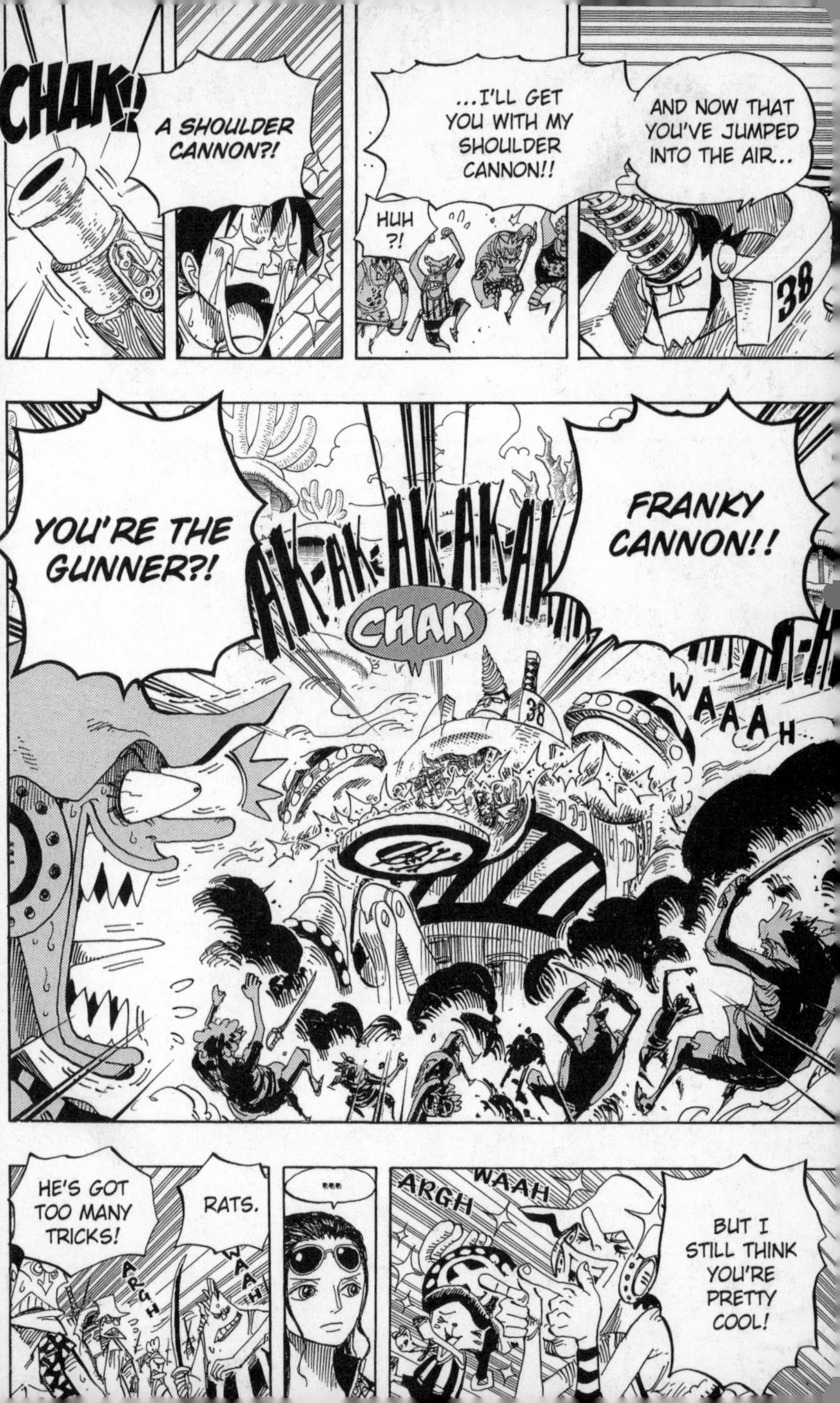
AND NOW THAT YOU'VE JUMPED INTO THE AIR...
...I'LL GET YOU WITH MY SHOULDER CANNON!!
HUH ?!
A SHOULDER CANNON?!
CHAK!!
FRANKY CANNON!!
WAAAH
AK-AK-AK-AK-AK
CHAK
YOU'RE THE GUNNER?!
BUT I STILL THINK YOU'RE PRETTY COOL!
WAAH
ARGH
...
RATS.
HE'S GOT TOO MANY TRICKS!
WAAH
ARGH

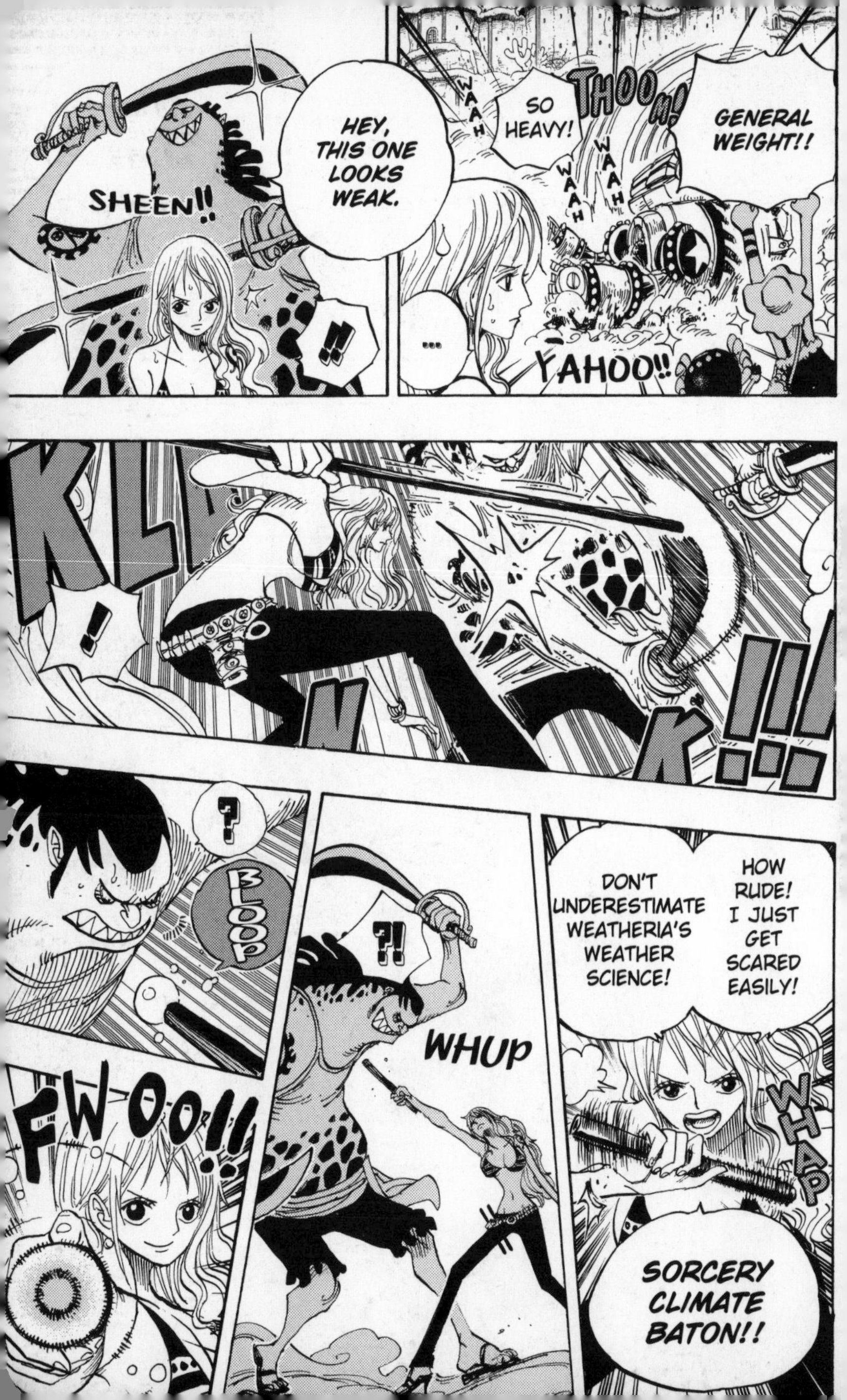
GENERAL WEIGHT!!
THOOM!
SO HEAVY!
WAAH
WAAH
WAAH
YAHOO!!
...
HEY, THIS ONE LOOKS WEAK.
SHEEN!!
!!
KL
!
N
K!!!
HOW RUDE! I JUST GET SCARED EASILY!
DON'T UNDERESTIMATE WEATHERIA'S WEATHER SCIENCE!
WHAP
SORCERY CLIMATE BATON!!
?!
WHUP
?
BLOOP
FWOO!!

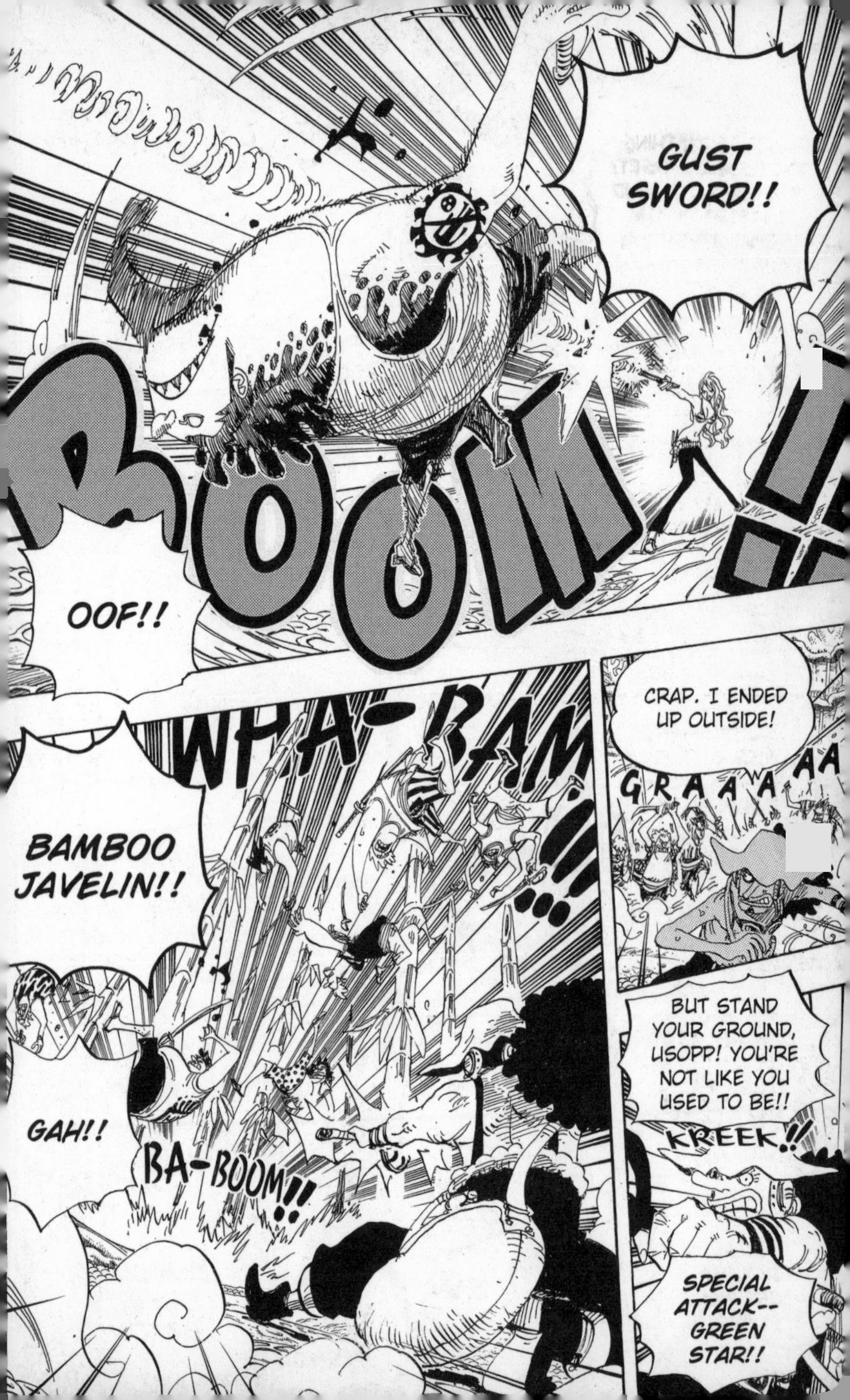
GUST SWORD!!
BOOM!!
OOF!!
CRAP. I ENDED UP OUTSIDE!
GRAAAAAA
BUT STAND YOUR GROUND, USOPP! YOU'RE NOT LIKE YOU USED TO BE!!
KREEK!!
SPECIAL ATTACK--GREEN STAR!!
WHA-BAM!!
BAMBOO JAVELIN!!
BA-BOOM!!
GAH!!

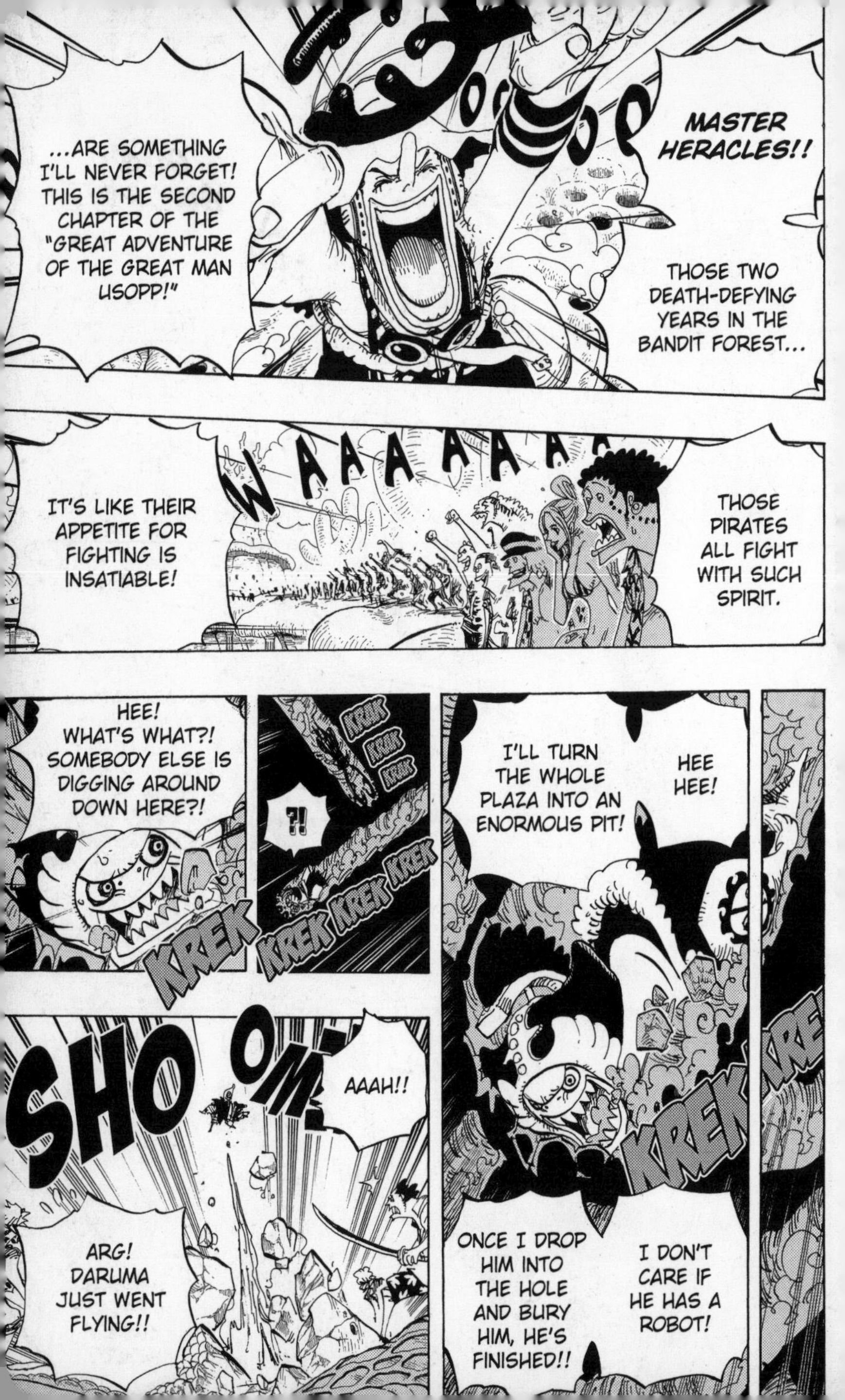
MASTER HERACLES!!
THOSE TWO DEATH-DEFYING YEARS IN THE BANDIT FOREST...
...ARE SOMETHING I'LL NEVER FORGET! THIS IS THE SECOND CHAPTER OF THE "GREAT ADVENTURE OF THE GREAT MAN USOPP!"
THOSE PIRATES ALL FIGHT WITH SUCH SPIRIT.
WAAAAAA
IT'S LIKE THEIR APPETITE FOR FIGHTING IS INSATIABLE!
HEE HEE!
I'LL TURN THE WHOLE PLAZA INTO AN ENORMOUS PIT!
KREK KRE
I DON'T CARE IF HE HAS A ROBOT!
ONCE I DROP HIM INTO THE HOLE AND BURY HIM, HE'S FINISHED!!
KRAK KRAK KRAK
?!
KREK KREK KREK
HEE! WHAT'S WHAT?! SOMEBODY ELSE IS DIGGING AROUND DOWN HERE?!
KREK
AAAH!!
SHOOM
ARG! DARUMA JUST WENT FLYING!!

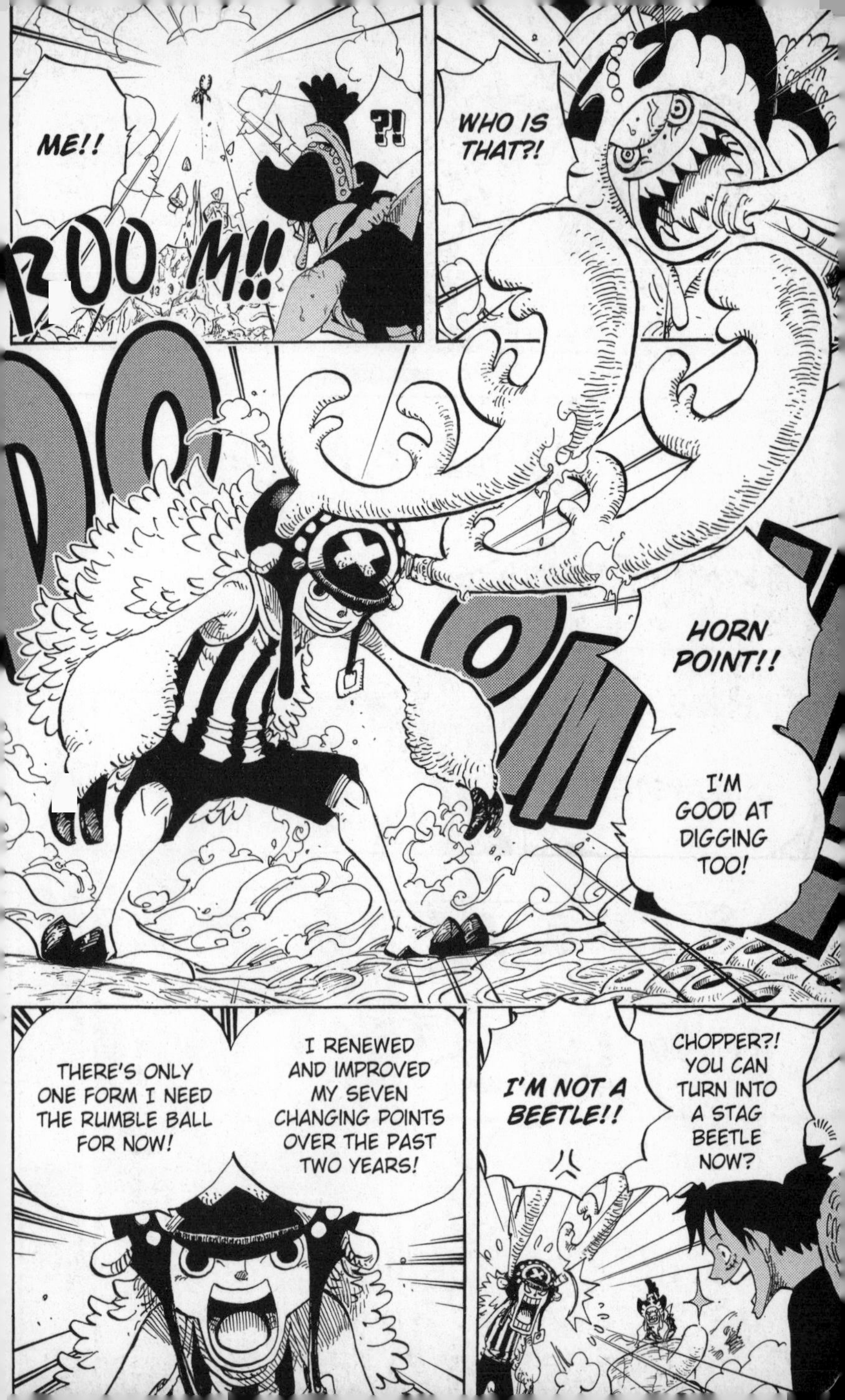
WHO IS THAT?!
?!
ME!!
HORN POINT!!
I'M GOOD AT DIGGING TOO!
CHOPPER?! YOU CAN TURN INTO A STAG BEETLE NOW?
I'M NOT A BEETLE!!
I RENEWED AND IMPROVED MY SEVEN CHANGING POINTS OVER THE PAST TWO YEARS!
THERE'S ONLY ONE FORM I NEED THE RUMBLE BALL FOR NOW!

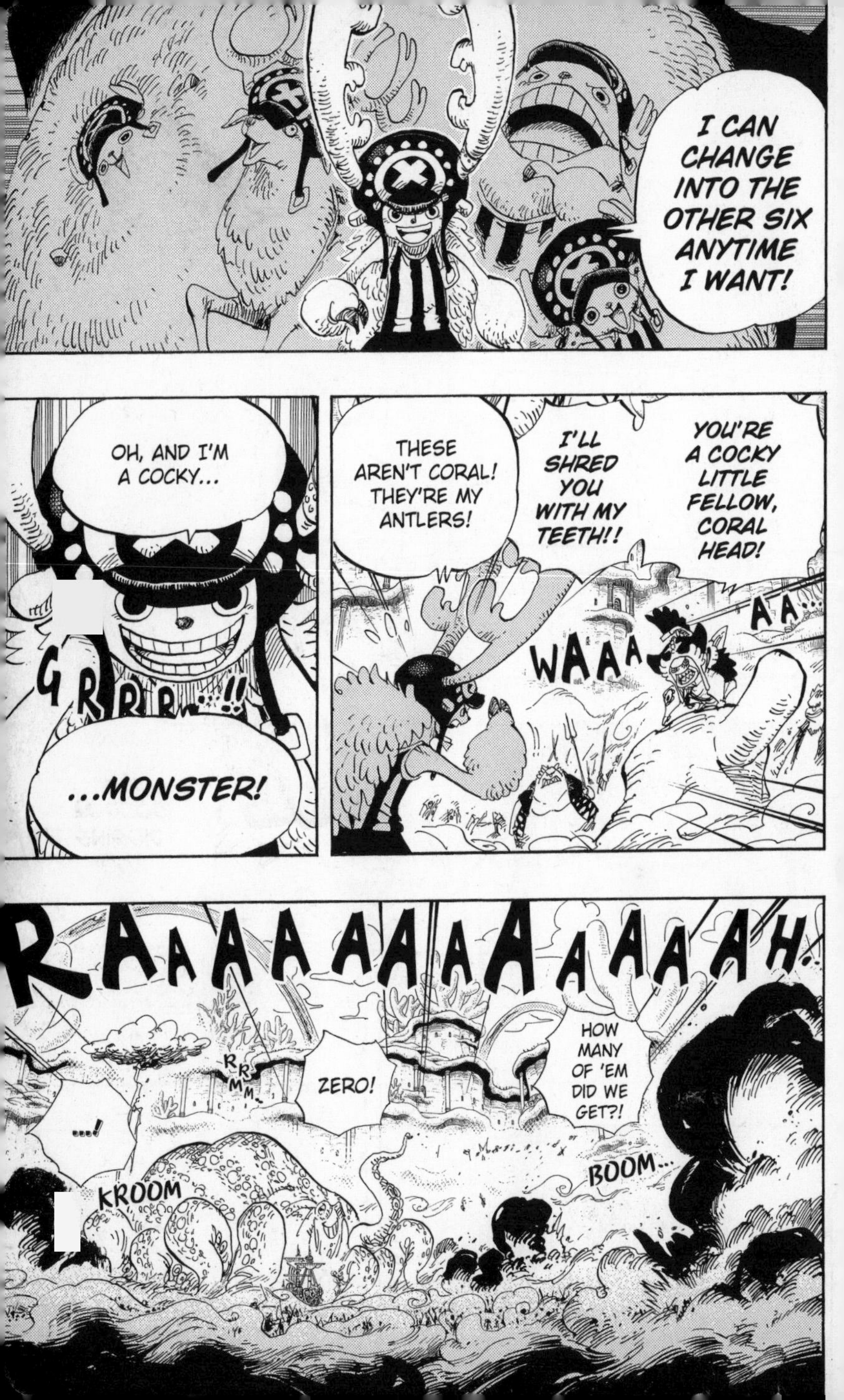
I CAN CHANGE INTO THE OTHER SIX ANYTIME I WANT!
YOU'RE A COCKY LITTLE FELLOW, CORAL HEAD!
I'LL SHRED YOU WITH MY TEETH!!
THESE AREN'T CORAL! THEY'RE MY ANTLERS!
WAAAAA...
OH, AND I'M A COCKY...
GRRR...!!
...MONSTER!
RAAAAAAAAAAAH...
HOW MANY OF 'EM DID WE GET?!
ZERO!
RRMM
...!
BOOM...
KROOM

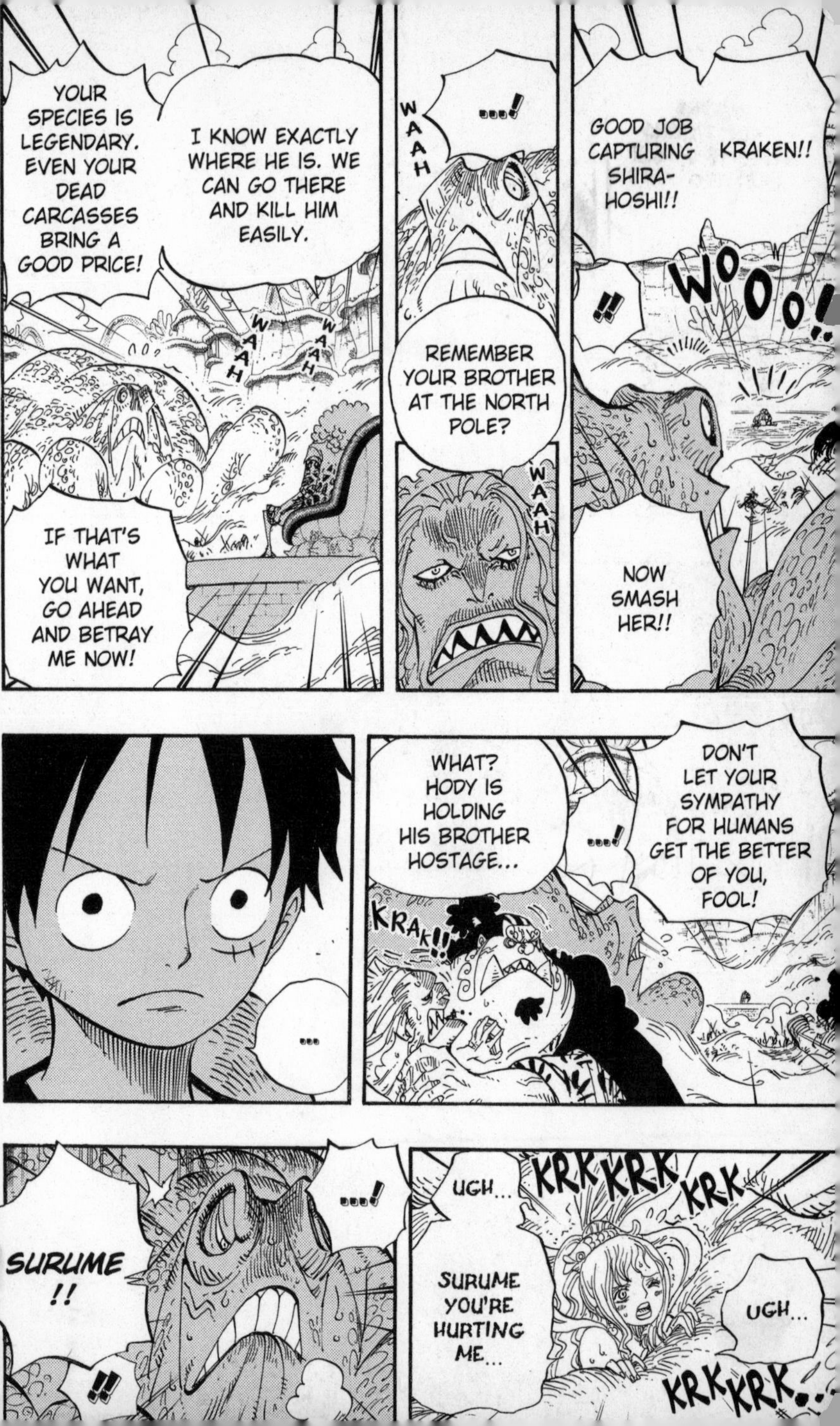
GOOD JOB CAPTURING KRAKEN!! SHIRAHOSHI!!
WOOO!!
!!
NOW SMASH HER!!
...!
WAAH
REMEMBER YOUR BROTHER AT THE NORTH POLE?
WAAH
I KNOW EXACTLY WHERE HE IS. WE CAN GO THERE AND KILL HIM EASILY.
YOUR SPECIES IS LEGENDARY. EVEN YOUR DEAD CARCASSES BRING A GOOD PRICE!
WAAH
WAAH
IF THAT'S WHAT YOU WANT, GO AHEAD AND BETRAY ME NOW!
DON'T LET YOUR SYMPATHY FOR HUMANS GET THE BETTER OF YOU, FOOL!
...!
WHAT? HODY IS HOLDING HIS BROTHER HOSTAGE...
KRAK!!
...
KRK
KRK KRK
UGH...
UGH...
SURUME YOU'RE HURTING ME...
KRK KRK...!
...!
SURUME!!
!!

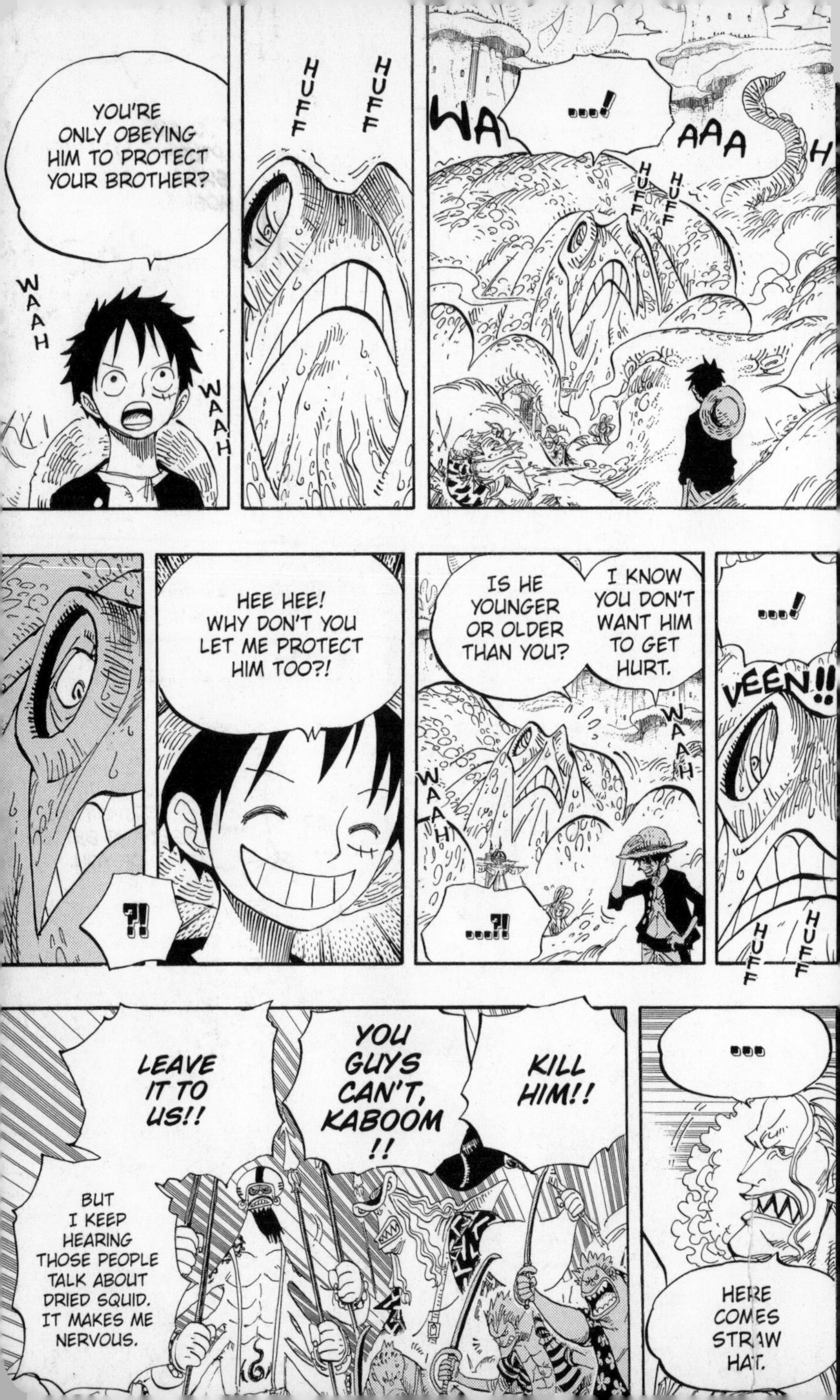

WA
...!
AAA
H
HUFF
HUFF
HUFF
HUFF
YOU'RE ONLY OBEYING HIM TO PROTECT YOUR BROTHER?
WAAH
WAAH
...!
VEEN!!
HUFF
HUFF
I KNOW YOU DON'T WANT HIM TO GET HURT.
IS HE YOUNGER OR OLDER THAN YOU?
WAAH
WAAH
...?!
HEE HEE! WHY DON'T YOU LET ME PROTECT HIM TOO?!
?!
...
HERE COMES STRAW HAT.
KILL HIM!!
YOU GUYS CAN'T, KABOOM!!
LEAVE IT TO US!!
BUT I KEEP HEARING THOSE PEOPLE TALK ABOUT DRIED SQUID. IT MAKES ME NERVOUS.

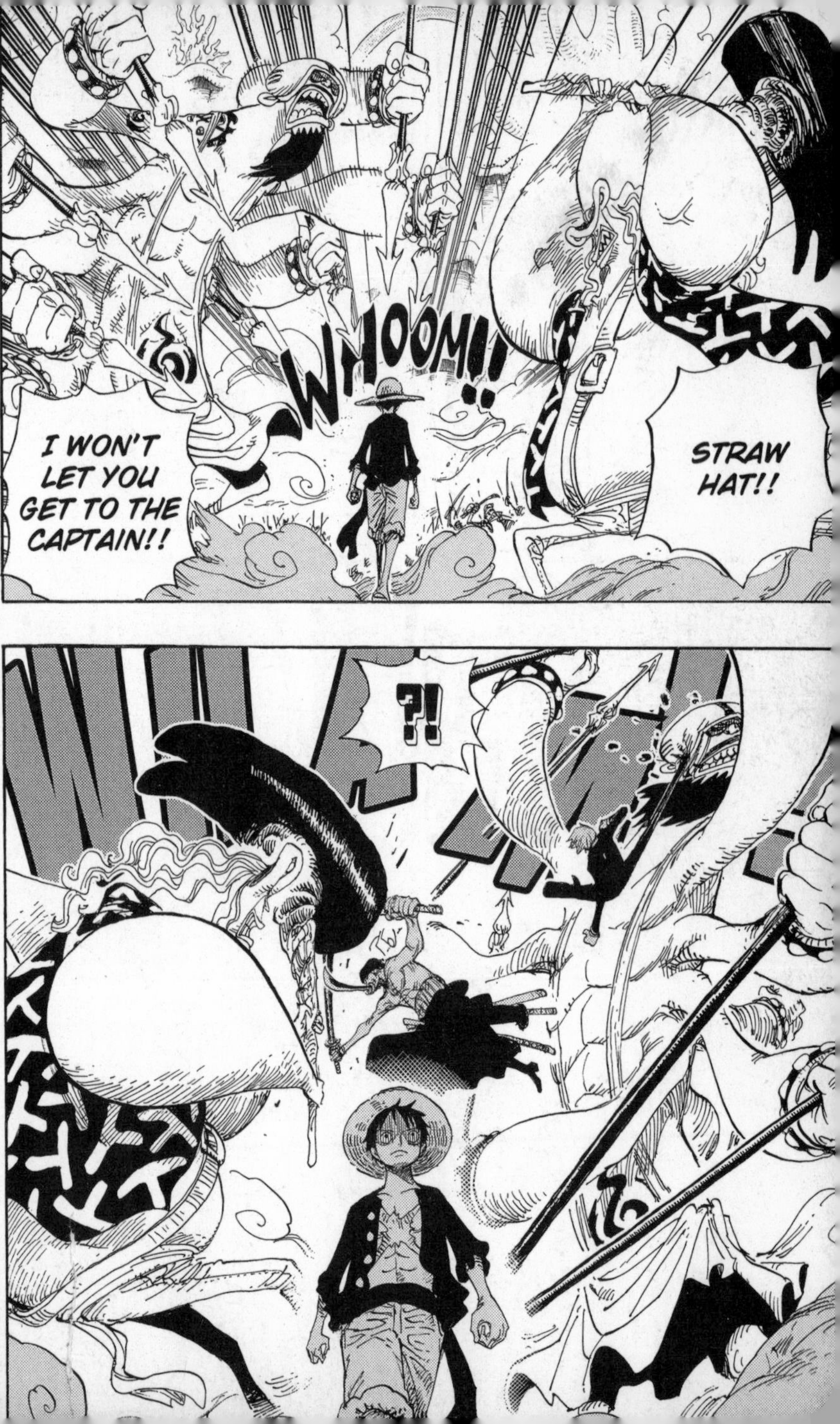
STRAW HAT!!
I WON'T LET YOU GET TO THE CAPTAIN!!
WHOOM!!
?!

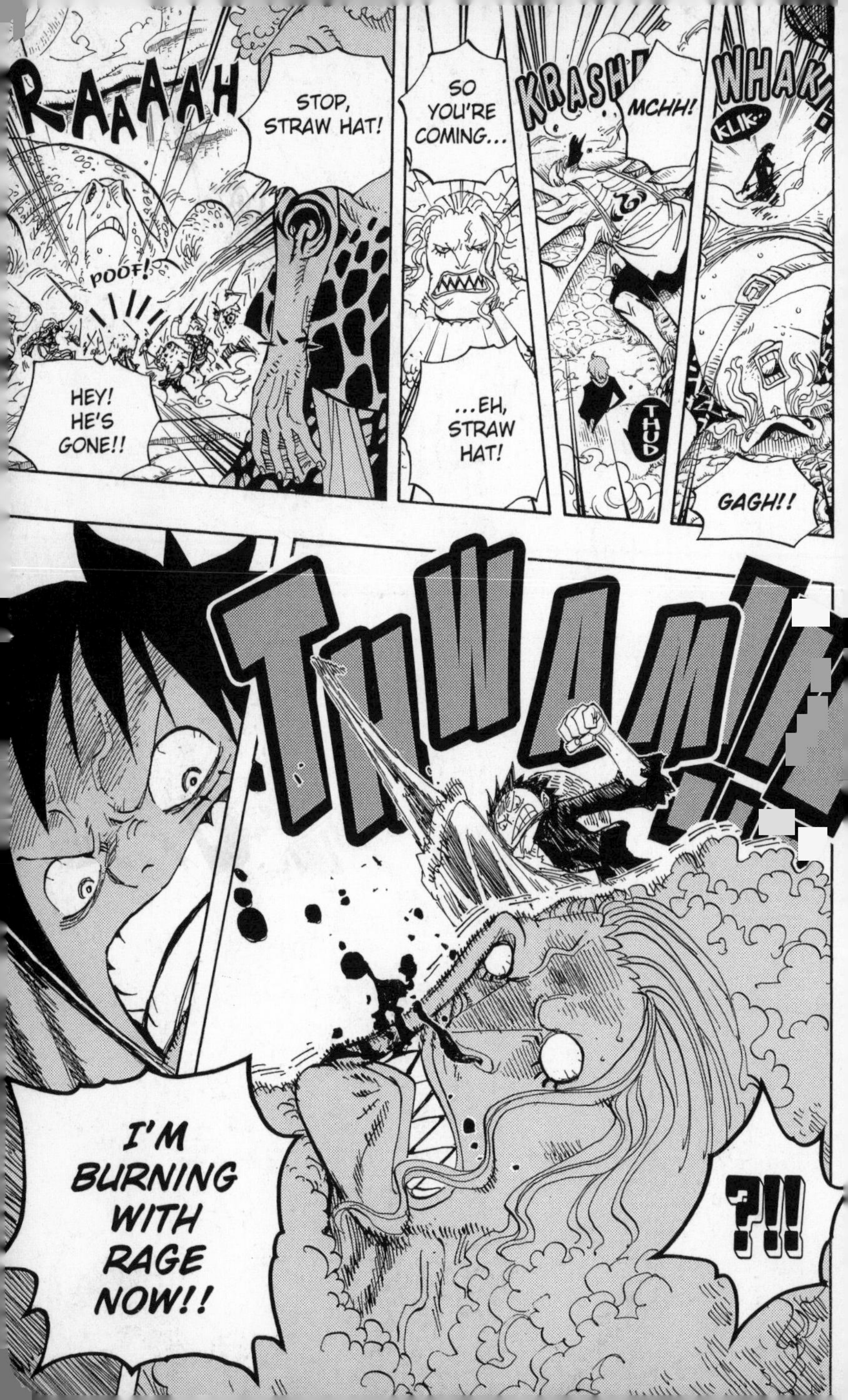
WHAK
KLIK
GAGH!!
KRASH
MCHH!
THUD
SO YOU'RE COMING...
...EH, STRAW HAT!
STOP, STRAW HAT!
RAAAAH
POOF!
HEY! HE'S GONE!!
THWAM!!
?!!
I'M BURNING WITH RAGE NOW!!

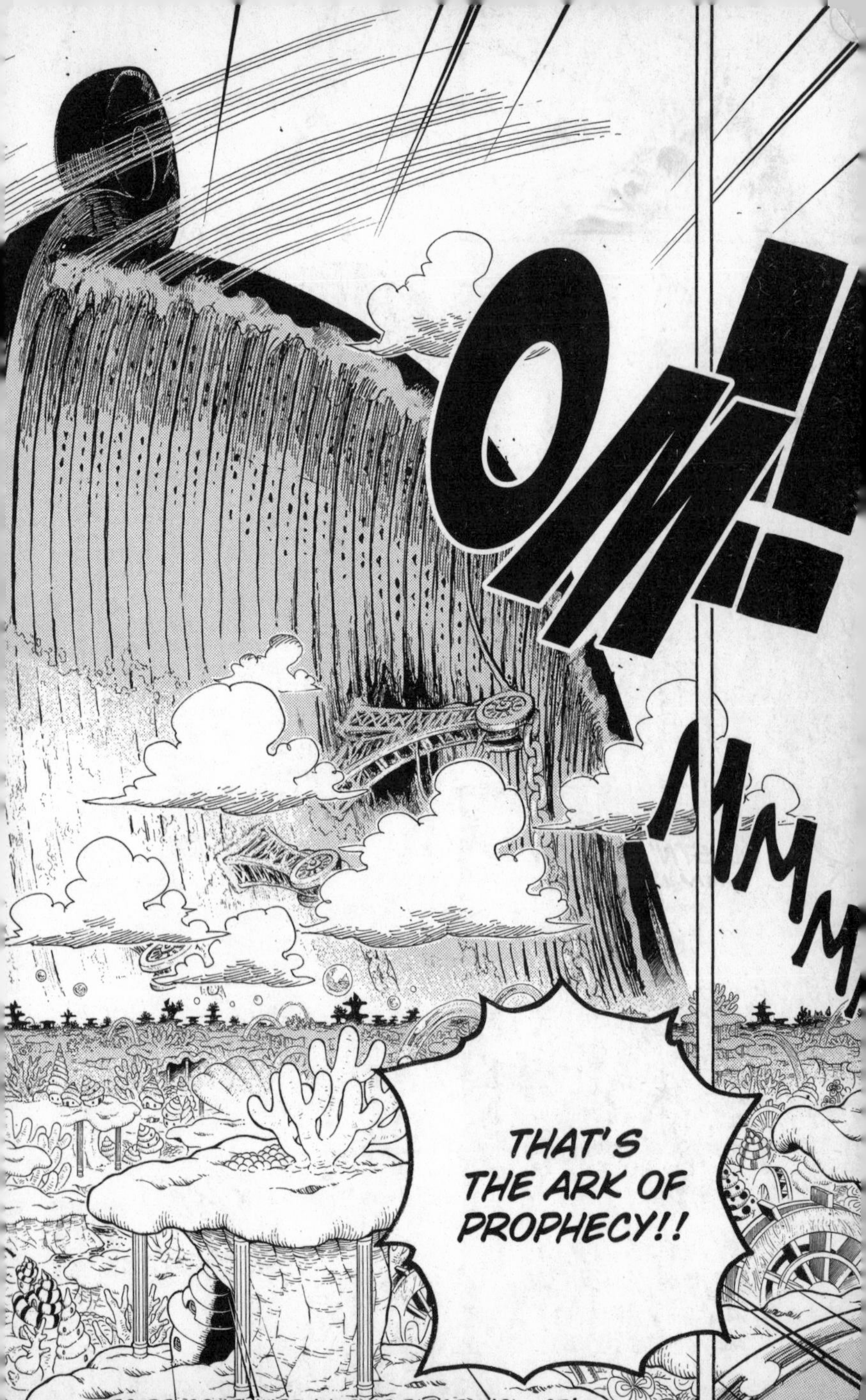
THAT'S THE ARK OF PROPHECY!!

TO BE CONTINUED IN *ONE PIECE*, VOL. 65!

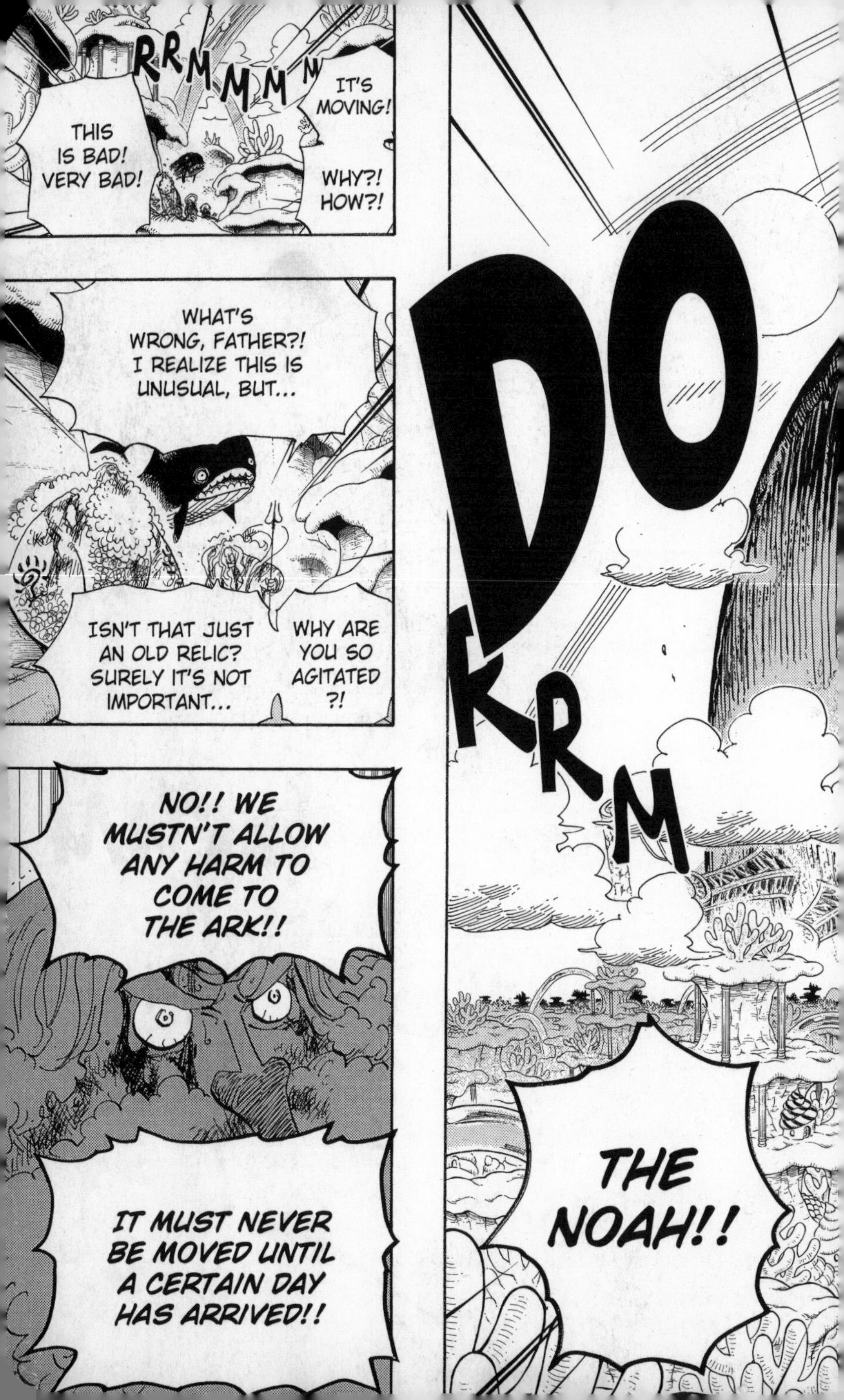

DO
KRM
THE NOAH!!
RRMMMMN
IT'S MOVING!
WHY?! HOW?!
THIS IS BAD! VERY BAD!
WHAT'S WRONG, FATHER?! I REALIZE THIS IS UNUSUAL, BUT...
WHY ARE YOU SO AGITATED ?!
ISN'T THAT JUST AN OLD RELIC? SURELY IT'S NOT IMPORTANT...
NO!! WE MUSTN'T ALLOW ANY HARM TO COME TO THE ARK!!
IT MUST NEVER BE MOVED UNTIL A CERTAIN DAY HAS ARRIVED!!

OUR VERY OWN MUSICIAN, CHO!

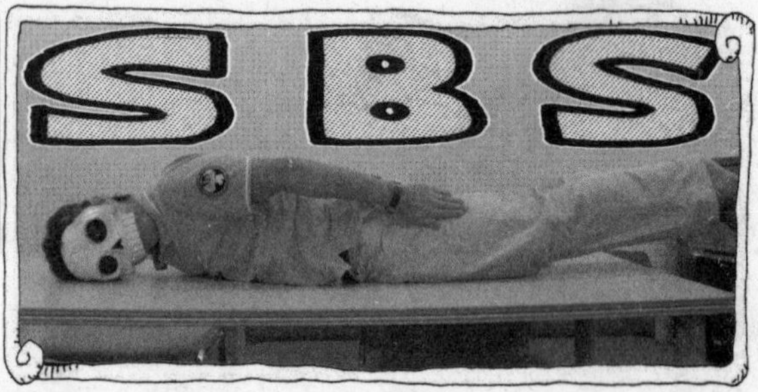
SBS

(Shigeru Nagashima, Tokyo)

Reader (Q): Cho, where did your name come from?

--Captain Nobuo

Cho (A): My real name is Shigeru Nagashima. The "Naga" part has an alternate reading of "Cho."

Q: I hear you run 10km every morning. Do you have a secret to your good health?

--If your name "Shigeru" changes to "Shigeo," you will be the same as "Mister"

A: Get some sun! The sun is great!

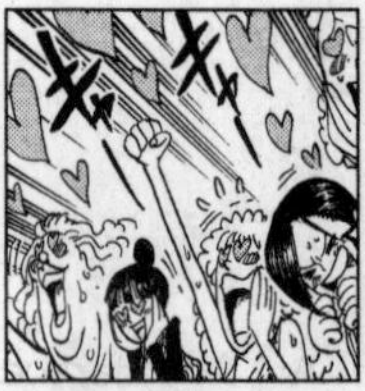

Q: I have a question. What was the best thing about being the voice actor for Brook? This is a serious question.

--Love Brook

A: I had some high school girls go "What?! No way! Wow!" Then again, I think they didn't think it was true.

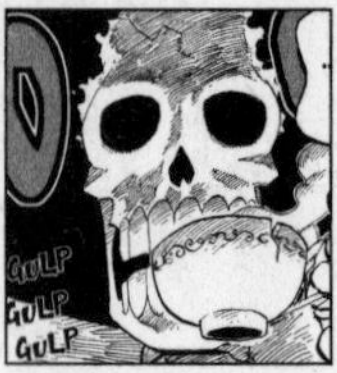
GULP
GULP
GULP

Q: Cho! I loved you ever since I was in the third grade! Marry me!♡♡ Whoops! I already have a husband! Oh, I have kids too! (Two of them) I guess for now, can you show me your underwear?

–Tanken Watashi no Machi

A: Sure. Oh, I'm not wearing any.

Q: Yo ho ho!♪ Is your method of maintaining realism in your acting to look at the female voice actresses' underwear?

--Nyonko

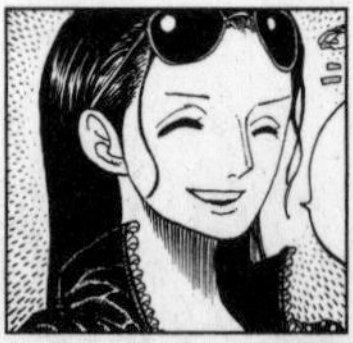

A: How did you know? Right? Right? Right? Right?

Q: What color is Yuriko Yamaguchi's (Robin) underwear today?

--Takaaki T

A: Color of a stray cat.

Q: Didn't you get irritated since they skipped your turn on SBS twice? Show your frustration to Oda! It's easy. Just open Oda's mouth when he's sleeping, jam some poo in his mouth and run!

--Ayaman Fishman

A: Oh, I don't poo. **Because I'm an idol.** You know the group AKB doesn't either. Momoe Yamaguchi doesn't either. Haruka Ayase doesn't either. Jang Geun-Suk doesn't either. **I'm sorry. I lied.**

YES, I DO POO, AS A MATTER OF FACT.

Q: If you were to teach Brook a new technique, what would it be?

--Red beard

A: **Ninty degrees on the side!** (Just lying down)

Q: You're the same Cho from that children's show on NHK, right? I loved it when I was a kid and I can even sing your songs now! I remember how you drew out an exploration map at the end. Since you're so good at drawing, can you draw the characters of *One Piece*?

–Kupante

A:

Q: Hey! Hey!! I have a favor to ask! Please make a song about the Soul King's favorite underwear! I know you love them too! ♡

--Rose Essence

A: ♪Underwear underwear!♫ Underwear doesn't walk to you! That's why you have to walk to the underwear to look yourself!♪ One on day one, two on day two!♫ When I see three, I think I'll get a nosebleed!♫

Oda: Okay, thank you! Time's up for Cho... He's still going!♨

Cho: Life is about one, two underwear!♫ Get all sweaty and cry all night!♫ But let's go see some underwear!♫ The underwear you showed me made my life all rosy!♡♫

Oda: Okay, thank you... Huh?!♨

Cho: Raise your legs!♪ Shake your butt!♫ Underwear! Underwear!♫ Don't let up and show it to me!♫
I think that's enough...
Sing with me, Odacchi!♪ Come on!♫

Oda/Cho: **I can see your underwear!♫ Tadah!♪**

Oda: What are you making me sing?!♨

Cho: Bye, everyone! See you again! *Runs*

Oda: **That's it?!♨** Well, I guess that's it. See you next volume!

COMING NEXT VOLUME:

OWW!!

The battle over Fish-Man Island escalates as the Straw Hat pirates take on Hody Jones and his minions. Luffy may be strong thanks to his new training, but how can he defeat a Fish-Man underwater? Especially since water is his greatest weakness!

ON SALE

**CALGARY PUBLIC LIBRARY
SEPTEMBER 2012**